A Land in Between

The Orontes Valley in the
Early Urban Age

Adapa Monographs

Series Editors: Alison Betts and Barbara Helwing
Executive Editor: Stephen Bourke

The Adapa Monographs series focuses on the archaeology of the ancient Near East and adjacent regions from North Africa to Central Asia. Archaeology in these regions is a vibrant and active field of research, further stimulated by issues relating to the loss of cultural heritage to war and other factors. The series is published in association with the Near Eastern Archaeology Foundation at the University of Sydney.

The ebb and flow of the Ghūrid empire
David C. Thomas

Game drives of the Aralo-Caspian region
Vadim N. Yagodin, edited by W. Paul van Pelt and Alison Betts

A land in between: the Orontes valley in the early urban age
Edited by Melissa A. Kennedy

A Land in Between

The Orontes Valley in the Early Urban Age

Edited by Melissa A. Kennedy

SYDNEY UNIVERSITY PRESS

This book is dedicated to Peter J. Parr, whose kindness and knowledge of this area inspired this and many other works on this important, yet often neglected region.

And to Madeline Parr for her tireless work in the background.

First published by Sydney University Press
© Individual contributors 2020
© Sydney University Press 2020

Reproduction and communication for other purposes
Except as permitted under the Act, no part of this edition may be reproduced, stored in a retrieval system, or communicated in any form or by any means without prior written permission. All requests for reproduction or communication should be made to Sydney University Press at the address below:

Sydney University Press
Fisher Library F03
University of Sydney NSW 2006
Australia
sup.info@sydney.edu.au
sydneyuniversitypress.com.au

 A catalogue record for this book is available from the National Library of Australia

ISBN 9781743327180 paperback
ISBN 9781743327197 epub
ISBN 9781743327296 mobi
ISBN 9781743327302 pdf

Cover image: The northern Orontes valley, © Jason Hermann

Contents

Introduction
Melissa A. Kennedy   1

1. **Northern Levantine spheres of interaction**
   The role of the ʿAmuq plain in the Late Chalcolithic and Early Bronze Age
   Lynn Welton   17

2. **The origin of Caliciform Ware in inland northern Syria during the mid-third millennium BC**
   A view from Tell Mardikh/Ebla and Hama
   Agnese Vacca   47

3. **Ebla in the third millennium BC**
   Architecture and urban planning
   Frances Pinnock   87

4. **A matter of style**
   Ceramic evidence of contacts between the Orontes valley and the southern Levant during the mid–late third millennium BC
   Marta D'Andrea   103

5. **Militarisation and the changing socio-political landscape of the northern Levant in the Early Bronze Age IVB**
   Melissa A. Kennedy   149

6. **Evolutions of pottery production over a millennium**
   Petrographic analysis of the EB ceramic assemblage from Tell Arqa
   Mathilde Jean   177

7. **The 1968 survey in the Beqaʿ of Lebanon and its relevance to the archaeology of the central Levant ca. 2500–2000/1900 BC**
   Kay Prag   199

8. **Sequence, chronology and culture at Tell Nebi Mend in the Middle and Late Bronze Ages**
   Stephen J. Bourke   229

Index   267

Introduction

A land in between – the Orontes valley in the early urban age

Melissa A. Kennedy

The Orontes valley

In the context of developing urban life and economic interaction in the northern Levant, the Orontes valley is often characterised as a 'land-in-between', flanked by the better-known coastal entrepot and the dense settlement landscapes of the Euphrates valley and beyond. Although generally treated within summaries of 'inland western Syria', the particular characteristics of the Orontes valley settlement and ceramic landscapes are frequently obscured and overshadowed, if not largely ignored, by a focus on the spectacular discoveries at Ebla and more recently Qatna. This book aims to explore the pivotal role played by the Orontes valley settlement system in the developing horizon of inter-regional activity that characterises the first urban age of western Syria, during the later fourth through to early second millennia BC. It also seeks to identify and explore key networks of interaction and to evaluate their varying intensities over this timeframe, while considering the impact of the nearby 'mega-sites', such as Ebla and Qatna, on the smaller regional settlements of the Orontes valley, such as Tell Nebi Mend. It is hoped that by focusing on both the smaller settlements as well as the larger 'mega-sites' of the region, this book will offer a more cohesive understanding of the Orontes and the surrounding regions and their role in the socio-cultural make-up of the first early urban age of Syria.

The workshop

The book itself grew out of the workshop 'The settlement landscape of the Orontes valley from the fourth through to the second millennia BC', held at the 9th International

Congress on the Archaeology of the Ancient Near East (Basel, Switzerland), on 11 and 12 June 2014.

Key themes of the workshop included:

- Articulating the settlement landscape of the Orontes catchment between the fourth and second millennia BC.
- Broader integration of archaeological and cultural sequences and the identification of key settlement phases throughout the region.
- Identifying and articulating major material cultural markers and their relative chronological proximity.
- Defining sub-regional settlement 'clusters' throughout the Orontes and its surrounds.
- Distinguishing key networks of communication and interaction and their varying impacts throughout the region.
- Assessing the role of 'nomads' and 'nomadic peoples' in the late third and early second millennia BC.
- Evaluating the scale and intensity of inter-regional interaction before, during and after the decline of the Eblaite state during the third millennium BC.
- Defining transitional horizons, in terms of material culture and stratigraphy.
- Exploring the rise and decline of 'Empires' in the third and second millennia BC and their wider impact on the settlement and cultural horizons of the Orontes valley.

Although not all of these themes are explored in the chapters presented here, these were the key themes explored in the papers presented at the time of the workshop. These contributions have since developed over time as research agendas have evolved.

Nomenclature and chronology

The nomenclature and chronology of the central and northern Levant vary considerably throughout scholarship. This is due to a number of factors, such as the nationality of scholars, as well as the geographical positioning of these regions between the more intensively studied areas of the southern Levant and Mesopotamia.[1] Along the Orontes corridor and the Mediterranean coast, Albright's and Wright's southern Levantine 'Early Bronze Age' periodisation has frequently been adopted;[2] while in the Euphrates and the Jezireh, quasi-historical Mesopotamian periodisation, such as Uruk, Early Dynastic, Akkadian and Ur III, has often been employed.[3] This scenario has been changing over the last few decades with the introduction of more region-specific periodisation[4] and

---

1   Kennedy 2015, 6.
2   See Höflmayer 2017; Matthiae et al. 2018.
3   Oates and Oates 2001; Margueron 2014.
4   See Jamieson 1993; Pfälzner 1995; Porter 2000; Cooper 2006.

the advent of the ARCANE project (Associated Regional Chronologies for the Ancient Near East and the Eastern Mediterranean). However, as the ARCANE study of the northern and central Levant is still currently underway, this book has for the most part retained the Early Bronze Age periodisation, with some reference to the ARCANE nomenclature. We have also chosen to use BC rather than BCE in order to effectively integrate and combine chronological and radiocarbon calibrated date ranges.

The chapters: some thoughts from the editor

As several chapters presented at the workshop were not able to be published in this book, additional chapters were solicited to cover aspects of study not represented in the original workshop. These additional chapters have considerably expanded the regional coverage of the book, which now includes studies centred on the Beqa' valley and the Akkar plain of the Lebanon. This expanded frame of reference allows for a more comprehensive view of the Orontes corridor, especially in the area of social and cultural connectivity. By foregrounding aspects of cultural, political and economic development critical to any attempt to re-evaluate the role and impact of the Orontes settlement landscape, its contribution to the development of early urban life in western Syria and the wider Near East is made clear.

The first chapter, 'Northern Levantine spheres of interaction: the role of the 'Amuq plain in the late Chalcolithic and Early Bronze Age' by Lynn Welton (Durham University), explores the origins of urbanism found in the 'Amuq valley, in the northern reaches of the Orontes corridor. This chapter outlines the developing horizons of ceramic and cultural fragmentation that appear to characterise this region during the latter part of the fourth through third millennia BC. It presents new insights into both the ceramic divergence of this region from the rest of the Orontes watershed and the developing horizon of cultural and socio-political interconnectivity that would ultimately come to characterise the region as a whole. In terms of this hypothesis, Welton opines that Phase H of the 'Amuq sequence witnessed an increase in socio-political centralisation, with the physical expansion of Tell Tayinat during this period, as well as an expansion and rural population dispersal into the surrounding hilly margins. However, the transition between Phases H and I appears to have been marked by a slowdown then contraction, ultimately culminating in Tell Tayinat being the only settlement to be occupied during Phase J. Although, as Welton asserts, defining ceramic distinctions between Phases G and H and Phases I and J is complex and not always readily apparent, this settlement stagnation, right at the height of the urban phenomenon, is of note. It perhaps suggests a thinning out of the rural landscape during the EB IV in this region. Settlement nucleation may in some instances be a hallmark of increased centralisation. A similar phenomenon is observable in the southern Levantine EB III, where the overall number of settlements declines significantly between the EB II and EB III.[5] Conversely, in the upper Orontes, the EB IV is marked by significant

---

5   Greenberg 2002, 97–100; Bradbury et al. 2014, 213–215.

settlement expansion into the marginal areas east of the Orontes.[6] Comparable data is also available from the middle Orontes[7] and the Ebla *chora*,[8] where an explosion in settlement is discernible throughout the EB IV. This identification of two distinct settlement trends in the Orontes is of note, and although the reasoning behind this remains unknown, it suggests there were multiple paths towards centralisation and 'urbanisation' during the third millennium BC.

Secondly, Welton notes a significant shift in the ceramic alignment of the 'Amuq between Phases G–H and Phases I–J, from a northern, Anatolian focus in the EB II–III to a more Levantine orientation from the EB IV, Phase I onwards. Welton stresses that this reorientation is far more complex than the rise of Ebla, as the political relationship between the two regions is somewhat opaque, although the socio-political/cultural gravitational pull of Ebla and the surrounding 'kingdoms' to the south appears undeniable. Interestingly, this feature is also mirrored in the southern extent of the Orontes and into the Hauran, where a cultural realignment can be seen from the EB IV. This reorientation ranges from subtle to radical during the EB I–III, where the ceramic horizons of sites such as Khirbet al-'Umbashi,[9] Khirbet ed-Dabab[10] and Tell Nebi Mend[11] appear to have a distinct southern Levantine flavour. Although this southern influence remains in the Hauran during the EB IV, it was tempered by the introduction of new 'northern' types, such as 'Caliciform' goblets. In the upper Orontes there is a radical shift, with a complete cultural realignment from south to north, characterised by the full adoption of the so-called 'Caliciform' tradition.[12] This shift in the material culture of the northern and southern peripheries suggests that these regions were beginning to be keyed into events and developments occurring in the northern Levantine heartland of urban florescence. Moreover, the parallel developmental trajectories of the northern and southern Orontes watershed and beyond highlights the impact that the changing socio-political landscape had upon the wider region in the third millennium BC.

Finally, Welton identified few connections/ceramic parallels between the 'Amuq and Euphrates valleys during the mid to late third millennium BC. This is in contrast to areas to the south, specifically around the Ebla *chora*, which have revealed a number of parallels.[13] Intriguingly, this phenomenon is also mirrored at the upper Orontean site of Tell Nebi Mend, where only broad parallels of form are identifiable between this site and the settlements of the Euphrates.[14] It would therefore appear that *both* the upper and lower extents of the Orontes valley were somewhat removed from this sphere of influence, further supporting Welton's assertion that cultural connections

---

6 Philip and Newson 2014, 35–36.
7 Bartl and al-Maqdissi 2014, 66.
8 Vacca, this book; Peyronel 2014.
9 Braemer et al. 2004, 298–335.
10 Braemer 2002, 11–12, pls I–IV.
11 Kennedy 2015, 148, 182.
12 Kennedy 2015, 184–189.
13 Mazzoni 2013, 96; Alkhalid 2018, 267–269; D'Andrea 2018, 231–232.
14 Kennedy 2015, 268–269.

Introduction

between western inland Syria and the Euphrates were not uni-dimensional. This aspect of the mid-to-late third millennium BC warrants further investigation.

The core focus of the book, the Orontes valley in the urban age of the third millennium BC, contains seven contributions spanning the entire Orontes watershed and adjacent lands to the south (Beqa' valley) and west (Akkar plain). These chapters focus on a variety of topics, such as differing sub-regional ceramic assemblages, urban development, the impact of the rise and fall of 'empires', and changing settlement landscapes over time. The first of these chapters, by Agnese Vacca (University of Milan), 'The origin of Caliciform Ware in inland northern Syria during the mid-third millennium BC: a view from Tell Mardikh/Ebla and Hama', examines the Caliciform tradition in the urban landscapes of western inland Syria, particularly with reference to the well-dated sequences at Ebla and the settlements within the Ebla *chora*. One of the most striking features of Vacca's chapter is her breakdown of the goblet to cup/bowl ratio across the EB III–IV boundary. Vacca states that cups/bowls account for 85% of the assemblage, while goblets account for a modest 8% of the corpus. This ratio is radically reversed during the EB IV, with cups/bowls accounting for 39% of the assemblage and goblets 60%. The importance of goblets in the socio-cultural and political landscape of the Levantine third millennium BC has been discussed at length,[15] and as such does not warrant further discussion here. However, this sixfold increase between the EB III and EB IV is remarkable. It suggests a profound if not sudden change in ceramic production and social practice during the mid-to-late third millennium BC at Ebla. This shift was also accompanied by a corresponding decline in platter-bowl numbers. Both these facets are mirrored across the ceramic sequences of the northern Levant at the EB III–IV transition,[16] further supporting the suggestion that this is a wider phenomenon which spans regional and geographic divides. Furthermore, Vacca highlights the high percentage of drinking and pouring vessels in the administrative/elite contexts of Palace G and Building G5, which further supports the supposition that communal drinking was a key tenet of the cultural (elite) lexicon of the region.

Finally, Vacca's identification of two distinct, yet contemporaneous, goblet traditions in northern inland Syria is also of note. She asserts that the first variant, the corrugated goblet, finds its origins in the Ebla region and its surrounds. The second variant, the painted goblet, appeared in the Orontes valley and was focused around Hama. According to Vacca, both of these variants have their origins early in the EB IV, at ca. 2550–2450 cal. BC. The identification of two coeval goblet traditions may go some way towards establishing the ultimate origins and spread of this tradition throughout the Levant, as well as providing greater insight into the various spheres of cultural influence and interaction that permeated this region throughout the third millennium BC.

Continuing this thread, the second chapter by Frances Pinnock (La Sapienza, University of Rome), 'Ebla in the third millennium BC: architecture and urban planning',

---

15 Mazzoni 1985; 1994; Bunimovitz and Greenberg 2004; Welton and Cooper 2014; Bechar 2015; Kennedy 2015; Cooper 2018; Kennedy et al. 2018.
16 Bikai 1978, 69–71; Thalmann 2006, 111–112, 130; Morandi Bonacossi 2008, 131–147; Kennedy 2015, 158, 182–183; Welton, this book.

details the architectural traditions at Ebla across the second half of the third millennium BC and outlines new information on foreign relations, offering fresh perspectives on trade and interaction in the third millennium BC. The identification of a large-scale cereal storage and possible (re)distribution centre in both the EB III and EB IV at Ebla is particularly interesting. A similar structure dating to the EB III (Mishrifeh II) has also been identified in Operation J at Qatna.[17] This large open-air storage facility was built upon a 50 cm thick deposit of pisé, which sealed the underlying deposits, effectively marking a break or realignment in the occupational/structural focus of the Operation J area.[18] The construction of at least two large, supra-domestic storage areas within the Orontes corridor and its surrounds during the EB III and EB IV is indicative of a developing centralised authority and increased sense of risk management. It also parallels developments in the southern Levant, such as the 'Circles Building' at Beth Yerah which has been interpreted as a granary.[19] Furthermore, the fact that these structures first appear at the same time is of particular note; it suggests that the growing concept of 'urbanism' and consolidated socio-political power was, at least initially, linked to food and its control, rather than high-status items. The idea that food equals power, and the role of food in the development of urbanism in the Early Bronze Age of the northern and central Levant, is a topic that requires further study. Similarly, Pinnock's (this book) identification of a votive, miniature goblet associated with the upper phase of Building B5 is also noteworthy. This ceramic type is ubiquitous across the northern Levant,[20] yet its miniaturisation and votive context, in this instance, suggests that the function and meaning of this ceramic type goes beyond the utilitarian to the symbolic. It is perhaps indicative of the ritualised aspect of drinking that has been hypothesised for the late third millennium BC.[21] The ritual and transformative characteristics of alcohol have long been discussed in archaeological scholarship.[22] However, the miniaturisation of the goblet form suggests that these ritual qualities go beyond the physical act of drinking, permeating all levels and aspects of society.

Finally, Pinnock's statement that the Temple of the Rock was spared from the conflagration that engulfed Ebla and Palace G at the end of the EB IVA is significant. It suggests that if the fire was intentionally lit, the Temple of the Rock may have been deliberately spared. If this is in fact the case it may indicate an ideological or religious link between the perpetrators of the fire and the ruling elite of Ebla, with perhaps the instigators of this disaster attempting to appease or not anger the gods by sparing the temple. This provides an interesting insight into the possible mindset of the individuals involved with this disaster.

Marta D'Andrea (La Sapienza, University of Rome) continues the exploration of inter-regional interaction in the third chapter, 'A matter of style: ceramic evidence of

---

17 Morandi Bonacossi 2008, 65–66, Vacca, in this book.
18 Morandi Bonacossi 2008, 65–67.
19 Genz 2003; Paz 2006, 56–79.
20 Welton and Cooper 2014.
21 Bunimovitz and Greenberg 2004; Prag 2009, 84–86.
22 Mandelbaun 1965; Bacon 1976; Sherrat 1987; Dietler 1990; Michalowski 1994.

Introduction

contacts between the Orontes valley and the southern Levant during the mid–late third millennium BC'. This chapter outlines ceramic connectivity and the socio-political relationships between northern and southern Levant in the second half of the third millennium BC. D'Andrea's chapter offers a number of interesting suggestions and proposals, offering new insights into the apparently related cultures of the Levant during this period. Firstly, her discussion of Hazor as a settlement positioned at a geographic and cultural crossroads is of note and this has been suggested previously for the EB IV,[23] as well as other periods, where the site has been referred to as the 'gateway' to the Hulah valley.[24] D'Andrea's argument and the available evidence suggest that Hazor is key to understanding the relationship(s) between the northern and southern Levant during the third millennium BC. Indeed, understanding Hazor may also be key to understanding the southern Levantine EB IV, with the burgeoning evidence from this site revealing greater ceramic and architectural complexity than previously supposed.[25]

Secondly, D'Andrea highlights the possibility that the 'Grey Ware' goblet tradition at Ebla may have been exogenous. If this is in fact the case, this presents an intriguing possibility. 'Grey Ware' goblets appear to have their origins and widest distribution in the central and upper Orontes, as well as in the marginal zones to the east of this watershed, although instances have been identified as far north as the 'Amuq.[26] D'Andrea's assertion reinforces the idea that multiple ceramic provinces were present in the northern and central Levant during the Bronze Age and that although the region was characterised by an overall ceramic homogeneity, distinct cultural/ceramic 'provinces' were discernible, particularly during the late third millennium BC.[27] In addition, it indicates that increased political centralisation and the rise of the region's first 'kingdoms' had little impact upon the growth and development of these 'provinces'. Furthermore, this supposition of an external origin for the 'Grey Ware' tradition at Ebla supports the idea that the Black Wheel-made Ware of the southern Levant has its origins in the headwaters of the Orontes watershed rather than in the traditional heartland of the Syrian Caliciform tradition.[28]

D'Andrea also opines that the cultural horizon of southern Syria is best described as a localised regional variant of western inland Syria and the central and upper Orontes valley. I would also argue that this is the case, although in my opinion this influence was tempered by cultural stimulus from the south, particularly from northern Transjordan. Indeed, the material culture from sites located in the Hauran appears to mirror cultural facets of both regions. This can be seen primarily in the ceramic repertoire, where northern goblet forms and southern holemouth and ledge handled storage jars are found side by side.[29] Finally, D'Andrea's hypothesis that the apparent lack of EB IVA

---

23 Bechar 2015, 28; 2017, 180.
24 Greenberg 2002, 35–36.
25 Bechar 2017.
26 Kennedy et al. 2018; Mouamar 2018; Welton, this book.
27 Mazzoni 2000; 2002.
28 Kennedy et al. 2018.
29 Braemer et al. 2004, figs 546–548, 556–562, 584; cf. Helms and McCreery 1988; Richard et al. 2010.

materials in southern Syria is linked to the collapse of the southern EB II–III settlement system is noteworthy, although as D'Andrea herself asserts this cannot be solved until more stratified sequences are published from this region. It presents a new challenge as to how this area should be viewed. Was this region more integrated with the north or with the south, or is it something entirely different? Although I do not have the answer to this question, it introduces a new and important avenue for future research.

The fourth contribution written by myself, 'Militarisation and the changing socio-political landscape of the northern Levant in the Early Bronze Age IVB', explores the settlement landscape of the northern Levant in the final centuries of the third millennium BC, concentrating on the socio-political realignment of south/central Syria after the fall of Ebla. This chapter builds upon some of my earlier works,[30] which focused on the importance of the steppe and the decline in Eblaite hegemony and the developing landscape of regional fragmentation that appears to have characterised the northern Levant during this period. However, it significantly expands these earlier discussions both in terms of chronological and geographic scope. Although our understanding of the pre-EB IV Orontes and its surrounds is limited, as few excavations have permeated below EB IV levels, the extant, albeit limited, evidence suggests that the fortification process as a whole occurred somewhat later in the northern Levant than in comparison to other regions such as the southern Levant and Mesopotamia and, as such, a discussion as to the reasoning behind these developments is worth pursuing.

The following two chapters explore the ceramic and settlement landscape of the Lebanon and its regional connections during the third and second millennia BC. Mathilde Jean (University of Paris I) in 'Evolutions of pottery production over a millennium: petrographic analysis of the Early Bronze Age ceramic assemblage from Tell Arqa', outlines EBA ceramic developments west of the Orontes valley, with special reference to the key site of Tell Arqa and its regional connections. Of particular note is Jean's identification of a significant change in the ceramic repertoire between Phases T and S of the Tell Arqa sequence, highlighting the decline in carinated platter-bowls with the coincident appearance of drinking vessels. This transition is mirrored throughout the Orontes corridor and its surrounds. At Tell Nebi Mend, an identical transition is also discernible in Trench I between Phases P and O.[31] Likewise, Agnese Vacca (this book) has also identified a similar trend in the Ebla *chora*. The identification of this ceramic transition at Tell Arqa reinforces the supposition that the third millennium BC witnessed an ideological/functional shift from eating/feasting to drinking. Furthermore, this repertoire transition was a pan-regional phenomenon with a similar, much discussed, shift paralleled in the southern Levant.[32] The identification of two identical trends in different geographic regions further reinforces the suggestion that the cultural connections between these two areas ran deep throughout the third millennium BC. Finally, Jean's exploration of the relationship between the petrography and chronology of the Tell Arqa sequence presents a new and important element to discussions of

---

30 Kennedy 2016; Kennedy, 2020.
31 Kennedy 2015, 148.
32 Bunimovitz and Greenberg 2004; Bechar 2015; Kennedy et al. 2018.

Introduction

ceramic technology and development in the northern and central Levant during the Early Bronze Age. Her work indicates that a steady evolution in ceramic technology occurred throughout the third millennium BC, in terms of raw material selection, production and development. This trajectory of steady, constant progression indicates that the Early Bronze Age was not just an era of revolution but one of experimentation and evolution.

The second chapter to treat Lebanese Early Bronze Age material, by Kay Prag (Manchester University Museum), 'The 1968 survey in the Beqaʿ of Lebanon and its relevance to the archaeology of the central Levant ca. 2500–2000/1900 BC', presents for the first time the results of an unpublished survey in the region, thereby offering important new information bearing on links between the Beqaʿ valley and regions to the east and south. This study is particularly pertinent as significant site destruction has occurred throughout Lebanon since this work was undertaken, with a number of these sites since destroyed or significantly damaged. As such, this survey offers some of the only available archaeological investigations of these sites. One of the most interesting finds from this survey is the apparent lack of 'Caliciform' and Grey Ware/Black Wheel-made Ware (henceforth BWW), although as Prag herself asserts this absence may be more apparent than real, as survey evidence is less likely to reveal such evidence. The absence of these ceramic types is interesting, as examples of these wares have been found on both sides of the 'Homs-Tripoli Gap', at Tell Nebi Mend in the east,[33] and Tell Arqa in the west.[34] Instances have also been identified at several tomb sites in the Beqaʿ and on the coast at Tyre,[35] and significant quantities of this material have also been recovered from Hazor in the Hulah valley.[36] Indeed, the Beqaʿ appears to have functioned as a conduit for the transmission of the BWW to the southern Levant, with BWW most probably an imitation of the Grey Ware vessels of the upper Orontes valley;[37] as such, the absence of this material from the sites surveyed by Prag is unusual. It may in fact support Marfoe's earlier supposition that the EB IV was a period of settlement contraction in the Beqaʿ valley.[38] However, this in itself raises more questions than answers. Why is the EB IV an era of settlement contraction in the Beqaʿ, and how does this area relate to the southern Levant, the coastal littoral and the upper Orontes? Unfortunately, these questions cannot be answered until more excavations are carried out in this important region.

Finally, Prag's identification of several Trickle-Painted Ware (henceforth TPW) vessels in the Damascus Museum offers a new and important insight into the distribution of TPW in the Levant. Although these examples are unprovenanced, Prag believes they originated in the Deraʾa region. Such an origin would make these vessels the

---

33 Kennedy 2015, 192–205.
34 Thalmann 2006, pl. 63: 6–12; Jean, this book.
35 Mansfeld 1970; Bikai 1978, pl. LVI: 12–13; Genz 2010, figs 2–4.
36 Bechar 2015.
37 Kennedy et al. 2018.
38 Marfoe 1979; 1998.

most northerly and easterly examples of this tradition.[39] That TPW was produced or traded into the Hauran has important ramifications for understanding the cultural relationship and interface between the northern and southern Levant during the late third millennium BC. It also potentially supports the supposition that the Hauran functioned as a borderland or interaction zone between these two regions, and that this area is key to understanding a wide variety of issues associated with the final centuries of the third millennium BC.[40]

The final chapter, bookending the largely EBA-focused studies, is by Stephen Bourke (University of Sydney), 'Sequence, chronology and culture at Tell Nebi Mend in the Middle and Late Bronze Ages'. This chapter explores the key upper Orontean site of Tell Nebi Mend (Qadesh on the Orontes) and the changing settlement and political landscapes of the second millennium BC. Bourke's chapter highlights the political and cultural importance of Tell Nebi Mend throughout the Middle and Late Bronze Ages. Of note is Bourke's assertion that the fortification of Tell Nebi Mend occurred early in the Middle Bronze and was contemporary with the construction of other early MBA defensive systems such as those at Ebla and Qatna.[41] The early refortification of Tell Nebi Mend suggests that the site occupied a prominent/key position within the Orontes watershed, functioning as a centre of power during this period. Similarly, the sudden and widespread fortification of the hinterland during this era, as identified by Philip and Bradbury and highlighted by Bourke,[42] is also striking, suggesting a significant shift in how the regional landscapes of the northern Levant were both viewed internally and orientated. Perhaps most salient is Bourke's statement that the occupational remains of the LB I do not appear to match the economic and political influence that the kingdom of Qadesh is believed to have wielded during this period. Although Bourke states that this disjunction may be more apparent than real, the result of excavation bias, a similar pattern is also discernible in the hinterland of Tell Nebi Mend as well as throughout the Orontes watershed, suggesting that this may in fact be indicative of a wider regional trend.[43] However, Bourke's comparison with the Mahdists in Sudan, and the possibility that political influence and power is not always mirrored in material culture, is intriguing. This suggestion challenges many of our assumptions regarding the association between power and material culture and suggests that the two need not go together, with such correlations perhaps reflecting our own inherent (modern) bias. Similarly, Bourke's suggestion that lowering the end date for the Middle Bronze Age and reducing the time span of the LB I to a 50-year period or so may alleviate some of the inconsistencies between the historical and archaeological record is interesting. Recent Bayesian analysis of the southern Levantine Early Bronze Age (High Chronology) has radically altered our chronological understanding of the period,[44] with a long EB I, a short EB II and a longer EB III and EB IV now advocated

---

39 See D'Andrea 2014, 169–181.
40 Kennedy, 2020.
41 Rey 2012, 29–46; Matthiae 2013, 286–291; Nadali 2018, 296.
42 Philip and Bradbury 2016.
43 Thuesen and Ribbe 2000; Morandi Bonacossi 2007, 82.
44 Bourke et al. 2009; Regev et al. 2012.

for. This new data highlights the fact that our understanding of the regional chronologies remains in a state of flux. Unfortunately, comparatively few radiocarbon dates are available for the MBA and LBA in the northern Levant. This being the case, our understanding of these periods can only be improved with the publication of more radiocarbon data. Finally, Bourke's assertion that Tell Nebi Mend witnessed a shift in cultural affiliation from Mesopotamia towards the Mediterranean during the twelfth century BC is also of note. This feature appears to be paralleled throughout the region, with comparable finds recovered from sites such as Qatna during the late MBA and LBA,[45] and Tyre[46] and Sidon during the Late Bronze Age and early Iron Age.[47] This apparent reorientation of the cultural horizon of the Levant at the LBA–Iron Age transition may potentially be associated with a wider socio-cultural and possible demographic shift in the region, which saw the 'appearance' of the so-called 'Sea Peoples', the 'Philistines', as well as the rise of the (indigenous) Phoenicians.[48] Although definitive correlations between these factors cannot yet be determined, and recognising 'pots do not equal people', this shift still offers an intriguing insight into the profound changes that marked the Late Bronze Age–Iron Age transition across the Levant.

Final remarks

By focusing on the Orontes watershed and the adjacent lands it is hoped that this modest book will build upon the earlier contributions of scholars such as Bartl and Al-Maqdissi,[49] and Turri,[50] offering new information and insights into this important but often neglected region. It is also hoped this book will contribute to the process of documentation and discovery in the Orontes corridor, arguably the chief conduit for interaction between the coastal and inland zones, and a region of impetus that fuelled the first urban age in western inland Syria. I would like to thank the three anonymous reviewers for all of their invaluable feedback, as well as Agata Mrva-Montoya for all of her hard work in bringing this book to print, and Guadalupe Cincunegui and Nadia Khalaf for producing several of the maps. Finally, as most of these chapters were written in 2016, I would like to thank all of the authors for their contributions and their patience in bringing this book finally to publication.

Melissa A. Kennedy
Department of Classics and Ancient History
University of Western Australia, Perth
9 August 2018

---

45   Luciani 2008.
46   Bikai 1978, 53–56.
47   Doumet-Serhal et al. 2008, 24–39.
48   Karageorghis 2008; Feldman et al. 2019.
49   Bartl and Al-Maqdissi 2014.
50   Turri 2015.

References

Alkhalid, M. (2018). One hundred years of change at Ebla: the pottery assemblages between the 3rd and 2nd millennium BC. In *Ebla and beyond: ancient Near Eastern studies after fifty years of discoveries at Tell Mardikh*. P. Matthiae, F. Pinnock and M. D'Andrea, eds. 257–282. Wiesbaden: Harrassowitz Verlag.

Bacon, M.K. (1976). Cross-cultural studies of drinking: integrated drinking and sex differences in the uses of alcoholic beverages. In *Cross-cultural approaches to the study of alcohol: an interdisciplinary perspective* M. Everett, J. Waddell and D. Heath, eds. 23–33. The Hague: Mouton.

Bartl, K. and Al-Maqdissi, M. eds. (2014). *New prospecting in the Orontes region, first results of archaeological fieldwork*. Rahden: Verlag Marie Leidorf GmbH.

Bechar, S. (2015). A re-analysis of the Black Wheel-Made Ware of the Intermediate Bronze Age. *Tel Aviv* 42(1–2): 27–58.

Bechar, S. with an appendix by D. Ben-Sholmo (2017). The Intermediate Bronze Age Pottery. In *Hazor VII: the 1990-2012 excavations, the Bronze Age*. A. Ben-Tor, S. Zuckerman, S. Bechar and D. Sandhaus, eds. 161–198. Jerusalem: Israel Exploration Society.

Bikai, P.M. (1978). *The pottery of Tyre*. Warminster: Aris & Phillips.

Bourke, S.J., Zoppi, U., Meadows, J., Quan, H. and Gibbins, S. (2009). The beginnings of the Early Bronze Age in the north Jordan valley: new 14C determinations from Pella in Jordan. *Radiocarbon* 51(3): 905–913.

Bradbury, J., Braemer, F. and Sala, M. (2014). Fitting upland, steppe, and desert into a 'big picture' perspective: a case study from northern Jordan. *Levant* 46(2): 206–229.

Braemer, F. (2002). La céramique du Bronze Ancien en Syrie du Sud. In *Céramique de l'âge du Bronze en Syrie, I: La Syrie du sud et le vallée de l'Oronte*. M. Al-Maqdissi, V. Matoïan and C. Nicolle, eds. 9–22. Bibliothèque Archéologique et Historique T.161. Beyrouth: Institut Français du Proche-Orient.

Braemer, F., Échallier, J-C. and Taraqji, A. (2004). *Khirbet al Umbashi. villages et campements de pasteurs dans le 'désert noir' (Syrie) à l'âge du Bronze*. Bibliothèque Archéologique et Historique T.171. Institut français du Proche Orient: Beirut.

Bunimovitz, S. and Greenberg, R. (2004). Revealed in their cups: Syrian drinking customs in Intermediate Bronze Age Canaan. *Bulletin of the American Schools of Oriental Research* 334: 19–31.

Cooper, L. (2006). *Early urbanism on the Syrian Euphrates*. New York: Routledge.

(2018). Half-empty or Half-full? Past and present research on EB IV Caliciform goblets and their chronological and socio-economic implications. In *Ebla and beyond: ancient Near Eastern studies after fifty years of discoveries at Tell Mardikh*. P. Matthiae, F. Pinnock and M. D'Andrea, eds. 181–208. Wiesbaden: Harrassowitz Verlag.

D'Andrea, M. (2014). *The southern Levant in Early Bronze IV. Issues and perspectives in the pottery evidence*. Contributi e Materiali di Archeologia Orientale XVII. Roma: Universita di Roma 'La Sapienza'.

(2018). The Early Bronze IVB pottery of Ebla: stratigraphy, chronology, typology, and style. Remarks from a work-in-progress. In *Ebla and Beyond: Ancient Near Eastern Studies after*

Fifty Years of Discoveries at Tell Mardikh. P. Matthiae, F. Pinnock and M. D'Andrea, eds. 221–256. Wiesbaden: Harrassowitz Verlag.

Dietler, M. (1990). Driven by drink: the role of drinking in the political economy and the case of Early Iron Age France. *Journal of Anthropological Archaeology* 9: 352–406.

Doumet-Serhal, C., in collaboration with Karageorghis, V., Loffet, H. and Coldstream, N. (2008). The kingdom of Sidon and its Mediterranean connections. In *Networking patterns of the Bronze Age and Iron Age Levant: the Lebanon and its Mediterranean connections*. C. Doumet-Serhal in collaboration with A. Rabate and A. Resek, eds. 1–70. Beirut: ACCP.

Feldman, M., Master, D.M., Bianco, R.A., Burri, M., Stockhammer, P.W., Mittnik, A., Aja, A.J., Jeong, C. and Krause, J. (2019). Ancient DNA sheds light of the genetic origins of Early Iron Age Philistines. *Science Advances* 5(7): doi: 10.1126/sciadv.aax0061.

Genz, H. (2003). Cash crop production and storage in the Early Bronze Age southern Levant. *Journal of Mediterranean Archaeology* 16: 59–78.

(2010). Reflections on the Early Bronze Age IV in Lebanon. In *Proceedings of the 6th International Congress of the Archaeology of the Ancient Near East 5–10 May 2009*, Sapienza, Università di Roma. Vol. 2. P. Matthiae, F. Pinnock, L. Nigro and N. Marchetti, eds. 205–217. Wiesbaden: Harrassowitz.

Greenberg, R. (2002). *Early urbanizations in the Levant: a regional narrative*. London: Leicester University Press.

Helms, S.W. and McCreery, D.W. (1988). Rescue excavations at Umm el-Bighal: the pottery. *Annual of the Department of Antiquities Jordan* 32: 319–347.

Höflmayer, F. ed. (2017). *The late third millennium in the ancient Near East: chronology, C14, and climate change*. Oriental Institute Seminars 11. Chicago: University of Chicago Press.

Jamieson, A.S. (1993). The Euphrates valley and Early Bronze Age ceramic traditions. *Abr-Nahrain* 31: 36–92.

Karageorghis, V. (2008). Les Phéniciens à Chypre. In *Networking patterns of the Bronze Age and Iron Age Levant: the Lebanon and its Mediterranean connections*. C. Doumet-Serhal in collaboration with A. Rabate and A. Resek, eds. 189–214. Beirut: ACCP.

Kennedy, M.A. (2015). *The late third millennium BCE in the upper Orontes valley, Syria: ceramics, chronology and cultural connections*. Ancient Near Eastern Studies Supplement 46. Peeters: Leuven.

(2016). The end of the third millennium BC in the Levant: new perspective and old ideas. *Levant* 48(1): 1–32.

(2020). Developing horizons of cultural connectivity: north–south interactions and interconnections during the EB IV. In *New horizons in the study of the Early Bronze III and Early Bronze IV in the Levant*. S. Richard, ed. 327–346. Winona Lake: Eisenbrauns.

Kennedy, M.A., Badreshany, K. and Philip, G. (2018). Drinking on the periphery: the Tell Nebi Mend goblets in their regional and archaeometric context. *Levant*, doi: 10.1080/00758914.2018.1442076.

Luciani, M. (2008). The late MB to early LBA in Qatna with special emphasis on decorated and imported pottery. In *The Bronze Age in Lebanon: studies in the archaeology and chronology of Lebanon, Syria and Egypt*. M. Bietak and E. Czerny, eds. 115–126. Vienna: Österreichischen Akademie der Wissenschaften.

Mandelbaum, D.G. (1965). Alcohol and culture. *Current Anthropology* 6: 281–288; 289–293.

Mansfeld, G. (1970). Ein bronzezeitliches Steinkammergrab bei Rafid im Wadi at-Taym. In *Bericht über d. ergebnisse d. ausgrabung in Kamid el-Loz (Libanon) in den Jahren 1966 und 1967.* R. Hachmann, ed. 117–128 and Tfl. 38–39. Saarbrücker Beiträge zur Altertumskunde 7. Bonn: Rudolf Habelt Verlag.

Marfoe, L. (1979). The integrative transformation: patterns of socio-political organization in southern Syria. *Bulletin of the American Schools of Oriental Research* 234: 1–44.

(1998). *Kamid el-Loz 14: settlement history of the Biqaʻ up to the Iron Age.* Revised by R. Hachmann and prepared for publication by C. Misamer and M. Froese. Saarbrücker Beiträge zur Altertumskunde Bd. 53. Bonn: Dr. Rudolf Habelt GMBH.

Margueron, J-C. (2014). *Mari: capital of northern Mesopotamia in the third millennium: the archaeology of Tell Hariri on the Euphrates.* Oxford: Oxbow Books.

Matthiae, P. (2013). The IIIrd millennium in north-western Syria: stratigraphy and architecture. In *Archéologie et histoire de la Syrie I: la Syrie de l'époque Néolithique à l'âge du Fer.* W. Orthmann, P. Matthiae and M. Al-Maqdissi, eds. 181–198. Weisbaden: Harrassowitz Verlag.

Matthiae, P., Pinnock, F. and D'Andrea, M. eds. (2018). *Ebla and beyond: ancient Near Eastern studies after fifty years of discoveries at Tell Mardikh.* Wiesbaden: Harrassowitz Verlag.

Mazzoni, S. (1985). Elements of the ceramic culture of early Syrian Ebla in comparison with Syro-Palestinian EB IV. *Bulletin of the American Schools of Oriental Research* 257: 1–18.

(1994). Drinking Vessels in Syria: Ebla and the Early Bronze Age. In *Drinking in ancient societies: history and culture of drinks in the ancient Near East (papers of a symposium held in Rome, May 17–19, 1990).* L. Milano, ed. 245–255. Padua: Sargon srl.

(2000). Pots, people and cultural borders in Syria. In *Landscapes: territories, frontiers and horizons in the ancient Near East: papers presented to the XLIV Rencontre Assyriologique Internationale, Venezia, 7–11 July 1997: Part II. geography and cultural landscape: history of the ancient Near East.* L. Milano, S. de Martino, F.M. Fales and G.B. Lanfranchi, eds. 139–152. Padova: Sargon srl.

(2002). The ancient Bronze Age pottery tradition in north-western central Syria. In *Céramique de l'âge du Bronze en Syrie, I: la Syrie du sud et le vallée de l'Oronte.* M. Al-Maqdissi, V. Matoïan and C. Nicolle, eds. 69–96. Bibliothéque Archéologique et Historique T.161. Beyrouth: Institut Français du Proche-Orient.

(2013). Centralization and redistribution: the pottery assemblage from Royal Palace G. In *Ebla and its landscape: early state formation in the ancient Near East.* P. Matthiae and N. Marchetti, eds. 89–110. Walnut Creek: Left Coast Press.

Michalowski, P. (1994). The drinking of the gods: alcohol in Mesopotamian ritual and mythology. In *Drinking in ancient societies: history and culture of drinks in the ancient Near East (papers of a symposium held in Rome, May 17–19, 1990).* L. Milano, ed. 27–44. Padua: Sargon srl.

Morandi Bonacossi, D. (2007). Qatna and its hinterland during the Bronze and Iron Ages: a preliminary reconstruction of urbanism and settlement in the Mishrifeh Region. In *Urban and natural landscapes of an ancient Syrian capital: settlement and environment at Tell Mishrifeh/Qatna and in central-western Syria.* D. Morandi-Bonacossi, ed. 65–93. Studi Archeologici su Qatna 01. Udine: Forum.

(2008). The EB-MB transition at Tell Mishrifeh: stratigraphy, ceramics and absolute chronology: a preliminary review. In *The Bronze Age in Lebanon: studies in the archaeology and chronology*

Introduction

of Lebanon, Syria and Egypt. M. Bietak and E. Czerny, eds. 127–152. Vienna: Österreichischen Akademie der Wissenschaften.

Mouamar, G. (2018). The Early Bronze IVB Painted Simple Ware from Tell Shʿaīrat: an integrated archaeometric approach. *Levant*, doi.org/10.1080/00758914.2018.1477295.

Nadali, D. (2018). Inward/outward: a re-examination of the city-gates at Ebla. In *Ebla and beyond: ancient Near Eastern studies after fifty years of discoveries at Tell Mardikh*. P. Matthiae, F. Pinnock and M. D'Andrea, eds. 295–316. Wiesbaden: Harrassowitz Verlag.

Oates, D. and Oates, J. eds. (2001). *Excavations at Tell Brak.* Vol. 2. *Nagar in the third millennium B.C.* Cambridge: McDonald Institute of Archaeological Research.

Paz, S. (2006). Area SA: The Stekelis-Avi-Yonah excavations (Circles Building), 1945–1946. In *Bet Yerah: The Early Bronze Age mound. Volume I: excavation report, 1933–1986.* R. Greenberg, E. Eisenberg, S. Paz and Y. Paz, eds. 53–104. Israel Antiquities Authority Reports 30. Jerusalem: Israel Antiquities Authority.

Pfälzner, P. (1995). *Mittanische und Mittelassyrische keramik: eine chronologische, funktionale und produktionsökonomische analyse.* Berlin: Dietrich Reimer Verlag.

Philip, G. and Bradbury, J. (2016). Settlement in the upper Orontes valley from the Neolithic to the Islamic period: an instance of punctuated equilibrium. In *La geographie historique de l'Oronte: De l'époque d'Ebla a l'époque Medieval.* D. Paravre, ed. 375–399. Syria Supplement IV. Beirut: Institute Francois du Proche Orient.

Philip, G. and Newson, P. (2014). Settlement in the upper Orontes valley: a preliminary statement. In *New prospecting in the Orontes region: first results of archaeological field work.* K. Bartl and M. Al-Maqdissi, eds. 33–40. Orient-Archäologie Band 30. Rahden: Verlag Marie Leidorf GmbH.

Peyronel, L. (2014). Living near the lake: the Matkh region (Syria) during the Early and Middle Bronze Ages. In *Tell Tuqan excavations and regional perspectives. Cultural developments in inner Syria from the Early Bronze Age to the Persian/Hellenistic period, proceedings of the international conference, May 15th-17th 2013, Lecce.* F. Baffi, R. Fiorentino and L. Peyronel, eds. 115–161. Lecce: Congedo Editore.

Porter, A. (2000). *Mortality, Monuments and Mobility: Ancestor Traditions and the Transcendence of Space.* PhD Thesis. The Oriental Institute of Chicago, University of Chicago, Chicago, Illinois.

Prag, K. (2009). The late third millennium in the Levant: a reappraisal of the north–south divide. In *The Levant in transition: proceeding of a conference held at the British Museum on 20-21 April 2004.* P.J. Parr, ed. 80–89. PEF Annual IX. Leeds: Maney Publishing.

Regev, J., Miroschedji, P., Greenberg, R., Braun, E., Greenhut, Z., Boaretto, E. (2012). Chronology of the Early Bronze Age in the southern Levant: new analysis for a High Chronology. *Radiocarbon* 54(3–4): 525–566.

Rey, S. (2012). *Poliorcétique au Proche-Orient à l'âge du Bronze: fortifications urbaines, procédés de siège et systèmes défensifs.* Bibliothéque Archéologique et Historique T.197. Beyrouth: Institut Français du Proche-Orient.

Richard, S., Long Jr, J.C., Holdorf, P.S., Peterman, G. (2010). *Khirbet Iskander: final report on the Early Bronze Age C gateways and cemeteries.* American Schools of Oriental Research Archaeological Reports 14. Boston: American Schools of Oriental Research.

Sherratt, A.G. (1987). Cups that cheered. In *Bell beakers of the western Mediterranean: definition, interpretation, theory and new site data*. W.H. Waldren and R.C. Kennard, eds. 81–114. British Archaeological Reports International Series 331. Oxford: British Archaeology Reports.

Thalmann, J-P. (2006). *Tell Arqa I. Les niveaux de l'Âge du Bronze*. Bibliothèque Archéologique and Historique T.177. Beyrouth: Institut Français du Proche-Orient.

Thuesen, I. and Ribbe, W. (2000). Hama, the Middle Bronze Age reconsidered ceramic typology of Periods, J, H and G. In *Proceedings of the 1st International Congress on the Archaeology of the Ancient Near East*, P. Matthiae, F. Pinnock, L. Nigro and N. Marchetti, eds. 1637–1664. Rome: La Sapienza.

Turri, L. 2015. *Vieni, lascia che ti dica di altre città. Ambiente naturale, umano e politico della Valle dell'Oronte nella tarda eta del Bronzo*. Studi archeologici su Qatna 3. Udine: Forum.

Welton, L. and Cooper, L. (2014). Caliciform Ware. In *Associated Regional Chronologies for the Ancient Near East and the Eastern Mediterranean Interregional 1: Ceramics*. M. Lebeau, ed. 295–323. Turnhout: Brepols.

1

Northern Levantine spheres of interaction

The role of the 'Amuq plain in the Late Chalcolithic and Early Bronze Age

Lynn Welton
Durham University

The 'Amuq plain, located in the Hatay region of southern Turkey (Figure 1.1), has long been described as existing at the crossroads of Near Eastern cultures.[1] It has been variously described as an 'interaction zone',[2] a 'bridge',[3] a 'transitional buffer zone',[4] and a 'frontier zone'.[5] The river valleys connecting the plain to neighbouring regions have consistently been referred to as 'corridors', suggesting the movement of people and goods to and from the region. Indeed, the notion of connectivity has been key to recent definitions of the role that this region played in antiquity. However, the 'Amuq's role as a connector of cultures has varied significantly through time, and the long-term evolution of its external connections has rarely been evaluated in detail.

Since the time of the original publication of the 'Amuq sequence,[6] which divided the third millennium BC into four phases (lettered G through J), it has been one of the foundational sequences for the Early Bronze Age (EBA) northern Levant, along with the sites of Tell Mardikh-Ebla and Hama. Despite their early dates, Braidwood's original survey[7] and the 1930s excavations in the 'Amuq still represent two of our main

---

1 Oriental Institute 1937, 4.
2 Yener et al. 2000, 163.
3 Yener 2005, 2.
4 Akar 2011, 20.
5 Eger 2015, 6.
6 Braidwood 1937; Braidwood and Braidwood 1960.
7 Braidwood 1937.

Table 1.1: Ceramic assemblage of Phases 1MR-G in Area JK3 at Tell Judaidah.

Level in JK3	Assigned to	Earlier Wares [i]	Phase F Wares [ii]	Phase G Wares [iii]
18	G	insignificant	insignificant	94–99%
19	G	6–11%	6–11%	81–86%
20	G	11–16%	17–23%	65–70%
21	F	19–24%	45–81% *est	13–18%
22 debris	F	29–33%	66–71%	0–1%
22	1MR	44–49%	51–56%	insignificant
23 debris	1MR	79–84%	16–21%	insignificant
23	1MR	88–93%	7–12%	insignificant

i   Earlier Wares: various, but including Dark-Faced Burnished/Un-burnished Wares, Halaf Painted Wares, and 'Ubaid-like Monochrome Painted Ware, Braidwood and Braidwood 1960, 104–105.
ii Phase F Wares: primarily Smoothed-Faced Simple Ware, Chaff-Faced Simple Ware, Chaff-Faced Red-Slip Ware, Red Double-Slipped Ware.
iii Phase G Wares: primarily Plain Simple Ware, Reserved Slip Ware, Multiple Brush Painted Ware, Incised and Impressed Ware.

sources of knowledge about the EBA in the 'Amuq.[8] More recently, new information has been produced by the 'Amuq Valley Regional Project (AVRP) survey, which began in 1995,[9] and new material has been excavated at the site of Tell Tayinat, pertaining mainly to the latest phase of the EBA (EB IVB or Phase J).[10]

Renewed focus on the EBA of the Near East was stimulated by the ARCANE Project (Associated Regional Chronologies for the Ancient Near East), which has aimed to create both regional and trans-regional chronological sequences for the third millennium using a variety of different forms of material culture.[11] The development of the ceramic chronology for the third millennium BC assemblages of the inland northern Levant as part of this project has allowed for better correlation between the assemblages of the 'Amuq, the Orontes valley and the Euphrates region.[12]

8   Braidwood and Braidwood 1960.
9   Yener et al. 2000; Casana 2003; Casana and Wilkinson 2005; Gerritsen et al. 2008.
10 Welton et al. 2011; Welton 2014.
11 Lebeau 2011; Lebeau 2014; Finkbeiner et al. 2015.
12 Welton and Cooper in preparation.

1 Northern Levantine spheres of interaction

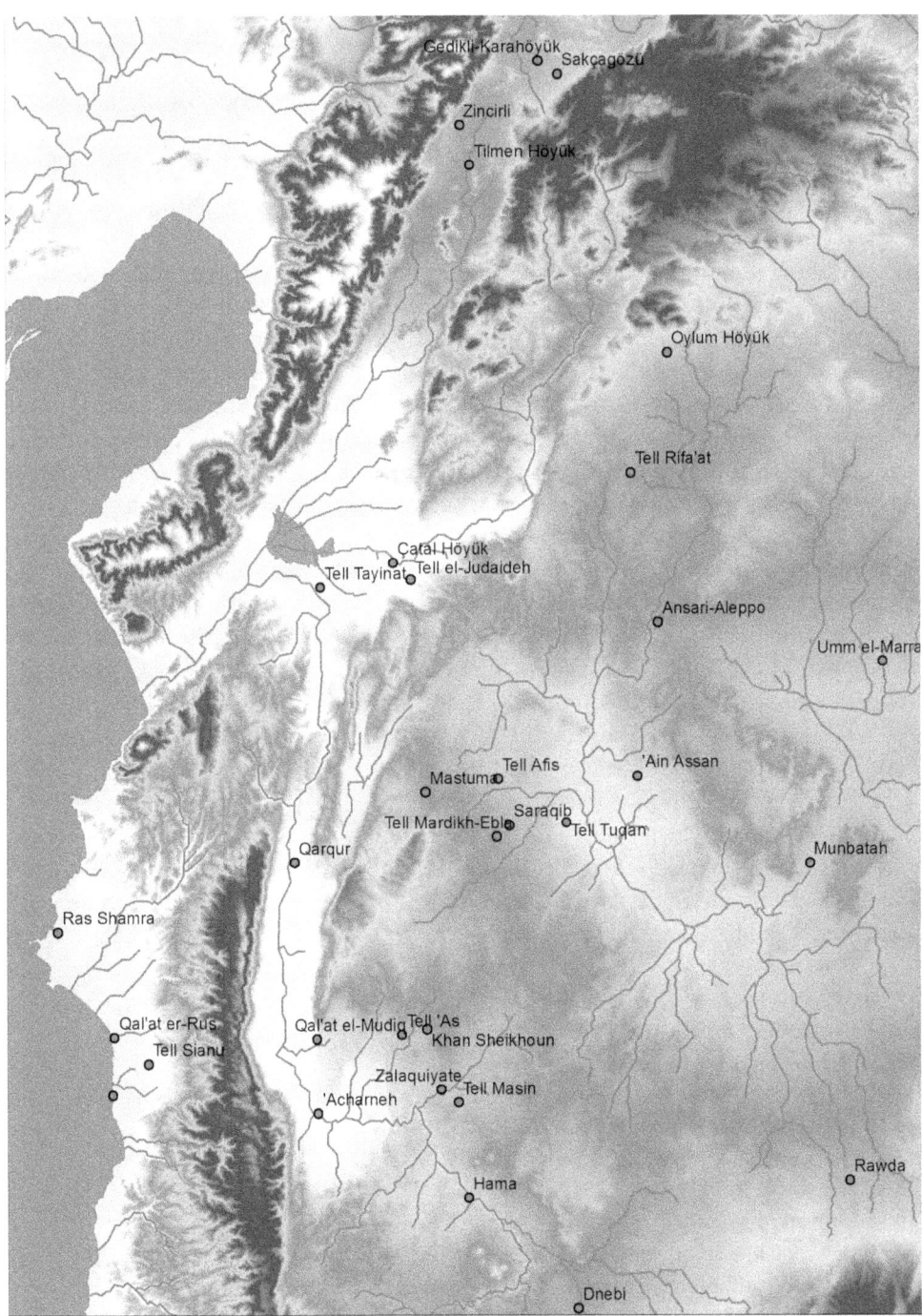

Figure 1.1: The 'Amuq and key northern Levantine EBA sites.

The 'Amuq plain in the Late Chalcolithic

The Late Chalcolithic is comparatively poorly understood in the Orontes region. Outside the 'Amuq plain, Late Chalcolithic remains are known in southern Turkey/western Syria from Sakçegözü, Gedikli-Karahöyük, Ras Shamra, Hama, Qal'at al-Mudiq and Tell Nebi Mend,[13] but the site with the most comprehensively published and secure contexts from this period is Tell Afis.[14]

Although identifying late fourth millennium BC sites in survey material can be difficult, the evidence from the AVRP provides a broad sense of settlement patterns during this period. The survey results suggest that the late fourth millennium BC lays the foundation for settlement trends that can be observed continuing into the third millennium.[15] In the 'Amuq, the Late Chalcolithic (Phase F) witnesses the beginning of a trend towards more agglomerated settlement into larger sites concentrated in the central part of the plain, in contrast to the more dispersed settlement patterns observed in the preceding periods.[16] This centralised pattern may be influenced at least to some degree by the window of low sedimentation located in the central part of the plain, which increases visibility of early sites in this area compared to other areas that experienced greater alluviation.[17] However, in addition to this tendency towards moderately sized centres, increasing numbers of smaller sites have also been observed.[18] Many Phase F sites appear to be new foundations in this phase, which may suggest an increasing population in the Late Chalcolithic period.[19]

As has been recognised previously, the stratified Late Chalcolithic (Phase F) contexts from the 1930s excavations in the 'Amuq are potentially problematic.[20] Phase F, as excavated at Tell Judaidah (JK3; see Table 1.1), did not overlie cleanly stratified material of Phase E, which dates to the fifth millennium BC and contains 'Ubaid-related ceramics. Rather, Phase F deposits lay above material of the 'First Mixed Range', a mixed level containing ceramic material dated between Phases C–E.[21] The deposits associated with Phase F are relatively shallow in depth (ca. 1 m), and although these levels

---

13 du Plat Taylor et al. 1950; Collon 1975; Thuesen 1988; de Contenson 1992; Mazzoni 1998, 21–23; Duru 2010.
14 Cecchini and Mazzoni 1998.
15 For a similar phenomenon in the Homs region, see Philip and Bradbury 2016, 381.
16 Casana 2003, 213; Gerritsen et al. 2008, 247–248.
17 Wilkinson 2000, 173; Casana and Wilkinson 2005, 36–38.
18 Gerritsen et al. 2008, 247–248; Casana and Wilkinson 2005, 39.
19 Gerritsen et al. 2008, 248.
20 Braidwood and Braidwood 1960, 228–229, 512–513; Mazzoni 1998, 22; Philip 2002, 212.
21 Braidwood and Braidwood 1960, 512–513; Welton 2017, 3–5. Although Phase F remains were also identified at Çatal Höyük and Tell Dhahab, these were also not well stratified. At the former, remains identified as belonging to Phase F lay above virgin soil, and at the latter, remains from this period were completely un-stratified. Late Chalcolithic materials may also be present at the excavations at Tabara al-Akrad Levels VII–VI (Hood 1951; Braidwood and Braidwood 1960, 512–513) and Tell esh-Sheikh (Mazzoni 1998, 22).

1 Northern Levantine spheres of interaction

were associated with architectural remains, Braidwood suggested that the associated assemblages (Floors 22 debris and 21) may represent mixed assemblages.[22] There is thus good evidence to suggest that there may be a stratigraphic gap in the 'Amuq sequence as published, between Phases E and F, which could cover a period spanning as long as the mid-fifth millennium through the first half of the fourth millennium BC.[23] Pottery types generally considered to represent the late fifth millennium and the earlier parts of the fourth millennium BC, such as the ubiquitous 'Coba bowls', are absent from the Judaidah material.[24]

Despite the problematic nature of stratified fourth millennium BC deposits in the region, Braidwood did isolate particular ceramic types that he identified with the Late Chalcolithic, most notably Chaff-Faced and Smooth-Faced Simple Wares (see Figure 1.2).[25] These ware types are generally considered diagnostic of this period across a wide area of the Near East, including western Syria, Cilicia and south-eastern Anatolia.[26] Algaze suggested on this basis that 'a surprising degree of material culture homogeneity existed over an exceedingly broad area'.[27] However, more recent discussions have tended to emphasise regional variability over homogeneity.[28] For example, Red-Slipped Wares, prevalent in the 'Amuq, are more common in this region compared to sites east of the Euphrates, extending as far to the north-east as Arslantepe (see Figure 1.2: 8).[29] Uruk elements (usually bevelled-rim bowls; Figure 2: 14–15), while present, are comparatively rare, and generally originate from contaminated or poorly stratified contexts.[30] Uruk influences appear to be completely absent further to the south in the upper Orontes, at Tell Nebi Mend,[31] while traces of red slip on examples of the vegetal-tempered Fabric C from the site may indicate that the Red-Slipped Wares extend this far south.[32] Other types are shared by sites throughout the Orontes valley, such as shallow bowls with reserved-slip on the interior, which are present in the 'Amuq, and at Hama and Nebi Mend, as

---

22 Braidwood and Braidwood 1960, 175, 228.
23 Welton 2017, 5–8.
24 Trentin suggested that the Chatal Höyük Phase F material may be chronologically differentiated from the Judaidah material from JK3 that was used as the primary basis for the definition of the sequence, based on parallels from Habuba Kabira and Sheikh Hassan (Trentin 1993, 192), an idea that was evaluated and further elaborated in Welton 2017, 8–13.
25 Braidwood and Braidwood 1960, 228–229.
26 Algaze 1993; Frangipane 1993; Mellink 1993; Trufelli 1997; Mazzoni 1998, 2000; Philip 2002.
27 Algaze 1993, 92.
28 Frangipane 1993, 153–156; Trufelli 1997, 24–25; Mazzoni 2000, 140–142; Philip 2002, 209.
29 Frangipane 1993, 148, 154; Trufelli 1997, 17; Mazzoni 1998, 22.
30 Braidwood and Braidwood 1960, 234, n. 10; Thuesen 1988, 182; Frangipane 1993, 156; Philip 2002, 212. Other forms that appear to be influenced by Uruk traditions, such as droop-spouted jars, appear in contexts and in ware types that clearly place them in Phase G (e.g. Late Reserved Slip Ware).
31 Philip 2002, 214.
32 Mathias and Parr 1989, 21; Mathias 2000, 419.

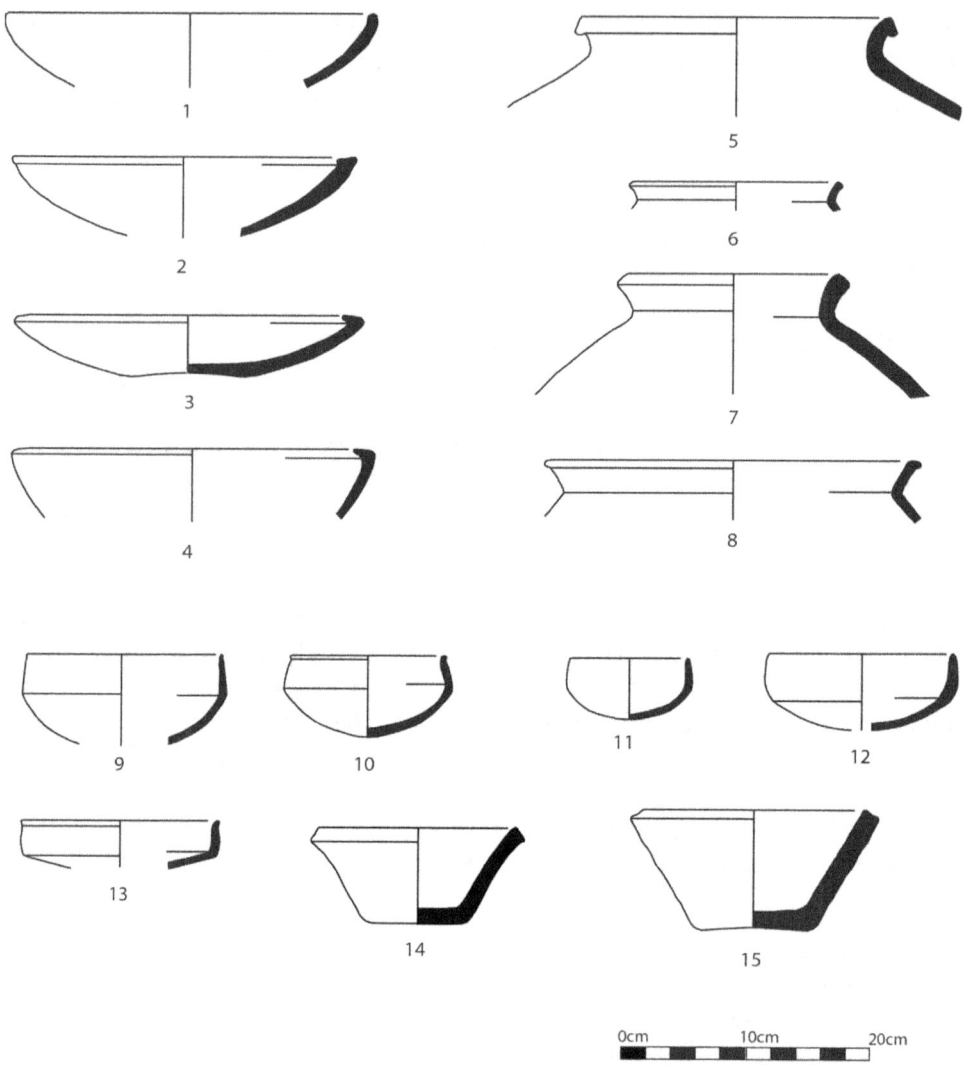

Figure 1.2: Diagnostic Phase F forms.

No.	Site and description	Reference
1.	'Amuq F, Chaff-Faced Simple Ware	Braidwood and Braidwood 1960, fig. 174: 4
2.	'Amuq F, Chaff-Faced Simple Ware	Braidwood and Braidwood 1960, fig. 174: 14
3.	Hama K3–2	Thuesen 1988, pl. LXII: 3 (4B998)
4.	Zeytinli Bahçe Höyük	Frangipane 2007, fig. 8.11: 1
5.	'Amuq F, Chaff-Faced Simple Ware	Braidwood and Braidwood 1960, fig. 176: 21

1 Northern Levantine spheres of interaction

No.	Site and description	Reference
6.	Tell Afis, Chaff-Faced Ware	Mazzoni 1998, fig. 4: 6
7.	Arslantepe VII	Frangipane 1993, fig. 10: 10
8.	'Amuq F, Red-Slipped and Burnished Ware	Braidwood and Braidwood 1960, fig. 179: 22
9.	'Amuq F, Chaff-Faced Simple Ware	Braidwood and Braidwood 1960, fig. 174: 20
10.	Hama K7–K5	Thuesen 1988, pl. XLIV: 9 (4B687)
11.	Hama K7–K5	Thuesen 1988, pl. XLIV: 7 (4C874)
12.	Qal'at er-Rus, Natural Un-burnished Ware	Ehrich 1939, pl. V: IIIB
13.	'Amuq F, Smooth-Faced Simple Ware	Braidwood and Braidwood 1960, fig. 171, 13
14.	Çatal Höyük W16, Chaff-Faced Simple Ware, Bevelled Rim Bowl	Braidwood and Braidwood 1960, fig. 175, 1
15.	Hama K 7–5, Bevelled Rim Bowl	Thuesen 1988, pl. XLIV:1 (4A882)

well as on the coast at Qal'at er-Rus.[33] The 'Amuq's external connections during Phase F are thus wide-ranging, reaching both to the north and east, towards the Euphrates region, and to the south and west, towards the coastal regions and the Orontes valley.[34]

Discussing the characteristics of the late fourth millennium BC assemblage in western Syria, Mazzoni pointed out the co-occurrence of Chaff-Faced pottery with Late 'Ubaid-like painted motifs at a number of other sites in western Syria, including Tell Afis, Ras Shamra, Hama and Tarsus,[35] suggesting that this may also be a regional feature. Although there is evidence for a stratigraphic gap in the 'Amuq sequence, the apparently mixed nature of the Phase F ceramic assemblage that was noted by Braidwood may partially be an indication of material conservatism and continuity in ceramic production.[36] Regardless of whether this is ultimately the case, it is clear that there is still much to understand about the dynamics of material culture in the 'Amuq (and western Syria in general) during the fifth and fourth millennia BC.

---

33 Ehrich 1939, 6; Braidwood and Braidwood 1960, 232, fig. 173; Thuesen 1988, 113; Philip 2002, 214, Table 5.
34 Welton 2017, 16–19.
35 de Contenson 1992, 178–183; Mazzoni 1998, 22–24; Thuesen 1998, 90–91.
36 Mazzoni 1998, 24; 2000, 140–141.

Table 1.2: ARCANE ENL Chronology.

Tentative Dates	Traditional	ENL	Tell Mardikh/Ebla	Amuq	TAP	Tell Tuqan	Hama	ECL	EME	EJZ	ESL	Ras Shamra	Tarsus
3200	LCH	LCH		Phase F					LCH	LCH	EBIB/ESL3	hiatus	Early Goldman EB I
3100				Phase G: Floors 20-18			K8	ECL1					
3000	EBI-II	ENL1	earlier levels	Phase G: Floors 17-12			K7 K6 K5	ECL2	EME1	EJZ0	EBII?/ESL4		
2900													
2700	EBIII	ENL2	Level IIA Building G2, Area CC	Phase H		Area P, IC1 (9-10) Area P, IC2 (7-8) Area P, IC3 (6)	K4 K3 K2 K1	ECL3	EME2	EJZ 1	EBIII/ESL5	IIIA1	Later Goldman EB I
2600										EJZ2			
2500	EBIVA1	ENL3	Building G5 Phase 1	Phase I		Area P, IC (5)	J8	ECL4	EME3	EJZ3a		IIIA2	Goldman EB II
2350	EBIVA2	ENL4	Building G5 Phase 2 Palace G, Building P4, FF2 T. of the Rock (HH1)		FP9?	hiatus	J7 J6-5	ECL5	EME4	EJZ3b	EBIV/ESL6		
2200	EBIVB	ENL5	Favissae, Private Houses, HH6?	Phase J	FP8	Area P, Ph. 4B	J4		EME5	EJZ4		IIIA3	Goldman EB III
2100	EB-MB Transition	ENL6	Temples HH4 & HH5, Temple D3?, Archaic Palace P Area T structure, HH squatters	?	FP7	Area P, Ph. 4A	J3	ECL6					
2000					hiatus?		J2 J1		EME6	EJZ5			?

The early third millennium BC

As observed for the preceding Late Chalcolithic phase, there are very few other excavated sites in the Orontes region that have produced excavated remains dating to the EB I–II (ARCANE ENL1; see Table 1.2) period. As a result, the sequence as it exists is heavily dependent on the evidence from the 'Amuq plain (Phase G) for understanding the early part of the third millennium BC in this region. Similarly, the best-described ceramic sequence for the EB III (ARCANE ENL2) originates from the 'Amuq (Phase H).[37] Although detailed ceramic data have been published for Level K at Hama, there is substantial evidence for problems of stratigraphy and artefact provenience at the site, rendering it less than reliable for discussions regarding chronological development.[38] A small amount of ENL1 material has been published from Tell Afis,[39] and recent publications have begun to greatly expand our knowledge of ENL2 occupations at both Tell Mardikh-Ebla and Tell Tuqan (i.e. Building G2 and Area CC at Ebla).[40]

The earliest third millennium BC phase in the 'Amuq, termed Phase G, is generally representative of the ARCANE ENL1 period, although its earliest floors in fact likely date to the late fourth millennium and may be considered transitional Late Chalcolithic–EB I.[41] The primary definition of this phase in the 'Amuq relied on stratified remains from Tell Judaidah.[42] This period is characterised by the appearance and proliferation of Plain Simple Ware (PLSW), a fine buff ware type that continues to appear, with some modifications, for more than a thousand years (see Figure 1.3: 1, 5–7 and 9).[43] Forms in this ware demonstrate strong continuity from the preceding period (see Figures 1.2: 1–4, 9–13; 1.3: 5–10). Other closely related wares with distinctive decoration types appear alongside it, such as Reserved Slip Ware and Incised and Impressed Ware. Certain features of the ceramic assemblage show chronological development that might allow the proposal of a distinction between early Phase G (represented by JK3: floors 20–18) and late Phase G (JK3: floors 17–12). These include the proliferation of painted decoration (Multiple-Brush Painted Ware) in the later part of Phase G, along with changes in the cooking pot assemblage.[44] Phase H (representing ARCANE ENL2) was marked by the continuation of Plain Simple Ware and other related wares in the same typical forms observed in Phase G. The primary changes to PLSW in ENL2 are the addition of a small number of chronologically specific forms, most notably Cyma Recta cups (see Figure 1.4: 1–3). As

---

37 Braidwood and Braidwood 1960.
38 Thuesen 1988, 11.
39 Mazzoni 1998, 30–31.
40 Vacca 2014; 2015; 2018; this book; Pinnock, this book.
41 Welton 2017, 15; Yener et al. 2000, 199.
42 Braidwood and Braidwood 1960, 259; see also Yener et al. 2000, 195–198.
43 Note, however, that PLSW shares many characteristics with the SFSW of the preceding Phase F, suggesting that the origins of this buff ware tradition in fact lie earlier in the fourth millennium (Welton 2017, 13).
44 Welton 2017, 22–23.

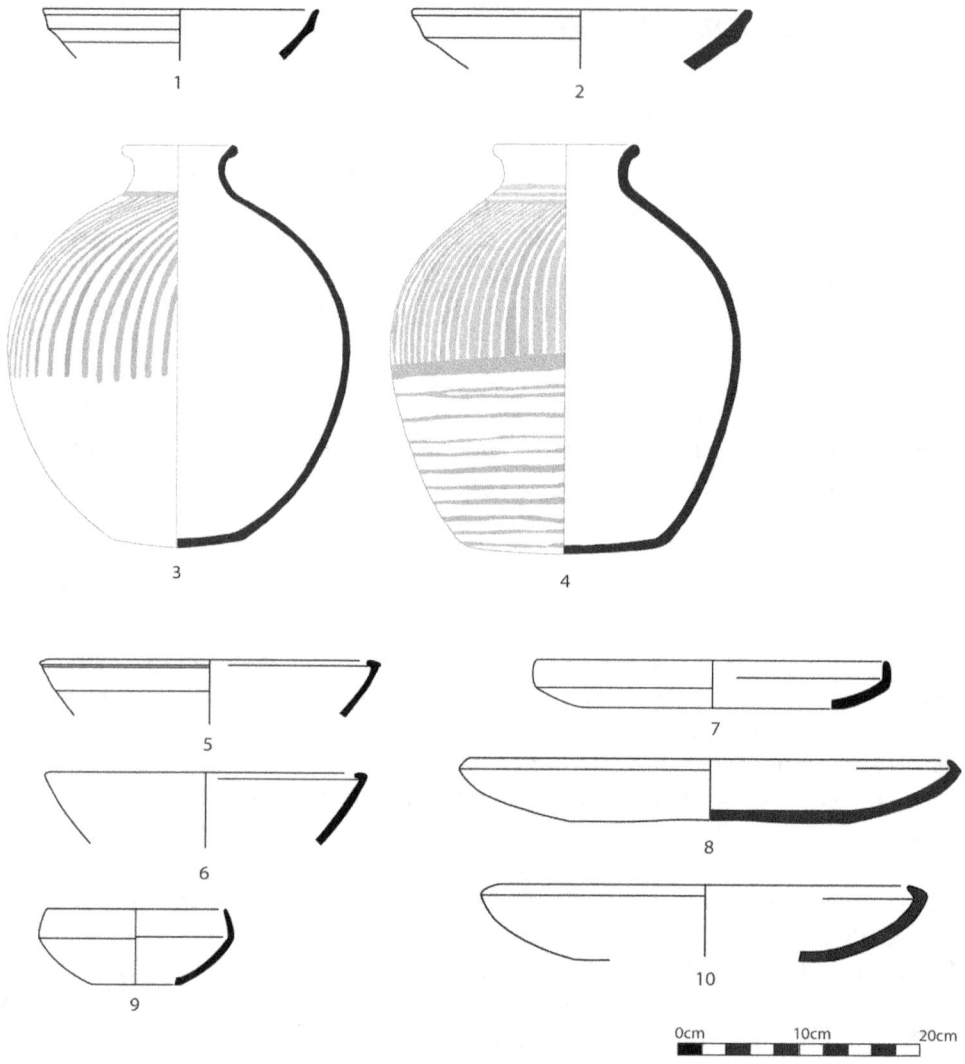

Figure 1.3: Diagnostic Phase G forms.

No.	Site and description	Reference
1.	Judaidah JK3 Plain Simple Ware	Braidwood and Braidwood 1960, fig. 205: 15
2.	Zeytinli Bahçe Höyük	Frangipane 1993, fig. 8.11: 8
3.	Judaidah JK3:15 Reserved Slip Ware	Braidwood and Braidwood 1960, fig. 219: 1
4.	Judaidah JK3:12 Reserved Slip Ware	Braidwood and Braidwood 1960, fig. 219: 2

1 Northern Levantine spheres of interaction

No.	Site and description	Reference
5.	Judaidah JK3 Plain Simple Ware	Braidwood and Braidwood 1960, fig. 205: 14
6.	Judaidah JK3 Plain Simple Ware	Braidwood and Braidwood 1960, fig. 205: 5
7.	Judaidah JK3 Plain Simple Ware	Braidwood and Braidwood 1960, fig. 202: 10
8.	Ras Shamra IIIA1	de Contenson 1969, fig. 20: 5
9.	Judaidah JK3 Plain Simple Ware	Braidwood and Braidwood 1960, fig. 202: 13
10.	Tell Sukas Level L2 Burnished Un-slipped Ware	Oldenberg 1991, fig. 36: 5

others have noted, these may begin to occur already in late Phase G,[45] but they remain particularly characteristic of Phase H.[46] Also characteristic of this period is the addition of significant amounts of Red-Black Burnished Ware (RBBW) and the first appearance of Brittle Orange Ware (BOW) (Figure 1.4: 4–16), although the appearance of RBBW in fact begins in the terminal floor of Phase G (JK3: floor 12).[47] These changes provide potential characteristics allowing for the division of the late fourth–early third millennium sequence into the traditional periodisation of EB I, II and III. However, these divisions have never mapped particularly well onto the 'Amuq sequence, and the general lack of synchronisation between the region's changes in material culture, coupled with the overwhelming evidence for continuity in ceramic production, must certainly lead us to question the utility of these divisions for describing the development of the Early Bronze Age sequence in the 'Amuq.

Survey data from the AVRP suggest that sites in Phase G commonly display continuity from the previous phase, including the concentration of population in a few larger sites located in the central part of the plain.[48] In contrast, the peripheral regions of the plain seem to have been more sparsely settled. A small number of larger sites in the range of 8–14 ha appear alongside a series of smaller sites, mostly measuring 1–3 ha in size. However, Phases G and H share virtually their entire range of wares, with the exception of the addition of RBBW in Phase H. As a result, it can be extremely difficult based on survey data alone to distinguish occupations that span both phases, making it problematic to evaluate settlement continuity from Phase G to H with a reliable degree of accuracy.

---

45 Algaze et al. 1990, 293, n. 2; Jamieson 2014b, 117, n. 3.
46 Braidwood and Braidwood 1960, 352; Conti and Persiani 1993, 380.
47 Braidwood and Braidwood 1960, 294. That the appearance of RBBW in Phase G occurs only in JK3: floor 12 has been confirmed by personal observation of the Judaidah ceramic collections held at the Oriental Institute.
48 Yener et al. 2000, 183; Welton 2012, 20.

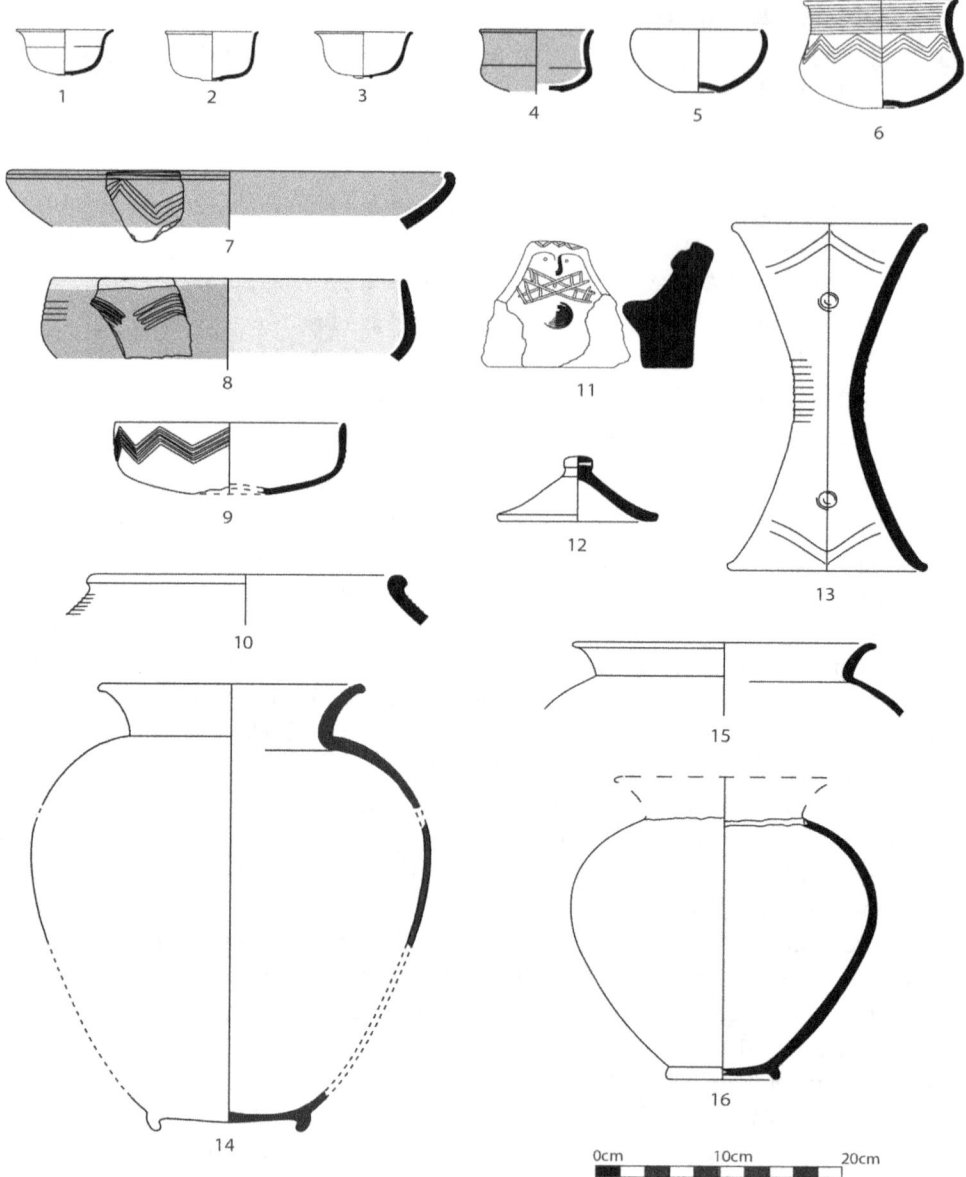

Figure 1.4: Diagnostic Phase H forms.

1 Northern Levantine spheres of interaction

No.	Site and description	Reference
1.	Judaidah JK3 Plain Simple Ware	Braidwood and Braidwood 1960, fig. 269: 9
2.	Judaidah JK3 Plain Simple Ware	Braidwood and Braidwood 1960, fig. 269: 10
3.	Judaidah JK3: 11 Plain Simple Ware	Braidwood and Braidwood 1960, fig. 271: 2
4.	Tayinat Red-Black Burnished Ware	Braidwood and Braidwood 1960, fig. 281: 22
5.	Judaidah JK3: 11 Red-Black Burnished Ware	Braidwood and Braidwood 1960, fig. 282: 3
6.	Tayinat T4 Red-Black Burnished Ware	Braidwood and Braidwood 1960, fig. 282: 8
7.	Judaidah JK3: 9 Red-Black Burnished Ware	Braidwood and Braidwood 1960, fig. 282: 6
8.	Tayinat Red-Black Burnished Ware	Braidwood and Braidwood 1960, fig. 281: 11
9.	Judaidah JK3: 11 Red-Black Burnished Ware	Braidwood and Braidwood 1960, fig. 282: 2
10.	Tell Dhahab Red-Black Burnished Ware	Braidwood and Braidwood 1960, fig. 283: 3
11.	Tayinat T4 Red-Black Burnished Ware	Braidwood and Braidwood 1960, fig. 290: 2
12.	Judaidah JK3: 11 Red-Black Burnished Ware	Braidwood and Braidwood 1960, fig. 282: 11
13.	Tell Dhahab Red-Black Burnished Ware	Braidwood and Braidwood 1960, fig. 282: 13
14.	Tarsus (EB II) Plain and Burnished Red Gritty Ware	Goldman 1956, pl. 350: 233
15.	Tayinat ('Amuq I) Brittle Orange Ware	Braidwood and Braidwood 1960, fig. 310: 7
16.	Tayinat T1 ('Amuq I) Brittle Orange Ware	Braidwood and Braidwood 1960, fig. 311: 1

Furthermore, due to the general conservatism and long continuity observed in RBBW in terms of both forms and fabric, there can also be difficulty in differentiating between Phase H and Phase I sites. Even so, a noticeable shift seems to occur during Phase H, with an increase in the number of sites. This increase seems to occur primarily in small sites measuring less than 3 ha in size.[49] Many of the larger sites occupied during Phase G are abandoned, although many of the smaller sites likely continued to be occupied. Replacing the moderately sized sites of Phase G is the single largest centre in this period, Tell Tayinat. Surface survey of the site produced Phase H wares around the base of the entire settlement, suggesting that at this time, the entire upper mound was likely already occupied, making the site ca. 18–20 ha in size and suggesting a trend towards greater centralisation.[50] Concurrently, however, settlements become more highly dispersed away from the centre of the plain and expand into hilly areas on its margins. This, along with the increase in small sites, has been interpreted to indicate a simultaneous dispersal of the population into smaller, more rural settlements.[51]

The general nature of the material assemblage gives us a sense of the ʿAmuq's larger regional connections during this period. The appearance of Late Reserved Slip Ware (RSW) in the ʿAmuq during Phase G is of particular note, as this ware is principally characteristic of the upper Euphrates (EME1–2),[52] but is comparatively poorly known in the northern Levantine region outside of the ʿAmuq (see Figure 1.3: 3–4).[53] Although the rarity of this ware may be due to our general lack of knowledge of this period in the region, the evidence from Hama and (slightly later, in ENL2) from Qalʾat el-Mudiq suggests, perhaps not surprisingly, that these areas had more distant relationships with the upper Euphrates. The frequency of RSW, as well as the occurrence of certain PLSW forms in the ʿAmuq in Phases G–H, suggests the continuation of connections to the north and east during this period. This connection appears to be strongest during the early to middle part of Phase G, perhaps tapering off later in the phase and into Phase H. Although these connections have received a fair amount of attention,[54] it is still important to recognise that ceramics demonstrating direct connections between the two regions represent only a small proportion of the respective assemblages, and the bulk of both assemblages remain quite distinct from each other.

Alongside the gradual separation in material culture between the ʿAmuq and its north-easterly neighbours that might be suggested to develop during this period in PLSW and RSW, the appearance of significant amounts of Red-Black Burnished Ware (henceforth RBBW; see Figure 1.4: 4–13) and the first appearance of Brittle Orange Ware (BOW; see Figure 1.4: 14–16) are both significant features of Phase H. Both of these ware types suggest a general northern orientation in material culture, with RBBW

---

49 Batiuk 2005, 99.
50 Batiuk et al. 2005, 176–177.
51 Batiuk 2007, 53; 2013, 452, 465; Welton 2012, 20.
52 Conti and Persiani 1993, 379–381; Sconzo 2015, 94.
53 Mazzoni 1980; Jamieson 2014a, 104. It is also found in small quantities at Ebla (Mazzoni 1985, 9, fig. 7:1–2, 5; 1991, 17) and Tell Tuqan (Vacca 2014, 62).
54 Trentin 1993; Abay 1997; Gerber 2005.

in particular demonstrating connections to a wide swathe of eastern and southeastern Anatolia. Brittle Orange Ware is not well attested in the northern Levant outside the 'Amuq, but is particularly characteristic of the Islahiye region and Cilicia, as well as being attested in the Maraş region (see Figure 1.4: 14).[55] With the exception of examples from the Qoueiq,[56] the 'Amuq appears to represent the most southerly appearance of this ware type. The broader regional connections of RBBW to the Early Transcaucasian Culture (ETC) have been widely discussed elsewhere, and are too complex to fully summarise here, but particularly relevant in this context is the idea that the 'Amuq represents a geographical transition point in the distribution of RBBW forms, with the most southerly examples of some Anatolian forms, and the most northerly examples of certain Levantine forms.[57] Thus, RBBW not only represents an indicator of the 'Amuq's northerly contacts during the early third millennium BC, but is also suggestive of its contemporary links towards the south and, more broadly, of its potential role in translating or transforming ETC ceramic forms for the Levantine *koine*.

The mid-late third millennium BC

The beginning of the EB IV period, in the mid-third millennium BC, represents the height of the centralisation and urbanisation processes of the Early Bronze Age of northern Syria, culminating with the period contemporary with the Ebla Palace G Complex and the Ebla archives. This period has traditionally been divided into the EB IVA (ARCANE ENL3–4) and EB IVB (ARCANE ENL5–6).

Of these phases, ENL3 (early EB IVA or EB IVA1) is only very sporadically attested in the northern Levant, but is known at both Ebla (Building G5)[58] and Tell Tuqan.[59] These levels demonstrate incipient goblet forms, as well as the continuation of small amounts of RBBW,[60] which then disappears in the levels associated with Palace G (ENL4). These levels also contain flaring neck, round bodied jars that have parallels in EME3 in the Euphrates.[61] ENL3 may thus be considered to represent an incipient phase of ENL4, which in turn can be taken to represent the height of Ebla's palatial complex immediately prior to its ultimate destruction. The chronological extent of the earlier phase in particular is not clear. It is with the ENL4 that we encounter a veritable explosion of available information in most regions of the northern Levant, as witnessed in the vast expansion of known settlements in the Orontes region and

---

55 von Luschan 1943, 38–41, pls. 15–16; Goldman 1956, 118–120; Steadman 1994, 98–99; Carter 1995, 334; Duru 2010, 142–146; Bell 2007.
56 Mellaart 1981, 159.
57 Batiuk 2005, Table 5, 169–170.
58 Matthiae 1993, 622; 2000, 576; Vacca 2015, 10; 2018; this book.
59 Vacca 2014, 66; this book.
60 Matthiae 1993, 623; Mazzoni 2002, 76; Vacca 2015, 8.
61 Mazzoni 2002, 76; Sconzo 2015, 123, pl. 12; Vacca 2015, 8–9.

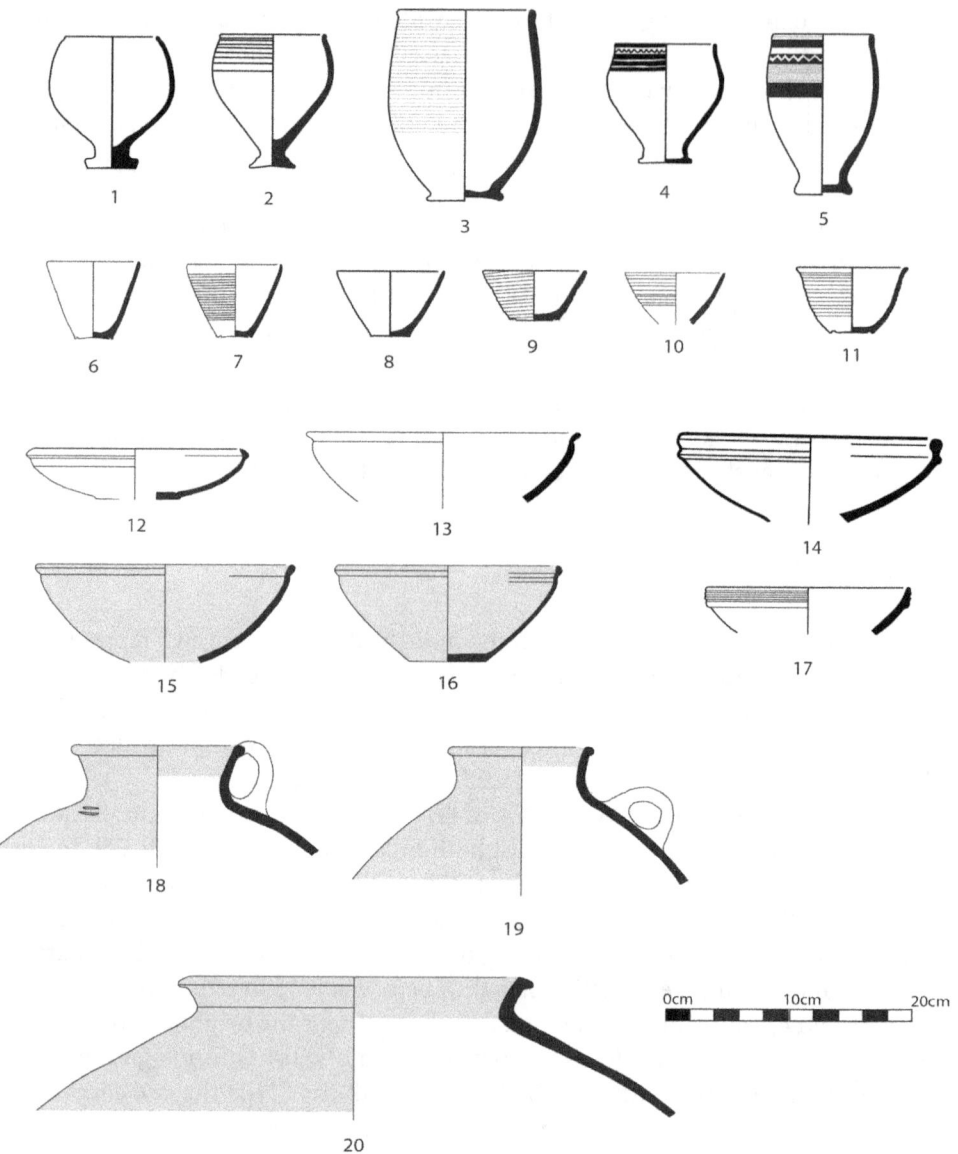

Figure 1.5: Diagnostic Phase I and J forms.

1 Northern Levantine spheres of interaction

No.	Site and description	Reference
1.	Tell Tayinat, Phase J, FP7 Simple Ware	TAP TT07.G4.55.352.1 L.205
2.	Tell Tayinat, Phase J, FP8b Simple Ware	TAP TT10.G4.55.586.4 L.263
3.	Hama J3	Fugmann 1958, fig. 93: 3F583
4.	Tell Tayinat, Phase J, FP7 Painted Simple Ware	TAP TT07.G4.65.290.1 L.108
5.	Tell Mardikh-Ebla Simple Painted Ware, P.9719	Sala 2012, fig. 11: 4, TM.07.HH.270/9
6.	Tayinat T4, Phase I Simple Ware	Braidwood and Braidwood 1960, fig. 315: 3
7.	Tayinat T4, Phase I Simple Ware	Braidwood and Braidwood 1960, fig. 315: 4
8.	Tayinat T8, Phase J Simple Ware	Braidwood and Braidwood 1960, fig. 338: 1
9.	Tayinat T8, Phase J Simple Ware	Braidwood and Braidwood 1960, fig. 338: 3
10.	Tell Mardikh-Ebla	Mazzoni 1991, fig. 7: 3, TM.89.G.399/1
11.	Ras Shamra IIIA3	de Contenson 1969, fig. 5: 12
12.	Tell Tayinat, Phase J, FP7 Simple Ware	TAP TT11.G4.56.703.37 L.308
13.	Tell Tayinat, Phase J, FP8a Simple Ware	TAP TT09.G4.55.496.1 L.271
14.	Tell Mardikh-Ebla Simple Ware, P. 9717	Sala 2012, fig. 8: 29, TM.07.HH.273/2
15.	Tell Tayinat, Phase J, FP8b Smeared Wash Ware	TAP TT09.G4.55.576.35 L.263
16.	Tell Tayinat, Phase J, FP8a Smeared Wash Ware	TAP TT09.G4.55.483.1 L.268
17.	Tell Afis (L.1112, Lev. 17b)	Mazzoni 2002, pl. XLIV: 123, TA.92.E.627/3
18.	Tell Tayinat, Phase J, FP8b Smeared Wash Ware	TAP TT08.G4.55.473.1 L.263
19.	Tell Tayinat, Phase J, FP8b Smeared Wash Ware, Phase J	TAP TT09.G4.55.560.1 L.263
20.	Tell Tayinat, Phase J, FP8b Smeared Wash Ware, Phase J	TAP TT10.G4.55.583.1 L.263

its neighbouring marginal areas.[62] In the 'Amuq, ENL3–4 are represented by Phase I, whose characteristics were defined primarily using stratified remains from Tell Tayinat.[63]

The final EBA phase, EB IVB (ENL5–6), corresponds to the period following the collapse of the Ebla Palace G Complex, when Ebla's power was significantly reduced, but it maintained its status as a regional centre. Ebla during this period is represented primarily by the Temple of the Rock sequence,[64] as well as by the Archaic Palace.[65] In the 'Amuq, remains from this period (Phase J) were excavated only at Tayinat, while other long-lived 'Amuq sites, such as Tell Judaidah, appear to display a hiatus.[66]

The EB IV is defined by the appearance of Simple Ware, a fine table ware characterised first by conical cup and later by goblet forms, as well as by the use of corrugated decoration (Figure 1.5: 1–2, 6–7). These general features are characteristic of ENL4 ceramic assemblages throughout the Orontes valley in Syria. Also characteristic of Phase I (ENL3–4) in the 'Amuq are the continuation of RBBW and BOW and the first appearance of Smeared Wash Ware (SWW). Phases I and J share virtually their entire range of wares, and Phase J is defined primarily by the substantial decrease in RBBW and the continuation of Simple Ware and SWW. The main form that appears to be unique to 'Amuq Phase J (ENL5–6) is the Painted Simple Ware goblet with reserved white-on-black painted decoration, but although it occurs regularly, this form still represents a comparatively minor component of excavated assemblages (see Figure 1.5: 4).[67]

In terms of settlement patterns, the trend towards increasing numbers of sites that began in Phase H continues into Phase I, although this growth slows somewhat in this period. The increase occurs primarily in mid-sized sites measuring between 3–8 ha in size. Despite various difficulties in distinguishing Phase H and I sites, there is clear evidence for continuity into this phase, suggesting that there was no obvious break in settlement, but rather that these phases form part of a long-term trend towards a more urbanised and highly populated landscape. Other areas of western Syria also display a trend towards increasing population and growing urbanisation in the EB IV. Many surveys have noted a proliferation in the numbers of sites observed in the EB IV period, compared to those represented in the EB I–III periods, corresponding to the rising population and the progressively more urbanised political situation that characterised the EB IV.[68]

The similarities in the ceramic assemblages of Phases I and J lead to difficulties in the evaluation of settlement continuity from Phase I to J, and Phase J sites are consequently likely underestimated in the survey data. Despite this, in Phase J, the number of settlements found in the region likely decreases. This decrease seems to

---

62 Wilkinson et al. 2014, 74–75.
63 Braidwood and Braidwood 1960, 397.
64 Matthiae 2007; Sala 2012; D'Andrea 2018; Pinnock, this book.
65 Matthiae 2006, 87–90, fig. 6.
66 Braidwood and Braidwood 1960, 429.
67 Welton 2014, 356.
68 Castel 2007; Castel and Peltenburg 2007; Geyer et al. 2007; Al-Maqdissi 2007; Morandi Bonacossi 2007; Wilkinson et al. 2014; Philip and Bradbury 2016.

1 Northern Levantine spheres of interaction

occur in both small and mid-sized sites, and the trend is largely confirmed by excavation results; sites like Çatal Höyük and Judaidah display a hiatus, with no evidence of stratified remains from this period. This may suggest a tendency towards even greater centralisation around a regional centre located at Tell Tayinat.

Phase I was defined by the appearance and proliferation of a 'standardised'[69] series of ceramics known as Simple Ware, a fine buff-coloured table ware characterised by the dominance of the goblet form, the use of corrugated decoration, and the appearance of distinctive painted motifs, particularly on goblets, in the EB IVB period. The widespread occurrence of these general features in ENL4 ceramic assemblages throughout the Orontes valley is likely a reflection of increasing intensity of intra-regional contact during this period.[70] However, despite the apparent existence of a shared cultural milieu, there remain significant differences between the 'Amuq assemblage and other Orontes sites, with only a minimal overlap between the most common recurring forms in each region.

This pattern continues into the EB IVB (Phase J), for which recent excavations at the site of Tell Tayinat have produced a large assemblage that allows a more detailed treatment of the relative frequencies of particular forms.[71] Many of the most common inland north Syrian forms are not present in the 'Amuq, or are only present in very small numbers. Vice versa, the majority of the most common forms observed in the 'Amuq are quite different from those observed in the rest of western Syria.[72] Goblet forms most common in the 'Amuq have wide, flaring bodies strongly tapering to a tall pedestal or wide bell-base (Figure 1.5: 1–2 and 4). In contrast, goblet forms to the south are generally narrow and barrel-shaped, with corrugated decoration in the EB IVA and painted decoration in the EB IVB (see Figure 1.5: 3 and 5).[73] This narrow form is comparatively rare in the 'Amuq, and while the widely flaring goblet occurs elsewhere in north-western Syria, it is generally less frequent than in the 'Amuq, where it is the dominant shape.[74] The 'Amuq also represents the core of the distribution of a contemporary drinking vessel, the conical cup (Figure 1.5: 6–11). These cups appear

---

69 The quotation marks here reflect the fact that the use of the word standardised to describe this assemblage may be somewhat misleading. Braidwood used this term (along with 'factory-made') originally to reflect a general decrease in variability in both form and fabric observed between the Plain Simple Ware of Phases G and H and the Simple Ware of Phases I and J (1960, 406, 520). Although it may have been implied, Braidwood's original characterisation of this ware type did not include any explicit discussion of the organisation of production of these ceramics. This word has since been regularly used to describe the Simple Ware of the EB IV period throughout western Syria, although often with quotation marks (i.e. Mazzoni 1985a; 2002; 2003). The assumed link between 'standardisation' and 'centralised production' has inevitably led to suggestions of centralised control of ceramic production by the Eblaite state, which the evidence in fact argues against. The more appropriate word to describe this assemblage would perhaps be 'specialised'.
70 Mazzoni 1985, 10–11; 2002, 70–71.
71 Welton et al. 2011; Welton 2014.
72 This issue is discussed in more depth in Welton 2014.
73 Welton and Cooper 2014; Welton 2014, figs. 10a–b.
74 Welton 2014, fig. 10c.

most commonly at other sites in the EB IVA, but the 'Amuq alone seems to demonstrate the continuation of significant numbers of these cups into the EB IVB, where they occur in somewhat lower frequencies than goblet forms.[75]

Likewise, the most common bowl forms in the 'Amuq in Phase J (Figure 1.5: 12–13 and 15–16) are not widely attested elsewhere in western Syria, and Tell Tayinat similarly demonstrates no evidence for bowl forms that occur widely at sites in inland north-western Syria in the EB IVB. Forms seemingly absent in the 'Amuq include bowls with vertical modelled rims, which are also widely distributed in the Euphrates region (Figure 1.5: 14).[76] One of the most characteristic forms of the late EB IVB, or ENL6, throughout northern Syria is the vertical grooved-rim bowl, which appears at almost all EB IVB sites in the region and along the Euphrates, but is thus far not attested in the 'Amuq (Figure 1.5: 17).[77]

Also characteristic of Phase I in the 'Amuq are the continuation of BOW and the first appearance of Smeared Wash Ware (henceforth SWW). Neither of these ware types are widespread in the northern Levant. As noted above, BOW is rare in the northern Levant, occurring almost exclusively in the 'Amuq, where it peaks in Phase I before virtually disappearing in Phase J. SWW is similarly limited in geographical distribution to a comparatively small core area between the Ebla region and the 'Amuq.[78] SWW first appears in the 'Amuq in the EB IVA (ca. 3–8% of the Phase I assemblage), earlier than its appearance elsewhere in western Syria, and is more frequent here than at almost all other sites, varying between 15–20% in most phases of the EB IVB (Figure 5: 15–16 and 18–20).[79] At Ebla, for example, SWW occurs predominantly in the EB IVB.[80] The only other site with a comparable amount of SWW is the site of Munbatah, where it reportedly formed 18% of the ceramic assemblage.[81] However, beyond this, SWW is comparatively rare outside the 'Amuq.

Phase I is also characterised by the continuation of RBBW, with some changes in decoration frequencies and the addition of some new forms. As discussed above, the occurrence of RBBW in small numbers in ENL3 can be observed at both Ebla and Tell Tuqan,[82] where its appearance may have been mediated through contacts with the 'Amuq. The persistence of RBBW into ENL4 is generally considered to be a feature unique to the 'Amuq, although it also occurs at Ras Shamra.[83] In both these cases, RBBW continues in significant quantities in EB IVA (e.g. in the 'Amuq, it forms 35–40% in Phase I).[84]

---

75 Welton 2014, 345.
76 Welton 2014, fig. 11a.
77 Welton 2014, fig. 11b.
78 Rova 1989; 2014, 207.
79 Welton 2014, fig. 13b.
80 Matthiae 1976, 201; Mazzoni 1985, 9; D'Andrea 2018, 5–6.
81 de Maigret 1974, 255.
82 Vacca 2014, 58; 2015, 8; this book.
83 Courtois 1962a–b; de Contenson 1963, 40.
84 Braidwood and Braidwood 1960, 398.

Although until recently it was suggested that RBBW disappeared completely in Phase J, excavations at Tell Tayinat have now demonstrated that it continues in very small but consistent frequencies in these levels.[85] Compared to Phases H–I, however, it is clear that the range of forms represented is by this time severely restricted, and is limited to large bowls and biconical pot-stands. Furthermore, elements of the coarse ware assemblage may reflect the continuity of the RBBW tradition, but in an altered form.[86] The limited range of forms, the alteration of the contexts in which these forms were used, and the lack of continuation of other features associated with the ETC 'package' (e.g. andirons, mud-plastered installations) together suggest that the cultural significance of this ware type had changed by the EB IVB. In this period, the longstanding conservatism witnessed in the ETC assemblage in the 'Amuq had broken down and the distinctiveness of the ETC 'community' was no longer maintained, at least at Tayinat. Similar persistence of RBBW-reminiscent influences into the EB IVB has recently also been proposed at Ebla.[87]

In terms of inter-regional relationships, the lack of evidence for sustained contacts between ETC communities is suggestive of decreasing northward-looking connections in the late third millennium BC; although in Phase H, the 'Amuq evidently played a role as a mediator between regions to the north and south, it is not clear that this role was sustained into the late third millennium. In contrast, links towards the north are rare by the end of the third millennium. One of the few clear late third millennium BC examples of Anatolian influence in the 'Amuq is the *depas* found in Phase J contexts at Tell Tayinat.[88]

Discussion: the position of the 'Amuq in the late third millennium

The ceramic data thus suggest a gradual shift in orientation throughout Phase I, from the more northerly connections observed in the late fourth and early third millennia BC (Phases G and H) to an almost exclusively southerly focus in Phase J. It is tempting to relate this shift in focus in the 'Amuq to the rise of Ebla as a major regional centre, but the situation is likely more complex. During the period of the Palace G archive, the site of Tell Tayinat may be identified with references to Alalaḫu, representing the major centre of the 'Amuq plain during this period.[89] Tell Atchana, the city of Alalakh in the second millennium BC, does not appear to have been occupied during this period, making it

---

85   Welton 2014, 355.
86   Braidwood and Braidwood 1960, 431; Welton 2014, 355.
87   D'Andrea 2018, 6.
88   Braidwood and Braidwood 1960, fig. 349. Note, however, that the reverse is not necessarily true. Ongoing contacts between the two regions, although they do not seem to appear directly in the 'Amuq ceramic repertoire, may be attested in the form of hybridised vessels at Tarsus combining Anatolian *depas*- or tankard-like forms with north Syrian goblets; see Goldman 1956; Mellink 1993. It is not clear, however, whether these connections are mediated through the 'Amuq, or appear via relationships with other more distant regions such as the Euphrates.
89   Archi 2006.

likely that this toponym in the Ebla archives refers to the site of Tayinat.⁹⁰ This suggests a long lifespan for this toponym as representative of the primary centre in the 'Amuq plain lasting until the late second millennium BC, despite the shift in settlement to Tell Atchana that occurs at the end of the third millennium BC. Various reconstructions have been suggested for the nature of the relationship between Alalaḫu and Ebla, ranging from direct control of the region from the early part of the archive period (in the reign of Irkab-Damu) to direct control of Alalaḫu only very late in the reign of Išar-Damu, during the tenure of the minister Ibbi-Zikir, when there is reference to a military conflict between the two cities.⁹¹ Prior to this time, we know that Alalaḫu periodically gave silver to Ebla, and that although no king was mentioned for the centre, it was under the control of an *ugula* or overseer. Although Archi has suggested that sites like Alalaḫu,⁹² which were controlled by an *ugula*, were under Ebla's direct control, Biga has more recently indicated that this need not always be the case.⁹³ There is little archaeological evidence to suggest any direct control by Ebla over the 'Amuq. In fact, although the two areas seem to share some common cultural preferences, there is still evidence of a noticeable disjuncture between the two assemblages. For example, it is reasonable to conclude that there is a lesser degree of similarity between the 'Amuq and Ebla in this period than there is between Ebla and the middle Euphrates. It may be that if the 'Amuq was ever under Ebla's direct control, it was likely for a relatively short period of time.⁹⁴

Although the broad similarities between the ceramic assemblages of the Orontes valley have often been assumed, whether implicitly or explicitly, to be tied to Eblaite political or cultural hegemony in the region, recent research has emphasised the variegated nature of the material culture in this region. Recent typological and petrographic studies of ceramics from Orontes valley sites suggest the development of different production sub-regions during the EBIV.⁹⁵ Both in terms of its morphological and its technological characteristics, it is clear that the 'Amuq represents one of several distinct 'provinces' or zones of production within the larger inland zone of the northern Levant. This suggests that within the Orontes valley, interconnections between regions were loose and flexible, despite evidence for shared cultural preferences and technological knowledge.

The assemblages of 'Amuq Phases I and J have limited parallels to the coastal assemblages, although connections do exist. Forms common at Tell Arqa, for example, occasionally occur in the 'Amuq, but while the forms demonstrate similarities, there are significant differences in fabrics and decorative techniques.⁹⁶ Other northern coastal sites such as Ras Shamra Level IIIA3–2, Qal'at er-Rus and Tell Sukas have somewhat

---

90   Batiuk and Horowitz 2010, 168; Welton 2012, 19.
91   Archi 2006; Biga 2008, 320.
92   Archi 2006.
93   Biga 2013, 260, 265.
94   For further discussion of the relationship between the 'Amuq and Ebla, see also Edwards 2018.
95   Welton and Cooper 2014, 332–335; Kennedy et al. 2018, 27–28; Welton 2018, 15–18.
96   See Thalmann 2006, figs 40 and 46: Type G1, fig. 47.

greater connections to the 'Amuq than are observed at Tell Arqa, but publication of the EBA artefacts from these sites remains sparsely illustrated.[97] At Ras Shamra, the appearance of Simple Ware goblets and conical cups and the longevity of Red-Black Burnished Ware demonstrate connections to the 'Amuq, but other diagnostic Phase J forms, such as white-on-black painted goblets and Smeared Wash Ware, are absent.[98] Coastal sites, furthermore, are generally characterised by Levantine 'Combed Ware', which is attested extremely infrequently in the 'Amuq, and never appears in the late third millennium BC.[99]

The evidence for restricted coastal connections is perhaps most pronounced in the 'Amuq, but also remains comparatively limited in the middle and lower Orontes valley,[100] suggesting a relative degree of separation between coastal and inland systems of exchange and circulation during this period. This may, however, not be true of the upper Orontes. An exception to the lack of evidence for direct connections between inland and coastal areas appears at Tell Nebi Mend, which demonstrates notable contacts with Tell Arqa during the late third millennium.[101] Similarly, examples of potential imports originating from inland Syria have been identified at Tell Arqa.[102] These connections, however, are likely to be due to direct contact occurring via the Homs-Tripoli gap, rather than to more systematic and wide-ranging coastal–inland connections during this period.

In contrast to many of the other sites in western Syria and the Orontes valley, the 'Amuq also demonstrates few direct ceramic connections to the Euphrates region. In the EB IVA, Ebla and other western Syrian sites begin to show more evidence for material connections to the Euphrates. This has often been implicated as an indication of Eblaite political control in the Euphrates during the period of Palace G, as suggested by textual sources. The ceramic influences between the regions, however, seem to be bi-directional rather than uni-directional, suggesting more complex relationships between these two areas. In contrast, the 'Amuq doesn't seem to be drawn into these interaction networks to the same degree as the areas to its south (in particular Ebla), and forms with direct connections to the Euphrates are very rare in the EB IVA, a feature that continues into the EB IVB.

Conclusions

To return to the idea that began this chapter, the 'Amuq's role as a connector or bridge is most evident in the fourth and earlier third millennium BC, beginning with its participation

---

97 Ehrich 1939; Courtois 1962a–b; de Contenson 1969; Oldenberg 1991; see also Sianu: al-Maqdissi 1993, figs 6–8.
98 de Contenson 1963, 40.
99 de Contenson 1969; Courtois 1962b; Thalmann 2006; Thalmann and Sowada 2014.
100 D'Andrea 2018, 19–20; Vacca 2018, 16.
101 Kennedy 2015, 258–260.
102 Thalmann 2006, 116; Jean 2018, 10–11.

in the widespread western Syrian milieu of the Late Chalcolithic, and continuing to be pronounced through the early third millennium (until Phase H, ENL2). It is during this period that its transitional role, as the southern participant in a northern cultural sphere, and the northern participant in more southerly regional interactions, is particularly clear. In Phases G and H, ware types like Reserved Slip Ware and Red-Black Burnished Ware suggest significant connections to northern regions like the upper Euphrates. In Phase I, however, these northerly connections begin to gradually shrink; no longer are there any direct connections to the upper Euphrates and Red-Black Burnished Ware no longer displays evidence for continuing interaction with the ongoing evolution of related wares to the north. Only Brittle Orange Ware suggests a continued connection to the north during Phase I, but over a more circumscribed area closer to the 'Amuq, in the region of Islahiye and possibly Cilicia. By Phase J, the shift in focus is complete, with the disappearance of this ware type. The ceramic data thus suggest a gradual shift in orientation throughout Phase I, from the more northerly connections observed in Phases G and H, to a more restricted and almost exclusively southerly focus by Phase J.

Concurrent with the general southerly shift in the 'Amuq's cultural focus during the late third millennium BC, however, is the appearance of notable differences in the details of its material culture from those observed in the Ebla region and other parts of inland western Syria. The continuing theme that emerges from the preceding observations is that while there are broad similarities between the ceramic assemblages of the 'Amuq and the rest of inland western Syria, which allow the proposal of chronological synchronisms between these regions, the 'Amuq is only comparatively loosely integrated into this larger region throughout the late third millennium. The 'Amuq, therefore, seems to consistently represent what might be termed an idiosyncratic local variant of the north Syrian assemblage. Its inhabitants subscribe to the same general ceramic preferences of EBA society, but communities in the 'Amuq interpret these patterns locally and separately from the remainder of inland Syria, suggesting that they retained a significant degree of regional independence throughout the period. Far from representing an isolated example, however, the evidence emerging from elsewhere in the Orontes valley suggests that this may have been a widespread phenomenon, with greater regionalisation of material culture than has been previously assumed.

References

Abay, E. (1997). *Die keramik der Frühbronzezeit in Anatolien: mit "Syrischen Affinitäten"*. Münster: Ugarit-Verlag.

Akar, M. (2011). *The Late Bronze Age II City of Alalakh and its social context in the northern Levant: a re-examination of the post-level IV stratigraphic sequence (I-III) based on new excavation results (2003–2010)*. PhD thesis, Universita' degli Studi di Firenze, Florence, Italy.

Algaze, G. (1993). *The Uruk world system: the dynamics of expansion of early Mesopotamian civilization*. Chicago: University of Chicago Press.

1 Northern Levantine spheres of interaction

Algaze, G., Evins, M.A., Ingraham, L., Marfoe, M. and Yener, K.A. eds. (1990). *Town and country in south eastern Anatolia II: the stratigraphic sequence at Kurban Höyük*. Oriental Institute Publications No. CX. Chicago: University of Chicago Press.

Al-Maqdissi, M. (1993). Chronique des activités archéologique en Syrie (I). *Syria* 70(3–4): 443–560.

(2007). Notes d'archéologie levantine X. Introduction au travaux archéologiques syriens à Mishrife-Qatna au nord-est de Homs (Emèse). In *Urban and natural landscapes of an ancient Syrian capital: settlement and environment at Tell Mishrifeh/Qatna and in central-western Syria*. D. Morandi-Bonacossi, ed. 19–27. Studi Archeologici su Qatna 01. Udine: Forum.

Archi, A. (2006). Alalah al tempo del regno di Ebla. In *Tra oriente e occidente: studi in onore di Elena di Filippo Balestrazzi*. D. Morandi Bonacossi, E. Rova, F. Veronese and P. Zanovello, eds. 2–5. Padova: S.A.R.G.O.N. Editrice e Libreria.

Batiuk, S.D. (2005). *Migration theory and the distribution of the early Transcaucasian culture*. PhD thesis. University of Toronto, Toronto, Canada.

Batiuk, S., Harrison, T.P. and Pavlish. L. (2005). The Taʻyinat survey, 1999–2002. In *The ʻAmuq valley regional projects. Vol. I: surveys in the Plain of Antioch and Orontes delta, Turkey, 1995–2002*. K.A. Yener, ed. 171–192. Oriental Institute Publications No. CXXXI. Chicago: University of Chicago Press.

Batiuk, S. (2007). Ancient landscapes of the ʻAmuq: geoarchaeological surveys of the ʻAmuq valley, 1999–2006. *Journal of the Canadian Society for Mesopotamian Studies* 2: 51–57.

(2013). The fruits of migration: understanding the 'longue durée' and the socio-economic relations of the early Transcaucasian culture. *Journal of Anthropological Archaeology* 32: 449–477.

Batiuk, S. and Horowitz, M. (2010). Temple deep sounding investigations 2001–2006. In *Tell Atchana, Ancient Alalakh, Volume 1: The 2003–2004 excavations seasons*. K.A. Yener, ed. 161–175. Istanbul: Koç University Press.

Bell, A. (2007). Tilmen Höyük'de Bulunan Anadolu'nun en Erken Yerli Çark Yapımı Mal Gruplarından Biri: Brittle Orange Ware. In *Refik duru'ya Armağan, Studies in Honour of Refik Duru*. G. Umurtak, Ş. Dönmez, and A. Yurtsever, eds. 115–125. Istanbul: Ege Yayınları.

Biga, M.G. (2008). Au-delà des frontières: guerre et diplomatie à Ebla. *Orientalia* 27: 289–334.

(2013). Defining the *chora* of Ebla: a textual perspective. In *Ebla and its landscape: early state formation in the ancient Near East*. P. Matthiae and N. Marchetti, eds. 259–267. Walnut Creek: Left Coast Press.

Braidwood, R.J. (1937). *Mounds in the Plain of Antioch: an archaeological survey*. Oriental Institute Publications No. XLVIII. Chicago: University of Chicago Press.

Braidwood, R.J. and Braidwood, L.S. (1960). *Excavations in the Plain of Antioch I: the earlier assemblages, Phases A to J*. Oriental Institute Publications No. LXI. Chicago: University of Chicago Press.

Carter, E. (1995). Report on the Kahramanmaraş archaeological survey project from 24.9.93 to 11.11.93. *Araştırma Sonuçları Toplantısı* XII: 331–341.

Casana, J. (2003). *From Alalakh to Antioch: settlement, land use, and environmental change in the ʻAmuq valley of southern Turkey*. PhD thesis. The Oriental Institute of Chicago, University of Chicago, Chicago, Illinois.

Casana, J. and Wilkinson, T.J. (2005). Settlement and landscapes in the 'Amuq region. In *The 'Amuq valley regional projects. Vol. I: surveys in the Plain of Antioch and Orontes delta, Turkey, 1995-2002.* K.A. Yener, ed. 25-65. Chicago: University of Chicago Press.

Castel, C. (2007). Stratégies de Subsistence et modes d'occupation de l'espace dans le micro-région d'al-Rawda au Bronze Ancien Final (Shamiyeh). In *Urban and natural landscapes of an ancient Syrian capital: settlement and environment at Tell Mishrifeh/Qatna and in central-western Syria.* D. Morandi-Bonacossi, ed. 283-294. Studi Archeologici su Qatna 01. Udine: Forum.

Castel, C. and Peltenburg, E. (2007). Urbanism on the margins: third millennium BC Rawda in the arid zone of Syria. *Antiquity* 81: 601-616.

Cecchini, S.M. and Mazzoni, S. eds. (1998). *Tell Afis (Siria): the 1988-1992 excavations on the acropolis.* Pisa: Edizioni Ets.

Collon, D. (1975). La céramique. In *Sondages au flanc sud du Tell de Qal'at el-Mudiq.* D. Collon, C. Otte, M. Otte and A. Zaqzouq, eds. 33-74. Brussels.

de Contenson, H. (1963). New Correlations between Ras Shamra and al-'Amuq. *Bulletin of the American Schools of Oriental Research* 172: 35-40.

(1969). Les couches du niveau III au sud de l'acropole de Ras Shamra. *Ugaritica IV.* C.F.A. Schaeffer, ed. 45-89. Paris: Librairie Orientalist Paul Geuthner.

(1992). *Préhistoire de Ras Shamra: les sondages stratigraphiques de 1955 à 1976.* Paris: Éditions Recherches sur les Civilisations.

Conti, A.M. and Persiani, C. (1993). When worlds collide: cultural developments in eastern Anatolia in the Early Bronze Age. In *Between the rivers and over the mountains: archaeologica Anatolica et Mesopotamica Alba Palmieri Dedicata.* M. Frangipane, H. Hauptmann, M. Liverani, P. Matthiae and M. Mellink, eds. 361-413. Rome: University of La Sapienza Press.

Courtois, J-C. (1962a). Contribution à l'étude des Niveaux II et III de Ras Shamra (sondages effectués à l'ouest de Temple de Baal, 1953). *Ugaritica IV.* C.F.A. Schaeffer, ed. 329-414. Paris: Librairie Orientalist Paul Geuthner.

(1962b). Contribution à l'étude des civilisations du Bronze Ancien à Ras Shamra-Ugarit – sondages 1959. *Ugaritica IV.* C.F.A. Schaeffer, ed. 414-475. Paris: Librairie Orientalist Paul Geuthner.

D'Andrea, M. (2018). The Early Bronze IVB pottery from Tell Mardikh/Ebla: chrono-typological and technological data for framing the site within the regional context. *Levant,* doi: 10.1080/00758914.2018.1449374.

Duru, R. (2010). *Gedikli-Karahöyük II.* Ankara: Turk Tarih Kurumu.

Eger, A.A. (2015). *The Islamic-Byzantine frontier: interaction and exchange among Muslim and Christian communities.* New York: I.B. Tauris.

Ehrich, A.M. (1939). *Early pottery of the Jebeleh plain.* Memoirs of the American Philosophical Society, Vol. 13. Philadelphia: American Philosophical Society.

Edwards, S. (2018). *Ebla's hegemony and its impact on the archaeology of the 'Amuq plain in the Third Millennium BCE.* PhD thesis. University of Toronto, Toronto, Canada.

Falb, C. (2009). *Untersuchungen an keramikwaren des dritten Jahrtausends v. Chr. aus Nordsyrien.* Münster: Ugarit-Verlag.

Finkbeiner, U., Novak, M., Sakal, F. and Sconzo, P. eds. (2015). *Associated Regional Chronologies for the Ancient Near East and the Eastern Mediterranean: Middle Euphrates*. Vol. IV. Turnhout: Brepols.

Frangipane, M. (1993). Local components in the development of centralized societies. In *Between the rivers and over the mountains: archaeologica Anatolica et Mesopotamica Alba Palmieri Dedicata*. M. Frangipane, H. Hauptmann, M. Liverani, P. Matthiae and M. Mellink, eds. 133–161. Rome: University of La Sapienza Press.

(2007). Establishment of a middle/upper Euphrates Early Bronze I culture from the fragmentation of the Uruk world: new data from Zeytinli Bahçe Höyük. In *Euphrates river valley settlement: The Carchemish sector in the third millennium BC*. E. Peltenburg, ed. 122–141. Levant Supplementary Series 5. Oxford: Oxbow Books.

Fugmann, E. (1958). *Hama: II.1. Fouilles et recherches de la Fondation Carlsberg 1931–1938: L'architecture des périodes pré-Hellénistiques*. Copenhagen: Nationalmuseet.

Gerritsen, F., de Giorgi, A., Eger, A., Özbal, R. and Vorderstrasse, T. (2008). Settlement and landscape transformations in the 'Amuq valley, Hatay: a long-term perspective. *Anatolica* 34: 241–314.

Gerber, J.C. (2005). *Hassek Höyük III: die frühbronzezeitliche keramik*. Tübingen: Ernst Wasmuth Verlag.

Geyer, B., al-Dbiyat, M., Awad, N., Barge, O., Besançon, J., Calvet, Y. and Jaubert, R. (2007). The arid margins of northern Syria: occupation of the land and modes of exploitation in the Bronze Age. In *Urban and natural landscapes of an ancient Syrian capital: settlement and environment at Tell Mishrifeh/Qatna and in central-western Syria*. D. Morandi-Bonacossi, ed. 269–281. Studi Archeologici su Qatna 01. Udine: Forum.

Goldman, H. (1956). *Excavations at Gözlü Kule, Tarsus, Vol. 2: from the Neolithic through the Bronze Age*. Princeton: Princeton University Press.

Hood, S. (1951). Excavations at Tabara al-Akrad, 1948–1949. *Anatolian Studies* 1: 113–147.

Jamieson, A. (2014a). Late Reserved Slip Ware. In *Associated Regional Chronologies for the Ancient Near East and the Eastern Mediterranean Interregional 1: Ceramics*. M. Lebeau, ed. 101–116. Turnhout: Brepols.

(2014b). Cyma-Recta Cups. In *Associated Regional Chronologies for the Ancient Near East and the Eastern Mediterranean Interregional 1: Ceramics*. M. Lebeau, ed. 117–130. Turnhout: Brepols Publishers.

Jean, M. (2018). Pottery production at Tell Arqa (Lebanon) during the 3rd millennium BC: preliminary results of petrographic analysis. *Levant*, doi: 10.1080/00758914.2018.1454239.

Kennedy, M.A. (2015). *The Late Third Millennium BCE in the upper Orontes valley, Syria: Ceramics, Chronology and Cultural Connections*. Ancient Near Eastern Studies Supplement 46. Peeters: Leuven.

Kennedy, M.A., Badreshany, K. and Philip, G. (2018). Drinking on the periphery: the Tell Nebi Mend goblets in their regional and archaeometric context. *Levant*, doi: 10.1080/00758914.2018.1442076.

Lebeau, M. ed. (2011). *Associated Regional Chronologies for the Ancient Near East and the Eastern Mediterranean: the Jezirah*. Vol. I. Turnhout: Brepols Publishers.

(2014). *Associated Regional Chronologies for the Ancient Near East and the Eastern Mediterranean Interregional 1: Ceramics*. Turnhout: Brepols.

de Maigret, A. (1974). Tell Munbatah: un nuovo sito della cultura "Caliciforme" nella Siria del nord. *Oriens Antiquus* 13: 249–297.

Mathias, V.T. and Parr, P.J. (1989). The early phases at Tell Nebi Mend: a preliminary account. *Levant* XXI: 13–32.

Mathias, V.T. (2000). The Early Bronze Age pottery of Tell Nebi Mend in its regional setting. In *Ceramics and change in the Early Bronze Age of the southern Levant*. G. Philip and D. Baird, eds. 411–427. Sheffield: Sheffield Academic Press.

Matthiae, P. (1976). Ebla à l'époque d'Akkad: archéologie et histoire, communication du 19 mars 1976. *Comptes-rendus des séances de l'Académie des Inscriptions et Belles-Lettres* 120(2): 190–215.

(1993). L'aire sacrée d'Ishtar à Ebla: résultats des fouilles de 1990–1992. *Comptes-rendus des séances de l'Académie des Inscriptions et Belles-Lettres* 137(3): 613–662.

(2006). The Archaic Palace at Ebla: a royal building between Early Bronze Age IVB and Middle Bronze Age I. In *Confronting the past: archaeological and historical essays on ancient Israel in honour of William G. Dever*. S.J. Gitin, E. Wright and J.P. Dessel, eds. 85–103. Winona Lake: Eisenbrauns.

(2007). Nouvelles fouilles à Ebla en 2006. le Temple du Rocher et ses successeurs protosyriens et paléosyriens. *Comptes-rendus des séances de l'Académie des Inscriptions et Belles-Lettres* 151(1): 481–525.

Mazzoni, S. (1980). Appunti sulla diffusione della ceramica "Reserved Slip" in Mesopotamia e in Siria. *Egitto e Vicino Oriente* 3: 241–258.

(1985). Elements of the ceramic culture of early Syrian Ebla in comparison with Syro-Palestinian EB IV. *Bulletin of the American Schools of Oriental Research* 257: 1–18.

(1991). Ebla e la formazione della cultura urbana in Siria. *La Parola del Passato* 46: 163–194.

(1998). Area E1, Late Chalcolithic, Early, Middle and Late Bronze I Ages: materials and chronology. In *Tell Afis (Siria): Scavi sull'acropoli 1988–1992*. S.M. Cecchini and S. Mazzoni, eds. 9–100. Pisa: Edizioni ETS.

(2000). Pots, people and cultural borders in Syria. In *Landscapes: territories, frontiers and horizons in the ancient Near East: papers presented to the XLIV Rencontre Assyriologique Internationale, Venezia, 7–11 July 1997: Part II. Geography and cultural landscape: history of the ancient Near East*. L. Milano, S. de Martino, F. M. Fales and G. B. Lanfranchi, eds. 139–152. Padova: Sargon srl.

(2002). The ancient Bronze Age pottery tradition in north-western central Syria. In *Céramique de l'Âge du Bronze en Syrie, I: La Syrie du sud et le vallée de l'Oronte*. M. Al-Maqdissi, V. Matoïan and C. Nicolle, eds. 69–96. Bibliothèque Archéologique et Historique T.161. Beyrouth: Institut Français du Proche-Orient.

(2003). Ebla: crafts and power in an emergent state of third millennium BC Syria. *Journal of Mediterranean Archaeology* 16(2): 173–191.

Mellaart, J. (1981). The prehistoric pottery from the Neolithic to the beginning of the EB IV (c. 7000–2500 BC). In *The river Qoueiq, northern Syria and its catchment*. J. Matthers, ed. 131–319. British Archaeological Reports, International Series 98. Oxford: British Archaeological Reports.

Mellink, M. (1993). The Anatolian south coast in the Early Bronze Age: the Cilician perspective. In *Between the rivers and over the mountains: archaeologica Anatolica et Mesopotamica*

Alba Palmieri Dedicata. M. Frangipane, H. Hauptmann, M. Liverani, P. Matthiae and M. Mellink, eds. 495–508. Rome: University of La Sapienza Press.

Morandi Bonacossi, D. (2007). Qatna and its hinterland during the Bronze and Iron Ages: a preliminary reconstruction of urbanism and settlement in the Mishrifeh Region. In *Urban and natural landscapes of an ancient Syrian capital: settlement and environment at Tell Mishrifeh/Qatna and in central-western Syria.* D. Morandi-Bonacossi, ed. 65–93. Studi Archeologici su Qatna 01. Udine: Forum.

Oldenburg, E. (1991). *Sukas IX: The Chalcolithic and Early Bronze Age periods.* Copenhagen: Det Kongelige Danske Videnskabernes Selskab.

Oriental Institute (1937). *Syrian Expedition: the Oriental Institute of the University of Chicago.* Oriental Institute Bulletin 1. Chicago: University of Chicago Press.

Philip, G. (2002). Contacts between the 'Uruk' world and the Levant during the fourth millennium BC: evidence and interpretation. In *Artifacts of complexity: tracking the Uruk in the Near East.* J. N. Postgate, ed. 207–236. Wiltshire: Aris & Philips.

Philip, G. and Bradbury, J. (2016). Settlement in the upper Orontes valley from the Neolithic to the Islamic period: an instance of punctuated equilibrium. In *Le Fleuve Rebelle: Géographie historique du moyen Oronte d'Ebla à l'époque médiévale.* D. Parayre, ed. 377–395. Syria Supplément IV. Beyrouth: Institut Français du Proche-Orient.

du Plat Taylor, J., Seton-Williams, M.W. and Waechter, J. (1950). The Excavations at Sakçe Gözü. *Iraq* 12(2): 53–138.

Rova, E. (1989). Die sogennante 'Smeared Wash Ware': ein beitrag zur Syrischen keramik des III, Jahrtausends V. Chr. *Baghdader Mitteilungen* 20: 139–196.

(2014). Combed Wash and Smeared Wash Wares. In *Associated Regional Chronologies for the Ancient Near East and the Eastern Mediterranean Interregional 1: Ceramics.* M. Lebeau, ed. 187–197. Turnhout: Brepols.

Sala, M. (2012). An Early Bronze IVB pottery repertoire from *favissae* P.9717 and P.9719 in the Temple of the Rock at Tell Mardikh/ancient Ebla. *Levant* 44(1): 51–81.

Sconzo, P. (2015). Ceramics. In *Associated Regional Chronologies of the Ancient Near East and the Eastern Mediterranean: Middle Euphrates.* Vol. IV. U. Finkbeiner, M. Novak, F. Sakal, and P. Sconzo, eds. 85–202. Turnhout: Brepols.

Steadman, S.R. (1994). Prehistoric sites on the Cilician coastal plain. *Anatolian Studies* XLIV: 85–103.

Thalmann, J-P. (2006). *Tell Arqa I. Les Niveaux de l'âge du Bronze.* Bibliothéque Archéologique et Historique T.177. Beyrouth: Institut Français du Proche-Orient.

Thalmann, J-P. and Sowada, K. (2014). Levantine Combed Ware. In *Associated Regional Chronologies for the Ancient Near East and the Eastern Mediterranean Interregional 1: Ceramics.* M. Lebeau, ed. 323–346. Turnhout: Brepols Publishers.

Thuesen, I. (1988). *Hama I: the pre- and proto-historic periods: fouilles et recherches de la foundation Carlsberg,* 1931–1938. Aarhus: Aarhus Universitetsforlag.

Trentin, M.G. (1993). The early Reserved Slip Wares horizon of the upper Euphrates basin and western Syria. In *Between the rivers and over the mountains: archaeologica Anatolica et Mesopotamica Alba Palmieri Dedicata.* M. Frangipane, H. Hauptmann, M. Liverani, P. Matthiae and M. Mellink, eds. 177–200. Rome: University of La Sapienza Press.

Trufelli, F. (1997). Ceramic correlations and cultural relations in IVth millennium eastern Anatolia and Syro-Mesopotamia. *Studi Micenei ed Egeo Anatolici* 39: 5–33.

Vacca, A. (2014). The Tuqan IC pottery sequence. In *Tell Tuqan excavations and regional perspectives: cultural developments in inner Syria from the the Early Bronze Age to the Persian/Hellenistic period. Proceedings of the international conference, May 15th-17th 2013, Lecce.* F. Baffi, R. Fiorentino, and L. Peyronel, eds. 45–84. Lecce: Congedo Editore.

(2015). Before the Royal Palace G: the stratigraphic and pottery sequence of the west unit of the central complex: the Building G5. *Studia Eblaitica* 1: 1–32.

(2018). Characterizing the Early Bronze III-IVA1 pottery of the northern Levant through typological and petrographic analyses: the case study of Tell Mardikh/Ebla and Tell Tuqan (Syria). *Levant*, doi: 10.1080/00758914.2018.1447208.

Von Luschan, F. (1943). *Die kleinfunde von sendschirli, ausgrabungen in sendschirli V.* Berlin: Verlag von Walter de Gruyter & Co.

Welton, L. (2012). The 'Amuq plain and Tell Tayinat in the third millennium BCE: the historical and socio-political context. *Journal of the Canadian Society for Mesopotamian Studies* 6: 15–27.

(2014). Revisiting the 'Amuq sequence: a preliminary investigation of the EB IVB ceramic assemblage from Tell Tayinat. *Levant* 46(3): 339–370.

(2017). Gap or transition? characterizing the Late Chalcolithic and Early Bronze I in the 'Amuq plain. *Studia Eblaitica* 3: 1–32.

(2018). EB IV ceramic production in the Orontes watershed: petrography from the 'Amuq and beyond. *Levant*, doi: 10.1080/00758914.2018.1470857.

Welton, L. and Cooper, L. (2014). Caliciform Ware. In *Associated Regional Chronologies for the Ancient Near East and the Eastern Mediterranean Interregional 1: Ceramics.* M. Lebeau, ed. 295–323. Turnhout: Brepols.

(In preparation). The inland ceramic sequence. In *Associated Regional Chronologies for the Ancient Near East and the Eastern Mediterranean: the northern Levant.* J-P. Thalmann and S. Mazzoni, eds. Turnhout: Brepols.

Welton, L., Harrison, T.P. and Batiuk, S. (2011). Tell Tayinat in the late third millennium: recent investigations of the Tayinat Archaeological Project, 2008-2010. *Anatolica* XXXVII: 147–185.

Wilkinson, T.J. (2000). Geoarchaeology of the 'Amuq plain. *American Journal of Archaeology* 104: 168–179.

Wilkinson, T.J., Philip, G., Bradbury, J., Dunford, R., Donoghue, D., Galiatsatos, N., Lawrence, D., Ricci, A. and Smith, S.L. (2014). Contextualizing early urbanization: settlement cores, early states and agro-pastoral strategies in the Fertile Crescent during the fourth and third millennia BC. *Journal of World Prehistory* 27(1): 43–109.

Yener, K.A., Edens, C., Harrison, T.P., Verstraete, J. and Wilkinson, T.J. (2000). The 'Amuq Valley Regional Project, 1995-1998. *American Journal of Archaeology* 104: 163–220.

Yener, K.A. (2005). The 'Amuq Valley Regional Projects. *The 'Amuq Valley Regional Projects, Volume 1: surveys in the Plain of Antioch and Orontes delta, Turkey, 1995-2002.* K.A. Yener, ed. 1–24. Oriental Institute Publications No. CXXXI. Chicago: University of Chicago Press.

2

The origin of Caliciform Ware in inland northern Syria during the mid-third millennium BC

A view from Tell Mardikh/Ebla and Hama

Agnese Vacca
Università degli Studi di Milano

Concurrent with urban expansion, a major change in ceramic production is observable in a number of sites within inland northern Syria during the third millennium BC. The marked regional character of pottery assemblages during the first half of the third millennium BC gives way to an increased homogenisation in the morphological repertoire and an improvement of manufacturing techniques in the second half of the millennium. Some general features characterising the EB IVA ceramic horizon of western inland Syria are the appearance of specialised fine wares (particularly the so-called 'Caliciform Ware' with its related repertoire of drinking and pouring vessels) and the high degree of standardisation in vessel production (well-controlled firing atmospheres, standardised vessel profiles and selected clay pastes). These major changes in pottery technology and morphological repertoires (with an emphasis on drinking vessels) occurring around the mid-third millennium BC argue in favour of similar developments taking place concurrently in northern and central Syria reflecting major socio-political changes.

The aim of this chapter is to analyse the evidence for the widespread diffusion of Caliciform Ware, signalling the fresh adoption of innovative commensality practices, and to address this relationship with the formation of urban elites. It will be shown that the diffusion of Caliciform Ware is a synchronic phenomenon, the origins of which can be traced back to the mid-third millennium BC both in the middle Orontes valley and in inland northern Syria.

Inland northern Syria and the Orontes valley around the mid-third millennium BC: an overview

The Orontes valley, crossing inland western Syria from south to north, represents a 'major geographical entity' in the northern Levant,[1] linking the Syrian upland (the 'Ebla region') and the coastal area with southern Syria and northern Lebanon. The northern sector of the Ghab basin (near Tell Qarqur) and its northernmost extension, the Ruj basin, have always provided an essential link between coastal Syria to the west and towns and villages of inland northern Syria and the middle Orontes valley to the east and south.

Settlement patterns

From around the mid-third millennium BC (EB IVA) the aforementioned areas were, in fact, intimately interconnected, displaying affinities in the material culture, as well as common trends in settlement patterns and urban growth. Intensive geological and archaeological surveys, focused on different sectors of the Orontes valley, from Homs downstream to the Ghab basin, have shown a remarkable increase in settlements during the EB III and, especially, during EB IVA (Figure 2.1). In the latter period, occupation expands in areas previously uninhabited, such as the rocky plateau bordering the river bend and the open plains located kilometres away from the course of the Orontes river.[2] It is, in fact, from around the mid-third millennium BC that nearly all the areas with a potential for agro-pastoral exploitation are occupied, including the arid region of the Syrian steppe, within the so-called 'zone of uncertainty' that is beyond the limit of rain-fed cultivation.[3] In this area, several towns are new foundations dating back from the mid-third millennium BC, such as Tell Sh'aīrat,[4] al-Rawda[5] and Tell Al-Ṣūr,[6] all circular towns sharing an elaborate pre-established plan.

Similar trends in human occupation are observable in the area defined as the *chora of Ebla*, extending from approximately the Ruj basin to the west, to the arid fringes of the Syrian steppe to the east.[7] A sharp increase in the number of sites is observable from at least the EB III period, while the peak of occupation corresponds to EB IVA.

---

1 Fortin 2007b.
2 Philip et al. 2002; Morandi Bonacossi 2008; Bartl and Al-Maqdissi 2014; Fortin 2007a; 2007b; Parayre (ed.) 2016.
3 Geyer et al. 1998; Wilkinson et al. 2014.
4 Al-Maqdissi 2010.
5 Castel 2007.
6 Al-Maqdissi 2007; Mouamar 2014.
7 Matthiae and Marchetti (eds) 2013.

2 The origin of Caliciform Ware in inland northern Syria during the mid-third millennium BC

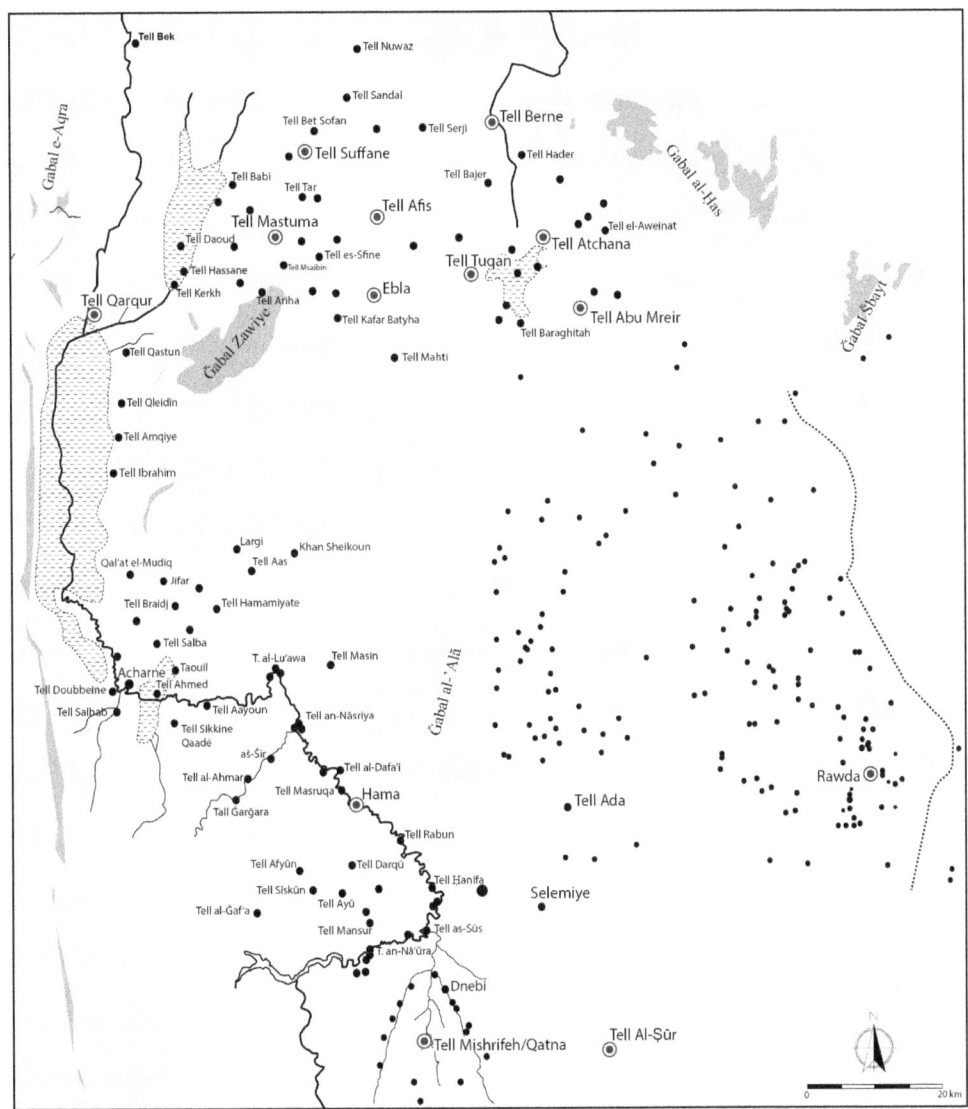

Figure 2.1: Map showing sites with an EB IVA (mainly EB IVA2) occupation.

In the latter phase, medium and small tell-sites spread across the fertile Matkh[8] and Jazr plains,[9] as well as in the area to the west of Ebla, around Tell Mastuma, and in the Ruj basin (see Figure 2.1).[10]

---

8   Mantellini et al. 2013; Peyronel 2014; Vacca 2019.
9   Mazzoni 2005.
10 Tsuneki 2009a; Iwasaki and Tsuneki 2003.

Similar paths towards urbanisation

The trend towards settlement increase and population growth, initiated during the EB III, goes along with a process of developing socio-economic complexity and the intensification of productive systems. At Tell Mardikh/Ebla, evidence, on the central mound, of large-scale storage facilities dating from EB III stands as indirect evidence for the intensification of agricultural production and its centralised management, performed by emerging elites who based their power upon the ability to control storable surplus.[11] Two extraordinary cuneiform texts from Palace G, mentioning the succession of 23 rulers before the last three kings who were active at the time of the State Archives, hint at the 'historicity' of such elites.[12] The concentration of large-scale facilities for cereal storage on the Acropolis during EB III was likely related to the formative process of urbanisation that culminated in the formation of the EB IVA polity. Emphasis on storage during this period is not limited to Ebla but is apparent at other sites in western inland Syria, such as Tell Tuqan,[13] Hama Level K4[14] and Tell Mishrifeh/Qatna, suggesting a wider regional trend. At the latter site, slightly later evidence (EB IVA: 2500–2300 cal. BC) of both centralised storage facilities located on the Acropolis – as at Ebla – and the recovery of a contemporary elite burial (Tomb IV), suggest the emergence of socio-political hierarchies at the site.[15]

While the roots of this process can be traced back to the first half of the third millennium BC (as suggested by the evidence from Mardikh IIA), its outcome is clearly visible in the following EB IVA period (EB IVA1–2: ca. 2550–2300 BC). From around the mid-third millennium BC, an increase in the number and geographical extent of urban communities and the full-fledged adoption of urban models are visible, with large-scale hierarchical political organisations ('states') and the establishment of Ebla as a centre of paramount importance.[16]

Caliciform Ware: a definition and research background

While the chronology of the first centuries of the third millennium BC (EB I–II) in the northern Levant is still imperfectly understood (due to the lack of extensively excavated sites and published sequences), more evidence is now available for the EB III–IVA period. In particular, the two key sites of Tell Mardikh/Ebla and Hama have both yielded continuous stratigraphic sequences and comparable pottery assemblages. These sequences allow us to outline similar developments and to address the issue of the emergence of a broader ceramic tradition by the mid-third millennium BC. This is

---

11   Vacca 2014a; 2015; 2016.
12   Archi 2001.
13   Peyronel 2011; Vacca 2014a.
14   Fugmann 1958, 37–38.
15   Morandi Bonacossi 2008.
16   Akkermans and Schwartz 2003, 233.

2 The origin of Caliciform Ware in inland northern Syria during the mid-third millennium BC

the result of broadly contemporary processes occurring in both western inland Syria and the middle Orontes valley. The analysis of the ceramic assemblages coming from well-stratified archaeological contexts at Ebla, anchored to radiocarbon dates, provides a solid basis to identify the roots of this process and the emergence of Caliciform Ware at the site. Conversely, the small number of published materials from Hama does not allow the same refined analysis. Nevertheless, some remarks can be put forward, based on the direct observation of a group of vessels stored at the National Museum of Denmark.[17] Moreover, recent data from several excavated sites within the northern Levant provide important benchmarks for assessing the regional chronology and pinpoint the emergence of a broader ceramic tradition, epitomised by the widespread introduction of Caliciform Ware drinking vessels in the local ceramic assemblages.

Terminological remarks: Simple Ware and Caliciform Ware

The high frequency of goblet forms among the EB IV ceramic assemblage of western inland Syria made the term 'Caliciform Ware' common in the archaeological literature.[18] In fact, the term has been usually employed in defining individual sites' ceramic assemblages (e.g. the Caliciform Ware at Ebla), as well as, in broader terms, the Caliciform Ware province of western inland Syria, characterised by the ubiquitous distribution of Simple and Simple Painted goblets, with specific local and regional features.[19]

Recently, Welton and Cooper have proposed a critical review of the term 'Caliciform Ware',[20] which sometimes lacked a general clear definition.[21] In particular, aspects related to typology, chronology and distribution have been taken into account as the main parameters in order to define the time span and the geographical distribution of this production. According to the authors, 'Caliciform Ware can be interpreted as the portion of the local assemblage of western inland Syria in ENL4–5 that expands out of this core and into neighbouring areas; this consists primarily of cups/goblets and teapots forms'.[22] With respect to this, the term assumes a morphological significance,

---

17 A selection of 30 vessels previously published by E. Fugmann (1958) and I. Thuesen (1988) and pertaining to Phases K1–6 and J7–8 of the Hama sequence has been registered, redrawn and photographed in 2014.
18 See Welton and Cooper 2014, with relevant bibliography.
19 Mazzoni 1985; 2002; Rova 1996.
20 Welton and Cooper 2014.
21 Mazzoni 2003.
22 See Welton and Cooper 2014; goblets and teapots documented outside the 'Caliciform Ware' core area occur particularly along the Euphrates river valley and in the southern Levant, suggesting an inter-regional network of interaction. While in the former area, the hallmark is usually known as the 'Hama goblet'; in the latter area goblets and teapots are more commonly defined as part of the local Black Wheel-made Ware repertoire of the EB IV southern Levant (Welton and Cooper 2014; D'Andrea 2014; see also D'Andrea, in this book, with relevant bibliography).

and allows definition of Caliciform Ware as a functional category within the Simple Ware (henceforth SW) assemblage, rather than a distinct ware type.

Moreover, the definition of a 'Caliciform ceramic province' of western Syria seems to be, recently, superseded by more precise terminologies, such as 'inland western Syria ceramic area' or 'ceramic tradition'.[23] This situation arises from the fact that the concept of 'ceramic province' is generally a problematic one, mainly because of the difficulties in tracing precise boundaries between different ceramic provinces (sometimes interpreted as cultural or political entities) and because of the existence of more of a vacuum than a continuum in the archaeological documentation.[24] With respect to this, we can talk about a broader northern Levantine SW ceramic tradition of the mid-late third millennium BC, characterised by similar technological aspects in manufacture and morphological repertoire, as well as by a certain degree of regional, sub-regional and local variability. Simple Ware is,[25] for instance, the most attested ware type (or class) in the 'Amuq assemblage throughout the entire EBA (Phases G–J), followed by Cooking Ware (henceforth CW) and other specialised production such as Brittle Orange Ware.[26] A similar trend is also documented at Ebla during the EB III–IVA2 (continuing in the EB IVB; see Figure 2.2). Simple Ware represents the main ware type, followed by CW, whereas other productions are documented only in small percentages (i.e. Red-Black Burnished Ware and Levantine Combed Ware).[27] At the site of Hama, Simple Fine Wares become more common in the late K period and particularly during Phase K1 (EB III), when light brown clays prevail and are often associated with the manufacture of goblets, which continue to be produced during the subsequent period J8.[28]

Simple Ware, being the predominant ware type in the northern Levant throughout the third millennium BC, is also the most sensitive to changes, which affect the ceramic production around the middle of the millennium. Two main trends have been detected through the observation of indirect evidence (i.e. finished objects). 1) The standardisation of fabrics (with finer and more homogeneous, exclusively mineral tempered clays, and highly fired vessels). 2) The functional specialisation of the morphological repertoire with a general reduction of types and an equivalent increase in functional shapes.[29] High-standardised products are generally interpreted as the result of mass production,

---

23 See Mazzoni 2002; Welton and Cooper 2014.
24 Welton and Cooper 2014, 365.
25 Within Simple Ware are included also Incised, Painted and Reserved Slip productions, which are considered as varieties of the Simple Ware, rather than distinct fabrics. In the case of the ceramic materials from Ebla this observation is, in fact, supported by archaeometric analyses, which do not allow the recognition of distinct pastes. This differentiation is more useful in terms of chronology and pottery decorative style and stylistic analysis.
26 Braidwood and Braidwood 1960; Welton 2014, 353–355; see Welton, this book.
27 Vacca 2014a; 2015, 9.
28 Thuesen 1988, 113.
29 See Braidwood and Braidwood 1960; Mazzoni 1994; Besana et al. 2008; see Welton, this book.

2 The origin of Caliciform Ware in inland northern Syria during the mid-third millennium BC

which can be related to a uniform process of manufacture, as well as to the ratio between producers and consumers (i.e. fewer producers per number of consumers); two aspects that can result in a low degree of variability in the ceramic assemblage.[30] While these aspects, and particularly the issue of standardisation, require an in-depth analysis, which is beyond the scope of this chapter, what I am concerned with here is the origin of Caliciform Ware and the widespread adoption of drinking sets, which is also linked to the introduction of specialised vessels for containing liquids and a change in social commensality.[31] Caliciform Ware, as a functional category within the SW assemblage, seems to appear around the mid-third millennium BC in different areas of the northern

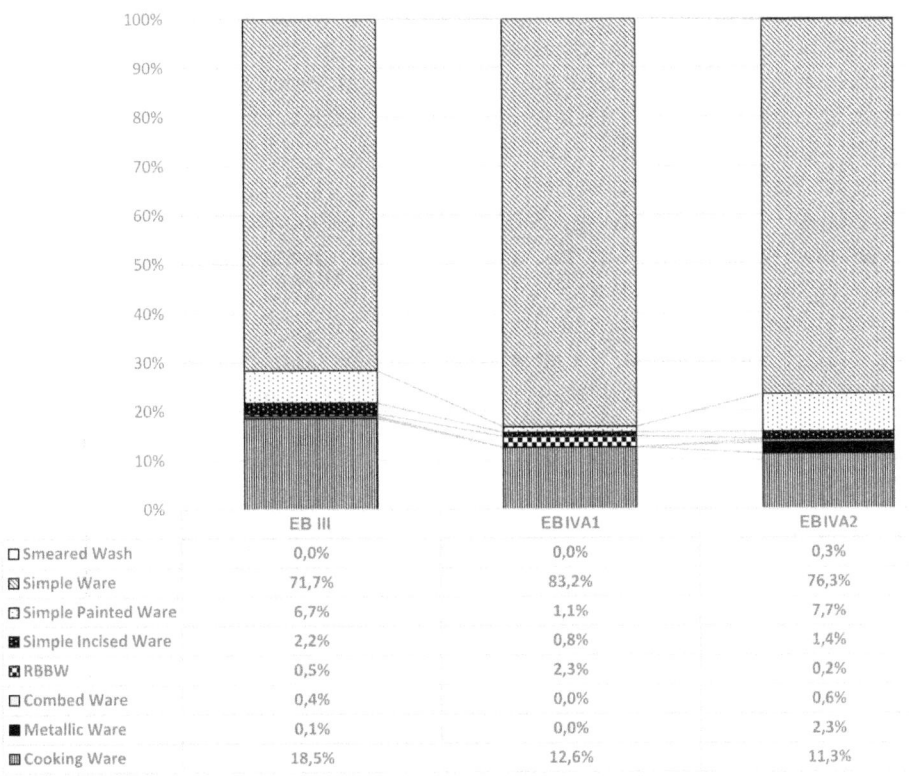

Figure 2.2: Percent histogram showing the different ware types documented in EB III, EB IVA1 (after Vacca 2018a, fig. 3) and EB IVA2 (after Mazzoni 1994) contexts at Tell Mardikh/Ebla. (Simple Incised and Simple Painted Wares, although considered as varieties of the Simple Ware, are counted separately in order to detect changes in terms of chronology and pottery decorative styles. N = 4413 of which 826 (EB III), 620 (EB IVA1), and 2967 (EB IVA2) vessels (including diagnostics, entire vessels and rim fragments, and wall fragments).

---

30 Rice 1981; Costin 1991.
31 Mazzoni 1994; Welton and Cooper 2014, 305.

Levant, from the middle Orontes valley to the 'Amuq plain and inland northern Syria, occurring predominantly in local fabrics and within local decorative traditions, which are maintained and further improved in the second half of the millennium. A brief overview of some key sites of inland northern Syria and the middle Orontes valley will be given, in order to provide the chronological background for the introduction of Caliciform Ware, and in particular of goblets, in the northern Levant, as well as to introduce some hypotheses on the socio-political and socio-economic structures at work during this period.

Data sources and key-sites sequences (EB III–IVA1): inland northern Syria

The site of Tell Mardikh/Ebla, excavated since 1964 by the Italian Archaeological Expedition to Syria (MAIS), headed by P. Matthiae, provided a continuous stratified sequence spanning the entire third millennium BC, mainly excavated on the central Acropolis. While the beginning of the Early Bronze Age (EB I–II) is still an ill-defined period in the site's periodisation, due to the lack of extensive excavations,[32] more evidence is now available for the following EB III–IV phases. In fact, in the last few decades, archaeological investigations on the central Acropolis led to the identification of a substantial multi-phase level pertaining to Palace G (EB IVA2) and two monumental public buildings preceding the construction of the palace, dating back from EB III and EB IVA1.[33] In particular, the stratigraphic sequence of EB III and EB IVA1 is clearly detectable on the north-western edge of the Acropolis (Building G5) and on its south-western slopes (Building G2), where the overlap of the two phases is well documented. The bulk of pottery materials coming from primary contexts (mainly sealed materials found on surfaces) allowed us to outline a ceramic chrono-typological sequence based on the statistical occurrence of different wares and vessel types in the different archaeological contexts. This ceramic-based relative sequence has been then anchored to radiocarbon dates.[34] The context of EB III materials (ca. 2750/2700–2550 BC) corresponds to Building G2, which is part of a large structure (with more than 1 m thick walls) lying below the later structures of Palace's G South Unit, and to Area CC, an open-air area for stockpiling with multi-phase EB III occupation.[35] As for the EB IVA1 (ca. 2550–2450 BC), the stratified sequence uncovered in Building G5, excavated beneath the West Unit of Palace G's Central Complex, is the most representative of this phase.[36] This large building consists of three rooms with thick walls and carefully laid floors; re-flooring suggests the existence of a sub-phase, within the same chronological

---

32 Scatter evidence dating from EB I–II are documented in a dump underlying the large terrace wall M.3117 in the Southern Unit of Royal Palace G; see Mazzoni 1985a, 9, fig. 7: 1–2, 5; Mazzoni 2002.
33 Matthiae 1987; 2000; Mazzoni 1991; Dolce 2009; Vacca 2015; Vacca 2016.
34 Vacca 2014b; Vacca 2016.
35 Matthiae 2000, 572; Vacca 2016; 2018b.
36 Matthiae 1990; Mazzoni 1991; Vacca 2015; 2018b.

2 The origin of Caliciform Ware in inland northern Syria during the mid-third millennium BC

and ceramic horizon (Building G5, Phases 1a–b).[37] The latest phase of occupation of Building G5, corresponding to a refurbishment of the structure, yielded a ceramic assemblage, which has been assigned to an earlier stage of EB IVA2 (or Palace G horizon), tentatively dated to ca. 2450 BC (Building G5, Phase 2).[38] Building G5 was ultimately abandoned and sealed under the construction of the Palace G Complex (Phase 3).[39]

Archaeological investigations at Tell Tuqan, resumed in 2006 by the Italian Expedition of the University of Salento headed by F. Baffi, provided new evidence on the earliest third millennium BC phases in the northern Levant.[40] The excavation of a deep sounding in Area P South (Lower City North) revealed a long EB III architectural sequence, including the earliest phase with a workshop for pottery manufacture (Phase 10) and the latest with large storage facilities and crop-processing areas (Phases 6–7).[41]

Another site which yielded a sequence of third millennium BC pottery is Tell Mastuma, investigated by the Japanese archaeological expedition of the Ancient Orient Museum of Tokyo. This small site (ca. 3 ha), located 15 km to the west of Ebla, yielded EB III materials in the deep stratigraphic sounding of Square 15Gc (Layer H).[42] Additional materials dating from the EB IVA were brought to light in the north trench (Strata XIII–X) and have consistent parallels in the ceramic repertoire of Ebla's Palace G.[43]

At the site of Tell Afis (Jazr plain), investigated by the Italian Expedition of the University of Florence under the direction of S. Mazzoni and S.M. Cecchini, excavations in Area E (on the western slope of the Acropolis) have provided evidence of EBA occupation corresponding to Afis III (EB I–III) and Afis IV (EB IVA–B) in the site's periodisation. The EB I–IVA occupation is relatively ephemeral compared to the later EB IVB evidence. Several pottery fragments dating from EB I–III have been found in a deposit covering the collapsed Late Chalcolithic fortification wall (Level 17),[44] whereas some EB IVA1 materials have been collected from secondary contexts (pits of Level 18a).

Further sites in inland northern Syria, which provide additional data, are: Tell Suffane in the Jazr plain;[45] Tell Atchana and Tell Abu Mreir in the Matkh plain;[46] and several tells along the Nahr el-Quweiq river.[47] All these sites have yielded pottery materials from surface collections, documenting an occupation during EB III–IVA (Figure 2.1).[48]

---

37 See Vacca 2015.
38 Vacca 2015, 9–10.
39 Vacca 2015, 5; Pinnock, this book.
40 Peyronel 2011.
41 Vacca 2014a.
42 See Tsuneki 2009b.
43 Wakita 2009.
44 Mazzoni 1998, fig. 16: 3–5, 9–11.
45 Mazzoni 2006.
46 de Maigret 1978.
47 Matthers 1981.
48 Vacca 2019.

The middle Orontes valley

The tell of Hama was investigated by the Carlsberg Expedition to Phoenicia, headed by H. Ingholt, between 1932 and 1938.[49] Archaeological investigations focused on a limited area (800m^2) located in the central part of the mound (Squares H–I 10–11) and in a small sounding opened in Square G11x, which was excavated down to bedrock. Early Bronze Age levels have been assigned to Period K (roughly covering the EB I–III time span) and Period J (corresponding to EB IVA–B).[50] The architectural sequence exposed in Squares H–I 10–11 yielded a multi-phase level of domestic structures forming part of housing estates rebuilt several times in the course of the third millennium BC. Three main destructions occurred at Hama, at the end of Level K7, K1 and of Level J5 respectively.[51] G. Schwartz pointed out that within the pottery assemblage of Hama K stratigraphic mixing is noticeable.[52] Thuesen suggested a threefold division for Period K (Hama K8–K10, K5–K7 and K1–K4), paralleled with Phases F, G and H of the 'Amuq sequence,[53] though admitting a certain degree of uncertainty in correlating finds and architecture.[54] Despite this uncertainty, an attribution of Phases K7–K8 and K5–K6 to the EB I and EB II periods, and Phases K1–K4 to EB III has been tentatively suggested based on architectural features and material culture correlates.[55] Coherent features in the architectural planning and the pottery assemblage characterise the latter four levels of Period K (K1–K4, EB III). In Levels K1–K4, the general layout of the domestic structures remained unaltered (except for two clusters of pits, interpreted as silos, restricted to Phase K4), with several small houses displaying a shift in orientation from the previous period (from a prevailing NNE–SSW orientation in K5–K7 to a NNW–SSE in K1–K4).[56] Conversely, a major change occurs between Period K and the following Period J. While the first level assigned to Period J (J8) displays aspects of continuity with the previous Phase K1 in terms of both pottery assemblage (lingering K1–K4 vessel shapes) and architecture (same orientation of the houses), some major changes are discernible in the following Phase J7. The settlement of Period K with detached houses is, in fact, replaced by agglomerated dwellings of variable size, flanking a main N–S road,[57] probably suggesting an increase in the population, resulting in high-density occupation. The pottery assemblage is characterised by several lingering EB III types (K1–K4), which continue into Levels J7–J8, but also by the introduction of new vessel shapes, such as Caliciform Ware goblets. The few radiocarbon dates available for Phase J suggest a chronological range spanning the second half of the third millennium BC

---

49   Ingholt 1940; Fugmann 1958.
50   See Fugmann 1958.
51   Fugmann 1958.
52   Schwartz 1993, 154.
53   Thuesen 1988, 94–185.
54   Thuesen 1988, 11.
55   Mazzoni 2002.
56   Thuesen 1988, 180.
57   Fugmann 1958, 49–50.

2 The origin of Caliciform Ware in inland northern Syria during the mid-third millennium BC

(2500–2000/1950 BC), with Phase Hama J6 yielding a calibrated date of 2310±140 BC (5570 half-life) or 2348±144 BC (5730 half-life).[58]

Recent excavations at other sites have provided ceramic assemblages from well-stratified and more reliable archaeological contexts. This is the case at Tell Mishrifeh/Qatna, south of Hama, which has yielded stratified EB III–IVA materials from two main soundings excavated on the central Acropolis (Operation J),[59] and beneath the Late Bronze Age Royal Palace (*Chantier R, Sondage B*, Mishrifeh IX–VIII).[60] In addition, an elite burial (Tomb IV) has been investigated in *Chantier C*, yielding 40 inhumations and a rich pottery assemblage.[61] A series of radiocarbon dates obtained from short-lived samples collected from stratified levels in Operation J shows a calibrated range between 2800–2500 BC for Levels J44–J39 (Mishrifeh II; EB III) and between 2500–2300 BC for Levels J38–J28 (Mishrifeh IIIA; EB IVA).[62] Levels assigned to the EB III–IVA (Phases J44–J28) are characterised by a change in the function of the area from domestic with storage units to an open-air area, with circular storage pits and freestanding mudbrick silos intended for the intensive and large-scale storage of agricultural products.[63] Excavation in *Chantier R* provided further evidence on the EB III–IV occupation, revealing a long sequence spanning the mid-late third millennium BC. A first occupation dating from the EB III (Mishrifeh IX, Level 16) consists of a series of silos cut into the bedrock. In the following levels assigned to EB III–IVA1 (Mishrifeh VIII, Levels 14–15), a small dwelling associated with beaten earth surfaces was discovered. A series of dwellings, rebuilt several times during the EB IVA1–2, characterises the following architectural levels (Mishrifeh VIIA–B, Levels 13–8), which were also marked by the appearance of Caliciform Ware goblets (Levels 13–10).[64]

Moving further east into the Syrian steppe, another site, which yielded stratified EBA materials, is Tell Al-Ṣūr, located 27 km east of Tell Mishrifeh/Qatna. It appears that the site was a new foundation dating from the mid-third millennium BC. The site was characterised by a circular, pre-established plan, a format reproduced across the Syrian steppe, as documented at al-Rawda and Tell Shʻaīrat (Al-Maqdissi 2007; Mouamar 2014). A sounding opened in *Chantier A* exposed the first occupation levels dating from EB III–IVA1 (Al-Ṣūr VIII, Level 3) characterised by two silos cut into the bedrock. A further level dating from EB IVA1 (Al-Ṣūr VIIA, Level 2) yielded heavily damaged architectural structures associated with beaten earth floors. This data is significant as it allows us to establish the first occupation, around 2600/2500 BC, of this type of settlement in the so-called 'zone of uncertainty' within the Syrian steppe. Moreover, the discovery of Caliciform Ware goblets in EB IVA1 contexts represents

---

58 Hopper 1975; Mouamar 2017, Table 1.
59 Morandi Bonacossi 2008; Besana et al. 2008, 80–81.
60 Al-Maqdissi 2008; Mouamar 2015.
61 du Mesnil du Buisson 1935; Mouamar 2012.
62 See Morandi Bonacossi 2008, Tables 2–3.
63 Morandi Bonacossi 2008.
64 Mouamar 2015.

another piece of evidence for the earlier attestation of this vessel type in inland western Syria and, especially, in the Orontes valley.

Another important EBA site is Tell Qarqur, located in the north Ghab sector. Materials dating from the EB I–III have been collected from secondary contexts in Area A, and particularly from Iron Age constructional fills.[65] Conversely, well-stratified EB IVA–B levels (Strata 14–12) have been excavated in Areas A, E and D, located on the southern upper mound (Areas A and E) and on the lower mound to the north (Area D). Excavations in Area A revealed a building with at least 12 architectural levels. Dornemann has assigned pottery materials collected from Stratum 14 to the EB IVA period, equated to Hama J8–J5, Mardikh IIB1, and 'Amuq I horizons.[66] Stratum 14 seems to cover a long time span and can be paralleled with the EB IVA1–2 horizons of Tell Mardikh/Ebla, based on the presence of some diagnostic Caliciform Ware goblets.[67]

Tell Mardikh/Ebla: absolute chronology

A series of new radiocarbon dates provide an absolute chronology for the EB III–IVA1 sequence at Ebla. A total amount of five radiocarbon determinations was obtained from charred seeds from Area CC (EB III) and Building G5 (EB IVA1) (Figure 2.3). In addition, the radiocarbon determinations available for the Palace G destruction (EB IVA2) have been also considered,[68] in order to better assess the boundaries between each phase and the next (Figure 2.3). Finally, two more samples from EB III contexts at Tell Tuqan (Phases 8A and 6) allow the combining of the relative sequences of the two sites. Organic samples selected from different archaeological contexts from Tell Mardikh/Ebla and Tell Tuqan were submitted to AMS radiocarbon dating at the Centre for Dating and Diagnostics of the University of Salento (CEDAD). Conventional radiocarbon ages were then calibrated using OxCal v4.2.4,[69] based on the atmospheric data.[70] All dates are arranged according to the stratigraphic position of the respective contexts (from the earliest to the latest) (Table 2.1, Figure 2.3).

Two measures from Ebla and Tell Tuqan, both coming from EB III sealed floors, provide widely overlapping ranges, with a probability concentration that is consistent with a chronology between 2750 (or 2700) and 2550 BC. Out of four samples from EB IVA1 contexts, only one comes from a sealed floor, while two of the remaining samples come from silos, and one from a floor disturbed by an Iron Age pit: the latter three samples, in fact, yielded dates that are either consistent with, or even later than, the chronological range ascertained for the Royal Palace G, belonging to EB IVA2: such late dates are, therefore, discarded. On the other hand, the sample from the EB

---

65 Dornemann 2003, 105, 113, figs. 210–211.
66 Dornemann 2008.
67 Vacca 2015, 12.
68 Calcagnile et al. 2013.
69 Bronk Ramsey and Lee 2013.
70 Reimer et al. 2013.

2 The origin of Caliciform Ware in inland northern Syria during the mid-third millennium BC

Table 2.1: Radiocarbon determinations from Tell Mardikh/Ebla and Tell Tuqan.

Site	Area	Context	Relative Chronology	Material	CEDAD Code	C14 yrs BP	BC range (95.4%)	BC range (68.2%)
Tell Mardikh	Area CC	L.7287 (floor)	EB III	Cerealia ind.	LTL14860A	4102±45	2872-2567 (91.9%); 2521-2498 (3.5%)	2853-2812 (15.7%); 2744-2762 (5.9%); 2696-2579 (46.5%)
Tell Tuqan	P South	I.981 (installation)	EB III	Olea europaea stone	LTL14863A	4060±45	2858-2810 (11.4%); 2750-2723 (3.8%); 2700-2474 (80.2%)	2835-2818 (6.2%); 2664-2645 (6.0%); 2639-2560 (37.1%); 2536-2491 (18.8%)
Tell Tuqan	P South	L.796 (floor)	EB III	Hordeum disticum	LTL4655A	4219±45	2911-2835 (35.2%); 2817-2665 (59.9%); 2643-2640 (0.3%)	2899-2860 (27.0%); 2809-2755 (33.1%); 2720-2704 (8.0%)
Tell Mardikh	Building G5	L.7704c (floor)	EB IVA1	Olea europaea stone	LTL14859A	4031±45	2849-2813 (4.9%); 2738-2735 (0.2%); 2693-2689 (0.2%); 2680-2464 (90.1%)	2617-2610 (3.3%); 2582-2481 (64.9%)
Tell Mardikh	Building G5	S.4843 (silo)	EB IVA1	Hordeum vulgare	LTL12327A	3918±35	2547-2542 (0.4%); 2489-2292 (95.0%)	2471-2397 (44.9%); 2385-2347 (23.3%)
Tell Mardikh	Building G5	S.4843 (silo)	EB IVA1	Olea europaea stone	LTL12326A	3833±45	2461-2196 (91.0%); 2172-2146 (4.4%)	2400-2382 (5.5%); 2348-2202 (62.7%)
Tell Mardikh	Building G5	L.4841 (floor, disturbed)	EB IVA1	charcol	LTL14858A	3904±45	2550-2538 (1.0%); 2491-2276 (90.4%); 2253-2210 (4.1%)	2468-2340 (68.2%)

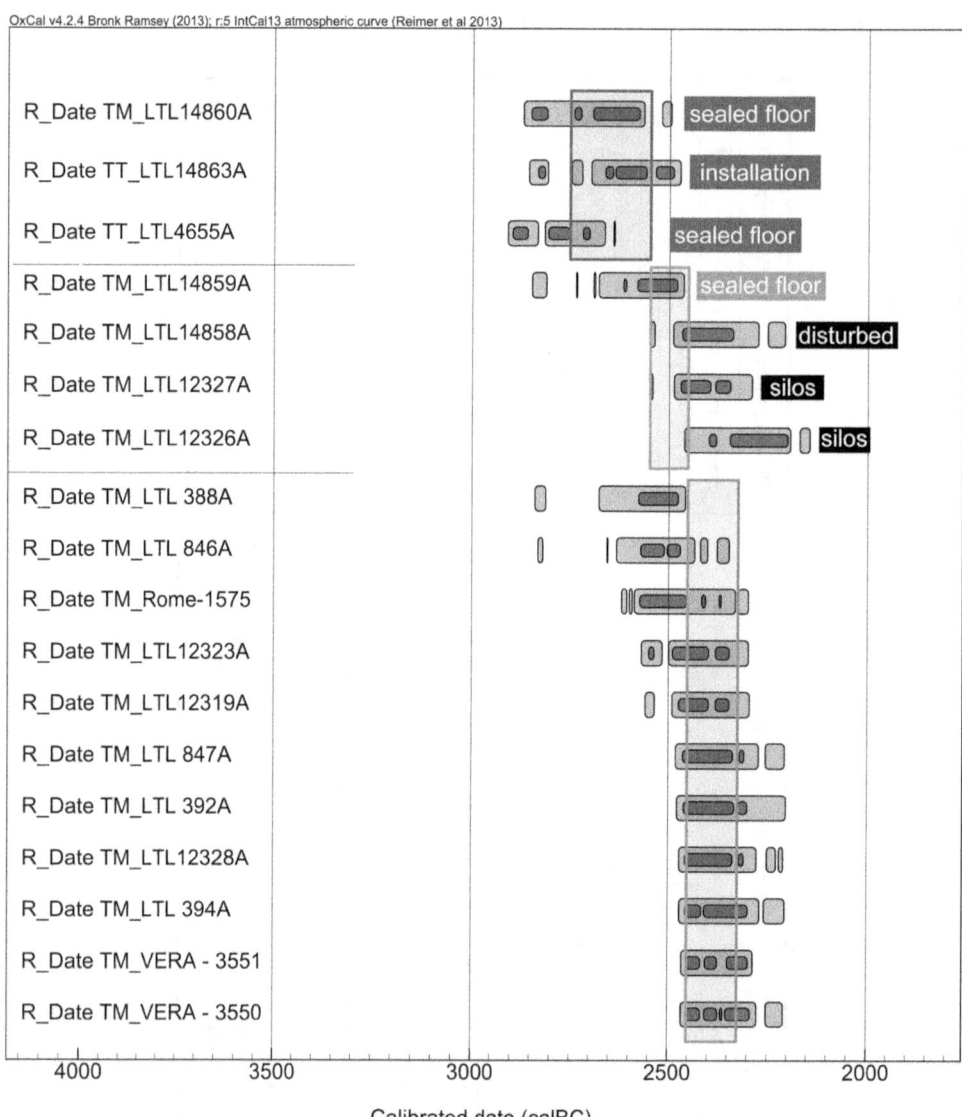

Figure 2.3: Calibrated age ranges from Tell Mardikh/Ebla and Tell Tuqan.

IVA1 sealed floor provides a date (2582–2481 cal. BC in the 1 sigma range) that fits well between the chronological ranges of EB III and EB IVA2 respectively. On the basis of this single date, therefore, the chronology of EB IVA1 will be tentatively set between 2550 (i.e. the lower end of the EB III range) and 2450 BC (approximately corresponding to the higher end of the EB IVA2 range).

2 The origin of Caliciform Ware in inland northern Syria during the mid-third millennium BC

The EB III–IVA1 pottery assemblage of western inland Syria and the origin of Caliciform Ware: local trends in ceramic production during EB III

The site of Tell Mardikh/Ebla represents the best reference point for revising the ceramic chronology and phasing of EB III–IVA1, providing a key-sequence, anchored to radiocarbon dates, for inland northern Syria. The bulk of ceramic materials coming from reliable contexts at Ebla and dating from EB III–IVA1 amounts to 1724 diagnostics collected in Building G2, Area CC, Building G5 and other stratified contexts.

A coherent pottery assemblage characterises the EB III phase. SW cups/bowls and jars dominate the ceramic repertoire, while goblets, teapots and platter-bowls represent only a smaller part of the assemblage. Cooking Ware is the second most attested ware type, including basic forms such as bowls and pots with out-flaring rims (Figures 2.2 and 2.6: 13–15). Among Table Ware, a wide range of bowl and cup types are attested, from shallow and large bowls to closed and deep cups (Figure 2.5: 1–7 and 9–12), suggesting that these forms fulfilled different functions as containers for solid and liquid products. Similar shapes documented at Ebla, Tell Tuqan and Tell Mastuma, as well as in sites along the Quweiq river (Quweiq H), argue in favour of a local production and circulation of these vessels (Figure 2.5: 1–13). The latter shapes, in particular, show affinities with the SW assemblage of the 'Amuq plain (Phase H) and of the Tabqa Dam basin, where bowls with curved profiles were characteristic during the first half of the third millennium BC.[71] Besides bowls, few proper goblet forms are documented. Some of these goblets show a peculiar feature, exhibiting the undulation of the outer surface (Figure 2.5: 14) with shallow grooves, spaced irregularly, in the upper part of the goblet. Such types of goblets, with this surface treatment, might be a forerunner of the later corrugated goblets, which appear in large amounts in the following EB IVA1 phase, outnumbering bowls (Figures 2.4 and 2.8). The EB III ceramic horizon detected at Ebla is directly comparable with sites located in the nearby Idlib (Tell Mastuma), Jazr (Tell Afis and Tell Suffane) and Matkh plains (Tell Tuqan, Tell Atchana and Tell Abu Mreir), suggesting a marked regional character of pottery production during this period, encompassing the ceramic area of inland northern Syria.[72] This is the case, for example, of Painted Simple Ware (henceforth PSW), characterised by similar monochrome painted patterns (mainly consisting of zigzags and crossing lines framed by horizontal bands) recurring on both open and closed forms (Figure 2.5: 2–9 and 19–23).[73] This local production, showing affinities in particular with the 'Multiple-Brush Painted Ware' of the 'Amuq plain, falls within the broader painted-ware tradition of the first half of the third millennium BC documented in northern Syria, south-eastern Anatolia and northern Iraq.[74] In the middle Orontes valley, PSW is documented in EB III contexts at Tell Mishrifeh/Qatna and Tell

---

71 Cooper 2006, 9–11; Vacca 2014a, 63; Sconzo 2015, 91, 100.
72 Vacca 2014a; 2018a; 2019.
73 See Vacca 2014a, fig. 5: 18–20.
74 Rova 2000.

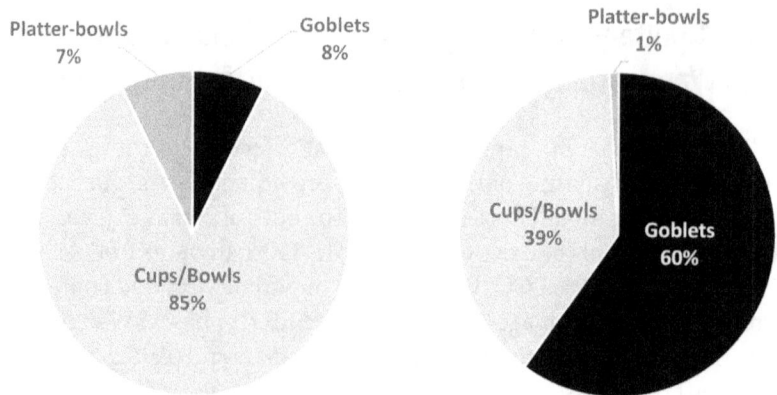

Figure 2.4: Pie chart showing the proportion of SW open shapes documented in EB III and EB IVA1 contexts from Tell Mardikh/Ebla. N= 566 of which 161 (EB III) and 405 (EB IVA1) vessels (including entire vessels and rim fragments).

Al-Ṣūr, showing similar decorative motifs to those described for inland northern Syria, combining superimposed bands with zigzags and crossing lines (see Figure 2.5: 24).[75]

EB III vessel forms that are common all over the northern Levant are shallow bowls and platter-bowls with protruding rounded or triangular rims (Figure 2.6: 1–10). Platter-bowls, with diameters ranging from a minimum of 15 cm to a maximum of 34 cm, occur sporadically in EB III contexts at Ebla (Figure 2.6: 5 and 8), as well as in other contemporary sites in the region, such as Tell Tuqan and Tell Mastuma.[76] While at Tell Tuqan and Tell Mastuma the plain SW variety is exclusively documented, at Ebla different surface treatments are present, such as painting, burnishing or slip and burnishing. Slipped and burnished exemplars (Figure 2.6: 5 and 8) are produced with pinkish-brown (2.5YR 5/6) mineral tempered fabrics, with the inner and outer surfaces white- or red-slipped and horizontally burnished.

The SW platter is a long-lasting type recurring in the 'Amuq pottery assemblages of both Phases G (middle and late) and H, mainly in the plain SW variety, although some burnished exemplars also exist.[77] Conversely, in the middle Orontes valley and the Syrian steppe (Hama K1–K4, Tell Mishrifeh/Qatna), in the coastal area (Tell Sukas L2, Ugarit/Ras-Shamra IIIA1, Qal'at ar-Rus),[78] in Lebanon (Tell Arqa, Phase S),[79] and in the

---

75 See Mouamar 2014, 101, fig. 15.
76 Vacca 2014a, fig. 5: 1; Tsuneki 2009b, fig. 3.24: 1–2.
77 Braidwood and Braidwood 1960, 265, figs 202: 1–9, 274–275, 216.
78 This production is named 'Burnished Un-slipped Ware' at Tell Sukas (Oldenburg 1991, 102, fig. 36.5–6, 104, fig. 38.1, 15) and 'Stone Ware Burnished' at Qal'at ar-Rus (Ehrich 1939, pl. VIII, fig. XI left). In the Orontes valley 'la céramique rouge lustrée' represents a diagnostic EB III production documented at Tell Mishrifeh/Qatna and Hama K1–4 (Mouamar 2015, 401).
79 Thalmann 2009.

2 The origin of Caliciform Ware in inland northern Syria during the mid-third millennium BC

southern Levant,[80] EB III carinated platters are mainly manufactured with red-orange or dark red clays, horizontally burnished outside and with radial burnishing on the inner surface. A further variety is represented by slip and burnished examples, mainly documented along the Syrian coast and in the middle Orontes valley.[81] A characteristic production of white-slipped platters (manufactured with light red pastes, mineral tempered and hard fired), so far documented only at the site of Hama (Figure 2.6: 7),[82] finds the best parallels in platter-bowls from Ebla, suggesting strong relationships between the two sites. Further similarities between the middle Orontes valley and inland northern Syria are observable in the production of Cooking Ware; a widely distributed type is the globular pot with everted thickened rim, which shows slightly local variations in fabrics and morphologies (Figure 2.6: 11–16).

Hama Levels K1–K4 have the most consistent parallels at the nearby site of Tell Mishrifeh/Qatna. Types attested at both sites are in-turned rim bowls with burnished surfaces and red-slipped and burnished bowls with rounded profiles, small jars with narrow neck, and cooking pots with vertical, slightly out-flared rim (Figure 2.6: 6–7, 9–11 and 16).[83] The most common ware type documented at both Hama K1–4 and Tell Mishrifeh/Qatna is the red polished ware.[84]

Sorting out 'ceramic traditions' during EB IVA1: shared trends and local peculiarities

During the EB III, a trend towards homogenisation in pottery production in the northern Levant begins, although the different areas still display a great degree of intra-regional differentiation. A few types show a supra-regional distribution, such as SW platter-bowls and CW pots. It is from the following EB IVA1 period that this process of homogenisation reaches its peak, resulting in technological and morphological similarities shared between the middle Orontes valley and inland northern Syria, particularly visible in the Simple Ware manufacture, with several locally produced types demonstrating a wide geographic distribution. The production of SW is improved, with finer pastes and highly fired vessels, a more varied functional repertoire and fewer, standardised, types.[85] Caliciform Ware is now introduced in the SW morphological repertoire, and goblets, in particular, become widespread all over western inland Syria.

---

80 In the southern Levant, platters are characteristic of the EB II–III pottery horizons; during the EB II these are mainly produced in 'Metallic Ware', whereas during the following EB III period platters are generally manufactured in Red Slipped and Pattern Burnished Ware, with some large specimens reaching 60 cm in diameter (Greenberg and Porat 1996).
81 This production is referred to as 'Pattern Burnished Ware' at Ugarit (Courtois 1962, 454, fig. 44E), 'Slip, and Burnished Ware' at Tell Sukas (Oldenburg 1991, 102).
82 Thuesen 1988, 144, 4B816.
83 Besana et al. 2008, fig. 1: 1–7; Mouamar 2015, 401, fig. 6: 19–21.
84 Mouamar 2015, 401, fn. 9.
85 See Welton, this book.

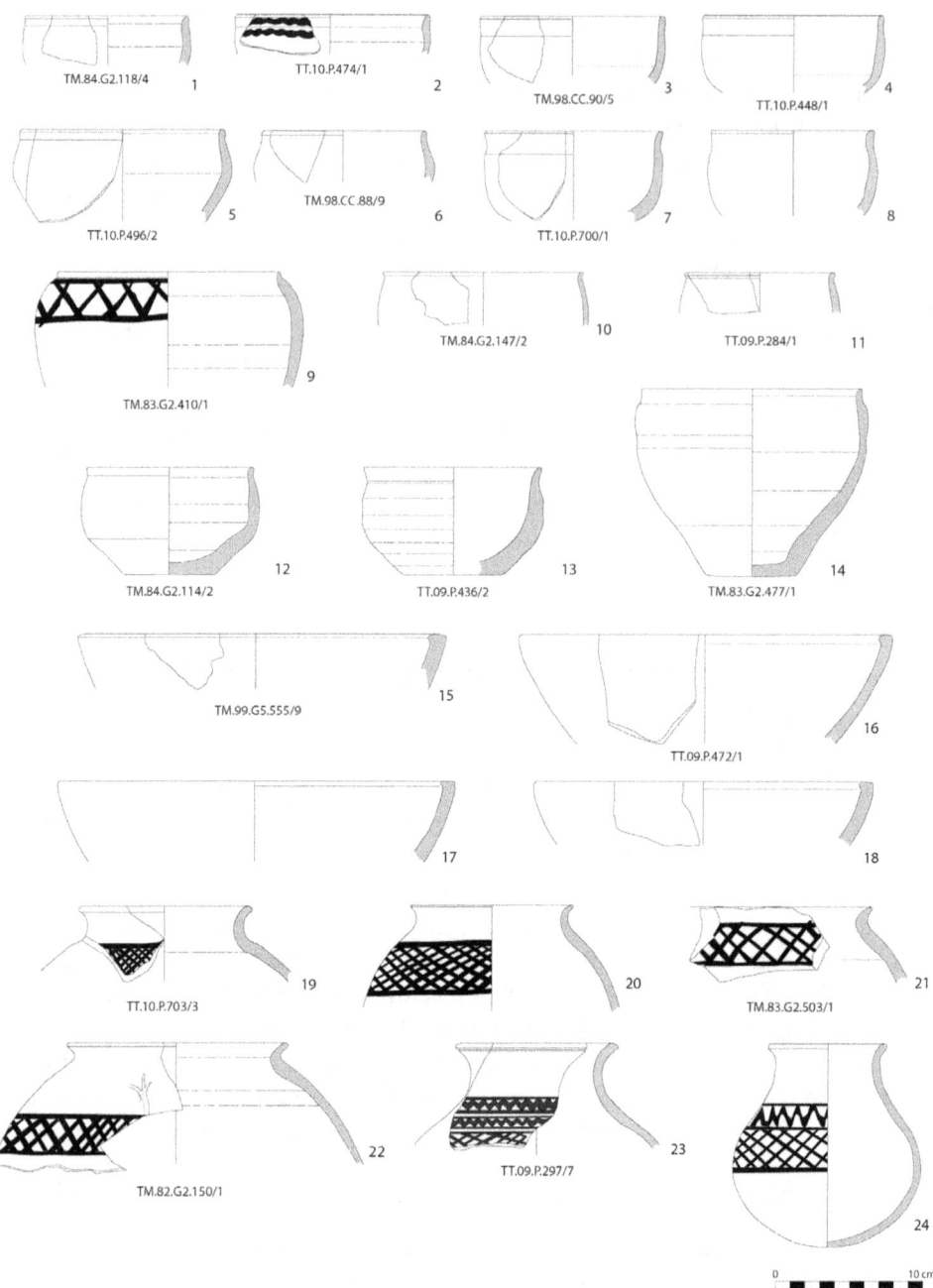

Figure 2.5: EB III SW and PSW pottery from different northern Levantine sites.

2 The origin of Caliciform Ware in inland northern Syria during the mid-third millennium BC

No.	Site and description	Reference
1.	Tell Mardikh/Ebla, Building G2 and Area CC	© MAIS
2.	Tell Tuqan, Area P South	© MAIS
3.	Tell Mardikh/Ebla, Building G2 and Area CC	© MAIS
4.	Tell Tuqan, Area P South	© MAIS
5.	Tell Tuqan, Area P South	© MAIS
6.	Tell Mardikh/Ebla, Building G2 and Area CC	© MAIS
7.	Tell Tuqan, Area P South	© MAIS
8.	Tell Mastuma, Square 15Gc, Layer H	re-drawn after Tsuneki 2009, fig. 3.24: 2
9.	Tell Mardikh/Ebla, Building G2 and Area CC	© MAIS
10.	Tell Mardikh/Ebla, Building G2 and Area CC	© MAIS
11.	Tell Tuqan, Area P South	© MAIS
12.	Tell Mardikh/Ebla, Building G2 and Area CC	© MAIS
13.	Tell Tuqan, Area P South	© MAIS
14.	Tell Mardikh/Ebla, Building G2 and Area CC	© MAIS
15.	Tell Mardikh/Ebla, Building G2 and Area CC	© MAIS
16.	Tell Tuqan, Area P South	© MAIS
17.	Tell Archaq, Quweiq H	re-drawn after Mellaart 1981, fig. 163: 925
18.	Tell 'Allush	re-drawn after de Maigret 1978, fig. 3: 4
19.	Tell Tuqan, Area P South	(© MAIS)
20.	Tell Mastuma, Square 15Gc, Layer H	re-drawn after Tsuneki 2009, fig. 3.24: 5
21.	Tell Mardikh/Ebla, Building G2 and Area CC	© MAIS
22.	Tell Mardikh/Ebla, Building G2 and Area CC	© MAIS
23.	Tell Tuqan, Area P South	© MAIS
24.	Tell Mishrifeh/Qatna, Chantier R, Niveaux 15–14	re-drawn after Mouamar 2015, fig. 6:16

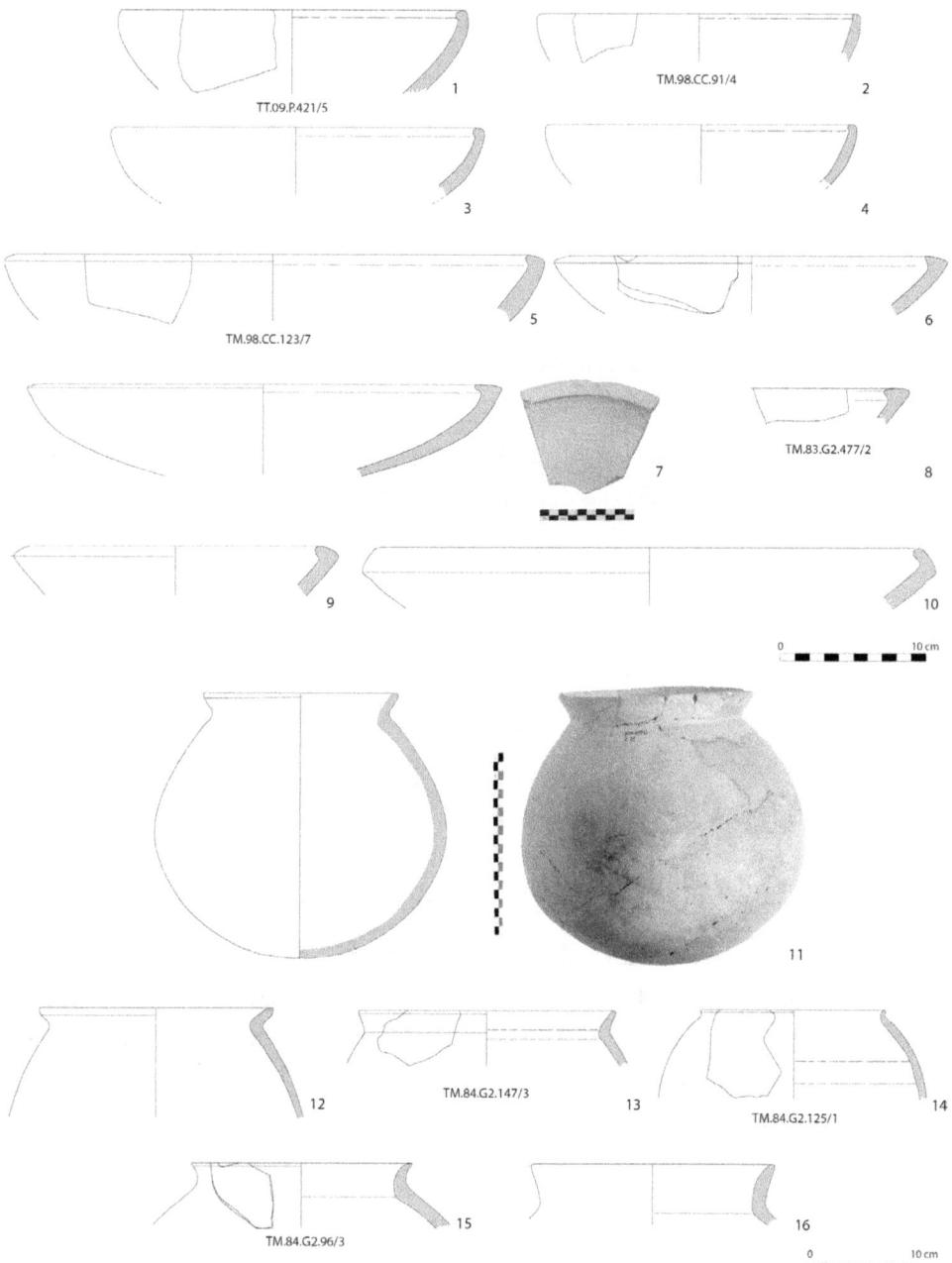

Figure 2.6: EB III SW (1–10) and CW (11–16) pottery from different northern Levantine sites.

2 The origin of Caliciform Ware in inland northern Syria during the mid-third millennium BC

No.	Site and description	Reference
1.	Tell Tuqan, Area P South	© MAIS
2.	Tell Mardikh/Ebla, Building G2, Area CC	© MAIS
3.	Tell Mastuma, Square 15Gc, Layer H	re-drawn after Tsuneki 2009, fig. 3.24: 1
4.	Tell Mishrifeh/Qatna, Operation J, Level 41	re-drawn after Besana et al. 2008, fig. 1: 1
5.	Tell Mardikh/Ebla, Building G2, Area CC	© MAIS
6.	Hama K1–2	Fugmann 1958, fig. 54: 4B816; reproduced courtesy of the National Museum of Denmark
7.	Hama K1–2	Fugmann 1958, fig. 54: 6B948; reproduced courtesy of the National Museum of Denmark
8.	Tell Mardikh/Ebla, Building G2, Area CC	(© MAIS)
9.	Tell Mishrifeh/Qatna, Operation J, Level 41	re-drawn after Besana et al. 2008, fig. 1: 7
10.	Chantier R, Niveau 16	re-drawn after Mouamar 2015, fig. 6: 19
11.	Hama K3	Fugmann 1958, fig. 49b: 7A650; reproduced courtesy of the National Museum of Denmark
12.	Tell Mastuma, Square 15Gc, Layer H	re-drawn after Tsuneki 2009, fig. 3.24: 11
13.	Tell Mardikh/Ebla, Building G2, Area CC	© MAIS
14.	Tell Mardikh/Ebla, Building G2, Area CC	© MAIS
15.	Tell Mardikh/Ebla, Building G2, Area CC	© MAIS
16.	Tell Mishrifeh/Qatna, Operation J, Level 41	re-drawn after Besana et al. 2008, fig. 1: 18

These trends are observable at Tell Mardikh/Ebla during the EB III–IVA1 transition. The ceramic horizon of EB IVA1 is characterised by the copious introduction of goblets, seldom attested in EB III levels. In fact, if we compare EB III and EB IVA1 SW open shapes, a difference can be observed in the proportion of goblets and bowls: during the EB III, cups/bowls account for 85%, while goblets amount to 8%. During the EB IVA1, the proportion is inverse, with 39% of cups/bowls and 60% of goblets (see Figure 2.4). Several types of goblets are attested, the majority of which were characterised by the marked corrugation of the outer surface and by greenish or cream-buff pastes (Figure 2.8: 1–3, 8, 11, 13–14, 16 and 19). Besides these forms, a limited range of standardised bowls, with swollen profiles and out-flared rim (similar to goblets' rim types) and deep carinated bowls characterise the assemblage (Figure 2.7: 1–8). Corrugation of the outer

A Land in Between

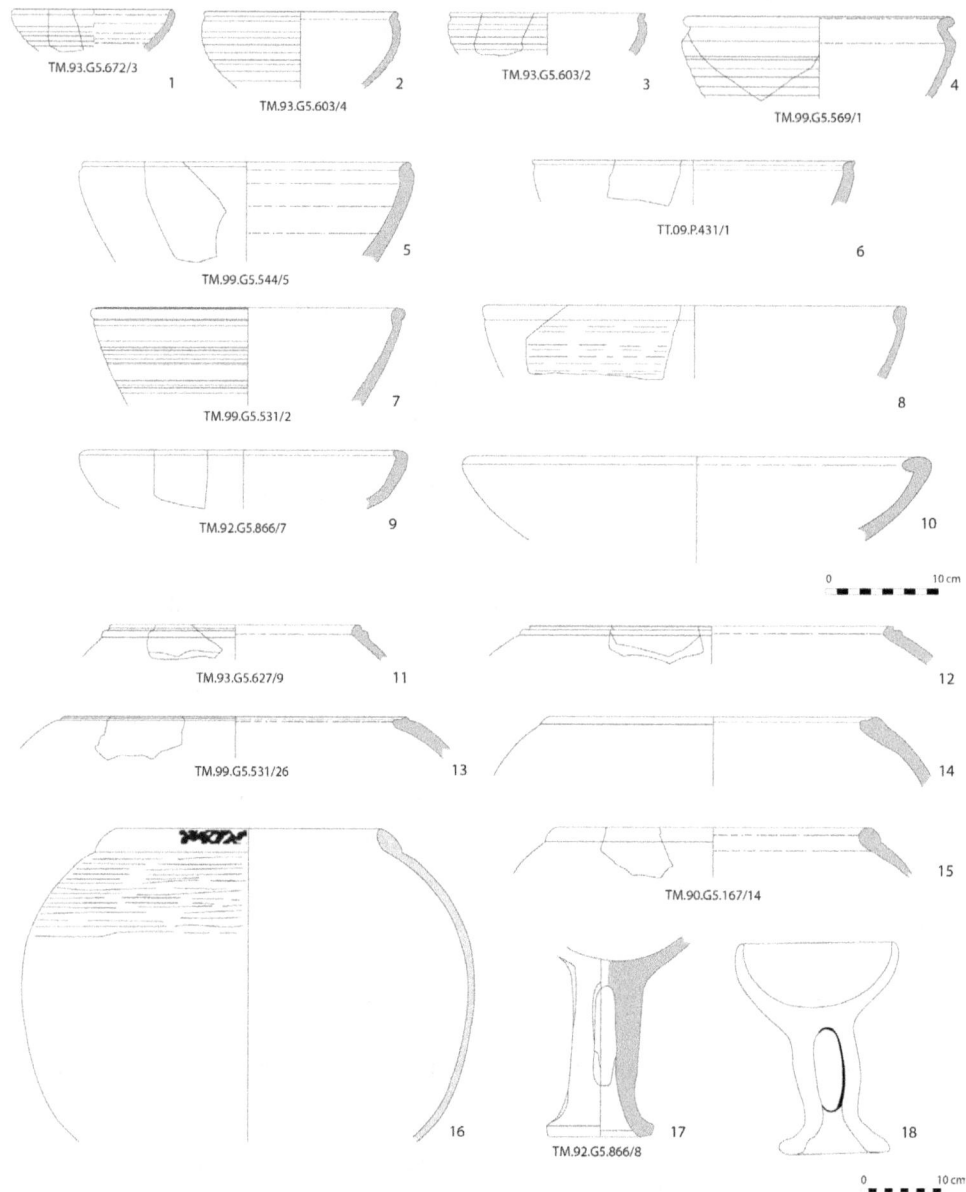

Figure 2.7: EB IVA1 SW (1-10) and CW (11-18) pottery from different northern Levantine sites.

No.	Site and description	Reference
1.	Tell Mardikh/Ebla, Building G5	© MAIS
2.	Tell Mardikh/Ebla, Building G5	© MAIS
3.	Tell Mardikh/Ebla, Building G5	© MAIS
4.	Tell Mardikh/Ebla, Building G5	© MAIS

2 The origin of Caliciform Ware in inland northern Syria during the mid-third millennium BC

No.	Site and description	Reference
5.	Tell Mardikh/Ebla, Building G5	© MAIS
6.	Tell Tuqan, Area P South	© MAIS
7.	Tell Mardikh/Ebla, Building G5	© MAIS
8.	Tell Afis, Area E, Level 18	re-drawn after Mazzoni 1998, fig. 16: 6
9.	Tell Mardikh/Ebla, Building G5	© MAIS
10.	Hama J8	re-drawn after Fugmann 1958, fig. 58: S.N°
11.	Tell Mardikh/Ebla, Building G5	© MAIS
12.	Tell Afis, Area E, Level 18	re-drawn after Mazzoni 1998, fig. 16: 6
13.	Tell Mardikh/Ebla, Building G5	© MAIS
14.	Tell Atchana	re-drawn after de Maigret 1978, fig. 3: 7
15.	Tell Mardikh/Ebla, Building G5	© MAIS
16.	Hama J8	re-drawn after Fugmann 1958, fig. 58: 3F183
17.	Tell Mardikh/Ebla, Building G5	© MAIS
18.	Hama J8	re-drawn after Fugmann 1958, fig. 58: 3E877

surface is a very common feature during this phase (recurring on ca. 1/3 of Building G5 assemblage), becoming the hallmark of the whole EB IVA period.[86] Some vessel shapes typical of the EB III, such as bowls with an incurving profile and platters with in-turned rims (Figure 2.7: 9), continue well into the EB IVA1, eventually declining and totally disappearing in the later Palace G ceramic horizon (EB IVA2). Another diagnostic type introduced from EB IVA1 is the holemouth CW pot (Figure 2.7: 11, 13 and 15), which is initially produced alongside EB III lingering types (Figure 2.6: 14), but ultimately becoming the prevalent CW shape of the Palace G assemblage.

Based on stratigraphic evidence, anchored to radiocarbon dates, it is possible to pinpoint the appearance of Caliciform goblets at Ebla around the mid-third millennium BC (EB IVA1, 2550–2450 cal. BC). Some diagnostic types, such as the goblets with out-turned inner-stepped rims (Figure 2.8: 1–3), restricted to EB IVA1 contexts at Ebla, appear at several sites within inland northern Syria, such as Tell Suffane, Tell Afis and Tell Qarqur (Figure 2.8: 4–6), also pointing to a regional production. In the 'Amuq plain, a local variant of drinking vessels is represented by conical cups with plain or corrugated surfaces, which develop out of Simple Ware at the beginning of Phase I (ENL 3, ca. 2600 BC), remaining the prevalent shape throughout late Phase I (ENL 4) – when the true goblet form is first introduced – and the beginning of Phase J (ENL 5).[87]

It seems that the two local Caliciform Ware traditions of the 'Amuq plain and the 'Ebla region' coexist, developing about the same time (ENL 3/EB IVA1). This is also

---

86 Mazzoni 2002, 76; Vacca 2015, 8.
87 Welton and Cooper 2014, 299–300; Welton, this book.

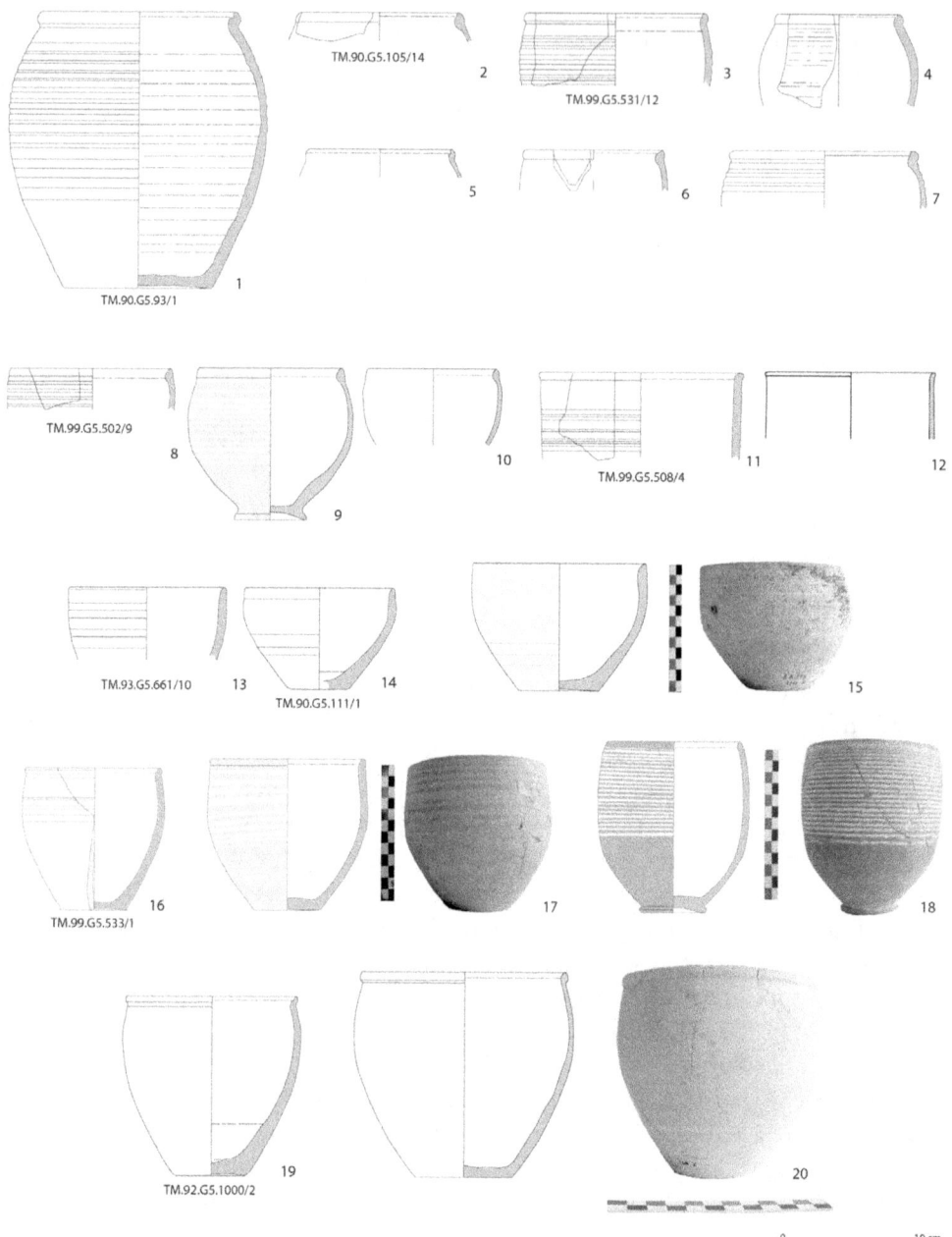

Figure 2.8: EB IVA1 goblets from different northern Levantine sites.

2 The origin of Caliciform Ware in inland northern Syria during the mid-third millennium BC

No.	Site and description	Reference
1.	Tell Mardikh/Ebla, Building G5	© MAIS
2.	Tell Mardikh/Ebla, Building G5	© MAIS
3.	Tell Mardikh/Ebla, Building G5	© MAIS
4.	Tell Afis Area E, Level 18	re-drawn after Mazzoni 1998, fig. 16: 1
5.	Tell Qarqur, Area A, Stratum 14	re-drawn after Dornemann 2008, fig. 3: 11
6.	Tell Suffane	re-drawn after Mazzoni 2006, fig. 4: k
7.	'Amuq, Phase I	re-drawn after Braidwood and Braidwood 1960, fig. 313: 10
8.	Tell Mardikh/Ebla, Building G5	© MAIS
9.	Hama J7	Fugmann 1958, fig. 62: SN°H10 IX; reproduced courtesy of the National Museum of Denmark
10.	Tell Qarqur, Area A, Stratum 14	re-drawn after Dornemann 2008, fig. 3: 16
11.	Tell Mardikh/Ebla, Building G5	© MAIS
12.	Tell Mishrifeh/Qatna, *Chantier R*, Niveaux 13–10	re-drawn after Mouamar 2015, fig. 6: 12
13.	Tell Mardikh/Ebla, Building G5	© MAIS
14.	Tell Mardikh/Ebla, Building G5	© MAIS
15.	Hama J8	Fugmann 1958, fig. 58: 3K243; reproduced courtesy of the National Museum of Denmark
16.	Tell Mardikh/Ebla, Building G5	© MAIS
17.	Hama J7	Fugmann 1958, fig. 62: 3G992; reproduced courtesy of the National Museum of Denmark
18.	Hama J7	Fugmann 1958, fig. 62: 3K219; reproduced courtesy of the National Museum of Denmark
19.	Tell Mardikh/Ebla, Building G5	© MAIS
20.	Hama J8	Fugmann 1958, fig. 58: 3K235; reproduced courtesy of the National Museum of Denmark

suggested by the presence of conical cups at Ebla,[88] and of goblets with out-turned inner-stepped rims (restricted to the EB IVA1) in the 'Amuq I assemblage.[89] A third Caliciform Ware tradition seems to emerge in the middle Orontes valley and the Syrian steppe at approximately the same time. At the sites of Tell Mishrifeh/Qatna (*Chantier R*, Levels 13–10) and Tell Al-Ṣūr, Caliciform Ware goblets are documented in levels assigned to the EB IVA1 period and are characterised by squat globular or cylindrical forms in plain

---

88 Mazzoni 1991, figs 7:3, 8:2.
89 Vacca 2015, 13.

SW, comparable with some goblet types documented also at Ebla (Figure 2.8: 11–12).[90] The only radiocarbon dates available for the EB III–IVA period at Tell Mishrifeh/Qatna come from Operation J, where Caliciform Ware goblets are not documented among published materials. However, the same overall features characterising the ceramic assemblages of the EB III (sets between 2800–2500 cal. BC) and EB IVA (2500–2300 cal. BC) in Operation J are also documented in other stratified contexts at the site assigned to the same time span,[91] indirectly suggesting a date around the mid-third millennium BC for the appearance of Caliciform Ware.

Evidence from Hama, although not very reliable due to its stratigraphic uncertainty, provides an important assemblage of goblet forms of the Syrian Caliciform Ware. The bulk of ceramic materials from Levels J7–J8 amounts to 72 almost complete vessels.[92] H. Ingholt identified four diagnostic goblet types (named GI–IV): goblets GI–II were produced from the earliest levels, J7–J8 up to Level J6, whereas goblets of Type GIII–IV appear only in a later phase, corresponding to Levels J1–J5.[93] Ingholt's Type GI includes grey ware goblets with spiral-incised decorations in the upper part of the vessel.[94] Type GII, although having a similar grey fabric, is characterised by a white spiral-painting or a white painted and reserved slip decoration. Actually, it seems that there is greater variability within each type or that more than four types of goblets exist. Phase J8 goblets are made either of pale-yellow mineral tempered clays (2.5Y 8/3), self-slipped (2.5Y 8/2) and horizontally reserved (Figure 2.8: 20), or pale-brown fabrics (10YR 6/3) combining spiral incised and white painted decoration (Figure 2.8: 15), or of dark grey clays and spiral-incised decoration (Type GI).[95] In Phase J7, light coloured fabrics continue to be attested,[96] alongside dark grey and red, non-oxidised, fabrics which characterised the white painted or reserved slip goblets of Type GII.[97] The 'grey goblets' are manufactured with black, red or brown pastes.[98] Two exemplars stored at the National Museum of Denmark show an oxidised fabric with yellowish-red fabric colour (5YR 5/6) and a dark grey surface (7.5YR 4/1) (Figure 2.8: 17–18).

A correlation between EB IVA1 at Ebla and Phases J8–J7 at Hama, already proposed by S. Mazzoni,[99] can be inferred from several comparisons, such as plain goblets with out-turned rims, and incense burners and hole-mouth cooking pots introduced from Level J8 (Figures 2.7: 15–18; 2.8: 8–9, 13–15 and 19–20). Moreover, Phases J8–J7 are

---

90 Mouamar 2014, 101; 2015, 404.
91 Besana et al. 2008.
92 Fugmann 1958, figs 58, 62.
93 Ingholt 1934, 34–35.
94 Ingholt 1934, 29–30.
95 Ingholt 1934, pl. VIII: 1. For a detailed analysis of goblets from Hama J, see Mouamar 2017. The author analysed a large sample of goblets from Phases J1–8, providing useful indicators for the dating of the Hama J goblets based on morpho-stylistics and technological criteria.
96 Fugmann 1958, pl. 62: 3H500.
97 Mouamar 2017; D'Andrea, this book.
98 Ingholt 1934, 30.
99 Mazzoni 2002, 76.

2 The origin of Caliciform Ware in inland northern Syria during the mid-third millennium BC

characterised by the presence of lingering Hama K4–K1 types (such as platters with in-turned rims; Figure 2.7: 10) and by the persistence of Red-Black Burnished Ware in Level J8.[100] As mentioned earlier, similar trends are also documented in the EB IVA1 ceramic horizon at Ebla, where some vessel types continue from the previous EB III period, such as large platter-bowls, with these totally disappearing in the later EB IVA2.[101] The introduction of a new cooking pot type (i.e. the hole-mouth) in Level J8 at Hama and in EB IVA1 contexts at Ebla bolsters our hypotheses about similarities in the ceramic horizons of these areas.

In particular Level J8, which marks the beginning of Phase J, can be paralleled with the EB IVA1 horizon of Tell Mardikh/Ebla and dated from the very start of EB IVA (ca. 2550–2450 BC).[102] As for Level J7, a slightly later date, probably matching the EB IVA1/beginning of EB IVA2 at Ebla, can be suggested based on some considerations.[103] Fugmann reports that in Phase J7, Type GI goblets are the most frequent, alongside fewer Types GII and GIII goblets, the latter characterising the late phases of the Phase J horizon (J1–J5).[104] Moreover, besides long-lasting J8 vessel types (comparable with the EB IVA1 horizon at Ebla), some new types appear to be introduced in Level J7 and continue into J5–J6. This is the case, for example, of grey ware deep bowls with triangular rim,[105] and ring-based slender goblets belonging to Type GII (Figure 2.8: 18),[106] comparable with similar early EB IVA2 types recurring at Ebla.[107]

Leaving aside the chronology of Level J7, the picture that emerges from this overview seems to suggest that the Caliciform Ware appeared in the middle Orontes valley around the mid-third millennium BC, like in inland northern Syria. Moreover, in the white painted Caliciform Ware documented at Hama, we can recognise a local tradition originating in central inland Syria, which continues during the second half of the third millennium BC.[108] With respect to this, the 'heartland of the Caliciform Culture', defined by Cooper and limited to the Orontes valley,[109] can be broadened by including the Ebla region. Therefore, we can track the emergence of the 'true' goblet form (i.e. the major component of the Caliciform Ware of the northern Levant) in these two regions, given its early attestation at both the sites of Hama and Tell Mardikh/Ebla, and identify two autonomous traditions: the corrugated Caliciform Ware of inland northern Syria and the painted Caliciform Ware of the middle Orontes valley. Despite the broadly contemporaneous appearance of these forms in the aforementioned areas, it cannot be assumed that the introduction of goblets was a simultaneous phenomenon; rather,

---

100 Fugmann 1958, 84.
101 Vacca 2015, fig. 7:13.
102 Mazzoni 2002, 76; Vacca 2014a; 2015, 11–12.
103 Vacca 2015, 9; see also Mouamar 2015, Table 2.
104 Fugmann 1958, 56.
105 Fugmann 1958, fig. 62: 3H189; J7, fig. 62:3G905, 3G919, J6.
106 J7; Fugmann 1958, fig. 3G903, J6.
107 Vacca 2015, figs 8: 2–5; Marchetti and Vacca 2018.
108 See D'Andrea 2014; D'Andrea, this book; Welton and Cooper 2014.
109 Copper 2007.

each case should be assessed based on contextual data. This is the case, for instance, of Tell Nebi Mend, in the upper Orontes valley, where it has been demonstrated that goblets appeared slightly later in the ceramic repertoire without local antecedents,[110] with these probably inspired by middle Orontes prototypes.[111]

Caliciform Ware and drinking practices during the mid-third millennium BC

The widespread adoption within local pottery assemblages ('Amuq plain, Ebla region, middle Orontes valley) of specialised drinking vessels, particularly cups and goblets, inspired by similar models but locally manufactured at different production centres, argues in favour of a wide regional phenomenon involving the whole northern Levant around the mid-third millennium BC. The introduction of standardised drinking vessels can be connected with increasing inter-regional contacts,[112] an intensified circulation and consumption of particular liquid products (wine and beer), as well as with a change in social commensality. This change is largely concurrent with the process of urbanisation and the formation of states so far outlined, and was probably linked to new needs, brought about by emergent elites, as a means of self-representation and a source for maintaining social and political relationships. While the convivial consumption of drinks is well attested in southern Mesopotamia from the onset of the third millennium BC,[113] drinking as a social practice seems to have quickly spread in northern Levantine and northern Mesopotamian societies in connection with the process of urbanisation around the mid-third millennium BC. The practice of convivial consumption of drinks has been widely discussed by several authors, who stressed the role of drinking as a means to gain social prestige and political power, to establish and maintain social and political ties, as well as to obtain economic advantage by means of the mobilisation of labour through work-party feasts.[114] The consumption of alcoholic beverages played an important role in Near Eastern societies at a feeding, economic and social level, as testified by the ever-growing amount of textual and archaeological evidence relating to beer and wine during the third millennium BC.[115] Beer, in particular, was consumed daily, and was produced at both a domestic and institutional level, while the circulation of wine appears more restricted and its consumption confined to specific contexts.[116] Wine production is documented in Syria and Anatolia through the recovery of carbonised grapevine seeds at several sites.[117] At Tilbeshar Höyük,

---

110 Kennedy et al. 2018.
111 See D'Andrea, this book.
112 See Welton, this book.
113 Benati 2019, with relevant bibliography.
114 Dietler 1990; Dietler and Hayden (eds) 2001; Bunimovitz and Greenberg 2004.
115 Joffee 1998.
116 See Joffee 1998; Powell 1996; Vacca 2020.
117 Zettler and Miller 1996, 128.

2 The origin of Caliciform Ware in inland northern Syria during the mid-third millennium BC

botanical analyses suggest local production of wine from Phase III C (2500–2300 BC).[118] Similarly, at Kurban Höyük a high number of pips of grapes were recovered in mid- to late-third millennium BC contexts.[119] At Titriş Höyük, plastered basins with a high concentration of tartaric acid, related to wine production, were found in late-third millennium BC private dwellings.[120]

In northern inland Syria, the production of wine is well documented in the archaeological and textual evidence from Palace G. *Vitis vinifera* pips have been identified among the botanic species collected in Palace G (Wachter-Sarkady 2013). Part of the incoming amount of wine (*geštin*) consumed by the Eblaite elite came from the 'royal fields' (*gána-kú*) as a tribute in return for the granting of land, or it was received by the palace in exchange for textiles. Wine income was also dispatched from different centres located to the north, north-east, east and south of Ebla, such as Gudanum, Kakmium, Dub, Ibal and Emar.[121]

The consumption of alcoholic beverages during feastings, or banquets, is well represented at the high-ranking levels, as can be inferred from numerous third millennium BC artistic representations, depicting a plurality of celebrations, such as sacred rituals or ceremonial-palatial occasions.[122] Moreover, the frequent recurrence of 'drinking sets' in funerary contexts along the Euphrates valley from the EB III[123] has been connected with a special drinking ritual during burial processes.[124]

From around the mid-third millennium BC, the specialisation of the Table Ware repertoire is suggested by the appearance of new morphological types for serving, pouring and consuming liquids, such as pitchers, spouted vessels, small necked jars and goblets.[125] According to the new chronologies (anchored to radiocarbon dates), developed within the framework of the ARCANE Project, it appears that the introduction of goblets and 'drinking sets' is largely concurrent in the Euphrates valley (EME 3–4),[126] in Jezirah (final EJZ 2–EJZ 3),[127] and in the northern Levant (ENL 3–6).

The evidence from Palace G at Ebla is very interesting; the high percentage of drinking and pouring vessels found in several sectors of the palace devoted to ceremonial activities or storage suggests a high-level demand for such commodities, likely employed in the redistribution and consumption of drinks within a large number of commensals.[128] A similar function can be hypothesised for Building G5, which

---

118 Kepinski 2007, 155–156.
119 Miller 1991, 150.
120 Algaze 1999, 549.
121 Archi 1993, 18; Milano 1994, 437; Fronzaroli 1994.
122 Pinnock 1994.
123 Sconzo 2007.
124 Porter 2002.
125 Joffee 1998; Bunimovitz and Greenberg 2004; Ünlü 2016; Laneri 2018; Vacca 2020.
126 Sconzo 2015.
127 Rova 2011.
128 Mazzoni 1994; Vacca 2020.

probably was a ceremonial sector of the EB IVA1 archaic palatial building.[129] The three excavated rooms yielded a large number of tableware (including 234 Caliciform Ware goblets and 15 SW bowls), followed by SW jars (mainly small jars with restricted necks and few storage jars), as well as some CW pots.[130] Moreover, the recovery of flint blades and disarticulated parts of skeletons pertaining to sheep and cattle[131] probably suggests butchering activities and food consumption within this sector of the building.

Elites consumed alcoholic beverages using both prized metal drinking sets made of precious stones, silver or copper alloy as well as ceramic vessels. Although they are rarely found, exemplars of metal beakers are known from contexts dating to the second half of the third millennium BC, for instance in an adult male grave of a probable military commander excavated on the Acropolis of Tell Beydar,[132] or in the rich mid-third millennium BC elite burial at Tell Ahmar/Til Barsip.[133]

Conversely, the patterns of distribution of ceramic goblets indicate that these vessels are ubiquitous in all kinds of contexts, from dwellings to large-scale/public buildings and burials, suggesting that the adoption of similar drinking practices was not restricted to political elites, but rather cut across different levels of the society.[134] This pattern of distribution in both public and domestic contexts testifies to the existence of differentiated circuits of distribution of the potters' production, responding to the common needs of the consumers, which stimulated a high-level demand for these mass-produced drinking vessels. A main distinction may rely in the low value of the goblet itself and the high social value of its use in feasting;[135] with respect to this, the goblet can be regarded as a socially valued good to which elites and all social classes accord the same basic need. Although elites had privileged access to alcoholic beverages, especially to wine (a rare commodity in cuneiform sources), the production of beer and wine occurred also at the private and familial level, as evidenced by the findings from third millennium BC contexts.[136] The widespread adoption of drinking practices might also reflect the desire to emulate the elite's convivial habits (i.e. the display of status through 'spending capacity', by sponsoring drinking feasts), as well as the incorporation of such habits into the private sphere in connection with shared ritual practices and beliefs. Some individuals displayed their high status, or 'purchase power', multiplying the drinking sets (for instance jars and goblets) in the domestic sphere or in burial equipment.[137]

---

129 Vacca 2018b.
130 Vacca 2018b, fig. 15.
131 Minniti 2013.
132 Bretschneider and Cunningham 2007.
133 Thureau-Dangin and Dunand 1936, pl. XXVIII: 1–3; Baccarin 2014.
134 Mazzoni 1994; Welton and Cooper 2014; Vacca 2020.
135 Aprile 2013.
136 Joffee 1998; Laneri 2008.
137 Vacca 2020.

2 The origin of Caliciform Ware in inland northern Syria during the mid-third millennium BC

Conclusion

The ubiquitous distribution of Caliciform Ware goblets, the most diagnostic shape within the SW assemblage of western inland Syria during the mid- to late-third millennium BC (EB IV), has been generally connected with the consumption of alcoholic beverages during elite-sponsored banquets and ceremonies.[138] Several artistic representations and the evidence, among others, from Royal Palace G at Ebla of hundreds of such goblets seem to support this reconstruction. Moreover, the presence of differentiated circuits of distribution of goblets, not restricted to political elites, suggests the incorporation of such habits at different levels of the society. Another important aspect is represented by the question of the origin of Caliciform Ware that is doubly linked to the issue of chronology and the introduction of new means of social commensality, accompanying important transformations and their relation with the process of urbanisation described above. The evidence, illustrated in this chapter, from the stratified sequence at Ebla, anchored to radiocarbon dates, shows that Caliciform Ware already appears at the site *before* the construction of Palace G, in association with an earlier monumental structure. Caliciform goblets are indeed introduced in bulk in the ceramic assemblage of Building G5, dating from EB IVA1 (2550–2450 BC), after an initial trial phase during EB III, when few goblet forms appear alongside the more numerous cup types. Furthermore, the correlation of the Hama and Ebla sequences, together with new data from other sites, shows that the appearance of Caliciform Ware was broadly contemporaneous in the middle Orontes valley and inland northern Syria, as well as in the 'Amuq valley, and can be placed around the mid-third millennium BC. It is, in fact, from this period that the northern Levant sees the emergence of a broader ceramic tradition, as the result of intensified contacts, similar paths towards urbanisation and similar modes of production and craft specialisation. The suggested synchronicity for the origin of Caliciform Ware in both the middle Orontes valley and inland northern Syria is supported by the coexistence of different local traditions (the painted ware of the middle Orontes valley and the corrugated ware of the Ebla region), which are maintained and further developed in the following late-third millennium BC.

Acknowledgements

I wish to thank warmly Dr Stephen Bourke and Dr Melissa Kennedy for kindly inviting me to take part in the workshop 'The Settlement Landscape of the Orontes valley in the Fourth to Second Millennia BCE', held at the University of Basel, Switzerland, during the 9th ICAANE in June 2014. I wish to thank also the former head of the collection of Classical and Near Eastern Antiquities, Dr Bodil Bundgaard Rasmussen, and the actual head of the collection, Dr Lasse Sørensen; Dr J. Lund (Assistant Keeper) and Dr Stephen Lumsden (Assistant Curator) of the Department of Classical and Near Eastern Antiquities of the National Museum of Denmark, Copenhagen, for allowing

---

138 Mazzoni 1994; Bunimovitz and Greenberg 2004; Cooper 2007.

me to study the Hama materials and for their invaluable help. I also wish to thank my colleague G. Mouamar for discussing with me materials from Hama and the sites of the Syrian steppe. My thanks go also to the anonymous peer reviewers for providing very helpful comments on the manuscript.

References

Al-Maqdissi, M. (2007). Notes d'archéologie Levantine X. Introduction aux travaux archéologiques syriens à Mishrifeh/Qatna au nord-est de Homs (Emèse). In *Urban and natural landscapes of an ancient Syrian capital: settlement and environment at Tell Mishrifeh/Qatna and in central-western Syria*. D. Morandi-Bonacossi, ed. 19–27. Studi Archeologici su Qatna 01. Udine: Forum.

(2008). Réflexions sur Qatna et sa region. *Studia Orontica* III: 3–41.

(2010). Matériel pour l'étude de la ville en Syrie (deuxième partie). In *Urban planning in Syria during the second urban revolution (mid third millennium BC). Formation of tribal communities. Integrated research in the Middle Euphrates, Syria*. K. Ohnuma, ed. 131–146. Hiroshima.

Algaze, G. (1999). Trends in the archaeological development of the upper Euphrates basin of southeastern Anatolia during the Late Chalcolithic and Early Bronze Ages. In *Archaeology of the upper Syrian Euphrates: the Tishrin Dam area. Proceedings of the international symposium held at Barcelona, January 28th-30th 1998*. G. del Olmo Lete and J.L. Montero Fenollós, eds. 535–572. Aula Orientalis-Supplementa 15. Barcelona: Sabadell.

Aprile, J.D. (2013). The new political economy of Nichoria: using intrasite distributional data to investigate regional institutions. *America Journal of Archaeology* 117(3): 429–36.

Archi, A. (1993). Five tablets from the Southern Wing of Palace G, Ebla. *Syro-Mesopotamian Studies* 5(2): 28–33.

(2001). The king-lists from Ebla. In *Historiography in the Cuneiform World I. Proceedings of the XLVe Rencontre Assyriologique Internationale*. I. T. Abusch, P. A. Beaulieu, J. Huehnergard, P. Machinist and P. Steinkeller, ed. 1–13. Bethesda: Harvard University.

Akkermans, P.M.M.G. and Schwartz, G.M. (2003). *The archaeology of Syria: from complex hunter-gatherers to early urban societies (ca. 16,000–300 BC)*. Cambridge: Cambridge University Press.

Baccarin, C. (2014). The Hypogeum of Tell Ahmar (North Syria). An Analysis of the Monumental Burial Complex in the Context of Early Bronze Age Funerary Practices. *Ancient Near Eastern Studies* 51: 213–225.

Bartl, K. and Al-Maqdissi, M. eds. (2014). *New prospecting in the Orontes region, first results of archaeological fieldwork*. Orient-Archäologie Band 30. Rahden: Verlag Marie Leidorf GmbH.

Benati, G. (2019). Shaping social dynamics in early third millennium BC Mesopotamia: solid-footed Goblets and the politics of drinking. In *Pearls of the Past. Studies in Honour of Frances Pinnock*. M. D'Andrea, M.G. Micale, D. Nadali, S. Pizzimenti and A. Vacca, eds. 53–76. Marru 8. Münster: Zaphon.

2 The origin of Caliciform Ware in inland northern Syria during the mid-third millennium BC

Besana, R., Da Ros, M. and Iamoni, M. (2008). Excavations on the Acropolis of Mishrifeh, Operation J. A new Early Bronze Age III – Iron Age III sequence for central inner Syria. Part II: The Pottery. *Akkadica* 129: 79–130.

Blackman, M.J., Stein, G.J. and Vandiver, P. (1993). The standardisation hypothesis and ceramic mass production: technological, compositional, and metric indices of craft specialisation at Tell Leilan, Syria. *American Antiquity* 58(1): 60–80.

Braidwood, R.J. and Braidwood, L.S. (1960). *Excavations in the plain of Antioch I: the early assemblages Phases A–J.* The University of Chicago Oriental Institute Publications No. LXI. Chicago: University of Chicago Press.

Bretschneider, J. and Cunningham, T. (2007). An elite Akkadian grave on the Acropolis at Tell Beydar. In *Tell Beydar: the 2000–2002 season of excavations, the 2003–2004 season of architectural restoration. A preliminary report.* M. Lebeau and A. Suleiman, eds. 99–158. Subartu 15. Turnhout: Brepols.

Bronk Ramsey, C. and Lee, S. (2013). Recent and planned developments of the program OxCal. *Radiocarbon* 55(3–4): 720–730.

Bunimovitz, S. and Greenberg, R. (2004). Revealed in their cups: Syrian drinking customs in Intermediate Bronze Age Canaan. *Bulletin of the American Schools of Oriental Research* 334: 19–31.

Calcagnile, L., Quarta, G. and D'Elia, M. (2013). Just at that time. 14C determinations and analysis from EB IVA layers. In *Ebla and its landscape: early state formation in the Ancient Near East.* P. Matthiae and N. Marchetti, eds. 450–458. Walnut Creek: Left Coast Press.

Castel, C. (2007). Stratégies de subsistence et modes d'occupation de l'espace dans la micro-région d'al-Rawda au Bronze Ancien Final (Shamiyeh). In *Urban and natural landscapes of an ancient Syrian capital: settlement and environment at Tell Mishrifeh/Qatna and in central-western Syria.* D. Morandi-Bonacossi, ed. 283–294. Studi Archeologici su Qatna 01. Udine: Forum.

Cooper, L. (2006). *Early urbanism on the Syrian Euphrates.* London: Routledge.

(2007). Exploring the heartland of the Early Bronze Age 'Caliciform' culture. *Journal of the Canadian Society for Mesopotamian Studies* 2: 43–50.

Courtois, J.C. (1962). Contribution à l'étude des niveaux II et III de Ras Shamra. In *Ugaritica IVC.* F.A. Schaeffer, ed. 329–414. Paris: Librairie Orientalist Paul Geuthner.

Costin, C.L. (1991). Craft specialisation: issues in defining, documenting, and explaining the organisation of production. *Archaeological Method and Theory,* Vol. 3. M.B. Schiffer, ed. 1–56. Tucson: University of Arizona Press.

D'Andrea, M. (2014). La Black Wheelmade Ware. Originalità e modelli stilistici, tipologici e tecnologici dalla Siria e dal Levante settentrionale in una peculiare produzione dipinta sud-levantina del tardo III millennio B.C. *Rendiconti Morali dell'Accademia Nazionale dei Lincei* IX: 181–220.

Dietler, M. (1990). Driven by drink: the role of drinking in the political economy and the case of early Iron Age France. *Journal of Anthropological Archaeology* 9: 352–406.

Dietler, M. and Hayden, B. eds. (2001). *Feasts: archaeological and ethnographic experiences on food, politics, and power.* Washington, D.C.: Smithsonian Institution Press.

Dolce, R. (2009). The archaeology of a long lasting power: the Ebla paradigm: a synthesis. *Studi Micenei ed Egeo-Anatolici* 51: 251–278.

Dornemann, R.H. (2003). Seven seasons of ASOR excavations at Tell Qarqur, Syria, 1993–1999. In *Preliminary excavation reports and other archaeological investigations: Tell Qarqur and Iron I sites in the north-central highlands of Palestine*. N. Lapp, ed. 1–141. Boston, MA: American Schools of Oriental Research.

(2008). Evidence from two transitional periods, Early Bronze IV and Iron I, at Tell Qarqur, Syria. In *Proceedings of the International Congress of the Archaeology of the Ancient Near East, 29 March – 3 April 2004, Freie Universität, Berlin. Volume 2: social and cultural transformation: the archaeology of transitional periods and dark ages, excavation reports*. H. Kühne, M. Czichon and F.J. Kreppner, eds. 81–95. Wiesbaden: Harrassowitz Verlag.

Ehrich, A.M.H. (1939). *Early pottery of Jebeleh region*. Memoirs of the American Philosophical Society 13. Philadelphia.

Fortin, M. (2007a). Reprise de la prospection de la moyenne vallée de l'Oronte (Syrie) par une mission Syro-Canadienne: 2004–2006. *Journal of the Canadian Society for Mesopotamian Studies* 2: 19–41.

(2007b). La vallée de l'Oronte: une entité géographique unique au Proche-Orient. *Journal of the Canadian Society for Mesopotamian Studies* 2: 7–18.

Fronzaroli, P. (1994). Osservazioni sul lessico delle bevande dei testi di Ebla. In *Drinking in ancient societies: history and culture of drinks in the Ancient Near East. Papers of a symposium held in Rome, May 17–19, 1990*. L. Milano, ed. 121–127. HANES 6. Padua: Sargon s.r.l.

Fugmann, E. (1958). *Hama: II.1. Fouilles et recherches de la Fondation Carlsberg 1931–1938: L'architecture des périodes pré-Hellénistiques*. Copenhagen: Nationalmuseet.

Geyer, B., Besancon, J., Calvet, Y. and Debaine, F. (1998). Les marges arides de la Syrie du nord: prospection géo-archéologique. *Bulletin de l'Association de Géographes Français* 75: 213–23.

Greenberg, R. and Porat, N. (1996). A third millennium Levantine pottery production center: typology, petrography, and provenance of the Metallic Ware of northern Israel and adjacent regions. *Bulletin of the American Schools of Oriental Research* 301: 5–24.

Ingholt, H. (1934). *Rapport préliminaire sur la première campagne des fouilles de Hama en Syrie*. Archæologisk-kunsthistoriske Meddelelser I,3. København: Gyldendal.

(1940). *Rapport préliminaire sur sept campagnes de fouilles de Hama en Syrie (1932–1938)*. Archæologisk-kunsthistoriske Meddelelser 3,1. København: Gyldendal.

Iwasaki, T. and Tsuneki, A. (2003). *Archaeology of the Rouj basin: a regional study of the transition from village to city in northwest Syria*, Vol. 1. Al-Shark 2. University of Tsukuba Press: Tsukuba.

Joffee, N. (1998). Alcohol and social complexity in ancient Western Asia. *Current Anthropology* 39(3): 297–322.

Kennedy, M., Badreshany, K. and Philip, G. (2018). Drinking on the periphery: the Tell Nebi Mend goblets in their regional and archaeometric Context. *Levant*, doi: 10.1080/00758914.2018.1442076.

Kepinski, C. (2007). Dynamics, diagnostic criteria and settlement patterns in the Carchemish area during the Early Bronze period. In *Euphrates river valley settlement: the Carchemish Sector in the Third Millennium BC*. E. Peltenburg, ed. 152–163. Levant Supplementary Series 5. Oxford: Oxbow.

Laneri, N. (2018). The impact of wine production in the social transformation of northern Mesopotamian societies during the third and second millennia BCE. *Die Welt des Orients* 48: 225–237.

de Maigret, A. (1978). Fluttuazioni territoriali e caratteristiche tipologiche degli insediamenti nella regione del Matah (Siria). Nota Preliminare. In *Atti del 1° Convegno Italiano sul Vicino Oriente Antico, Roma, 22–24 Aprile 1976*. 83–94. Orientis Antiqui Collectio 13. Roma.

Mantellini, S., Micale, M.G. and Peyronel, L. (2013). Exploiting diversity: the archaeological landscape of the Eblaite *Chora*. In *Ebla and its landscape: early state formation in the ancient Near East*. P. Matthiae and N. Marchetti, eds. 163–194. Walnut Creek: Left Coast Press.

Marchetti, N. and Vacca, A. (2018). Building complexity: layers from initial EB IVA2 in Area P South at Ebla. In *A Oriente del Delta. Scritti sull'Egitto ed il Vicino Oriente antico in onore di Gabriella Scandone Matthiae*. A. Vacca, S. Pizzimenti and M.G. Micale, eds. 317–358. CMAO XVIII. Roma: Arbor Sapientiae.

Matthers, J. ed. (1981). *The river Qoueiq, northern Syria and its catchment*. British Archaeological Reports International Series 98. Oxford: British Archaeological Reports.

Matthiae, P. and Marchetti, N. eds. (2013). *Ebla and its landscape: early state formation in the ancient Near East*. Walnut Creek: Left Coast Press.

Matthiae, P. (1987). Les dernières découvertes d'Ebla en 1983–1986. *Comptes rendus des séances de l'Académie des Inscriptions et Belles Lettres* 1987(1): 135–161.

(1990). Nouvelles fouilles à Ebla en 1987–1989. *Comptes Rendus de l'Académie des Inscriptions et Belles-Lettres* 1990: 1–431.

(2000). Nouvelles fouilles à Ébla (1998–1999): forts et palais de l'enceinte urbaine. *Comptes rendus des séances de l'Académie des Inscriptions et Belles-Lettres* 2000(2): 567–610.

Mazzoni, S. (1985). Elements of the ceramic culture of early Syrian Ebla in comparison with Syro-Palestinian EB IV. *Bulletin of the American Schools of Oriental Research* 257: 1–18.

(1991). Ebla e la formazione della cultura urbana in Siria. *La Parola del Passato* 46: 163–194.

(1994). Drinking vessels in Syria: Ebla and the Early Bronze Age. In *Drinking in ancient societies: history and culture of drinks in the Ancient Near East. Papers of a symposium held in Rome, May 17–19, 1990*. L. Milano, ed. 245–255. HANES 6. Padua: Sargon s.r.l.

(1998). Materials and chronology. In *Tell Afis (Siria): the 1988–1992 excavations on the acropolis*. S. M. Cecchini and S. Mazzoni, eds. 101–122. Pisa: Edizioni Ets.

(2002). The ancient Bronze Age pottery tradition in north-western central Syria. In *Céramique de l'Âge du Bronze en Syrie, I: la Syrie du sud et le vallée de l'Oronte*. M. Al-Maqdissi, V. Matoïan and C. Nicolle, eds. 69–96. Bibliothéque Archéologique et Historique T.161. Beyrouth: Institut Français du Proche-Orient.

(2003). Ebla: crafts and power in an emergent state of 3rd millennium Syria. *Journal of Mediterranean Archaeology* 16(2): 173–191.

(2005). Tell Afis, the survey and the regional sequence. *Egitto e Vicino Oriente* 28: 5–14.

(2006). Tell Suffane, an Early and Middle Bronze Age site in the Idlib plain. *Baghdader Mitteilungen* 37: 381–392.

Mellaart, J. (1981). The prehistoric pottery from the Neolithic to the beginning of the EB IV (c. 7000–2500 BC). In *The river Qoueiq, northern Syria and its catchment*. J. Matthers, ed. 131–319. British Archaeological Reports International Series 98. Oxford: British Archaeological Reports.

du Mesnil du Buisson, R. (1935). *Le site archéologique du Mishrifé-Qatna*. Paris.
Milano, L. (1994). Vino e birra in Oriente. Confini geografici e confini culturali. In *Drinking in ancient societies: history and culture of drinks in the Ancient Near East. Papers of a symposium held in Rome, May 17–19, 1990*. L. Milano, ed. 421–440. HANES 6. Padua: Sargon s.r.l.
Miller, N.F. (1991). The Near East. In *Progress in Old World palaeoethnobotany: a retrospective view on the occasion of 20 years of the international workgroup for palaeoethnobotany*. W. van Zeist, K. Wasylikowa, and K-E. Behre, eds. 133–160. Rotterdam: A Balkema Publishers.
Minniti, C. (2013). Exploiting animals. The zooarchaeological evidence through the Early Bronze Age at Ebla. In *Ebla and its landscape: early state formation in the ancient Near East*. P. Matthiae and N. Marchetti, eds. 413–430. Walnut Creek: Left Coast Press.
Morandi Bonacossi, D. (2008). Excavations on the Acropolis of Mishrifeh, Operation J. A new Early Bronze Age III – Iron Age III sequence for central inner Syria. Part 1: stratigraphy, chronology and architecture. *Akkadica* 129: 55–127.
Mouamar, G. (2012). Nouvelles données sur les inhumations en jarre du site de Mishrifeh/Qatna au Bronze ancien IV. In *L'Heure immobile. Entre ciel et terre, Mélanges en l'honneur d'Antoine Souleiman*. Ph. Quenet and M. Al-Maqdissi, eds. 77–92. Subartu 31. Turnhout: Brepols.
(2014). Tell Al-Ṣūr/Al-Sankarī: une nouvelle agglomération circulaire du Bronze ancien IV à la lisière de la steppe syrienne. In *Tell Tuqan excavations and regional perspectives: cultural developments in inner Syria from the Early Bronze Age to the Persian/Hellenistic period. Proceedings of the international conference, May 15th–17th 2013, Lecce*. F. Baffi, R. Fiorentino and L. Peyronel, eds. 95–114. Lecce: Congedo Editore.
(2015). Mishrifeh au troisième millénaire av. J-C. bilan provisoire des travaux du Chantier (R) 'cour du trône'. In *Networks of Bronze Age globalism proceedings of an international conference in Stuttgart and Tübingen in October 2009*. P. Pfälzner and M. Al-Maqdissi, eds. 399–406. Wiesbaden: Harrassowitz Verlag.
(2017). De nouvelles données sur les gobelets de Hama: marqueurs de la chronologie et des échanges de Syrie centrale pendant la seconde moitié du 3e millénaire avant J-C. *Paléorient* 43(2): 69–89.
Oldenburg, E. (1991). *Sukas IX: the Chalcolithic and Early Bronze Age periods*. Publications of the Carlsberg Expedition to Phoenicia 11. Copenhagen: Nationalmuseet.
Parayre, D. ed. (2016). *La Geographie Historique de l'Oronte. De l'Epoque d'Ebla a l'Epoque Medieval*. Syria Supplement IV. Beirut: Institute Francois du Proche Orient.
Peyronel, L. (2011). Area P. In *Tell Tuqan. Excavations 2008–2010*. F. Baffi, ed. 61–110, Galatina-Lecce.
(2014). Living near the lake. The Matkh region (Syria) during the Early and Middle Bronze Ages. In *Tell Tuqan excavations and regional perspectives: cultural developments in inner Syria from the Early Bronze Age to the Persian/Hellenistic period. Proceedings of the international conference, May 15th–17th 2013, Lecce*. F. Baffi, R. Fiorentino and L. Peyronel, eds. 115–161. Lecce: Congedo Editore.
Philip, G., Jabour, F., Beck, A., Bshesh, M., Grove, J., Kirk, A. and Millard, A. (2002). Settlement and landscape development in the Homs Region, Syria: research questions, preliminary results 1999–2000 and future potential. *Levant* 34: 1–23.
Pinnock, F. (1994). Consideration on the 'banquet theme' in the figurative art of Mesopotamia and Syria. In *Drinking in ancient societies: history and culture of drinks in the Ancient Near*

2 The origin of Caliciform Ware in inland northern Syria during the mid-third millennium BC

East. Papers of a symposium held in Rome, May 17–19, 1990. L. Milano, ed. 15–26. HANES 6. Padua: Sargon s.r.l.

Porter, A. (2002). The dynamics of death: ancestors, pastoralism, and the origins of a third-millennium city in Syria. *Bulletin of the American Schools of Oriental Research* 325: 1–36.

Powell, M.A. (1996). Wine and the vine in ancient Mesopotamia: the Cuneiform evidence. In *The origins and ancient history of wine.* P.E. McGovern, S.J. Fleming and S.H. Kats, eds. 97–122. Food and Nutrition in History and Anthropology 11. Amsterdam: Routledge.

Reimer, P.J., Bard, E., Bayliss, A., Warren Beck, J. and Blackwell, P.G. (2013). Intcal13 and Marine13 radiocarbon age calibration curves 0–50,000 years cal BP. *Radiocarbon* 55(4): 1869–1887.

Rice, P.M. (1981). Evolution of specialised pottery production: a trial model. *Current Anthropology* 22(3): 219–240.

Rova, E. (1996). Ceramic provinces along the middle and upper Euphrates: Late Chalcolithic-Early Bronze Age, a diachronic view. *Baghdader Mitteilungen* 27: 13–37.

(2000). Early third millennium B.C. painted pottery tradition in the Jezireh. In *Chronologie des pays du Caucase et de l'Euphrate aux IVe-IIIe millénaires, actes du colloque, d'Istanbul, 16-19 Décembre 1998.* C. Marro and H. Hauptmann, eds. 231–253. Varia Anatolica 11. Paris: Institut Français d'Etudes Anatoliennes d'Istanbul.

Schwartz, G.M. (1993). Review of Thuesen 1988. *Journal of Near Eastern Studies* 52(2): 153–155.

Schwartz, G.M., Curvers, H.H., Dunham, S.S. and Weber, J.A. (2012). From urban origins to imperial integration in western Syria: Umm el-Marra 2006, 2008. *American Journal of Archaeology* 116: 157–193.

Sconzo, P. (2007). Plain and luxury wares of the third millennium BC in the Carchemish region: two case-studies from Tell Shiyukh Tahtani. In *Euphrates river valley settlement: the Carchemish sector in the third millennium BC.* E. Peltenburg, ed. 250–266. Levant Supplementary Series 5. Oxford: Oxbow Books.

(2015). Ceramics. In *Associated regional chronologies for the ancient Near East IV: the middle Euphrates region.* U. Finkbeiner, M. Novák, F. Sakal and P. Sconzo, eds. 85–202. Turnhout: Brepols.

Thalmann, J-P. (2009). The Early Bronze Age: foreign relations in the light of recent excavations at Tell Arqa. In *Interconnections in the eastern Mediterranean. Lebanon in the Bronze and Iron Ages. Proceedings of the international symposium, Beirut 2008.* A.M. Afeiche, ed. 15–28. Beirut.

Thuesen, I. (1988). *Hama: the pre- and proto-historic periods: fouilles et recherches de la foundation Carlsberg, 1931–1938.* Copenhagen: Nationalmuseet.

Thureau-Dangin, F. and Dunand, M. (1936). *Til-Barsib.* Paris: Paul Geuthner.

Tsuneki, S. (2009a). Tell-type settlements around Tell Mastuma. In *Tell Mastuma: an Iron Age settlement in the northwest Syria.* T. Iwasaki, S. Wakita, K. Ishida, H. Wada, eds. 13–52. Memoirs of the Ancient Orient Museum 3. Tokyo: Ancient Orient Museum.

(2009b). Neolithic and Early Bronze Age layers in Square 15Gc. In *Tell Mastuma: an Iron Age settlement in the northwest Syria.* T. Iwasaki, S. Wakita, K. Ishida and H. Wada, eds. 69–88. Memoirs of the Ancient Orient Museum 3. Tokyo: Ancient Orient Museum.

Ünlü, E. (2016). The handle wagging the cup. Formal aspects of alcohol consumption in the transfer of ideology: Anatolia and the Aegean towards the end of the third millennium BC. *Oxford Journal of Archaeology* 35(4): 345–358.

Vacca, A. (2014a). The Tuqan IC pottery sequence from Area P South. In *Tell Tuqan excavations and regional perspectives: cultural developments in inner Syria from the Early Bronze Age to the Persian/Hellenistic period. Proceedings of the international conference, May 15th–17th 2013, Lecce.* F. Baffi, R. Fiorentino and L. Peyronel, eds. 45–84. Lecce: Congedo Editore.

(2014b). *La sequenza ceramica del BA III-IV della Siria interna attraverso lo studio dei contesti di Tell Mardikh/Ebla e Tell Tuqan (Siria).* PhD thesis, Sapienza University of Rome, Italy.

(2015). Before the royal Palace G. The stratigraphic and pottery sequence of the West Unit of the Central Complex: the Building G5. *Studia Eblaitica* 1: 1–32.

(2016). New Data on the EB III of northern inner Syria in the light of old and recent excavations at Tell Mardikh/Ebla and Tell Tuqan (Syria). In *Proceedings of the 9th International Congress on the Archaeology of the Ancient Near East, 9–13 June 2014, University of Basel.* R.A. Stucky, O. Kaelin and H-P. Mathys, eds. 269–282. Wiesbaden: Harrassowitz Verlag.

(2018a). Characterizing the Early Bronze III-IVA1 pottery from northern Levant through typological and petrographic analyses. New data from Tell Mardikh/Ebla and Tell Tuqan (Syria). *Levant*, doi:10.1080/00758914.2018.1447208.

(2018b). Centralization before the palace. The EB III-IVA1 sequence on the Acropolis of Tell Mardikh/Ebla. In *Ebla and Beyond. Ancient Near Eastern studies after fifty years of discoveries at Tell Mardikh.* P. Matthiae, F. Pinnock and M. D'Andrea, eds. 35–73. Wiesbaden: Harrassowitz Verlag.

(2019). Some reflections about the *Chora* of Ebla during the EB III and IVA1 periods. In *Pearls of the Past. Studies in Honour of Frances Pinnock.* M. D'Andrea, M.G. Micale, D. Nadali, S. Pizzimenti and A. Vacca, eds. 869–898. Marru 8. Münster: Zaphon.

(2020). What did it taste like? Consuming liquids in 3rd millennium BC Syria and Mesopotamia. In *Sensing the past. Detecting the use of the five senses in ancient contexts. proceedings of the congress held at the Sapienza University of Rome, 4th June 2018.* F. Pinnock and D. Nadali, eds. 131–165. Wiesbaden: Harrassowitz-Verlag.

Wachter-Sarkady, C. (2013). Consuming Plants. Archaeobotanical Samples from Royal Palace G and Building P4. In *Ebla and its landscape: early state formation in the ancient Near East.* P. Matthiae and N. Marchetti, eds. 376–402. Walnut Creek: Left Coast Press.

Wakita, S. (2009). North Trench. In *Tell Mastuma: An Iron Age settlement in the northwest Syria.* T. Iwasaki, S. Wakita, K. Ishida and H. Wada, eds. 62–68. Memoirs of the Ancient Orient Museum 3. Tokyo: Ancient Orient Museum.

Welton, L. (2014). Revisiting the 'Amuq sequence: a preliminary investigation of the EBIVB ceramic assemblage from Tell Tayinat. *Levant* 46: 339–370.

Welton, L. and Cooper. L. (2014). Caliciform Ware. In *Associated Regional Chronologies for the Ancient Near East and the Eastern Mediterranean: Interregional I. Ceramics.* M. Lebeau, ed. 325–354. Turnhout: Brepols.

Wilkinson, T.J., Philip, G., Bradbury, J., Dunford, R., Donoghue, D., Galiatsatos, N., Lawrence, D., Ricci, A. and Smith, S.L. (2014). Contextualizing early urbanization: settlement cores, early states and agro-pastoral strategies in the Fertile Crescent during the fourth and third millennia BC. *Journal of World Prehistory* 27(1): 43–109.

Zettler, R. and Miller, N.F. (1996). Searching for wine in the archaeological record of ancient Mesopotamia of the third and second millennia B.C. in the Near East. In *The origins and ancient history of wine.* P.E. McGovern, S.J. Fleming and S.H. Kats, eds. 125–134. Food and Nutrition in History and Anthropology 11. Amsterdam: Routledge.

3

Ebla in the third millennium BC

Architecture and urban planning

Frances Pinnock
Sapienza Università di Roma

As is well known, the development of urbanisation in north inner Syria was considered a somewhat later development, as compared to urbanisation in southern Mesopotamia: a phenomenon probably related to the presence of Uruk colonies in northern Mesopotamia and northern Syria, and possibly inspired by this presence in close relation with local communities.[1] These ideas are nowadays being questioned, on the basis of recent discoveries, and more autonomous developments are proposed for north inner Syria. Within this frame, it would be of the greatest importance to analyse the foundation of the most important urban centres of the Early Syrian period, among which Ebla is certainly one of the most relevant, and yet this is often problematic, or rather impossible, due to the superimposed phases of these flourishing centres, which makes it extremely hard to reach the deepest levels of occupation over large areas.

In the Ebla region, two sites yielded conspicuous evidence for the Uruk and Late Chalcolithic periods – Tell Afis and Tell Tuqan – whereas Ebla apparently did not have a proper occupation before the flourishing of the mature Early Syrian period.[2] In fact, besides the important superimpositions of the Early and Old Syrian periods, one main problem is the geological structure of the region where Ebla was founded: an outcrop of the limestone layer typical of the north inner Syrian plateau, quite irregular, so that

---

1   Matthiae 1993.
2   Matthiae 2014, 39. About the early phases of Tell Tuqan; see Vacca 2014; Mazzoni 2006, 321, 326, 328. Recently a member of the Ebla Project, A. Vacca, devoted a PhD dissertation to the formative phases of the urban culture at Ebla, which will be published as a volume in the series *Materiali e Studi Archeologici di Ebla*. Preliminary results of her research are presented in Vacca 2015, Vacca in preparation. I rely on her observations for the presentation of the earliest phases of Tell Mardikh.

it still sometimes surfaces in several spots of the modern tell. As the site was levelled at the beginning of Middle Bronze I, in order to use the soil from inside the town to build up the massive earthen-work ramparts of the outer fortification, in the Lower Town of Ebla traces of the settlements prior to Middle Bronze I–II can be found only in the spots where the limestone layer level drops abruptly, and where the older ruins were filled up in order to create a base for the later ones.[3]

Being far away from any river – the Orontes flows some 40 km away – Ebla appears as a typical elaboration of a secondary urban culture. The underground water-bearing stratum was quite close to the surface,[4] and it was probably very easy to detect and to reach in the region south-east of the actual Acropolis, where the Temple of the Rock was built later,[5] and to the south, where a well is still visible, and where water was present at a depth of less than 30 m still in the 1980s. Thus, Ebla developed exploiting all the different resources provided by the region: rainfall was particularly suitable for the practice of extensive agriculture (dry agriculture), integrated with the cultivation of olive trees and vines; the nearby mountains of the Jebel Arbayin provided wood and fruits; and cattle, sheep and goats were easily bred in the Matkh region.[6] The place where the town was founded, moreover, was strategic in order to control important trade routes, of local and medium range, as well as the main route of the so-called Long Distance Trade, connecting the Euphrates valley with the Mediterranean coast.[7]

The formative phases

The formative phases of the settlement of Ebla have not been identified, yet, based on some sporadic finds, it was possible to indicate as the first phase of occupation – Mardikh I – a period when some kind of settlement was present on the site. No architectural evidence was preserved, but three stamp seals were found in Area B, in the Lower Town south-west, for which S. Mazzoni proposed a date between the Uruk and Jemdet Nasr periods.[8] According to S. Mazzoni, the seals, which were found in the Middle Bronze I–II levels of the private houses in that region of the site, were actually in use, although not for administration, but probably as ornaments or amulets. Further evidence is offered by the finding of some fragments of Bevelled Rim Bowls, from the southern slopes of the Acropolis.[9] The presence of these two kinds of evidence – seals and vases – implies that already by the Late Uruk and Jemdet Nasr periods, there was at Ebla a succession of settlements, with some form of administrative control.[10] Due to

---

3   Pinnock 2004, 93–94.
4   Arnoldus-Huyzendveld 2013, 325–326.
5   Matthiae 2010, 387; Matthiae 2013a, 208.
6   Mantellini et al. 2013, 171.
7   See Quenet 2008, 224–227.
8   Mazzoni 1980; Matthews 1997, 57.
9   Vacca 2016.
10 Mazzoni 2006, 330.

the location of the findings, it is quite difficult to ascertain where the settlement was. The Acropolis seems of course a likely spot, but sweet water was easier to reach, as already mentioned, in the south-east and south Lower Town, so it is possible that these first settlements stretched from the Acropolis at least to the spots where the well was, and, therefore, the older artefacts might have been found during the construction of the private quarter in Area B.[11] If, on the other hand, the settlement occupied only the central hill of the site, they might have been found during the huge building activities for the erection of the massive stone fortification of the Acropolis.[12]

In our terminology, these phases would correspond to Mardikh I, whereas Mardikh IIA would include all the phases of Early Bronze I–IVA1, and Mardikh IIB1 would include Early Bronze IVA2, namely all the phases of the ceramic horizon of the Royal Palace G. At the time when this periodisation was proposed, in fact, only poor traces of these occupations had been identified, leading us to consider these periods as a rather indistinct pre-palace phase.[13] Nowadays, on the contrary, it is possible to ascertain that the EB III represents a definitely different *facies* from the EB I and EB II, which, in their turn, were certainly represented by settlements, albeit less important than the EB III one.[14] The EB I is represented by rare findings of sherds of the Reserved Slip Ware, whereas the EB II produced a few fragments of Cyma Recta Bowls, from a pit in the region of the Central Complex of the Royal Palace G of EB IVA. Also, this evidence points to some continuity of settlement on the actual Acropolis, though probably always at a village level.[15]

The urban development

During the Early Bronze III (Figure 3.1), on the other hand, Ebla witnessed a true urban development, with the erection of an important building, identified in two extended sectors, G2 and CC, nearly 40 m apart from each other, yet certainly belonging to the same building, as the orientation and building technique show. The first, better-preserved sector, G2, is located at the southern foot of the Acropolis, while Area CC, featuring less preserved structures, is located further to the north-east, along the same south sector of the Acropolis. The building yielded a large amount of pottery, including preservation

---

11 Due to the already mentioned characteristics of the limestone layer, on which Ebla was built, the private quarter of Area B, which was certainly related to the cult Area B, and in particular to Resheph's Temple (Temple B1), is located in a region definitely lower than the platform on which Temple B1 stands; thus, it is possible that earlier levels had been better preserved there (Matthiae 2010, 464–468).
12 The inner fortification of the Acropolis included a massive stone escarp at the foot of the hill, completed by a sloping mudbrick wall on its top (see Matthiae 1990, 414–417; Matthiae 2004, 319, fig. 18).
13 Matthiae 1995, 52–53.
14 For the new periodisation of Early Bronze Age I–IVA, and for the 14C dating of Early Bronze III–IVA1, see A. Vacca's contribution in this book.
15 Vacca 2016.

jars, hinting at some form of incipient centralisation of agricultural products. Other EB III remains were identified in the Lower Town north, in the region of Building P4, whose foundations cut into previous architecture, leaving some floor trace exposed, particularly along the east side of the building.[16] This evidence demonstrates, on the one hand, that quite important buildings had been erected on the Acropolis, and, on the other hand, that the settlement reached to the north and east into Area P, though it is quite unlikely that the town extended as far as the later settlements of EB IVA–B and MB I–II.[17]

The proto-palatial phases

During the Early Bronze III–Early Bronze IV transition (= Mardikh IIA3/IIB1), the building G2+CC was abandoned, and its place was taken by insubstantial architectural phases.[18] On the other hand, in the same transitional period, EB III/EB IV, the monumentalisation of the Acropolis becomes quite clear. The so-called Building G5 dates from this period, identified in Sector G West of the Acropolis, where the Royal Palace G structures were not well preserved. A few walls, with an orientation slightly different from that of the Royal Palace G, remains of floors and a silo, in association with sherds of *Khirbet Kerak Ware*, testify for activities of cereals storage on a large scale. This building was supported, along the slopes of the Acropolis, by an imposing terracing wall, still visible in the pit, which was cut in the same region during the Iron Age, and reached to the floor of hypogeum G4 of EB IVA2. Building G5, featuring two phases, is quite likely the direct predecessor of the Royal Palace G, as is proved by their topographic contiguity, and by the evolution of the pottery found in the building, which, in its last phase, presented features already anticipating the EB IVA horizon of the mature phase of the palace. Probably to the second phase of this same Building G5 belonged the large inlaid panel, the so-called Victory Standard, made of wooden planks and limestone inlays, which was found re-employed in later structures already belonging to the Royal Palace G. The building quite likely stretched further to the west, where a fragment of a votive plaque was found, with a miniature goblet dating from the second and later phase of the structure. The presence of imposing terracing walls shows that they were built following a plan of definite enlargement of the Acropolis surface, and they probably had to support, and/or level, earlier ruins. The presence of the silos and the evidence for monumental art testify for a well-developed central organisation, not yet fully palatine,[19] but already featuring a definite capacity to control

---

16   Marchetti and Nigro 1995–1996, 10.
17   For the details about this reconstruction, see Vacca 2016.
18   This late phase in the area was completely obliterated by the huge works made at the beginning of Middle Bronze I for the construction of the massive earthen-work rampart of the outer fortification.
19   Too little is preserved of the building to allow a full understanding of its structure and nature; in particular, the small sector thus far brought to light does not belong to a ceremonial region, but rather to a storage area.

3 Ebla in the third millennium BC

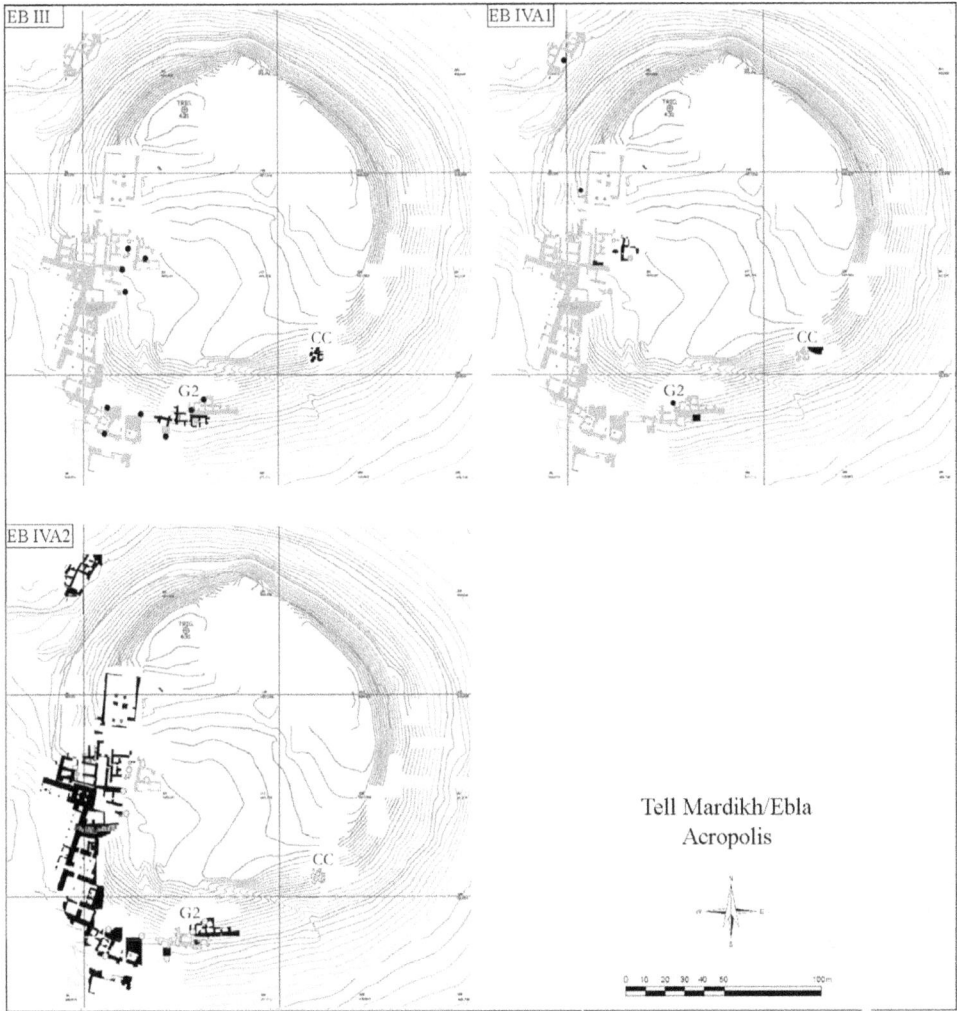

Figure 3.1: Development of the occupation of the Acropolis of Ebla between EB III and EB IVA2 (© Missione Archeologica Italiana in Siria).

agricultural production, and a definite repertoire of visual representation of power, with characteristics clearly forerunning those of the mature phase of Early Bronze IVA, as represented by Palace G.

Ebla in the Early Bronze Age IVA

For these reasons, these structures, whose chronological span stretches to the archaic phase of Early Bronze IVA, may be defined proto-palatial, and over them the true palace structure of the Royal Palace G was built during Early Bronze IVA = Mardikh IIB1. Two phases can be identified for this period, which we might call PG1 and PG2; the last one, moreover, can include two sub-phases, PG2a and PG2b. The oldest phase, PG1, can be identified in the north-west edge of the Acropolis, corresponding to and below the Red Temple, where the refurbishing, made in order to build the temple, razed and sealed it. PG1 has two phases, which were basically re-employments of service rooms, in a region which also included one sector, with larger and more regular spaces, probably with a ritual or ceremonial function, where the wooden planks of the Victory Standard were found re-employed as a floor decoration, with the inlaid elements still largely in place, face down in the grooves created in order to host the planks.[20] Though the identified part of the building is basically devoted to services, and particularly to food processing, the amount of working places identified for grinding flour leads to the proposal that in this sector food was prepared for a large proportion of the palace inhabitants.[21] Yet, this is not a kitchen, as no cooking facility was found, but rather a place for the preparation and possibly delivery of food rations. This hypothesis is also supported by the presence of the sector with a ceremonial function, closely related with the service rooms. The ceremonial nature of these rooms was probably retained over time, and even enhanced by the later construction of the Red Temple at the end of EB IVA.

Most of the Royal Palace G, as we actually know it, belongs to PG2a, including the core of the building on the Acropolis, but not the parts stretching at the foot of the Acropolis, as the final layout of the Court of Audience dates from a time between PG2a and PG2b, while the formulation of the Administrative Quarter, and most of all of the State Archives, built under the porch of the Court of Audience and encasing some columns in their walls, certainly dates from PG2b, the period to which the largest majority of the Archives texts refer. Also Building P4 is contemporary with PG2, and was probably founded during PG2a, or slightly earlier, as its foundation, as already stated, directly cut EB III levels. Another important feature of this period, although chronology is not so easy to pinpoint, is the so-called Sanctuary of the Painted Plaster – FF2 – located south of the Acropolis, along the line leading to the well in the Lower Town south.[22] This building was razed during the huge building activities of Middle Bronze I, for the construction of the massive stone foundation of the defence wall of the Acropolis and of the Southern Palace, so it yielded only a few sherds, which belong to the Palace G horizon.[23]

---

20 Matthiae 1990, 392–405; 2013b, 498–507.
21 Matthiae 2008, 45–46. The dwelling quarters and other services were probably in the central part of the Acropolis, in the sector called Central Quarter, whose outskirts were singled out on the south slope of the Acropolis; there a set of small rooms was identified, which were used for the storage of food and vases for table service.
22 The Sanctuary yielded a number of fragments of painted plaster, in red, black and white, which were probably part of a recessed niche, painted with geometric motifs, among which some rosettes; a large stone rosette was found on the floor in the same building. It is possible, therefore, that the chapel was dedicated to a form of Ishtar, and that it was related to the nearby well.
23 Matthiae 2004, 321–326.

3 Ebla in the third millennium BC

The Temple of the Rock is certainly contemporary with this phase, though probably not with PG1. Yet, it should belong to PG2a, as it is certainly older than the Red Temple, which was built, as just mentioned, over the razed structures of the first phase of the Royal Palace G. One text of the State Archives, moreover, dating from Ishar-Damu's reign, dating from PG2b, registers the delivery by the king of a large amount of silver for the erection of Kura's Temple.[24] So, it seems quite likely that a minor cult place stood on the Acropolis of Ebla, perhaps the place where the Victory Standard was originally kept (proto-palatial phase, EB IV1); later on, it was transformed in the probable cult, or ceremonial place, inside the palace, where the standard was re-employed (Phases PG1, EB IVA2). Lastly, during Ishar-Damu's reign (PG2b), the new monumental building was erected outside the palace, albeit still related with it, not only for the topographic closeness, but also for ritual and ceremonial functions. The older service rooms and the ceremonial sector of PG1 were razed and sealed, but this did not lead to the erection of a boundary wall for the palace. There probably was a kind of osmosis between the north-western sectors of the palace and the cult area, thus marking the nature of the Red Temple as a real palatine chapel.[25] The main residential quarters, as well as the service rooms and storerooms, stretching over most of the Acropolis, should belong to PG2a.

Sections of a huge mudbrick wall, 6 m wide, were found in a few spots, included in the earthen-work ramparts of the Middle Bronze town walls. The wall was certainly in use during EB IVB, but it is quite likely that it had been founded in EB IVA, though it is not possible to better define the phase to which it belongs within the period.[26]

---

24 Matthiae 2010.
25 In fact, it is quite likely that this temple was the last stop in the long trip the king and queen of Ebla had to perform in order to renew their kingship, according to the ritual preserved in the third and latest of three important texts of the Royal archive: see Fronzaroli 1993, 87–88; Pinnock 2016a; 2016b. The fact that this temple is mentioned only in the third text of the Eblaic Ritual of Kingship is further proof of its belonging to the latest phase of life of EB IVA Ebla.
26 The only chronological element we have in order to date this wall is the presence, on the inner floor of the structure, of a few EB IVB shards, whereas the bricks feature the shape and size typical of the Royal Palace G of EB IVA. Besides, if the hypothesis is that the erection of Building G5 marks the beginning of the development of Ebla as a big administrative centre, it is quite likely that a fortification was built in that period, though it is impossible to say which extension the town had at the time. So, it is quite likely that the first fortification of Ebla was built at the same time as Building G5, not necessarily in the same place as the later town walls, and that it was rebuilt, or refurbished at least in parts, after EB IVA.

Table 3.1: Chronological and architectural phasing of EB IV Ebla.

Chronology	Phase	Period	Architectural evidence
ca. 3500 BC	Mardikh I	Uruk Jemdet Nasr	No architectural evidence Stamp seals Bevelled rim bowls
ca. 3000–2750 BC	Mardikh IIA1	Early Bronze I-II	No architectural evidence Reserved Slip Ware Fragments of Cyrna Recta bowls
ca. 2750–2550 BC	Mardikh IIA2	Early Bronze III	Building G2+CC
ca. 2550–2450 BC	Mardikh IIA3	Early Bronze IVA1	Building G5 (Phase 1)
ca. 2450–2400 BC	Mardikh IIB1a	Early Bronze IVA2	Building G5 (Phase 2)
ca. 2450–2400 BC	Mardikh IIB1b	Early Bronze IVA2	PG1a-b North sector of the building Town wall (?)
ca. 2400–2350 BC	Mardikh IIB1b	Early Bronze IVA2	PG2a Main core of the Royal Palace G Building P4 Sanctuary FF2? Temple of the Rock
ca. 2350–2300 BC	Mardikh IIB1b	Early Bronze IVA2	PG2a/b Court of Audience
ca. 2350–2300 BC	Mardikh IIB1b	Early Bronze IVA2	PG2b Administrative Quarter Red Temple Royal Hypogeum (G4)
ca. 2300–2250 BC	Mardikh IIB2a	Early Bronze IVB1a	No architectural evidence Votive deposits in the Temple of the Rock Sealing of the cella of the Temple of the Rock
ca. 2300–2250 BC	Mardikh IIB2b	Early Bronze IVB1b	Mudbrick revetment of the outer wall of the Temple of the Rock Residential units along the wall of the Temple of the Rock
ca. 2250 BC	Mardikh IIB2c	Early Bronze IVB2	Intermediate level Levelling of Area HH with light structures

3 Ebla in the third millennium BC

Chronology	Phase	Period	Architectural evidence
ca. 2250–2030 BC	Mardikh IIB2d	Early Bronze IVB3	Temples HH4 and HH5 Monumental stairway to the Acropolis Temple D3 Archaic Palace Residential Quarter in Area T
ca. 2030–2000 BC	Mardikh IIB2e	Early Bronze IVB4	Re-use of part of the structures by squatters

The end of the Early Syrian period

The destruction of 2300 BC affected the whole settlement, though with different modes: Palace G was sacked and set on fire, while the Temple of the Rock was probably spared from fire.[27] Though the destruction was widespread, there was not a very long hiatus in the settlement life, as is proved quite clearly by the sequence in Area HH.[28] The late Early Syrian period, EB IVB = Mardikh IIB2, included five stratigraphic phases, as was possible to ascertain in the region of the Temple of the Rock (Area HH), where an important succession of ritual actions and cult buildings is preserved, but also a residential quarter.

The first phase, Mardikh IIB2a, immediately follows the destruction of 2300 BC, and it is not related to a building phase. It is the time when the cella of the Temple of the Rock was cleaned, a votive deposit (L.9719) was created, and, lastly, the cella of the temple was sealed with 15 courses of mudbricks. This phase is certainly later than the destruction of Palace G, and, as the pottery from the votive deposit shows, definitely belongs to an EB IVB horizon.

In the second phase, Mardikh IIB2b, a mudbrick revetment was built against the outer wall of the ruined Temple of the Rock, as well as a number of quite small rooms, of probable residential function, which were brought to light along the north and west walls of the temple.

---

27 Only one small trace of burnt wood was found in the filling of the door between cella and vestibule, but it is rather the trace of one burnt log, and not a typical trace of destruction. This presence is quite difficult to explain in archaeological terms; it might be casual and belong only to the filling of the door, in which possibly the burnt log belonged.

28 Matthiae (2007, 488) proposed a first periodisation for EB IVB, based on the observations made in Area HH. Later on, taking also into account the other EB IVB levels at Ebla, he slightly modified that proposal. Furthermore, an important contribution to the definition of the subdivision and relative chronology of the period is coming from M. D'Andrea's ongoing analysis of the pottery (D'Andrea 2015). Thus, what we propose here is the actual state of the art of our interpretation of EB IVB at Ebla, and I wish to thank both P. Matthiae and M. D'Andrea for a very fruitful discussion on the subject.

In the third phase, Mardikh IIB2c, the only known activity is the levelling of the eastern region over the Temple of the Rock, where some light structures were detected, whose real shape and function were impossible to ascertain, as they were completely razed by the later structures.

In the fourth phase, Mardikh IIB2d, the true renaissance of the late Early Syrian Ebla starts. Temples HH4 and HH5 were erected over the ruins of the Temple of the Rock. The finding of a long double-conoid carnelian bead, of a well-known type and probably coming from the Indus valley, is clear evidence of the economic importance of the town, in the period when 'men from Ebla' are mentioned in Ur III texts.[29] At the same time, they felt the need for a new palace. The region of the Royal Palace G was neglected. It was probably considered too dangerous, due to the large amount of crumbling ruins; so the steepest parts were filled up, like the site of the previous Throne Room, where the use of large amounts of soil, regularly thrown into it in oblique layers, is quite evident, and on top of the ruins, on the western edge of the Acropolis, a monumental stone staircase was built, leading to the cult area to the north-west (Area D, Temple D3).[30] A new royal residence, on the other hand, was built in the Lower Town north. The Archaic Palace, which was at least partially in use until the beginning of Middle Bronze I, features a monumental elaboration, which foreshadows aspects of the Reception Suite which will become canonical in the Old Syrian period.[31] The final phase of EB IVB is represented by the very scanty remains, mainly of floors, of a residential quarter in Area T, in the Lower Town west, whose pottery already alludes to typical Middle Bronze I shapes,[32] and by the last phase of the small rooms in Area HH, which bear very evident traces of the destruction which put an end to the Early Syrian period, shortly before 2000 BC. Taking into account the fact that the Archaic Palace building was not accomplished, and that the pottery in Area T seems to be very late in the period, it is most likely that the palace and the private quarter in Area T were the latest building activities of the phase.

The fifth phase, Mardikh IIB2e, is the unsuccessful attempt to rebuild the town after the destruction that put an end to the life of all the previous buildings. Its only traces are the remains of poor dwellings in the north region of Area HH.

Sporadic findings of groups of pottery sherds are the evidence of the extension of the EB IVB town over the whole area of Tell Mardikh as included in the perimeter of the MB I–II rampart (probably corresponding to the perimeter of the mudbrick wall of EB IVA–B). They were found at the foot of the huge section of the town wall, included in the Middle Bronze earthen-work rampart in Area AA, below the floors of the Western Palace, with rarer EB IVA fragments, and in a waste pit in the Lower

---

29 Peyronel 2015.
30 Matthiae 1995, 126–128.
31 Matthiae 2013c, 248. It is quite interesting that, in building the new throne room, the model of the mature Early Syrian period was abandoned (for which see Matthiae 2013d) in favour of a new type, possibly derived from a contemporary south Mesopotamian typology, identified in the *giparku* of Ur (Matthiae 2013e, 351–354; Pinnock 2006, 93).
32 Pinnock 2009, 69, figs 2–6.

Town North, east of Temple N.[33] Temple N, as already mentioned, was certainly built over an older structure, whose foundation appeared in a deep sounding along its north wall, with a texture definitely different from the Middle Bronze one. It is thus possible to propose that the town of Ebla reached its largest extension in the mature Early Syrian period, corresponding to PG2a–b, and that it kept its size also in the late Early Syrian period, though with less imposing architecture.

Chronology

As concerns absolute chronology, the results of the 14C analyses made on samples from the Royal Palace G are in agreement with the dates proposed by the Italian Archaeological Expedition for a life of Palace G, namely PG2a–b, spanning between 2400 and 2300 BC,[34] while we are still waiting for the results on the EB III samples. On the base of this fixed element it will be possible in the near future to propose a more sound hypothesis about the whole chronological setting of third millennium BC Ebla.[35] Thus far, we can only maintain with some certainty that Building G5 was in use for some time around 2500 BC, and that the first settlement in Ebla started around 3500 BC or later, but not later than 2900 BC.

Conclusion

Summing up, Ebla was most probably founded during the Late Uruk period, the result of so-called secondary urbanisation, according to the most recent interpretations of this phenomenon. It was sited in a location strategically suitable for the control of long-distance trade routes, in particular connections between the middle Euphrates valley and the Syrian coast. The region chosen, though lacking primary water sources, was quite close to the Matkh marshes, had an easily reachable water-bearing stratum, and important subsistence resources could be exploited, from extensive agriculture, integrated with the cultivation of vine and olives, to cattle breeding. The true structure of the town as a centre of administrative control probably dates from EB III, the phase when kingship also started, as might be inferred from the Ebla king list, which includes 26 names,[36] three of whom cover the Archives' time span.[37] At the same time as the Royal Palace G flourished in Ebla, there was a definite increase in settlements east of

---

33 Matthiae 1995, 128–129.
34 Calcagnile et al. 2013, 452–454.
35 The results of the analyses were presented by A. Vacca at the 2015 ASOR meeting in Atlanta, published in the volume edited by S. Richard. See also A. Vacca in this same volume.
36 Archi 2015, 164.
37 Archi 2001.

Ebla, in the Matkh region and in the direction of the Jabbul lake, with minor centres, like al-Rawda, built as probable intermediate stops along the main trade routes.[38]

After the destruction of 2300 BC, the general north inner Syrian system did not suffer from a final crisis, with the system resuming quite quickly, and with Ebla again playing an important international role; although a strong reduction in the settlements in the innermost regions, and a probable diminution of political importance of the whole region, is evidenced. On the other hand, the end of EB IVB was more dramatic, and it brought a drastic population decrease, particularly east of Ebla; while the new renaissance, at the beginning of the Middle Bronze period, brought on very different occupation modes and ideological forms, albeit with some strong links with the previous assessments. Due to the lack of written evidence, the end of EB IVB is difficult to set in absolute chronology, but it probably took place slightly earlier than 2000 BC.

The Ebla texts enlighten much of the political relations of the town at the age of the State Archives. Based on this evidence, it is quite clear that the main economic and political interests of Ebla were in the Euphrates valley, with different modes of action, from domination, as with Karkemish, to an alternation of good relations and clashes, such as with Mari. On the other hand, the political relations between Ebla and the Orontes valley seem to have been marked by a reciprocal respect, based on diplomatic relations, inferred by the pilgrimages to the sanctuaries of the god 'Adabal, where the town of Ebla was represented at the highest level by the members of a special religious confraternity,[39] who were sometimes joined by the king, queen and vizier,[40] thus demonstrating their interest in religious ceremonies, and, at the same time, their respect for the roles of other local rulers. Political and economic relations may produce cultural contacts, as may be inferred from similarities in architectural and artistic models, which are different from, and sometimes superimposed on, the diffusion and developments of material culture.

References

Archi, A. (2001). The king-lists from Ebla. In *Historiography in the Cuneiform world*. T. Abusch, C. Noyes and W.W. Hallo, eds. 1–13. Proceedings of the XLVème RAI. Bethesda: Harvard University.

(2002). Šeš-II-ib: a religious confraternity. In *Eblaitica: essays on the Ebla archives and Eblaite language*, 4. C.H. Gordon and G.A. Rendsburg, eds. 23–55. Eisenbrauns: Winona Lake.

(2015). The chronology of Ebla and the synchronism with Abarsal, Tuttul, Nagar and Nabada, Mari, Kish. In *Associated Regional Chronologies for the Ancient Near East and the Eastern Mediterranean: history and philology*. Vol. III. W. Sallaberger and I. Schrakamp, eds. 163–178. Turnhout: Brepols.

---

38 Mouamar 2014, 102–105.
39 Šeš-II-ib: Archi 2002, in particular on pp. 26–27 for the participants in 'Adabal's (there NIdabal) festival.
40 Ristvet 2011, 11–13, 23.

3 Ebla in the third millennium BC

Arnoldus-Huyzendveld, A. (2013). A thin basis: the soil landscape of Ebla and Tell Tuqan. In *Ebla and its landscape: early state formation in the ancient Near East*. P. Matthiae and N. Marchetti, eds. 324–331.Walnut Creek: Left Coast Press.

Baffi, F., Fiorentino, R. and Peyronel, L. eds. (2014) *Tell Tuqan excavations and regional perspectives. Cultural developments in inner Syria from the Early Bronze Age to the Persian/ Hellenistic Period. Proceedings of the international conference, May 15th–17th 2013, Lecce*. Lecce: Congedo Editore.

Calcagnile, L., Quarta, G. and D'Elia, M. (2013). Just at that time. 14C determinations and analysis from EB IVA layers. In *Ebla and its landscape: early state formation in the ancient Near East*. P. Matthiae and N. Marchetti, eds. 450–458. Walnut Creek: Left Coast Press.

D'Andrea, M. (2015). Preliminary notes on some EB IVB Painted Simple Ware shards from Ebla. *Studia Eblaitica* 1: 205–209.

Fronzaroli, P. (1993). *Archivi Reali di Ebla, Testi XI. Testi rituali della regalità* (Archivio L.2769). Roma.

Mantellini, S., Micale, M.G. and Peyronel, L. (2013). Exploiting diversity: The archaeological landscape of the Eblaite *chora*. In *Ebla and its landscape: early state formation in the ancient Near East*. P. Matthiae and N. Marchetti, eds. 164–194. Walnut Creek: Left Coast Press.

Marchetti, N. and Nigro, L. (1995–1996). Handicraft production, secondary food transformation and storage in the Public Building P4 at EVB IVA Ebla. *Berytus* 42: 9–36.

Matthews, D.M. (1997). *The early glyptic of Tell Brak: Cylinder seals of third millennium Syria* (= OBO SA 5). Fribourg-Göttingen Press.

Matthiae, P. (1990). Nouvelles fouilles à Ébla en 1987–1989. *Comptes-Rendus de l'Académie des Inscriptions et Belles-Lettres* 134: 384–431.

(1993). On this side of the Euphrates: a note on the urban origins of inner Syria. In *Between the rivers and over the mountains: archaeologica Anatolica et Mesopotamica Alba Palmieri Dedicata*. M. Frangipane, H. Hauptmann, M. Liverani, P. Matthiae and M. Mellink, eds. 523–530. Rome: University of La Sapienzia Press.

(1995). *Ebla. Un impero ritrovato. Dai primi scavi alle ultime scoperte*. Torino.

(2004). Le palais méridional dans la ville basse d'Ébla paléosyrienne: fouilles à Tell Mardikh (2002–2003). *Comptes-Rendus de l'Académie des Inscriptions et Belles-Lettres* 148: 301–346.

(2007). Nouvelles fouilles à Ébla en 2006. Le temple du rocher et ses successeurs protosyriens et paléosyriens. *Comptes-Rendus de l'Académie des Inscriptions et Belles-Lettres* 151: 481–525.

(2008). *Gli Archivi Reali di Ebla. La scoperta, i testi, il significato*. Milano.

(2010). *Ebla. La città del trono. Archeologia e storia*. Torino.

(2013a). The Temple of the Rock of Early Bronze IVA-B at Ebla: structure, chronology, continuity. In *Studies on the archaeology of Ebla 1980–2010 by P. Matthiae*. F. Pinnock, ed. 203–215. Wiesbaden: Harrassowitz Verlag.

(2013b). Masterpieces of Early and Old Syrian art: discoveries of the 1988 Ebla excavations in a historical perspective. In *Studies on the archaeology of Ebla 1980–2010 by P. Matthiae*. F. Pinnock, ed. 495–516. Wiesbaden: Harrassowitz Verlag.

(2013c). The Archaic Palace at Ebla: a royal building between Early Bronze Age IVB and Middle Bronze Age I. In *Studies on the archaeology of Ebla 1980–2010 by P. Matthiae*. F. Pinnock, ed. 243–257. Wiesbaden: Harrassowitzn Verlag.

(2013d). Early Syrian palatial architecture: Some thoughts about its unity. In *Studies on the archaeology of Ebla 1980-2010 by P. Matthiae*. F. Pinnock, ed. 235-242. Wiesbaden: Harrassowitz Verlag.

(2013e). About the formation of Old Syrian architectural tradition. In *Studies on the archaeology of Ebla 1980-2010 by P. Matthiae*. F. Pinnock, ed. 347-364. Wiesbaden: Harrassowitz Verlag.

(2014). A note on Tell Tuqan and the archaic urbanization in western Syria. Some clue for future reflection. In *Tell Tuqan excavations and regional perspectives. Cultural developments in inner Syria from the early Bronze Age to the Persian/Hellenistic period. Proceedings of the international conference, May 15th-17th 2013, Lecce*. F. Baffi, R. Fiorentino and L. Peyronel, eds. 35-44. Lecce: Congedo Editore.

Matthiae, P. and Marchetti, N. eds. (2013) *Ebla and its Landscape: early state formation in the ancient Near East*. Walnut Creek: Left Coast Press.

Mazzoni, S. (1980). Sigilli a stampo protostorici di Mardikh I. *Studi Eblaiti* 2: 53-80.

(2006). Syria and the emergence of cultural complexity. In *Ina kibrāt erbetti. Studi di Archeologia Orientale dedicati a Paolo Matthiae*. F. Baffi, R. Dolce, S. Mazzoni and F. Pinnock, eds. 321-347. Roma.

Mouamar, G. (2014). Tell al-Ṣūr/al-Sankarī: une nouvelle agglomération circulaire du Bronze Ancien IV à la lisière de la steppe Syrienne. In *Tell Tuqan excavations and regional perspectives. Cultural developments in inner Syria from the early Bronze Age to the Persian/Hellenistic period. Proceedings of the international conference, May 15th-17th 2013, Lecce*. F. Baffi, R. Fiorentino and L. Peyronel, eds. 95-114. Lecce: Congedo Editore.

Peyronel, L. (2015). A long-barrel carnelian bead from Ebla: a new evidence for long-distance contacts between the Indus valley and the Near East. *Studia Eblaitica* 1: 217-220.

Pinnock, F. (2004). Change and continuity of art in Syria viewed from Ebla. In *2000 v. Chr. - politische, wirtschaftliche und kulturelle entwicklung im zeichen einer jahrtausenwende. 3. Internationales colloquium der Deutschen Orient-Gesellschaft 4-7 April 2000 in Frankfurt/Main und Marburg/Lahn*. J-W. Meyer and W. Sommerfeld, eds. 87-118. Saarbrücken.

(2006). Ebla and Ur: exchanges and contacts between two great capitals of the ancient Near East. *Iraq* 68: 85-97.

(2009). EB IVB-MB I in northern Syria: crisis and change of a mature urban civilization. In *The Levant in transition: proceeding of a conference held at the British Museum on 20-21 April 2004*. P.J. Parr, ed. 69-79. PEF Annual IX. Leeds: Maney Publishing.

(2016a). Dealing with the past at Ebla: ancestors' cults and foreign relations. In *Proceedings of the 9th International Congress on the Archaeology of the Ancient Near East, 9-13 June 2014, University of Basel*, R.A. Stucky, O. Kaelin and H-P. Mathys, eds. 395-406. Wiesbaden: Harrassowitz Verlag.

(2016b). Royal images and kingship rituals in Early Syrian Ebla: a multi-faceted strategy of territorial control in EB IVA north inner Syria. *Zeitschrift für Orient-Archäologie* 9: 98-116.

Pinnock, F. ed. (2013). *Studies on the Archaeology of Ebla 1980-2010 by P. Matthiae*. Wiesbaden: Harrassowitz-Verlag.

Ristvet, L. (2011). Travel and the making of north Mesopotamian polities. *Bulletin of the American Schools of Oriental Research* 361(2): 1-31.

Quenet, P. (2008). *Les échanges du nord de la Mésopotamie avec ses voisins proche-orientaux au IIIe millénaire (ca 3100-2300 av. J-C)*. Subartu 22. Turnhout.

Vacca, A. (2014). The Tuqan IC pottery sequence from Area P south. In *Tell Tuqan excavations and regional perspectives: cultural developments in inner Syria from the Early Bronze Age to the Persian/Hellenistic period. Proceedings of the international conference, May 15th–17th 2013, Lecce*. F. Baffi, R. Fiorentino and L. Peyronel, eds. 45–84. Lecce: Congedo Editore.

(2015). Before the Royal Palace G. The stratigraphic and pottery sequence of the west unit of the central complex: the Building G5. *Studia Eblaitica* 1: 1–32.

(2016). New data on the EB III of northern inner Syria in the light of old and recent excavations at Tell Mardikh/Ebla and Tell Tuqan (Syria). In *Proceedings of the 9th International Congress on the Archaeology of the Ancient Near East, 9-13 June 2014, University of Basel*. R.A. Stucky, O. Kaelin and H-P. Mathys, eds. 269–282. Wiesbaden: Harrassowitz Verlag.

4

A matter of style

Ceramic evidence of contacts between the Orontes valley and the southern Levant during the mid-late third millennium BC

Marta D'Andrea
Sapienza Università di Roma

Between the 1920s and the 1970s, invasionist and migrationist interpretations of connections between the northern and southern Levant were widely accepted.[1] Later on, between the 1970s and the 1990s, W.G. Dever,[2] K. Prag,[3] S. Mazzoni,[4] S. Richard[5] and G. Palumbo[6] provided in-depth analyses from different points of views of what came to be called the 'Syrian connection' in the material culture of the southern Levant.[7] During the past decade, several reappraisals of the subject have been put forward, renewing interest in the topic.[8]

It has been acknowledged for some time that similarities in pottery types and styles in the northern and southern Levant mirror interactions between these regions during the last phase of the Early Bronze Age (EBA). Conventionally, Early Bronze IV (EB IV, also referred to as Intermediate Bronze Age/IBA) in the southern Levant has been dated to ca. 2300–2000 BC, corresponding to EB IVB in the northern Levant. Recent proposals of a

---

1 Wright 1938, 34; Albright 1940, 119; de Vaux 1946; Kenyon 1966, 76; Dever 1970, 140–141; 1971, 210–224.
2 Dever 1980, 50–52.
3 Prag 1974, 102–107.
4 Mazzoni 1985a, 12–15.
5 Richard 1980, 20, 21–26.
6 Palumbo 1990, 118–119.
7 Dever 1980, 52; Mazzoni 1985a, 12; Palumbo 1990, 118–119.
8 Bunimovitz and Greenberg 2004; 2006; Prag 2009; 2011; 2014; Welton and Cooper 2014, 305; D'Andrea 2014a; 2014b, Volume 1, 153–166, 169, 256–264; 2017; 2018a; 2019; 2020a; Richard and D'Andrea 2016; D'Andrea and Vacca 2015; Bechar 2015, 43–47; 2020; Greenberg 2017; Schloen 2017; Cooper 2018.

Table 4.1: Traditional and new inter-regional synchronisation of the northern and southern Levant.

Absolute dates BC	Southern Levant / Old Periodization	Southern Levant / New Periodization	Northern Levant / Traditional Periodization	Northern Levant / New Proposals
2750/2700			(↑ up to ca.3050/3000 BC) Early Bronze II	
2600	Early Bronze IIIA	Early Bronze IIIB	Early Bronze III	Early Bronze III
2500/2450			Early Bronze IVA1	Early Bronze IVA1
2300	Early Bronze IIIB / Early Bronze IV/Intermediate Bronze Age	Early Bronze IV/Intermediate Bronze Age	Early Bronze IVA2 / Early Bronze IVB	Early Bronze IVA2 / Early Bronze IVB
2000	Early Middle Bronze I (=MB IIA)		Early Middle Bronze I	Early Middle Bronze I
1950				
1900		Early Middle Bronze I		Early Middle Bronze I

higher absolute chronology for the southern Levantine EBA,[9] based on Bayesian modelling of 14C dates, have raised the end of Early Bronze III (EB III) in the southern Levant to ca. 2550/2500 BC. The absolute chronology for the northern Levantine EB III and EB IV has remained relatively unchanged (with only slight adjustments for the beginning of EB III see Table 1).[10] Conversely, compared to traditional chronology, the time lapse proposed for the southern Levantine EB IV is substantially longer, that is, ca. 2500–2000/1950 (or even 1920) BC.[11] This change influences both inter-regional synchronisation and historical interpretation, as with the revised chronology the EB III and EB IV in the northern and southern Levant are now largely parallel and contemporaneous (Table 4.1).[12]

Employing these insights, this chapter seeks to re-analyse the Black Wheel-made Ware[13] – the well-known hallmark of the 'Syrian connection' in the pottery repertoire of the southern Levant during EB IV. In the past, this ceramic type has been considered as

---

9   See Regev et al. 2012; Regev et al. 2014, 259–263; Höflmayer 2014a, 128–133; 2014b; 2017, 3–12.
10 See Vacca 2014; 2015.
11 Absolute dates for the lower boundary take into account the 14C dates for the beginning of the MBA in the region (see Marcus 2003; 2010) as well as synchronisms with Egypt at the time of the 12th Dynasty (Cohen 2002, 11–19, 137–138; 2012; 2017; Marcus 2013); see also Maeir (2010, 127–128), with relevant bibliography on this topic.
12 See with differing interpretations, Greenberg 2017; Schloen 2017; D'Andrea 2020a; Vacca and D'Andrea 2020.
13 In the past, it was called Megiddo Ware, due to its first identification at Tell el-Mutesellim/Megiddo (Guy 1938, 148), subsequently Black Wheelmade Ware (Greenberg 2002, 53; Bunimovitz and Greenberg 2004, 23-25) and more recently Black Wheel-made Ware (e.g. Welton and Cooper 2014, 335; Bechar 2015; 2020; Cohen-Weinberger 2016; Kennedy et al. 2018, 29).

4 A matter of style

a regional variant and the southernmost manifestation of the Syrian painted 'Caliciform culture'. This tradition spread over north-western inland Syria during the local EB IVB, that is, 2300–2000 BC.[14] We, therefore, present a short overview of Syrian EB IV pottery, in order to re-examine contacts between the ceramic traditions of the northern and southern Levant and identify a possible area of origin for the stylistic and technological traditions that reached the northern areas of the southern Levant during EB IV. This will allow us to re-discuss the definition of regional ceramic developments, patterns of interconnectivity between the northern and southern Levant, and their changes through time in connection to major socio-political transformations in the mid-late third millennium BC, as well as issues in inter-regional synchronisation.

In particular, building on previous works, we suggest possible areas of origin for the stylistic and technological transfer that reached the northern areas of the southern Levant during EB IV.[15] We reaffirm that the central and upper sectors of the Orontes valley might have played an important role in receiving, re-elaborating and transmitting to the south techno-stylistic and cultural information.[16] This chapter will also propose a preliminary interpretive framework.

The Black Wheel-made Ware: typology and decorative styles

The Black Wheel-made Ware is a fine ware distributed over southern Syria, southern Lebanon and the northern southern Levant,[17] with a few finds further north,[18] and possibly south (Figure 4.1).[19] Black Wheel-made Ware vessels (Figures 4.2–3) are made of compact, hard-textured and highly fired grey or more rarely reddish-brown

---

14 Tadmor 1978, 10; Bunimovitz and Greenberg 2004, 23; Welton and Cooper 2014.
15 D'Andrea 2017.
16 Ascalone and D'Andrea 2013, 226; D'Andrea 2014a, 206–212; 2014b: Volume 1, 158, 164–166; 2017; 2020a, 212–215 and fig. 3; D'Andrea and Vacca 2015, 49.
17 See Bunimovitz and Greenberg 2004, 23; Genz 2010, 210; D'Andrea 2014a, 195–203; 2014b, Volume 1, 153, 157, fig. 5.3 and see footnote 89 with relevant bibliography for each site; D'Andrea and Vacca 2015, 47–49; see Bechar 2015, 20, fig. 1, also with references to previously unpublished finds.
18 Byblos: Dunand 1954, 117, fig. 114:7585; Saghieh 1983, pl. XLII: 7585; Mengez: Tallon 1964, pl. II; Tell Fadous-Kfarabida: Genz et al. forthcoming; Hama: Vacca et al. 2018: 32–34, 54, fig. 3 (3G 678).
19 A Black Wheel-made Ware goblet may have been found in a tomb near Madaba, in central Transjordan, as is related by Kay Prag, personal communication reported by Braemer and Échallier (2000, 409; Braemer 2002, 15, note 22). A goblet base from Cave G23 at Jebel Qa'aqir, in the Shephelah (Gitin 1975, fig. 4.14; Dever 2014, fig. 3.29: 11) was ascribed to the Black Wheel-made Ware, but the description of the fabric does not seem to match with this ware. The attribution of a teapot from Be'er Resisim/Bir er-Resisiyeh, in the central Negev, to the Black Wheel-made Ware has been recently called into question (Dever 2014, 271–273).

fabrics and are entirely wheel-fashioned on the slow wheel.[20] Goblets and spouted vessels are the dominant vessel shapes in the repertoire, but other types are present, such as necked jars and kraters. Both decorated and undecorated vessels are attested, although decorated ones (characterised by the white paint) are more frequent than undecorated variants.

In the past, the Black Wheel-made Ware vessels found in the southern Levant have been considered as imports from the central Orontes valley by Dever[21] and Mazzoni.[22] Subsequently, based on petrographic analyses of Black Wheel-made Ware vessels from Khirbat an-Na'ima/Tel Na'ama, in the Hula valley, S. Bunimovitz and R. Greenberg suggested that Lower Cretaceous clays outcropping in the area of the Mount Hermon and Anti-Lebanon had been used for the vessels.[23] Based on petrographic analyses of Black Wheel-made Ware from Tell el-Waqqas/Hazor and surrounding sites, S. Bechar[24] proposed that the Hula valley might have been another area of production.[25] In addition, K. Badreshany suggested that the Lebanese Beqa' might also have been an area of production during EB IV.[26] Therefore, although workshops have not been identified and places of production have not been located precisely thus far, it seems likely that the production of the Black Wheel-made Ware was an articulated phenomenon, with various centres of production, using different petrographic recipes on the basis of local geological availability in order to achieve similar aesthetic results.[27] Although regional petrographic differences may lead us to question the use of a wholesale definition 'Black-Wheel-made Ware' for all of those grey ceramics found in the Lebanese Beqa' and the northern areas of the southern Levant, striking typological homogeneity allows us to retain such a general definition.

Black Wheel-made Ware from southern Syria has not been analysed thus far, but it cannot be excluded that either this region had its own core(s) of local production or received Black Wheel-made Ware and/or other types of grey wares from neighbouring regions (see below). In fact, during the EB IV, the production of grey wares, of which the Black Wheel-made Ware was part, was a phenomenon involving the whole of central Syria, as is discussed below.[28]

---

20   D'Andrea 2014a, 194; 2014b, Volume 1, 157; Bechar 2015, 39–40, figs 8–9. On pottery manufacturing techniques in the southern Levant during EB IV, see D'Andrea 2012, 21–25; 2014b, Volume 1, 54–57, 59–94, 2015a, 33, figs 1–4.
21   Dever 1970, 137; 1971, 211; 1980, 50. On possible relations with the Orontes see Amiran 1960, 219, 221.
22   Mazzoni 1985a, 15 refers to 'Syrian ceramics imitated or imported in Palestine', mentioning the area around Qatna as a possible place of origin for the vessels.
23   Greenberg et al. 1998, 23; Greenberg 2002, 53–54; Bunimovitz and Greenberg 2004, 23.
24   Bechar 2013, 75; 2015, 41–43, 53–54.
25   See Cohen-Weinberger 2016.
26   See Genz et al. forthcoming.
27   D'Andrea 2017, 180–181.
28   Kennedy 2015, 151–152, 154–156; 2019; Mouamar 2017a, 82–83, fig. 14, 85–87; 2017b, 82–83, 98, fig. 6: 8–11; 2018, 6–8, fig. 7; D'Andrea 2017, 177–181; Kennedy et al. 2018, 25–29; Boileau 2018, 1–2, 5–6; Vacca et al. 2018, 28–34.

4 A matter of style

Figure 4.1: The main area of distribution of Levantine 'grey wares' during Early Bronze IVB (marked with a dashed line; the grey area highlights the region of central Syria where Grey Wares were produced and distributed in this period).

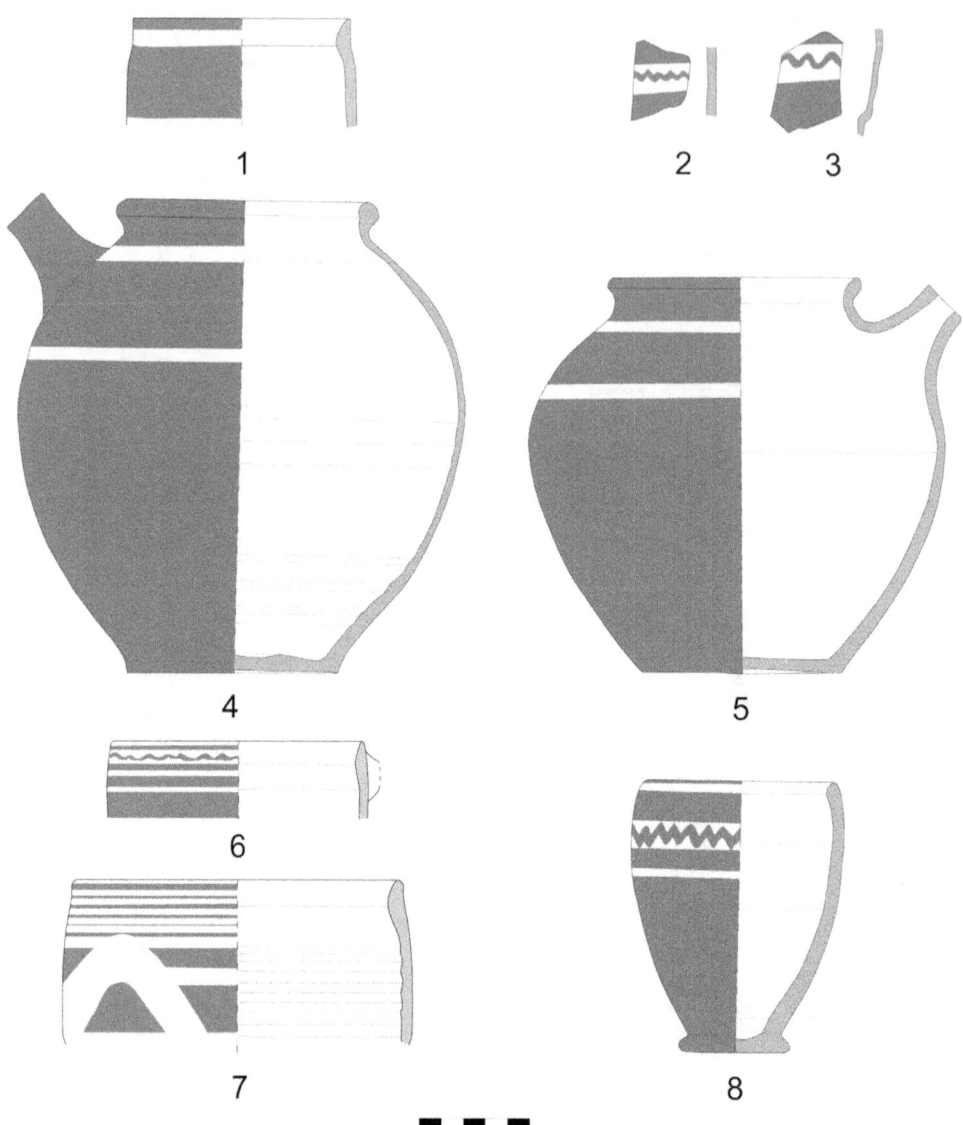

Figure 4.2: Black Wheel-made Ware, vessels reflecting an 'eastern' tradition (nos 1–6 and 8) and mixing eastern typological traits and western styles (no. 7), Early Bronze IV.

No.	Site	Reference
1.	Khirbet al-'Umbashi	re-drawn after Échallier and Braemer 2004, fig. 584: C.157
2.	Khirbet al-'Umbashi	re-drawn after Échallier and Braemer 2004, fig. 584: C.182
3.	Khirbet al-'Umbashi	re-drawn after Échallier and Braemer 2004, fig. 584: C.183
4.	Yabroud	re-drawn after Abou Assaf 1967, pl. III: 23
5.	Yabroud	re-drawn after Abou Assaf 1967, pl. III: 24

4 A matter of style

No.	Site	Reference
6.	Tell el-Waqqas/Hazor	re-drawn after Bechar 2015, fig. 5: 10
7.	Tell el-Waqqas/Hazor	re-drawn after Bechar 2015, fig. 5: 9
8.	Tell el-Mutesellim/Megiddo	re-drawn after Guy 1938, pl. 22: 19

In previous studies, which we recall here, we have identified two different 'traditions' of Black Wheel-made Ware, based on vessel morphology and decorative styles (see Figures 4.2–3).[29] The eastern tradition (Figure 4.2) is characterised by goblets with an elongated, cylindrical body and bell-shaped base, with a swollen inner rim (Figure 4.2: 1),[30] and by spouted jars with a very short neck and ovoid-shaped body with a flat base, generally taller than the teapots of the western tradition.[31] As for decoration, white painted parallel bands are the most common style (Figure 4.2: 1 and 4–5), although a variety of decorative techniques were used. They include white thin spiral-painted parallel lines, white painted bands reserved through multiple thin comb incisions (Figure 4.2: 2 and 4), white painted bands reserved through wavy incisions (Figure 4.2: 2–3), or a combination of these techniques and styles. Vessels made according to the 'eastern tradition' are found in southern Syria, in the Hula valley at Tell el-Waqqas/Hazor, and occasionally at other sites in the northern southern Levant, like the isolated find of a goblet in a tomb group at Tell el-Mutesellim/Megiddo.

The 'western tradition' (Figure 4.3) is characterised by much shorter goblets than in the 'eastern tradition', either with a globular body and simple, slightly upright, or flaring rims (see Figure 4.3: 1 and 3),[32] or with incurving walls and upright, slightly flaring outward, or swollen inner rims (see Figure 4.3: 2 and 4),[33] as well as by teapots of the hole-mouth type,[34] with a flat-based body, either biconic or globular (see Figure 4.3: 8–9).[35] Bottles are characterised by a narrow neck with an inner-stepped rim and

---

29 D'Andrea 2014a, 197–203, figs 8–9, 11; 2014b, Volume 1, 159–166, 169, figs 5.1–5.3; D'Andrea and Vacca 2015, 47–49, figs 3: 2–5, 8, 19–22, 4: 1, 5, 7, 5, 6–7, 10–12.
30 D'Andrea 2014a, 200–202, fig. 11: a–b, e; 2014b, Volume 2, 189, Types G1.1A–B, pl. XXVII: 1–3, 6–8, with relevant bibliography. See here fig. 2 nos 1 and nos 6–8.
31 D'Andrea 2014a, 200–202, fig. 11: f, h–i; 2014b, Volume 2, 242. Type T61.1Aii, 242, pl. LVI:4–7, with relevant bibliography. See here fig. 2 nos 4–5.
32 D'Andrea 2014b, Volume 2, 189–190, Types G1.2A–C, pl. XXVIII: 1–5, with relevant bibliography.
33 D'Andrea 2014b, Volume 2, 190, Types G1.3A–B, pl. XVIII: 6–12, with relevant bibliography. A tall cup with tapered flat base from Khirbet Qadish/Qedesh (Tadmor 1978: fig. 8: 74–1202) is a unicum (see also D'Andrea 2014b, Volume 2, 180, Type 5.1i, pl. XXI:19).
34 Only one necked teapot has been found in Megiddo, Tomb 1014 A (Guy 1938: pl. 22:3); see also D'Andrea 2014b, Volume 2, 239, Type 5.1A, pl. LXVIII:5.
35 D'Andrea 2014b, Volume 2, 233–234, Type T1.1A, pl. LX: 1, p. 236, Type 3.1A, pl. LXXII: 1, with relevant bibliography.

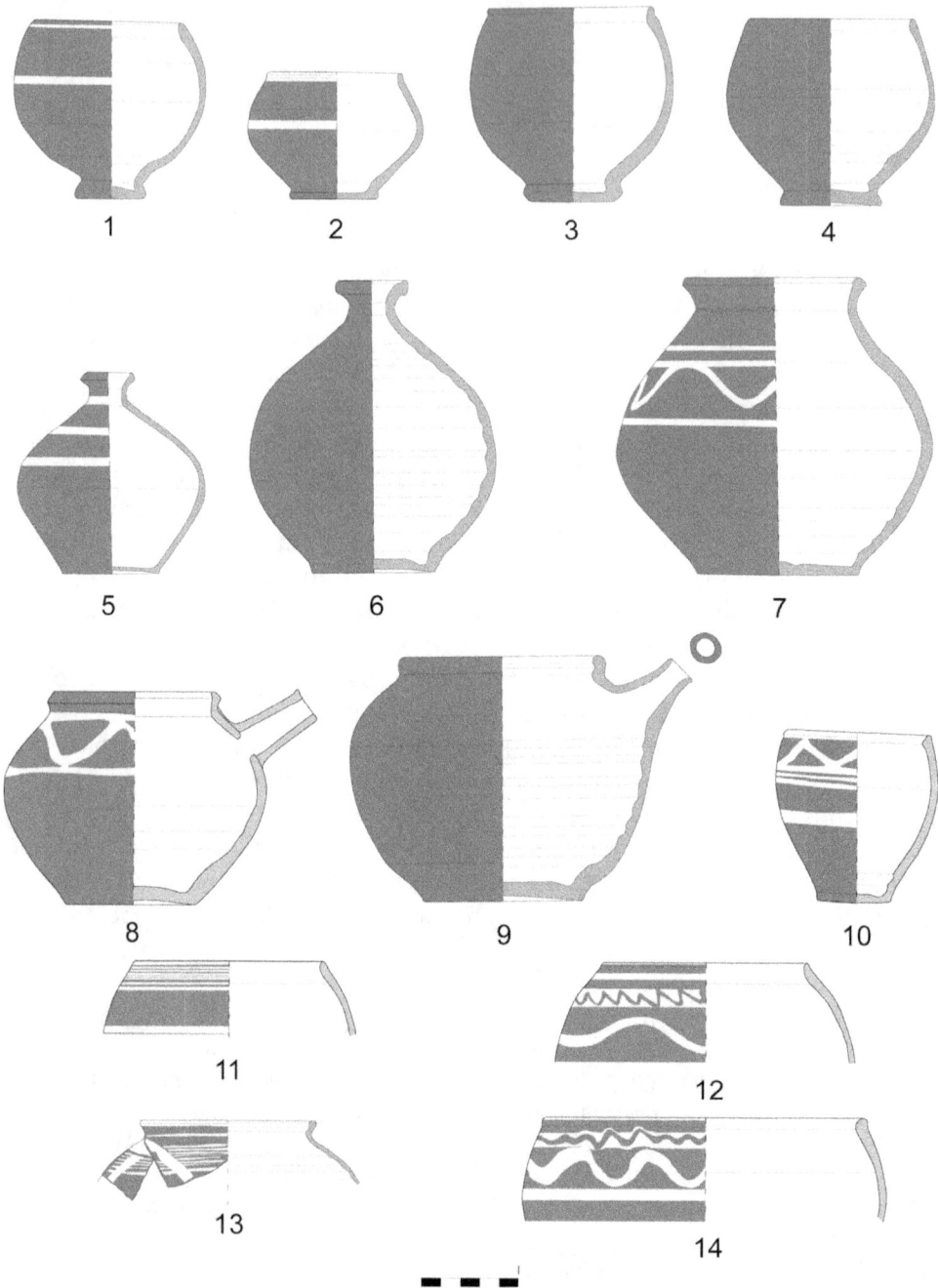

Figure 4.3: Black Wheel-made Ware, 'western' tradition (nos 1-10) and mixing western typological traits with eastern decorative styles (nos 11-14), Early Bronze IV.

4 A matter of style

No.	Site	Reference
1.	Khirbet Qadish/Qedesh	re-drawn after Tadmor 1978, fig. 8: 70-417
2.	Tell el-Mutesellim/Megiddo	re-drawn after Guy 1938, pl. 11: 26
3.	Rafid	re-drawn after Mansfeld 1970, pl. 38: 5
4.	Rafid	re-drawn after Mansfeld 1970, pl. 39: 7
5.	Khirbet Qadish/Qedesh	re-drawn after Tadmor 1978, fig. 8: 70-388
6.	Rafid	re-drawn after Mansfeld 1970, pl. 39: 5
7.	Khirbet Qadish/Qedesh	re-drawn after Tadmor 1978, fig. 8: 70-414
8.	Khirbet Qadish/Qedesh	re-drawn after Tadmor 1978, fig. 8: 70-225
9.	Rafid	re-drawn after Mansfeld 1970, pl. 39: 8
10.	Khirbet Qadish/Qedesh	re-drawn after Tadmor 1978, fig. 8: 74-1202
11.	Tell el-Waqqas/Hazor	re-drawn after Bechar 2015, fig. 5: 6
12.	Tell el-Waqqas/Hazor	re-drawn after Bechar 2015, fig. 5: 17
13.	Tell el-Waqqas/Hazor	re-drawn after Garfinkel 1997, fig. III: 5
14.	Tell el-Waqqas/Hazor	re-drawn after Bechar 2015, fig. 5: 20

the lenticular or globular body shape (see Figure 4.3: 5–6).[36] Jars are characterised by a slightly biconic body with a wide mouth and slightly flaring rim (Figure 4.3: 7).[37] As for decoration, the 'western tradition' is characterised by painted parallel bands either isolated or framing or intersecting wavy lines (Figure 4.3: 1–2, 5 and 7–8). Vessels in the 'western tradition' appear mostly in the Lebanese Beqa' and in the northern regions of the southern Levant.

Although the proposal to identify two traditions relies on a speculative basis, the typological and techno-stylistic differences between the two groups described above, albeit slight, are clearly visible. In fact, the 'western tradition' seems more connected to the EB IV ceramic development of the region of central Syria between Hama and Tell Nebi Mend, while the 'eastern tradition' adopts and adapts vessel types and decorative styles more typical of the EB IV development in the region between Hama and Ebla.[38] This observation on the one hand may indicate that the Hama/Homs region was the area where different EB IV ceramic industries intersected,[39] but it may also suggest that these elements were selectively incorporated in the Black Wheel-made Ware repertoires of different areas, following differentiated 'paths of interconnectivity'.[40] Moreover, it is possible that individual areas of production of the Black Wheel-made Ware adopted and adapted

---

36 D'Andrea 2014b, Volume 2, 254–255, Type Bt1.1B, pl. LXXVII: 3, 255, Type Bt1.2B, pl. LXXVIII: 6–7, with relevant bibliography; see also Vacca 2014, 256, flasks type 1d, fig. 3: 12–13.
37 D'Andrea 2014b, Volume 2, 265, Type NJ2, pl. LXXXV: 1–2, with relevant bibliography.
38 See D'Andrea 2014a; 2017; D'Andrea and Vacca 2015.
39 Vacca et al. 2018, 37.
40 Cooper 2018, 195.

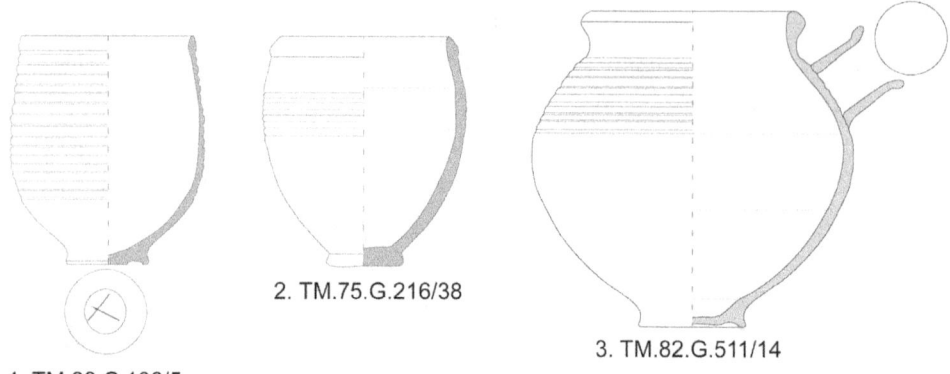

1. TM.83.G.106/5
2. TM.75.G.216/38
3. TM.82.G.511/14

Figure 4.4: Corrugated ware from Ebla, Palace G, Early Bronze IVA (© MAIS).

4 A matter of style

elements of both traditions, likely because the respective paths of interconnectivity might have overlapped or intersected at those places. This might be the case of Tell el-Waqqas/Hazor, which has yielded a varied and eclectic repertoire of Black Wheel-made Ware in terms of both vessel shapes and styles that seem to be petrographically homogeneous though distinct from other Black Wheel-made Ware assemblages analysed thus far.[41]

In fact, the Black Wheel-made Ware corpus from Hazor includes a variety of different decorative styles (see Figures 4.2: 6–7 and 4.3: 11–14),[42] the horizontal and wavy bands typical of the western tradition as well as the painted bands reserved through band-combing or single wavy incisions (Figures 4.2: 6–7 and 4.3: 11–14), and the thin spiral-painted parallel bands (Figure 4.3: 13) matching the decorative styles attested in southern Syria (Figure 4.2: 7–8). Also, from a typological point of view, the Black Wheel-made Ware corpus from Hazor includes globular goblets with incurving walls and hole-mouth teapots in the 'western tradition' as well as cylindrical goblets comparable to those found in southern Syria (Figure 4.2: 6–7).[43] In addition, a very interesting characteristic of the Black Wheel-made Ware vessels from Hazor is the combination of typological and stylistic components belonging to both Black Wheel-made Ware 'traditions' (Figures 4.2: 6–7 and 4.3: 12–14). In fact, wavy white painted bands intersecting thin parallel lines obtained by wiping off the paint from a horizontal band through combing are found on cylindrical goblets (see Figures 4.2: 7 and 4.3: 13),[44] and white painted bands reserved through band-combing or wavy stick incisions appear on short globular goblets (see Figures 4.2: 6 and 4.3: 12, 14).[45] Such combinations of motifs appear occasionally also at Khirbet Qadish/Qedesh (see Figure 4.3: 10)[46] and Khirbet Kishron/Horbat Qishron.[47] In addition, as stated above, a cylindrical goblet in the 'eastern tradition' has been found at Tell el-Mutesellim/Megiddo (Figure 4.2: 8),[48] and ovoid-shaped necked spouted jars similar to those of the 'eastern tradition' were found in a tomb group al-Sanbariyya/Ma'ayan Barukh[49] and Megiddo.[50] The eclectic Black Wheel-made Ware repertoire of Hazor might be due to the geographical position of the site in the Hula valley of the Upper Galilee, at the crossroad between the Lebanese Beqa' and southern Syria. The particular Black Wheel-made Ware vessels from Khirbet Qadish/Qadesh, Megiddo, Beth Shean and Khirbet Kishron/Horbat Qishron might have been distributed by Hazor, if, as recently hypothesised,[51] the site served as a 'regional centre' during EB IV. However, our suggestion would need verification through petrographic analyses.

---

41   Bechar 2020, 366–367.
42   Yadin et al. 1961, pls CLVI: 1–7, CCC: 28–32, CCXXX: 9–10; Garfinkel 1997, 194, fig. III.5; Bechar 2012, fig. on p. 12; 2013, fig. 9; 2015, 30–31, figs 2: 5–8, 5: 2, 4–6, 8–12, 14–17, 19–20, 6: 1–2, 6–8, 10; 12: 1, 6–7, 9, 13: 9; 2017, figs 6.9–6.10.
43   Bechar 2015, fig. 5: 8–10; 2017, 173–180, figs 6.9–6.10.
44   Bechar 2015, fig. 5: 9.
45   Yadin et al. 1961, pl. CLVI: 1; Bechar 2015, fig. 5: 10, 17, 20.
46   Tadmor 1978, fig. 8: 70–385, 74–1202.
47   Smithline 2002, fig. 17: 18.
48   Tomb 1120 B – see Guy 1938, pl. 22: 19.
49   Tomb III – see Amiran 1961, fig. 6: 1 and 4.
50   Tomb 41 – see Guy 1938, pl. 10: 5.
51   Bechar 2015, 54; 2020, 372–373.

Painted wares in the northern Levant in the second half of the third millennium BC

As is well known, the EB IVA in the northern Levant, ca. 2500–2300 BC, is characterised by the spread of corrugated wares over the entire area, between the 'Amuq plain, the Ebla and the Homs regions and up to the middle Euphrates valley (see Figure 4.4).[52] However, during this period, a particular painted ware is diffused in the sites of the central Orontes valley (Figure 4.5–7). This ware is characterised by multiple thin white painted parallel bands, made either by spiral-painting or by painting and wiping off the paint on a tournette; these vessels are also generally made of dark grey fabrics (Figures 4.6: 2 and 5–11), although a red, oxidised, variant is well attested (Figures 4.6: 1 and 3–4). This ware includes Ingholt's Type GII ring-based goblets (Figure 4.6: 5–7),[53] bowls,[54] bottles (Figure 4.6: 8),[55] and jars with white painted bands (Figure 4.6: 9–10) found at Hama.[56] Similar goblets were found in Tomb II at Tell 'As.[57] This ware was called White-on-Black Ware by Mazzoni (Figures 4.6: 1–4)[58] and, more recently, White-on-Black/Red Ware by Mouamar because of the presence of red, oxidised vessels.[59] Imported White-on-Black Ware vessels were found at al-Rawda in the eastern steppe,[60] at Tell Umm el-Marra in the region of the Lake Jabbul,[61] at Ebla in north-west inland Syria (Figures 4.6: 1–4),[62] at Tell Taynat in the 'Amuq plain,[63] and at Tell 'Arqa in the Akkar plain (Figure 4.6: 11–12).[64]

---

52 Mazzoni 1985a; 1985b; 2002; Welton and Cooper 2014, 299–300.
53 Ingholt 1934, 30, pl. VIII: 4; Fugmann 1958, figs 64: 3G 216, 65: 3D 313 [J6], 74: 3D 967, 75: 3D 318 [J5].
54 Ingholt 1934, 30–31, pl. VIII: 5; Vacca et al. 2018, 29, 52, fig. 6: 1, 3G 919 [J6].
55 Fugmann 1958, fig. 74: 3A 736 [J5]; Vacca et al. 2018, 29, 53; fig. 6: 2, 3A 736 [J5].
56 Ingholt 1934, 30–31, pl. IX: 3; Fugmann 1958, figs 74: 3H122, 75: 3E221 [J5].
57 du Mesnil du Buisson 1932, pls XXIX: 32, 36, XLI: II.36.
58 Mazzoni 1985a, 1, fig. 2: 4; 1985b, 563, fig. 2: 2; 2002, 77, pl. XXXVIII: 82.
59 Mouamar 2017a, 80–81, figs 10–11; Vacca et al. 2018, 28–29.
60 Only one (RW1.6140.1) of the published sherds from the settlement has been ascribed to this ware, citing parallels with Ingholt's Type GII goblets (Castel et al. 2014, 30, figs 20:5, 23: 9). However, from the photographs another goblet (RW1.6131.2) seems to belong to the same ware (Castel et al. 2014, 40, figs 21: 21, 23: 10). The excavators ascribed these finds to a time span extended from the end of EB IVA and the beginning of EB IVB or even to just EB IVB (Castel et al. 2014, 30 and 40).
61 Schwartz et al. 2006, 625.
62 A White-on-Black goblet published by Mazzoni (1982, fig. XXIX: 5; 1985a, fig. 2: 4; 1985b, fig. 1: 4; 2002, pl. XXXVIII: 82; see Figure 4.6: 2), was analysed by L. Lazzarini and C. Colombo (1995, 21), who determined its non-local provenance based on the nature of the tempering materials. M. Laritan and others later on confirmed this, since the Ebla goblet could be highly correlated chemically and petrographically to materials from Qatna (Maritan et al. 2005, 735, fig. 4).
63 Braidwood and Braidwood 1960, pl. 88: 2.
64 Phase P, Level 16; goblets: Thalmann 2006, 118–119, pl. 56: 12, 14, fig. 6: 12–13; medium-sized jars with grey fabrics and white paint: Thalmann 2006, pl. 65: 2, 4–9 and 11–13.

4 A matter of style

Figure 4.5: Production and distribution of the White-on-Black Ware/'Grey Ware' during Early Bronze IVA.

A Land in Between

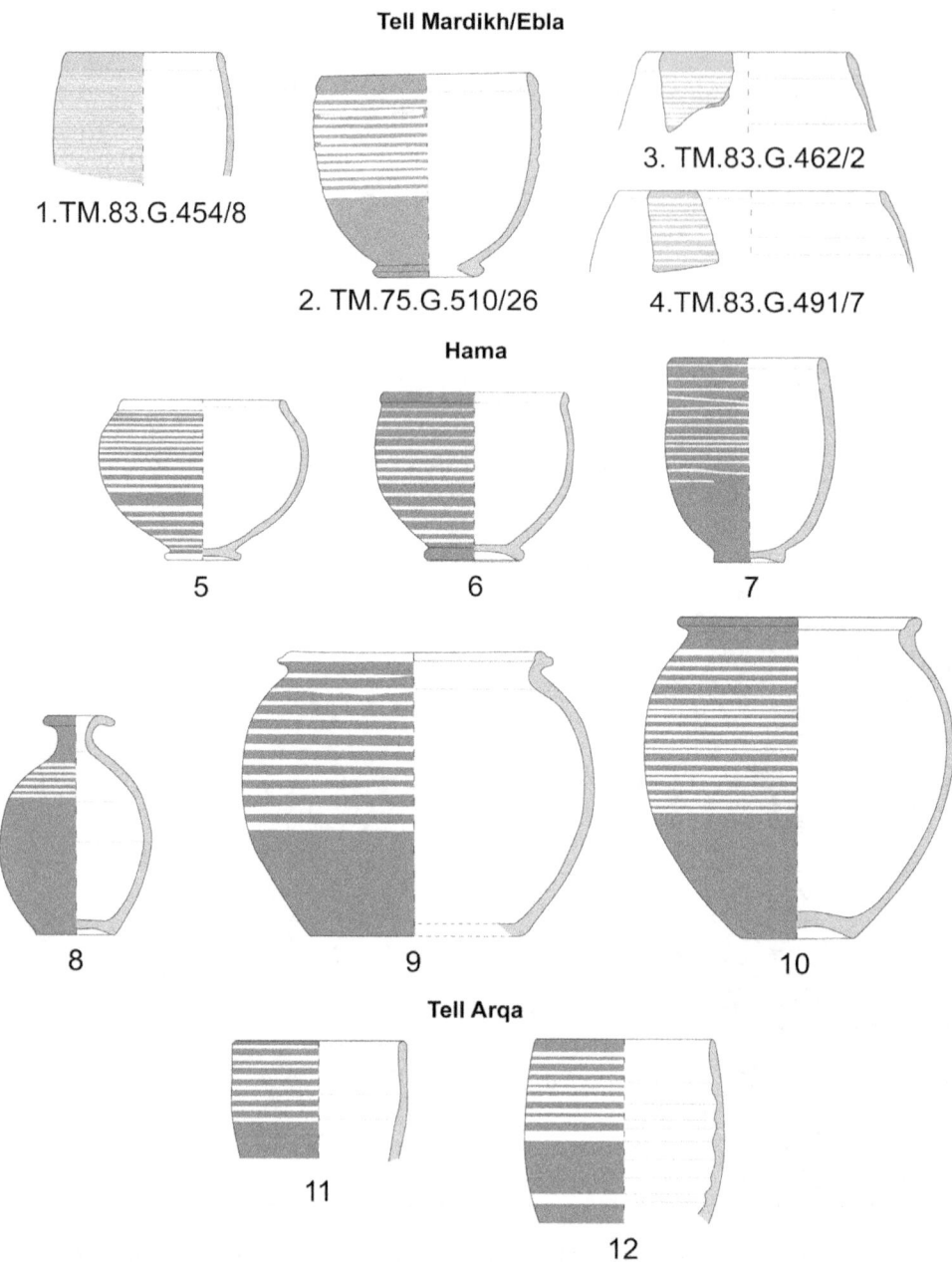

Figure 4.6: White-on-Black Ware from Tell Mardikh/Ebla, Palace G, Phase Mardikh IIB1, Hama J6–J5, and Tell Arqa Phase P, Level 16, Early Bronze IVA.

4 A matter of style

No.	Site	Reference
1.	Tell Mardikh/Ebla	© MAIS
2.	Tell Mardikh/Ebla	© MAIS
3.	Tell Mardikh/Ebla	© MAIS
4.	Tell Mardikh/Ebla	© MAIS
5.	Hama J5	re-drawn after Fugmann 1958, fig. 75: 3D 318
6.	Hama J5	re-drawn after Fugmann 1958, fig. 74: 3D 967
7.	Hama J6	re-drawn after Fugmann 1958, fig. 65: 3D 313
8.	Hama J5	re-drawn after Fugmann 1958, fig. 74: 3A 736
9.	Hama J5	re-drawn after Fugmann 1958, fig. 74: 3H 122
10.	Hama J5	re-drawn after Fugmann 1958, fig. 75: 3E 221
11.	Tell Arqa, Level 16	re-drawn after Thalmann 2006, pl. 56: 14
12.	Tell Arqa, Level 16	re-drawn after Thalmann 2006, pl. 56: 12

During EB IVA, the Hama/Homs regions were likely the areas where the tradition of the corrugated ware of the Ebla region and White-on-Black/Red Ware typical of the central Orontes valley intersected.[65] In addition, the publication of the EB IV pottery from Tell Nebi Mend by M. Kennedy has shown that this site in the upper Orontes valley was located within the core area of grey ware production (with or without white decorations) from the EB III/IV transition and through EB IVA and IVB.[66] As will be elaborated later on, the EB IVA White-on-Black/Red Ware and the grey wares play an important role in the analysis of the connections between the Orontes valley and the southern Levant.

Ceramic developments in north-central Syria during the following EB IVB are marked by the spread of Painted Simple Ware, characterised by light-coloured fabrics and brownish-red, blackish or grey painted decorations (Figures 4.8–9). These include multiple bands of paint (Figures 4.8: 7–8, 10–11 and 4.9: 2, 5–7), which is often wiped off through horizontal combing, single or multiple wavy incisions, or a combination of such motifs with different schemas (Figures 4.8: 1–2, 4–6, 9 and 4.9: 1, 3–4). Net-patterned triangles and stylised animal figures are more rarely found (Figures 4.8: 3–4, 6 and 4.9: 5 and 7).[67] Syrian Painted Simple Ware includes a broad range of vessel types that are decorated replicas of most vessel types of the plain Simple Ware repertoire of north-western inland Syria (Figures 4.8–9). We will focus on goblets, bottles and spouted jars for comparison, since none of the other Painted Simple Ware vessel types finds a counterpart in the southern Levantine EB IV pottery repertoire.[68] Goblets (Figures 4.8: 1–4 and 4.9: 1) are characterised by their bell-shaped base, a typological feature that appears at the beginning of EB IVB. They can be roughly divided into two broad typological classes, one with a tall cylindrical body and

---

65 Vacca et al. 2018, 37.
66 Kennedy 2015, 151–152, 154–156; 2019; Kennedy et al. 2018, 4–5.
67 D'Andrea 2015; 2016, 209, fig. 7: 7, 10–14; 2018b, 225, fig. 7: 1–3.
68 D'Andrea 2014a, 209.

1. TM.83.G.491/7   2. TM.83.G.462/2

3. TM.83.G.454/8

Figure 4.7: White-on-Black Ware from Tell Mardikh/Ebla, Palace G, Phase Mardikh IIB1, Early Bronze IVA (© MAIS).

slightly thickened inside rims (Figure 4.8: 1, 3–4) and one with a shorter and larger, roughly globular body with incurved walls and upright, often thickened inside rims (Figure 4.8: 2). Spouted jars are characterised by flat-based, ovoid-shaped bodies and flaring necks and folded rims (Figures 4.8: 11 and 4.9: 3).[69] Bottles are characterised by either globular or ovoid flat-based bodies, and narrow necks with simple flaring, out-turned/thickened outside, or inner-stepped rims (Figure 4.9: 6).[70]

---

69 D'Andrea and Vacca 2015, 48, fig. 5: 15.16.
70 Vacca 2014, 254–259, flasks type 1a-e, figs 2: 10–21; 3: 1–6, 9, 11, 17, 19, 21; D'Andrea and Vacca 2015, fig. 4: 10–16.

4 A matter of style

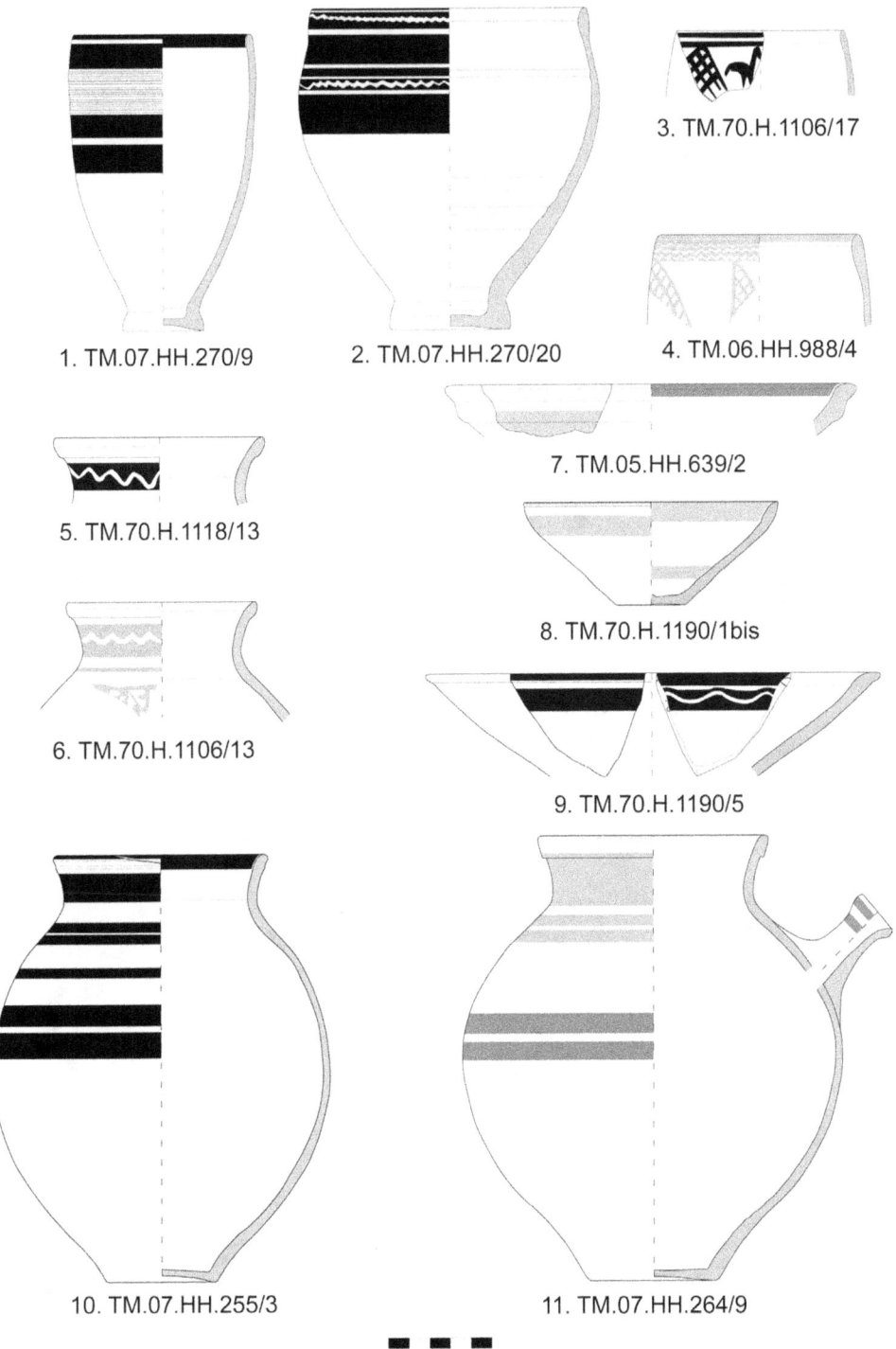

Figure 4.8: Syrian Painted Simple Ware from Ebla: selection of representative vessel types and styles from Areas H and HH, Early Bronze IVB (© MAIS).

A Land in Between

Figure 4.9: Syrian Painted Simple Ware from Ebla: selection of representative complete vessels from Area HH, Early Bronze IVB (© MAIS).

4 A matter of style

Painted Simple Ware spreads over virtually all of north-western inland Syria up to the south-east steppe and the 'Amuq plain. Occasionally, isolated finds reach neighbouring areas – Cilicia, the northern Syrian coast, the Akkar plain, the Jabbul plain, the west bank of the Euphrates river, and southern Syria – but Painted Simple Ware has thus far not been found in the Lebanese Beqaʿ and the southern Levant.[71]

In the central and upper Orontes valley, another painted ware is attested during the EB IVB (Figure 4.10: 1–9). It is characterised by grey, hard-textured fabrics and white painted decorations consisting of parallel painted bands (Figure 4.10: 3 and 7), parallel bands of white paint wiped off through combing, spiral-painted thin lines, or a combination of these motifs (Figure 4.10: 1–2, 4–6 and 8). The typological repertoire includes tall cylindrical goblets with a bell-shaped base (Figure 4.10: 5); shorter goblets with bell-shaped bases, incurving walls and thickened inside rims (Figure 4.10: 1–3); flat-based goblets with simple pointed rims (Figure 4.10: 4); several types of bowls (Figure 4.10: 8–9); spouted jars and necked jars (Figure 4.10: 7). Similar grey vessels were found at Hama (Figure 4.10: 8),[72] Tell Mishrifeh/Qatna,[73] Tell Shaʿirat[74] and Tell Nebi Mend (Figure 4.10: 3–7 and 9).[75] At Tell ʿAcharneh, EB IV grey vessels have been divided into three categories called, respectively, 'Grey Ware',[76] grey Hama Goblet Ware, and Reserved Slip Ware,[77] with these including goblets and medium-sized jars.[78] Unfortunately, all the EB IV materials from Tell ʿAcharneh are from secondary contexts; therefore, it is difficult to categorise them according to EB IVA and EB IVB dates. However, it seems likely that the latter site and other sites in the Ghab basin (e.g. Tell Sikkin Qaʿdah, Tell Ahmed and Tell ʿAmourin) were part and parcel of the grey ware phenomenon of the EB IVB, and perhaps as early as the EB IVA period.[79] Moreover, during EB IVB, imported grey wares are found occasionally at Simiriyan on the Syrian coast,[80] and at Tell ʿArqa in the Akkar plain (see Figure 4.10: 10–13).[81]

At some sites in central Syria, such as Tell Mishrifeh/Qatna,[82] Tell Shaʿirat[83] and Tell ʿAcharneh, and several sites in the Ghab basin, grey white-painted ware and the

---

71 D'Andrea 2014a, 187–191.
72 Fugmann 1958, fig. 103: 3C642 [J1]; Vacca et al. 2018, 30, 53, fig. 7: 1 3E 314 [J4], 2, 3F 596 [J3].
73 Besana et al. 2008, fig 3: 6.
74 Al-Maqdissi 1995, fig. 57: 3; Mouamar 2017a, 87; 2017b, fig. 8: 8–11; 2018, 6–8, fig. 7.
75 Mathias 2000, 425, figs 23.5: 86–91, 93–96; 23.6: 99 and 111; Kennedy 2015, 184–186; 2019, figs 3: 2, 4–5 and 10, 4: 2, 5: 1–5; Kennedy et al. 2018, 5, 29, fig 4: 3–10.
76 Boileau 2006, 193; Cooper 2006, 150, 152, 155; 2007, 47; 2018, fig. 6: e and g.
77 Boileau 2018, fig. 1.
78 Boileau 2006, pl. 4; Cooper 2006, 147, 150, pls 18: 3–4, 19: 1–3, 22: 9–10, 19–20; 2007, fig. 8; Welton and Cooper 2014, 298.
79 Cooper 2007; Fortin and Cooper 2014, figs 9: 4, 15: 4–6, 18: 1; D'Andrea 2017, 175; Vacca et al. 2018, 29.
80 Braidwood 1940, fig. 20: 2–3 and 6.
81 Phase P, Level 15 = EB IVB: Thalmann 2006, 123–124, pls 64, 65: 1, 3, 10 and 14, 129: 1–4.
82 Besana et al. 2008, fig. 3: 6–14.
83 Al-Maqdissi 1995a, fig. 57: 1; 3–8; Mouamar 2017b, fig. 8; 2018, 5–9, figs 5–8.

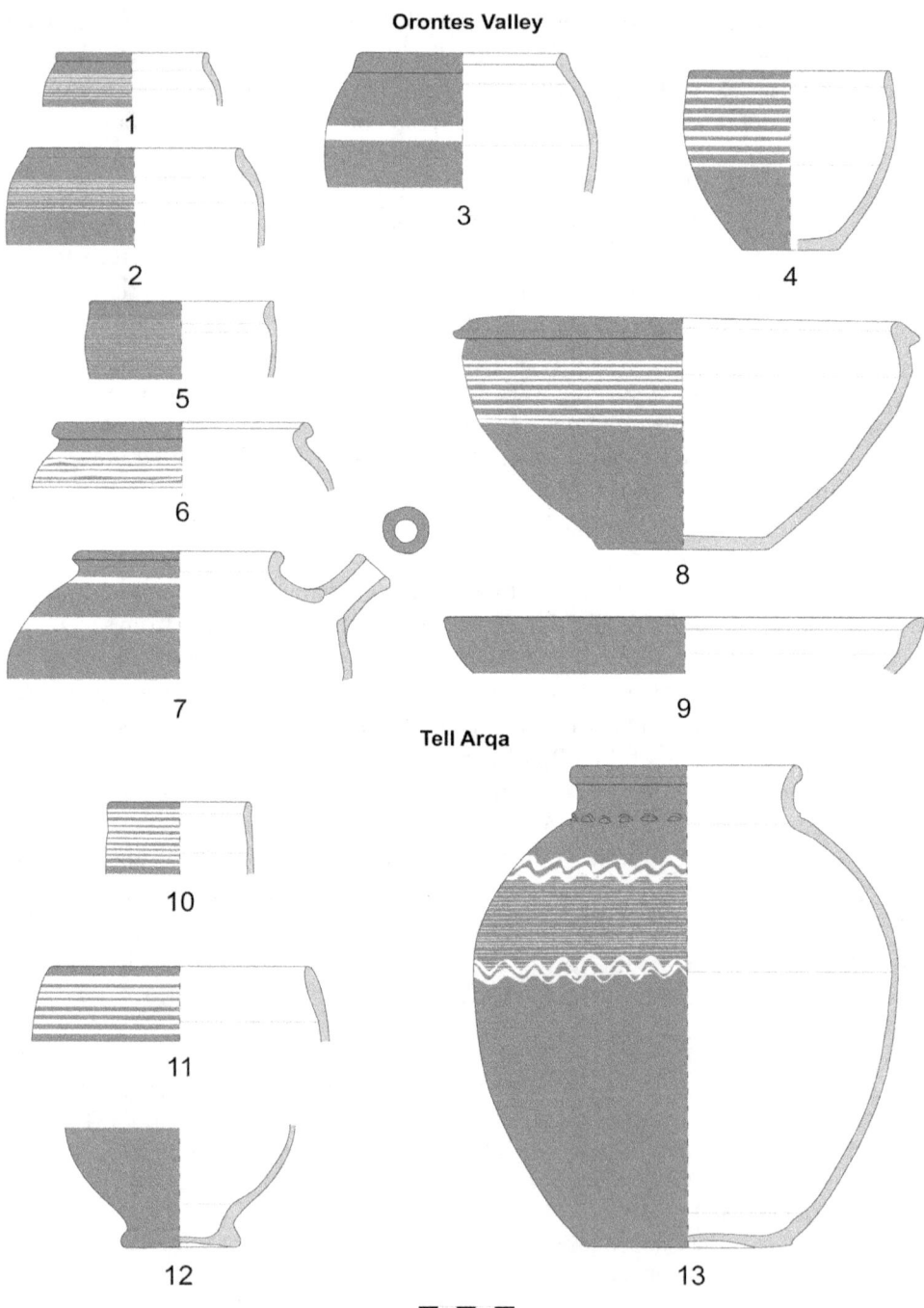

Figure 4.10: Vessels made of grey wares decorated with white paint.

4 A matter of style

No.	Site	Reference
1.	Tell Nebi Mend	re-drawn after Mathias 2000, fig. 23.5: 87
2.	Tell Nebi Mend	re-drawn after Mathias 2000, fig. 23.5: 88
3.	Tell Nebi Mend	re-drawn after Mathias 2000, fig. 23.5: 91
4.	Tell Nebi Mend	re-drawn after Mathias 2000, fig. 23.5: 93
5.	Tell Nebi Mend	re-drawn after Mathias 2000, fig. 23.5: 90
6.	Tell Nebi Mend	re-drawn after Mathias 2000, fig. 23.5: 89
7.	Tell Nebi Mend	re-drawn after Mathias 2000, fig. 23.5: 86
8.	Hama J1	re-drawn after Fugmann 1958, fig. 103: 3C 642
9.	Tell Nebi Mend	re-drawn after Mathias 2000, fig. 23.6: 111
10.	Tell Arqa, Phase P, Level 15	re-drawn after Thalmann 2006, pl. 56: 15
11.	Tell Arqa, Phase P, Level 15	re-drawn after Thalmann 2006, pl. 56: 13
12.	Tell Arqa, Phase P, Level 15	re-drawn after Thalmann 2006, pl. 56: 18
13.	Tell Arqa, Phase P, Level 16	re-drawn after Thalmann 2006, pl. 64: 1

Painted Simple Ware coexist.[84] However, at Tell Nebi Mend, only the grey ware with white paint is found,[85] and although other vessel types belonging to the standard EB IVB pottery repertoire of north-western inland Syria are attested at the site,[86] there is none of the Painted Simple Ware typical of north-central Syria during EB IVB.[87] As shown by the recent analysis by M. Kennedy, the typological and techno-stylistic developments of the grey wares at Tell Nebi Mend are continuous throughout the EB IV period, reaffirming the hypothesis that the site was one of the core areas of production.[88] Conversely, the recent work of G. Mouamar at Tell Shaʿirat, in the Syrian steppe at the east edge of the upper Orontes valley, demonstrated that only in the EB IVB period does the characteristic grey ware appear.[89] The so-called 'Shaʿirat Grey Ware', considered typical of the desert margins between Tell Mishrifeh/Qatna and Tell Shaʿirat,[90] produced goblets and jars with characteristic white painted motifs, either two thicker parallel horizontal bands or multiple upper thin horizontal bands and a lower thicker parallel line.[91] These vessels were also seemingly imported to other sites in central Syria,[92] and may have reached southern Syria. Interestingly, not only is the resemblance between

---

84 Cooper 2007; 2018, figs 5, 6: e and g.
85 Mathias 2000, figs 23.5: 86–91, 93–96; Kennedy 2019, 438; Kennedy et al. 2018, 27–29.
86 Mathias 2000, figs 23.6: 98, 105–113.
87 With regard to the site's repertoire compared to the surrounding sub-regional areas, see also Ascalone and D'Andrea 2013, 226.
88 Kennedy 2015; 2019; Kennedy et al. 2018, 4–5.
89 Mouamar 2017b, 82–84, fig. 8: 8–11; 2018, 6–8, fig. 7.
90 Mouamar 2017a, 87; 2017b, 82–84; 2018, 6–8, fig. 7.
91 Mouamar 2017b, fig. 8: 8–9; 2018, figs 7, 9: Group B.
92 Hama: Vacca et al. 2018, 31, 54, fig. 8: 1, 3E 677, 2, 3G 936+3 H2.

the EB IVB grey ware repertoires of Tell Shaʿirat[93] and Tell Nebi Mend (Figure 4.10: 1–6 and 9) striking,[94] but also petrography suggests close similarities between the grey ware assemblages of the two sites.[95]

From the short discussion of the evidence above it is clear that, during the EB IVB as in EB IVA, the central Orontes valley was an area where two EB IVB sub-regional ceramic traditions intersected in western inland Syria – that is, the light ware with dark paint and the dark ware with light paint (Painted Simple Ware), as exemplified by Hama and Tell Mishrifeh/Qatna. Tell Shaʿirat and the sites of the steppe margin east of Tell Mishrifeh/Qatna also seem to be located in this region where the two EB IV traditions – the light-coloured ware with dark paint (in various regional varieties) and the dark-coloured ware with white painted decoration – merge.[96] On the other hand, Tell Nebi Mend seems, rather, to be located south of the boundary of this region where the two different developments intersect although it lies within the core area of the original EB IVA elaboration, with continuous production of the grey wares during EB IVB, and is possibly a separate, autonomous, ceramic development.[97]

The Black Wheel-made Ware: origin, ancestry and ceramic regionalism

The short overview of the EB IV traditions of painted wares in north-central western inland Syria above allows us to analyse the question of origin and ancestry of the two typological and techno-stylistic developments which we have identified within Black Wheel-made Ware and the so-called 'eastern and western traditions' (Figures 4.2–3).

The cylindrical goblets (Figure 4.2: 1, 6–8) and the ovoid spouted jars with a wide flaring neck (Figure 4.2: 4–5) seem to be regional variants, made of grey fabrics and painted in white. These vessel shapes occur in the Painted Simple Ware repertoire of north-western inland Syria, where they are made of light fabrics and painted in dark colours (compare with Figures 4.8: 1 and 4.9: 1 for goblets and with Figures 4.8: 11 and 4. 9: 3 for necked spouted jars). Similarly, some decorative techniques used on the Black Wheel-made Ware vessels of the 'eastern tradition' (Figure 4.2: 6–7) are the same as those attested in Painted Simple Ware of north-central western inland Syria, such as painted bands wiped off through wavy incisions made with a stick (Figures 4.8: 2, 4–6, 9 and 4.9: 3–4). These decorative schemas are never found on the grey ware vessels from the central and upper Orontes valley. Conversely, as we have seen before, Painted Simple Ware with these motifs was produced in EB IVB in the region between Ebla and Homs and was imported into steppe margin sites like Tell Shaʿirat and, occasionally, at sites in the Qalamun region north-east of Damascus, like Moumassakhin. Therefore, their incorporation within the decorative schemas of the grey ware of southern Syria

---

93 Mouamar 2018, fig. 7.
94 Kennedy 2019, figs 3: 2, 4–5, 10; 4: 2, 5: 1–5.
95 Kennedy et al. 2018, 28–29; Mouamar 2018, 15.
96 See Mouamar 2017b, 82–84; 2018, 5–9 and figs 5–8.
97 See recently Kennedy et al. 2018, 27–30; Kennedy 2019, 438.

4 A matter of style

and, above all, of Tell el-Waqqas/Hazor, may indicate a different connection, through a path running on a north–south axis through the Syrian Desert and connecting to the upper Galilee.[98] As for the relative chronology of the appearance of these new typological and stylistic features, a good *terminus ante quem non* is suggested by the observation that, in their heartland region between Ebla and Homs, these features characterise only the second half of the EB IV period, that is, EB IVB, as noticed earlier by Tadmor and Bunimovitz and Greenberg.[99]

The ancestry of the 'western tradition' of Black Wheel-made Ware apparently lies in prototypes from the central Orontes valley. Bottles reproduce prototypes attested in north-central western inland Syria during local EB IVB, as already pointed out by Vacca and D'Andrea (compare Figures 4.3: 5–6 and 4.9: 6).[100] Teapots (Figure 4.3: 8–9) show an EB IVA ancestry as well, and once again find close parallels in the EB IVA pottery repertoire of the central Orontes valley (Hama, Qatna Tomb IV, Tell Masin and Tell Ada; see Figure 4.11),[101] as noted already by Dever[102] and Mazzoni,[103] rather than reproduce the body shape of the EB IVB Syrian spouted jars (Figures 4.8: 10 and 4.9: 3). Bell-shaped goblets (Figure 4.3: 1–4) recall the shorter type of goblets attested in the central and upper Orontes valley during EB IVB (Figure 4.10: 1–3), which seem to descend from the local EB IVA goblets (Figure 4.6: 3–7) belonging to the 'White-on-Black Ware' (now with bell-shaped and no longer ring-shaped bases) and 'Grey Ware' after continuous local development throughout the EB IV period. These typological similarities suggest connections along a western path of connectivity, also running along a north–south axis, but, in this case, parallel to the course of the Orontes river and thence crossing the Beqa' and reaching the upper Galilee at Hazor.[104]

It is difficult to determine the timing of the appearance of the new typological and techno-stylistic features that we have ascribed to the 'western tradition' of the Black Wheel-made Ware. The pottery repertoire of the northern areas of the southern Levant in the period preceding EB IV is well known,[105] thus far, to exclude these vessel types as deriving from the local EB III tradition. The EB III ceramic repertoire of the Lebanese Beqa' is known basically from survey materials, but it seems that, even in this area, such vessels were not represented in the EB III inventory.[106] However, in the absence of long EB IV sequences for both the Lebanese Beqa' and the northern southern Levant,

---

98 See Cooper 2018, 195, fig. 12.
99 Tadmor 1978, 9–10; Bunimovitz and Greenberg 2004, 23; see, recently, Greenberg 2019, 139.
100 D'Andrea and Vacca 2015, 47–48, fig. 4; D'Andrea 2014a, 198, figs 3: b, 9: e–f; 2014b, Volume 1, 159, fig. 5.1: 5–6; Vacca 2014, 254–259, fig. 3.
101 Hama, Level J8: Fugmann 1958, fig. 58: 4A 859; Qatna, Tomb IV: du Mesnil du Buisson 1930, pl. XXXI: the last vessel at the bottom of the first column; Tell Masin: du Mesnil du Buisson 1935, pl. XLIX: 9; Tell Ada: du Mesnil du Buisson 1930, fig. 6. Also see Mazzoni 1985a, 15; Genz 2010, 210; D'Andrea 2014a, 199; D'Andrea and Vacca 2015, 48, fig. 5:3–7.
102 Dever 1980, 50, fig. 5.
103 Mazzoni 1985a, 15.
104 See D'Andrea and Vacca 2015, 49; Cooper 2018, 195, fig. 11.
105 Greenberg 2002, 48–51, figs 3.16–3.17.
106 Badreshany 2013, 263–288, figs 3.34–3.44.

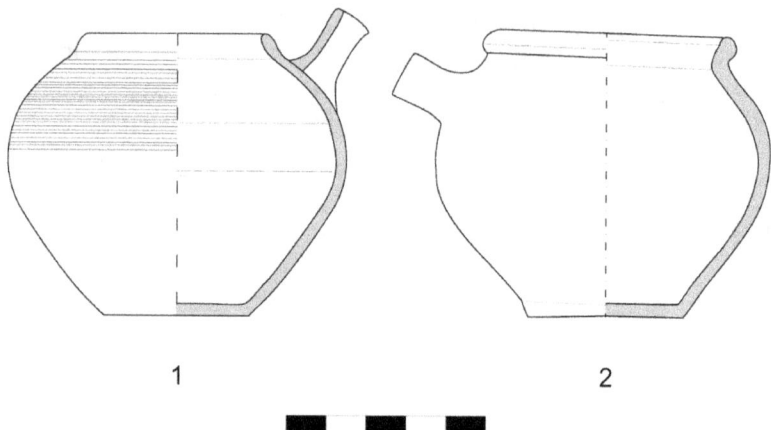

Figure 4.11: Early Bronze IVA Simple Ware teapots from the Orontes Valley.

No.	Site	Reference
1.	Tell Masin	re-drawn after du Mesnil du Buisson 1935, pl. XLIX: 9
2.	Tell Mishrifeh/Qatna Tomb IV	re-drawn after du Mesnil du Buisson 1930, pl. XXXI, bottom left in the first column

it is impossible to pinpoint the appearance of those vessel types in the latter areas to a relative EB IV chronological sequence. Therefore, on the one hand, it is clear that the EB IV goblet shapes found in the Lebanese Beqa' and the northern regions of the southern Levant that we have ascribed to a 'western tradition' of the Black Wheel-made Ware show typological and techno-stylistic proximity to the EB IVB grey goblets of the upper and central Orontes valley.[107] As we have seen before, the EB IVB goblets of the latter regions derive from local EB IVA prototypes developing throughout the EB IV periods and, during EB IVB, appear in the Syrian steppe margin bordering the central and upper Orontes valley. However, we are currently unable to define the EB IV periodisation for the Beqa' and the upper Galilee, and to determine whether, in these areas, the Black Wheel-made Ware 'western' goblets were elaborated locally during an early EB IV phase, or were adopted during a later EB IV phase, once they had been already developed in the central and upper Orontes valley and following on contacts with the latter regions.[108]

Interestingly, in terms of circulation of techno-stylistic information, white painted decoration was common during EB IVB on the northern Lebanese coast (see Tell 'Arqa,

---

107 On the techno-stylistic link between the southern Levantine BWMW and the White-on-Black Ware of the Orontes valley, see Welton and Cooper 2014, 303. See also Dever 1980, 50, fig. 5.
108 D'Andrea 2014b Volume 1, 162–166; 2017, 178.

4 A matter of style

Tell Fadous-Kfarabida and Byblos),[109] where it appears on vessel shapes peculiar to the regional pottery repertoire (Figure 4.12: 7). With regard to this, it is important that vessels made of grey fabrics and decorated with white paint were imported to Tell 'Arqa from the Orontes valley in both the EB IVA and EB IVB (here Figures 4.6: 12–13 and 4.10: 10–13).[110]

Therefore, the central and upper Orontes valley might have been the starting point of technological and stylistic elements that spread over the neighbouring areas – the northern coast of Lebanon, the Beqa', the northern southern Levant and southern Syria – following different paths of connectivity during the mid-to-late EBA. However, despite the circulation of technological and stylistic information, these areas belonged to different ceramic regions during EB IV.

The northern coast of Lebanon forms a discrete group characterised by local ceramic developments (Figure 4.12) that are different from those of the Beqa'.[111] The central Orontes valley and the western edge of the Syrian steppe bordering it are located at the intersection between two EB IV ceramic developments: the Painted Simple Ware of the region between Ebla and Homs and the tradition of grey wares of the region between Hama and Tell Nebi Mend. The latter site seems, thus far, characterised by remarkable connections with the region of Tell Sha'irat in relation to the grey wares,[112] but differs from the neighbouring areas in the development of the other ware classes, suggesting that it might have had a particular, localised development.[113] On the other hand, although there are visible connections between the grey ware goblets from Tell Nebi Mend and those of the 'western tradition' of the Black Wheel-made Ware of the Beqa' and the upper Galilee,[114] these areas do not belong altogether to a homogenous ceramic region.[115] In fact, not only is the Black Wheel-made Ware tradition of the Beqa' and upper Galilee very homogenous, but also similar vessel types in the common wares of the two areas make up a distinctive pottery repertoire (Figure 4.14), which is not found at Tell Nebi Mend or at any site in central Syria, but extends to the Jawlan.[116]

Southern Syria is traditionally considered as part of the same ceramic region as the Beqa' and Galilee.[117] However, the specific pottery types and styles found in the Beqa' and Galilee (Figure 4.14) are not thus far attested in the EB IV ceramic tradition of southern Syria, and the EB IV assemblages from the Beqa' and Galilee suggest that southern Syria might constitute a discrete sub-region in terms of ceramic development.[118] In fact, it shows ceramic types that are a local subset of the pottery horizon of western inland

---

109 For example, Thalmann 2008; Thalmann and Roux 2016, 104, 119, fig. 16; D'Andrea 2017.
110 Thalmann 2009.
111 Thalmann 2006, 220–223; 2008, 63–72; 2009, 10–12.
112 Kennedy et al. 2018, 28–29; Mouamar 2018, 7, footnotes 4–5, 15.
113 See Mathias 2000, 426; Kennedy 2019, 438–439.
114 D'Andrea 2014b, Volume 1, 159–160; 2017; Kennedy et al. 2018, 29.
115 D'Andrea 2014a, 208–212.
116 D'Andrea 2014b, Voulme 1, 193–194, figs 5.25–5.26.
117 Braemer and Échallier 2000, 409; Braemer 2002, 15; Genz 2010, 210–211.
118 D'Andrea 2014b, Volume 1, 193, fig. 5.24.

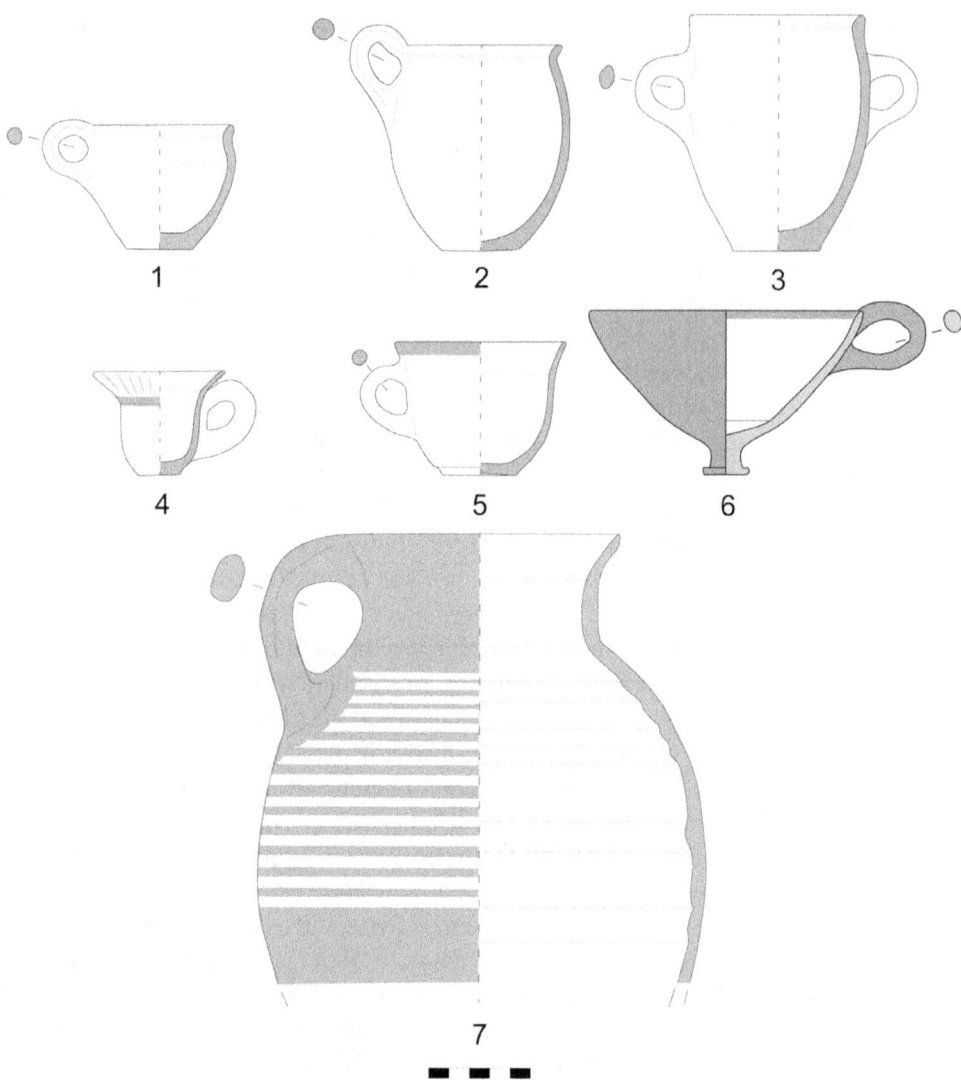

Figure 4.12: Early Bronze IVB pottery repertoire of the northern Lebanese coast.

No.	Site	Reference
1.	Tell 'Arqa	re-drawn after Thalmann 2008, fig. 6: 25
2.	Tell 'Arqa	re-drawn after Thalmann 2008, fig. 6: 28
3.	Tell 'Arqa	re-drawn after Thalmann 2008, fig. 6: 33
4.	Byblos	re-drawn after Thalmann 2008, fig. 6: 4
5.	Tell 'Arqa	re-drawn after Thalmann 2008, fig. 6: 31
6.	Tell Fadous-Kfarabida	re-drawn after Genz et al. 2010, pl. 1: 2
7.	Tell Fadous-Kfarabida	re-drawn after Genz et al. 2010, pl. 1: 7

4 A matter of style

Syria (Figure 4.12: 1–7), even in the local version of the Black Wheel-made Ware, with vessel shapes that connect it to the northern area of the southern Levant.[119] Actually, the latter ceramics might come from the northern plateau of Transjordan and/or even from upper Galilee, but this hypothesis would need verification through petrographic analyses. Future data might considerably change this proposition, in particular when more information becomes available from the Damascene, which is virtually unknown thus far.[120] As proposed in previous studies based on typological and techno-stylistic elements and the parallels in stratified assemblages of north-central western inland Syria, the suggested chronology of the available ceramic assemblages from southern Syria is parallel to the EB IVB.[121] In the Beqaʿ and the northern southern Levant, we do not as yet have data on ceramic developments from EB III, when the region's material culture was definitely oriented to the south,[122] but in EB IV, it incorporated both northern (from central Syria and the western steppe margin) and southern (local) elements. Moreover, petrographic analyses are needed to distinguish local and non-local components of the EB pottery repertoire.

The Black Wheel-made Ware: chronology and inter-regional synchronisation

Stratified assemblages and survey materials from Lebanon (the Akkar plain and the Beqaʿ) and southern Syria show clearly that a ceramic phase corresponding to EB II–III in the northern southern Levant is attested in these regions.[123] However, the current lack of long stratigraphic sequences in the Beqaʿ and the Hula valley hinders the definition of the archaeological periodisation of the following EB IV period.[124] The EB IV assemblages from the Beqaʿ mostly originate from tombs, with the EB IV not yet excavated within settlement sites.[125] The EB IV in the Hula valley is attested by tomb groups and by the stratified evidence of Tell el-Waqqas/Hazor and Khirbet an-Naʿima/Tel Naʿama; however, only one phase has been documented within the period. Therefore, there are no stratigraphic lynchpins to ascribe the evidence to a

---

119 See Braemer and Échallier 2001, 407, figs 22.3: 12, 408; Braemer 2002; Échallier and Braemer 2004, 303, fig. 552, 306, 307, fig. 556: C.953, C.672, 311, fig. 562; D'Andrea 2014b, Volume 1, 192–194, with references.
120 Braemer 2002; Al-Maqdissi 2008–2009.
121 D'Andrea 2014a, 203–206; 2014b, Volume 1, 114–117; D'Andrea 2020b, 406.
122 Genz 2010, 208–210.
123 For Tell Arqa, Phases S and R, see Thalmann 2009, 5–10; 2010, 88–90, fig. 7; Köhler and Thalmann 2014; for Tell Fadous-Kfarabida Phases III–IV, see Genz 2014. For survey materials, see Marfoe 1998, 88–92, figs 49–53.
124 D'Andrea 2014b, Volume 1, 117–120, Table 6.
125 Genz 2010, 208–210.

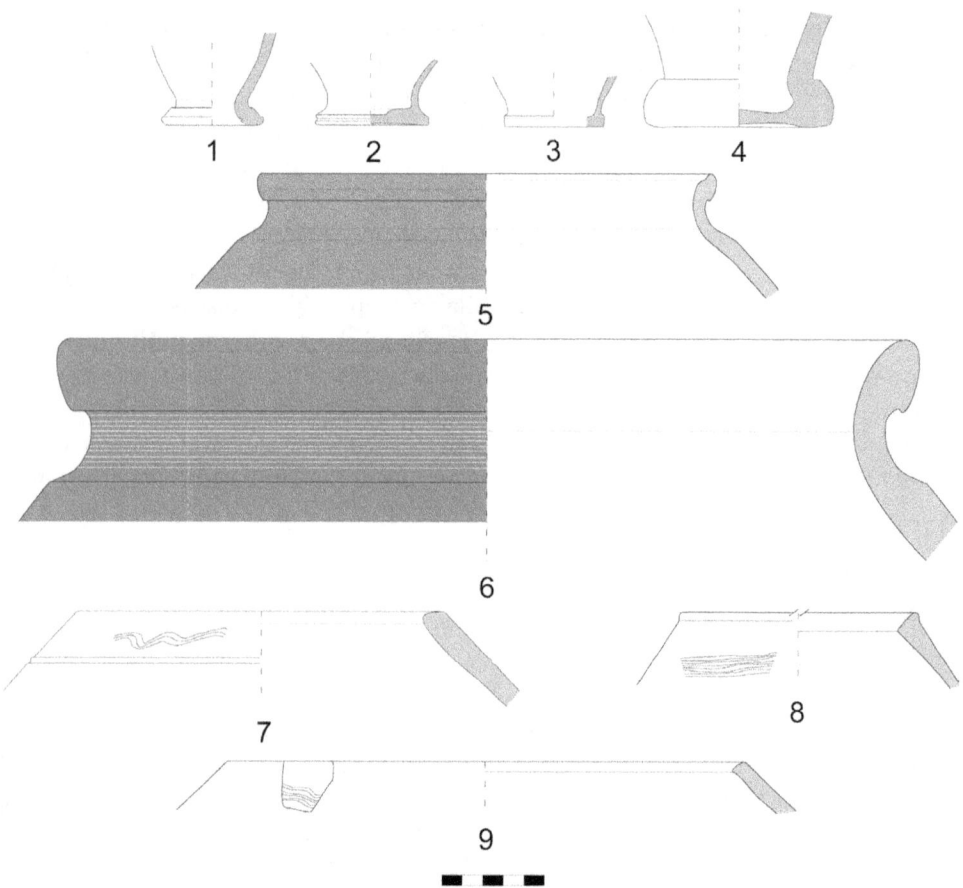

Figure 4.13: Early Bronze IV pottery repertoire typical of southern Syria.

No.	Site	Reference
1.	Khirbet al-'Umbashi	re-drawn after Échallier and Braemer 2004, fig. 584: C.489
2.	Yabroud	re-drawn after Abou Assaf 1967, pl. VI: 34
3.	Moumassakhin	re-drawn after Al-Maqdissi 1989, fig. 21: 159
4.	Moumassakhin	re-drawn after Al-Maqdissi 1989, fig. 20b: 140
5.	Moumassakhin	re-drawn after Al-Maqdissi 1989, fig. 4: 15
6.	Moumassakhin	re-drawn after Al-Maqdissi 1989, fig. 15: 81
7	Khirbet al-'Umbashi	re-drawn after Échallier and Braemer 2004, fig. 552: C.956
8.	Khirbet al-'Umbashi	re-drawn after Échallier and Braemer 2004, fig. 552: C.609
9.	Khirbet al-'Umbashi	re-drawn after Échallier and Braemer 2004, fig. 552: C.658

given EB IV phase, although there are techno-stylistic elements pointing towards a date in the second half of the EB IV period for the Hazor Stratum XVIII assemblage.[126]

Bunimovitz and Greenberg pointed out that the Black Wheel-made Ware should have been elaborated in these regions only after its Syrian prototypes – which they considered to be the EB IVB Syrian Painted Simple Ware vessels – had been well established in their homeland, that is, during the northern Levantine EB IVB, after ca. 2300 BC.[127] This was the beginning of EB IV in the southern Levant according to the traditional chronology, but, within the higher chronology, it now corresponds to the central phase of EB IV. As we have discussed before, the Syrian counterparts of the Black Wheel-made Ware goblets found in the Beqa' and the northern southern Levant appear in the central and upper Orontes valley and the adjacent steppe margin at sites such as Tell Mishrifeh/Qatna, Tell Sha'irat and Tell Nebi Mend (Figure 4.10: 1–7) in the local EB IVB pottery horizon, ca. 2300–2000 BC. Therefore, they might have first appeared in the northern southern Levant in this phase too. In the latter areas, Black Wheel-made Ware vessels occasionally occur along with band- and wavy-combed pottery,[128] making a date of the assemblages in a relatively 'late' EB IV phase feasible, since combed vessels are late in the Levantine EB IV sequence.[129] However, this is too little evidence to say that *all* the Black Wheel-made Ware vessels found in the southern Levant *should* date from a 'late' EB IV phase within the longer time span proposed for the period. Interestingly, a Black Wheel-made Ware sherd has been recently identified in the Hama EB IV assemblages,[130] dating from Level J5, which corresponds to the EB IVA/IVB cusp.[131] This currently represents, if not the earliest Black Wheel-made Ware sherd thus far uncovered within a stratified deposit, the only one that can be attributed to a long EB IV stratigraphic sequence.[132]

As we have seen, the chronological question is complicated by the observation that the ancestry of the Black Wheel-made Ware tradition of the Beqa' and the northern southern Levant finds its origins in mid-third millennium BC prototypes of the Orontes valley (Figures 4.6: 5–11 and 4.11), suggesting a long elaboration of this ware. As for the Black Wheel-made Ware from the Hula valley, the presence of the wavy incised motifs that parallel those of the EB IVB Painted Simple Ware of north-central western inland Syria may provide a reliable *terminus ante quem non* for dating the assemblages.[133] However, this style might simply have come into use in a later EB IVB phase following

---

126 D'Andrea 2014b, Volume 1, 160; 2020b, 404, fig. 22.5: 4–7; Bechar 2015, fig 5: 10, 17, 20, 6:7; 2020, 366, fig. 20.1.
127 Bunimovitz and Greenberg 2004, 23.
128 Hanita: Singer and Dar 1986, pl. on p. 65.
129 Helms 1986, 46, fig. 18: 8; Nigro 2003, 134, fig. 20: 4–6; Richard 2010, 71, figs 4.7: 7–8, 4.10: 3, 6; D'Andrea 2012, 24; 2014b, Volume 1, 102, figs 3.58–3.67, 2015a, 33, fig. 5.5–5.7.
130 Vacca et al. 2018, 32–34, fig. 6:3, 3G 678.
131 Vacca et al. 2018, 34, fn 105.
132 Vacca et al. 2018, 34.
133 D'Andrea 2014a, 204–206; 2017, 178.

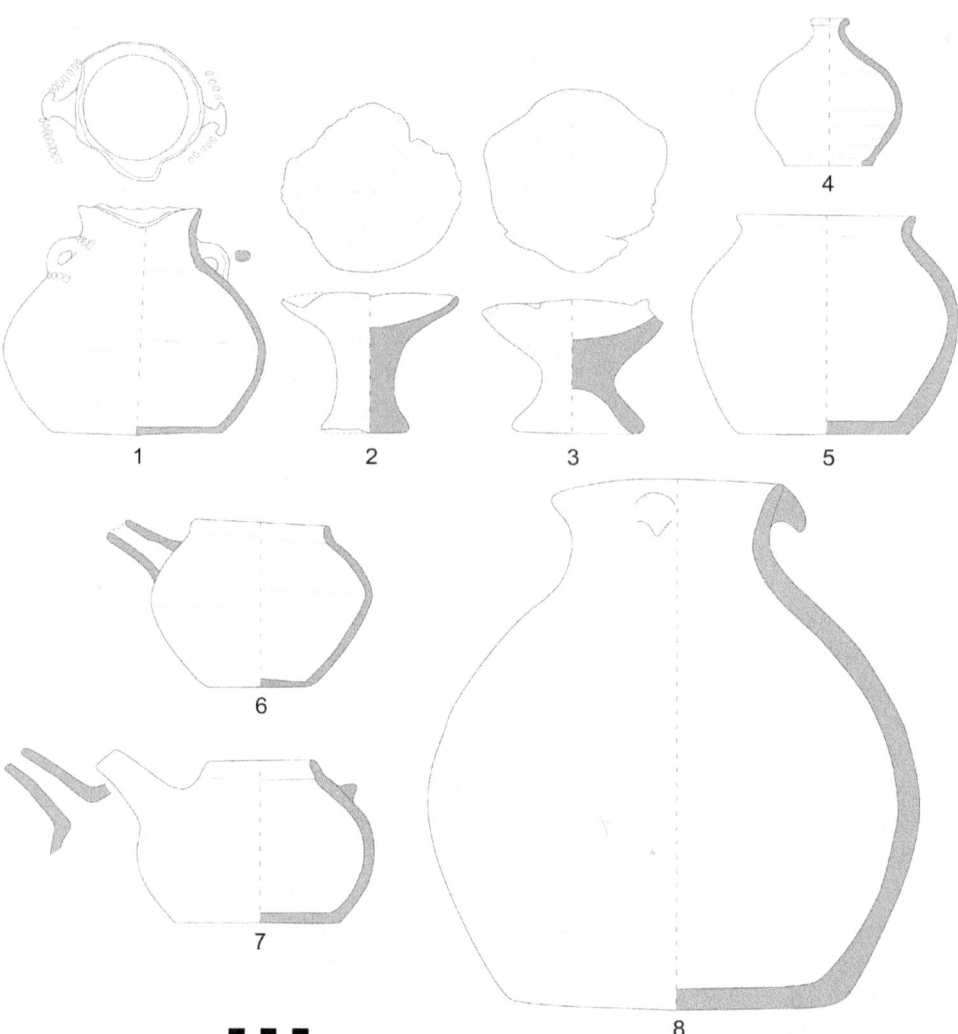

Figure 4.14: Early Bronze IV pottery repertoire typical of the upper Galilee, the southern Lebanese Beqa', and the Jawlan (From D'Andrea 2014b, Volume 1, fig. 5.26.).

No.	Site	Reference
1.	Khirbet Qadish/Qedesh	re-drawn after Tadmor 1978, fig. 4: 70-223
2.	Khirbet Qadish/Qedesh	re-drawn after Tadmor 1978, fig. 10: 70-526
3.	Khirbet Qadish/Qedesh	re-drawn after Tadmor 1978, fig. 10: 70-1105
4.	Deir Saras	re-drawn after Epstein 1985, fig. 3: 16
5.	Nahf (Tomb 3)	re-drawn after Getzov 1995, fig. 8: 10
6.	Khirbet Qadish/Qedesh	re-drawn after Tadmor 1978, fig. 7: 70-214

4 A matter of style

No.	Site	Reference
7.	ʿAin Mallaha/ʾEnan	re-drawn after Eisenberg 1985, fig. 3: 9
8.	as-Sanbariyya/Maʿayan Barukh (Tomb III)	re-drawn after Amiran 1961, fig. 6: 8

on the opening of a new eastern route, as suggested by Cooper,[134] and have been merged to the local Black Wheel-made Ware repertoire developed already in the EB IVA period.

However, given the current lack of long stratigraphic sequences spanning the whole EB IV period for the Beqaʿ and the northern southern Levant, we cannot determine when it was actually elaborated, if it might have appeared earlier within local EB IV, and how long it remained in use. Only when long stratigraphic sequences spanning the whole of the EB IV period are excavated will it be possible to determine whether the production of Black Wheel-made Ware started in EB IVA or in EB IVB, and clarify whether visible Syrian EB IVA ancestry of the southern Levantine Black Wheel-made Ware vessels derives from the local early EB IV cultural horizon,[135] or from the Syrian EB IVB grey vessels that developed from EB IVA models.[136]

Moving eastward, archaeological research in southern Syria demonstrated that the EB II–III was a period of growth for fortified settlements in this region, possibly following the sedentarisation of pastoralists,[137] and contacts with the northern southern Levant, suggested by the material culture.[138] However, it is currently difficult to isolate an early EB IV phase following that EB III horizon within the regional archaeological evidence available for the EB IV period, thus far represented by settlement assemblages from Yabroud, Moumassakhin and Khirbet al-ʿUmbashi and by tomb groups from Yabroud, Tell el-ʿAshari and Deraʿa.[139]

Based on typological and techno-stylistic grounds – the goblets and spouted jars in the 'eastern tradition' and the wavy incised motifs – the Black Wheel-made Ware of this region may be considered as a local variant of the Painted Simple Ware of western inland Syria dating from EB IVB, though borrowing techno-stylistic elements from central Syria – the use of grey fabrics and whitish decorations. An EB IVB date for this ware class is supported also by the presence of other vessel types which refer to other ceramic traditions. Thus, for instance, at Moumassakhin, the 'eastern' grey ware occurs alongside limited amounts of imported EB IVB Painted Simple Ware, and grey ware vessels comparable with the EB IVB Shaʿirat Grey Ware. Likewise, Khirbet al-ʿUmbashi yielded both grey ware vessels and EB IV vessels comparable to those

---

134 Cooper 2018, 195, fig. 12.
135 Cooper 2018, 194–195, fig. 11.
136 D'Andrea 2017, 178.
137 Braemer et al. 2004, 361–372; Braemer 2011, 42–44.
138 Fiaccavento 2013.
139 D'Andrea 2014b, Volume 1, 114–117, Table 5.

found in northern Transjordan bearing combed decoration (here Figure 4.13: 7–9),[140] which date to a 'late' EB IV phase in the local sequence.[141] However, no typical EB IVA vessel types (see Figure 4.4) have been found in the region so far, making it difficult to recognise this cultural and chronological horizon in southern Syria. On the one hand, this might be due to low-resolution regional ceramic chronology; on the other hand, this might reflect lack of permanent settlement in this region during an early EB IV phase, following the crisis of urbanism, given that, as we have seen, the local EB III was connected to the south. This issue will remain unsolved until new stratified data is available.

Conclusion: the significance of the Black Wheel-made Ware in the southern Levantine EB IV

When we first isolated two groups within the Black Wheel-made Ware vessels of southern Syria, the Lebanese Beqa' and the northern regions of the southern Levant,[142] there was much less data available than there is now. During the last five years, our knowledge has been increased by the publication of the Black Wheel-made Ware assemblage from Tell el-Waqqas/Hazor,[143] and the appearance of studies on the grey wares of central Syria, which we have discussed in the paragraphs above. These studies have allowed us to refine our previous hypothesis, to redefine typological and stylistic elements that can be assigned to an 'eastern' and a 'western' tradition, as well as a better understanding of the nature of these two developments.[144] Clearly, our working hypothesis that a western and an eastern tradition may be discerned within the Black Wheel-made Ware assemblages will need extensive petrographic research to be properly tested. However, the typological and techno-stylistic differences between the two groups, although not striking, are clearly evident (compare Figures 4.2 and 4.3). Indisputably, the western tradition shows closer ties to the ceramic developments of the central and upper sectors of the Orontes valley, which are characterised by remarkable continuity throughout the EB IV period, while the eastern tradition retains greater connections to the ceramic developments of north-central western inland Syria during EB IVB.[145]

L. Cooper has recently further articulated our hypotheses, proposing that the two groups might reflect not only a geographical differentiation, but also a chronological

---

140 Échallier and Braemer 2004, figs 552: C.065, C.305, C.609, C.678, C.954, C.955, C.956; D'Andrea 2014b, Volume 2, pl. LVIII: 6–11.
141 D'Andrea 2014b, Volume 1, 116 and 193.
142 D'Andrea 2014a.
143 Bechar 2015; 2017, 173–180.
144 Moreover, now that the ceramic assemblages from the steppe margin and Tell Nebi Mend are published, it might well be that goblets from Moumassakhin may belong to the grey production from those areas rather than to an 'eastern' Black Wheel-made Ware tradition (see, e.g. D'Andrea 2014a, 201, fig. 11: g; 2014b, Volume 1, 155, fig. 5.2:6).
145 D'Andrea 2014a, 192–203; 2014b, Volume 1, 158–166.

4 A matter of style

distinction.[146] The western tradition would represent an EB IVA development following a western path of connectivity reaching the northern southern Levant through central Syria and central Lebanon at that time.[147] The eastern tradition would mirror an EB IVB development following an eastern route cutting through the steppe margin and the Damascene,[148] more intensively used during the latter part of the period.[149]

While a date parallel to the EB IVB period for the eastern tradition of the Black Wheel-made Ware seems very likely based on typological and techno-stylistic grounds, it is currently difficult to determine when the western tradition of the Black Wheel-made Ware appeared in the Beqaʽ and in the northern valleys of the southern Levant. The presence of a single imported Black Wheel-made Ware sherd with a white painted motif within the Hama Level J5 pottery assemblages allows for cross dating. In fact, Hama Level J5 has good parallels in the ceramic horizon of Ebla's Royal Palace G of the EB IVA period, but seems to better fit a phase immediately after its destruction, thus corresponding to the EB IVA/B cusp,[150] around 2300 BC.[151] Moreover, the EB IV assemblage from Hazor including Black Wheel-made Ware seems to date to the second half of the period, during the last quarter of the third millennium BC. This proposal is corroborated by the presence of wavy motifs incised through the white paint that are derived from the EB IVB tradition of central Syria, which also appear in the eastern Black Wheel-made Ware tradition. Clearly, these considerations do not per se imply that *all* the Black Wheel-made Ware found in the Beqaʽ and the upper Galilee dates from a later EB IV phase; and this will need more stratified evidence to be demonstrated. Likewise, it cannot be excluded that the 'western' route was used earlier than the eastern path, as suggested by Cooper.[152] However, the confluence of the two traditions in the Black Wheel-made Ware assemblages at Tell el-Waqqas/Hazor suggests that these two 'traditions' and the paths of connectivity through which they were transferred to the south might have been used simultaneously at least during the second half of the EB IV period. At that time, the two routes might have intersected at the height of Hazor when the site had some regional relevance.[153]

Elite emulation has been used as an interpretive framework for the appearance, in the de-urbanised south, of drinking paraphernalia associated with the sophisticated EB IV urban cultures of the northern Levant for some time,[154] and still resonates in

---

146 Cooper 2018, 194.
147 Cooper 2018, 195, fig. 11.
148 See Wilkinson et al. 2014, 92; D'Andrea and Vacca 2015, 49.
149 Cooper 2018, 195, fig. 12.
150 Mazzoni 1982, 185; Vacca et al. 2018, 34, fn. 105.
151 Based on average mean of radiocarbon dates for the destruction level – see Calcagnile, Quarta and D'Elia 2013.
152 Cooper 2018, 194–195, figs 11–12.
153 Bechar 2020, 372–374.
154 Bunimovitz and Greenberg 2004; 2006.

recent literature.¹⁵⁵ However, this might not be the only way to understand socio-cultural transformations in the regions located at the interface between the northern and southern Levant during the EB IV period.¹⁵⁶ Although chronological, historical and socio-cultural developments in the Lebanese Beqaʻ are still obscure, we can start setting some firm points.

During EB IV, the region encompassing the Lebanese Beqaʻ, the Jawlan and upper Galilee shared a homogeneous, discrete and very particular cultural horizon, connecting it to the southern Levant on the one hand (Simple Ware, Cooking Ware, and Storage Ware; Figure 4.13: 7–9) and to central Syria on the other (the Black Wheel-made Ware; Figure 4.13: 1–6), highlighting its nature as a transition zone between the northern and the southern Levant. The observation that, in the EB IV period, these regions were intersected by the distribution of locally produced Black Wheel-made Ware, with at least two possible distinct areas of production, probably one in the Beqaʻ¹⁵⁷ and one in the upper Galilee,¹⁵⁸ suggests an explanation different from elite emulation. It might be more likely that, during EB IV, these regions were integrated into and became part of a broader 'technological milieu' that extended up to the Hama region to the north, represented by the production of grey ware often decorated with white paint and descending from the EB IVA ceramic tradition of central Syria.¹⁵⁹ The Beqaʻ and the upper Galilee were places of specialised ware production since the EB II–III (Metallic Ware),¹⁶⁰ which may have facilitated the inclusion of these regions within the area of production of grey wares possibly from the EB IVA/B transition and certainly during EB IVB. However, this phenomenon probably resulted from greater integration of the latter areas with central Syria during the EB IVB. In fact, the archaeological evidence shows that the sites of the middle and upper Orontes sectors and the steppe margins were expanding during EB IVB.¹⁶¹ Unfortunately, the current lack of stratigraphic sequences does not allow us to refine the chronology of the occupation of the Beqaʻ during EB IV and settlement sites dating from this period have not been identified thus far; future research will hopefully shed light on regional patterns of settlement and landscape use during EB IV. However, it seems possible to identify a drop in permanent settlement in the Hula valley at the beginning of the EB IV period (which might account for the absence of Hazor in the EB IVA Syrian sources),¹⁶² following changes in patterns of settlement observed during EB III.¹⁶³ During the last quarter of the

---

155 See Wilkinson et al. 2014, 91–92; Bechar 2015; 2020; Kennedy 2015, 195–197, 203–204; Greenberg 2017; Schloen 2017; Kennedy et al. 2018, 29.
156 See D'Andrea 2018a, 81–84.
157 Genz et al. forthcoming.
158 Bechar 2013, 75; Cohen-Weinberger 2016.
159 D'Andrea 2017, 180–181.
160 Greengberg and Porat 1996. See also the recent re-examination by Badreshany et al. 2019.
161 Mouamar 2017b, 88, 96, fig. 6; Kennedy 2015, 64; 2016, 3; 2019: 439; 2020, 337.
162 D'Andrea 2020a, 209–211.
163 Greenberg 2017, 46–48.

4 A matter of style

third millennium BC, sedentary settlements were re-established in upper Galilee[164] and a developed permanent village grew at Hazor that, in all likelihood, functioned as a regional centre.[165] As we said above, this chronological proposal is supported by techno-stylistic elements in the Black Wheel-made Ware that are markers of a later EB IV phase.

The aggrandisement of sites in central Syria noticeable during a later phase of the EB IV period has been connected to changed socio-political balances between the EB IVA and EB IVB, due to the crisis of the Ebla kingdom around 2300 BC (2367–2293 cal. BC, 2-sigma[166]), allowing sites in central Syria to prosper.[167] In particular, consensus has grown that the area between Tell Mishrifeh/Qatna and the steppe margins, where also Tell Sha'irat is located, may correspond to the territory of Ibal.[168] Ibal was a tribal confederation, mentioned in the EB IVA texts from Ebla,[169] that was at some point subjugated by Ebla during EB IVA,[170] and that might have enjoyed political autonomy after the wane of the northern dominating polity.[171]

During the last quarter of the third millennium BC there was a considerable sociopolitical reconfiguration in the central and upper Orontes sectors, the western margins of the Syrian steppe, and at least the Hula valley, with more or less large territories reorganising around regional settlements; likely still at a 'cantonal' scale in this early phase in terms of size and economic and political control exerted. This new configuration would somehow pre-figure the regional developments of the following Middle Bronze Age.[172] From north to south, the regional settlements might have been Tell Mishrifeh/Qatna and/or Tell Sha'irat, Tell Nebi Mend and Tell el-Waqqas/Hazor. All of these sites belonged to different ceramic provinces during EB IV, but might have found a means to fuel interactions (quite likely economic) in the production of different but similar grey wares, as a visually distinctive unifying element in the material culture. Therefore, the various grey wares might be interpreted differently than markers of southern emulation of northern elite behaviours and as elements mirroring the new socio-political and socio-economic order of the later EB IV period.[173] These wares were made with different petrographic recipes according to the local geological availability, but with the aim of making aesthetically homogeneous products to visually show connections among regional areas that were

---

164 D'Andrea 2014b, Volume 1, 117–120, Tab. 6; 2020a, 213–215; Greenberg 2019, 141; Bechar 2020, 369.
165 Bechar 2013, 75; 2015, 54; 2020, 373–374.
166 Calcagnile, Quarta and D'Elia 2013.
167 Kennedy 2015, 316–317; 2016, 3; 2019; D'Andrea 2017, 181; 2019, 17–19; 2020a, 211–214.
168 Morandi Bonacossi 2009, 56–57; Mouamar 2016, 189; 2017b, 87–88; Vacca et al. 2018, 20.
169 Fronzaroli 2003; Biga 2008; 2014.
170 Catagnoti 1997, 123–124; Archi 2013, 83; Biga 2014, 201–205.
171 D'Andrea 2019, 18–192; 2020a, 208–209, 212–213; for the region of Tell Nebi Mend, see Kennedy 2019, 438–439.
172 See Wilkinson et al. 2014, 96.
173 Differently, Bechar (2020) has recently suggested that the visual connection to Syria in the southern Levantine Black Wheel-made Ware was used by the local community at Hazor as an exclusionary strategy to separate elite groups from non-elite groups.

otherwise part of differentiated cultural horizons and, possibly, of different socio-political organisations.[174] A support to this hypothesis may come from the observation that grey wares were produced in the later EB IV phase not only at Hazor but also at sites in the Syrian steppe margin, like Tell Shaʻirat, where they appear only in EB IVB. Since the central and upper sectors of the Orontes valley were the original core of elaboration and the heartland of the production of grey wares from the EB IVA, these areas might have played a leading role in transferring cultural and techno-stylistic information to the neighbouring regions. This suggests that the central and upper sectors of the Orontes valley may have also played a major role in regional reorganisation around 2300 BC.

Finally, the placement of southern Syria within the inter-regional framework that we have just delineated deserves a few words. It is, in fact, of the greatest interest that EB IV activities in the latter area are noticeable in the later part of the period, when permanent sedentary settlements are established at Yabroud and Moumassakhin, north-east of Damascus. As said above, these villages yielded ceramic materials that include: 1) a local version of the grey ware (the 'eastern Black Wheel-made Ware tradition') that adopts and adapts vessel types and styles typical of the EB IVB Painted Simple Ware of north-central western inland Syria; 2) Painted Simple Ware possibly imported from north-central inland western Syria and/or from the Mishrifeh/Shaʻirat region; 3) EB IVB grey wares possibly imported from the regions of Tell Shaʻirat and/or Tell Nebi Mend. Although very little is known about Damascus and its hinterland in the third millennium BC,[175] it is not impossible that the Damascene was another EB IVB 'cantonal' entity.[176]

Sites farther south, such as Khirbet al-ʻUmbashi in the Black Desert, might mirror a different situation. In fact, the region is traditionally connected to pastoralism and its sedentary occupation may depend on the creation of given socio-political and socio-economic preconditions (on 'sub-optimal zones'),[177] as it was the case with the appearance of EB II–III fortified settlements, possibly prompted by incipient urbanisation in the southern Levant.[178] It is likely that this region during the EB IV was influenced by materials from areas to its north-west (central Syria, the Damascene and/or the Beqaʻ) and south (the northern Jordanian plateau and/or the upper Galilee), serving as a true interface between the northern and the southern Levant, although this hypothesis would need confirmation through petrographic analyses. It might have been used as a 'buffer' region where sedentists and (semi)nomadic pastoralists interacted and the ending point of the paths through which elements of the 'eastern tradition'

---

174 D'Andrea 2017, 180–181.

175 Klengel 1985; Al-Maqdissi 2008–2009.

176 As for the Beqaʻ, Kamid el-Loz was an important regional centre during the Middle Bronze Age, but no EB IV materials have been thus far found, because the layers below the second millennium BC settlement have not been investigated thus far. Some EB IV sherds were found at Baalbeck in a sounding below the cella of the Temple of Bel (van Ess 2008, 110–111 and pl. 2:9), but this is too little evidence for defining the nature of the settlement during EB IV.

177 See Philip and Bradbury 2010, 138; Wilkinson et al. 2014, 52–53.

178 Braemer 2011; Braemer et al. 2011.

reached western sites located within one core area of production of Black Wheel-made Ware,[179] like Hazor,[180] in EB IVB during the last quarter of the third millennium BC.

Acknowledgements

This chapter is a revised, re-elaborated and expanded version of a paper given at the workshop 'The settlement landscape of the Orontes valley in the fourth to second millennia BC', held during the 9th International Congress on the Archaeology of the Ancient Near East at the University of Basel, Switzerland, in June 2014. I wish to thank warmly Stephen Bourke and Melissa Kennedy for kindly inviting me to take part in the workshop and to contribute to its publication. I wish to thank also Suzanne Richard, for reading an earlier version of the manuscript and giving valuable suggestions, Frances Pinnock for commenting on the final draft, and Lisa Cooper for information on EB IV pottery from Tell 'Acharneh. Photographic material from Ebla is reproduced here by courtesy of the Missione Archeologica Italiana in Siria (MAIS).

References

Abou Assaf, A. (1967). Der Friedhof von Yabrud. *Annales Archéologiques Arabes Syriennes* 17: 55–68.
Albright, W.F. (1940). *From the Stone Age to Christianity*. John Hopkins Press: Baltimore.
Al-Maqdissi, M. (1989). Essai préliminaire de la céramique de la poterie de Moumassakhin (Campagnes de 1987 et 1988). *Notes de céramologie Syrienne* 5.
(1990). La poterie de Moumassakhin (note explicative à propos du Décor). *Aula Orientalis* 8: 251–254.
(1993). Les tombes de Tell Ash'ari. *Syria* LXX(3–4): 470–473.
(1995a). Tell Sh'airat (region de Homs). *Syria* LXXII(1–2): 196–198.
(1995b). La Tombe de Dera'a, *Syria* LXXII(1–2): 199–201.
(2008–2009). Damas au IIIe millénaire av. J.-C. *Notes d'archéologie Levantine* XXIV: 17–22.
(2013). Notes d'archéologie Levantine XXXI. Moumassakhin, remarques sur l'organisation interne d'une agglomération de la deuxième moitié du troisième millénaire av. J.-C., *Hauran V. La Syrie du sud dans le Néolithique à l'antiquité tardive*, Volume 2. M. al-Maqdissi, F. Braemer, J-M. Dentzer and E. Ishaq eds. 12–32. Bibliothèque Archéologique et Historique T.202, Beyrouth: Institut Français du Proche-Orient.
Amiran, R. (1960). The pottery of the Middle Bronze I in Palestine. *Israel Exploration Journal* 10: 204–225.
(1961). Tombs of the Middle Bronze Age I at Ma'ayan Barukh. *'Atiqot* 3: 84–92.
Ascalone, E. and D'Andrea, M. (2013). Assembling the evidence. Excavated sites dating from the Early Bronze Age in and around the *chora* of Ebla. In *Ebla and its landscape: early state*

---

179 Philip and Bradbury 2010, 162–164.
180 See Bechar 2015, 53.

organization in the Near East. P. Matthiae and N. Marchetti, eds. 215–237. Walnut Creek, CA: Left Coast Press.

Badreshany, K.P. (2013). *Urbanization in the Levant: an archaeometric approach to understanding the social and economic impact of settlement nucleation in the Biqaʿ valley*, PhD thesis. The Oriental Institute of Chicago. Chicago: United States of America.

Badreshany, K., Philip, G. and Kennedy, M. (2019). The development of integrated regional economies in the Early Bronze Age Levant: new evidence from 'Combed Ware' jars. *Levant*, doi: 10.1080/00758914.2019.1641009.

Bechar, S. (2012). Tel Hazor: a key site during the Intermediate Bronze Age. *Qadmoniot* 45/143: 11–12.

(2013). Tel Hazor: a key site of the Intermediate Bronze Age. *Near Eastern Archaeology* 76(2): 73–75.

(2015). A reanalysis of the Black Wheel-Made Ware of the Intermediate Bronze Age. *Tel Aviv* 42(1–2): 27–58.

(2017). The Intermediate Bronze Age pottery. In *Hazor VII. The 1990–2012 Excavations: the Bronze Age*. A. Ben-Tor, S. Zuckerman, S. Bechar and D. Sandhaus, eds. 161–198. Israel Exploration Society: Jerusalem.

(2020). It's in the style: Black Wheelmade Ware and its social meaning. In *New horizons in the study of the Early Bronze III and Early Bronze IV in the Levant*. S. Richard, ed. 365–375. University Park, PA: Eisenbrauns.

Besana, M. Da Ros, M. and Iamoni, M. (2008). Excavations on the acropolis of Mishrifeh, Operation J: a new Early Bronze Age III-Iron Age III sequence for central inner Syria. Part 2: The Pottery. *Akkadica* 129(2): 129–179.

Boileau, M-C. (2006). The pottery from Tell ʿAcharneh, Part II: technological considerations. In *Tell ʿAcharneh 1998–2004: Preliminary reports on excavation campaigns and study season*. M. Fortin, ed. 191–213. Subartu XVIII. Turnhout: Brepols.

(2018). Petrographic signatures of the Tell ʿAcharneh ceramics: a diachronic perspective. *Levant*, doi:10.1080/00758914.2018.1477296.

Braemer, F. (2002). La céramique du Bronze Ancien en Syrie du sud. In *Céramique de l'Âge du Bronze en Syrie, I: la Syrie du sud et le vallée de l'Oronte*. M. Al-Maqdissi, V. Matoïan and C. Nicolle, ed. 9–22. Bibliothèque Archéologique et Historique T.161. Beyrouth: Institut Français du Proche-Orient.

(2011). Badia and Maamoura, the Jawlan/Hawran regions during the Bronze Age: landscapes and hypothetical territories. *Syria* 88: 23–30.

Braemer, F. and Échallier, J-C. (2000). A summary statement on the EBA ceramics from southern Syria, and the relationship of this material with that of neighbouring regions. In *Ceramics and change in the Early Bronze Age of the southern Levant*. G. Philip and D. Baird, eds. 430–410. Sheffield: Sheffield Academic Press.

Braemer, F., Échallier, J-C. and Taraqji, A. eds. (2004). *Khirbet al-ʿUmbashi: villages et campements de pasteurs dans le "Désert Noir" (Syrie) à l'Âge du Bronze*. Bibliothéque Archéologique et Historique T.171. Beyrouth: Institut Français du Proche-Orient.

Braemer, F., Criaud, H., Davtian, G., Fiaccavento, C., Flambeaux, A., Ghanem, G., Herveux, L., Ibáñez, J.J., Liétar, C., Nicolle, C., Shaarani, W. and Vila, E. (2011). Qarassa, un site du Bronze Ancien et Moyen en Syrie du sud. *Syria* 88: 225–250.

Braidwood, R.J. (1940). Report on two sondages on the coast of Syria, south of Tartous. *Syria* XXI: 183–226.

Braidwood, R.J. and Braidwood, L.S. (1960). *Excavations in the plain of Antioch I: the earlier assemblages Phases A–J.* Oriental Institute Publications 61. Chicago: The University of Chicago Press.

Bunimovitz, S. and Greenberg, R. (2004). Revealed in their cups: Syrian drinking customs in Intermediate Bronze Age Canaan. *Bulletin of the American Schools of Oriental Research* 334: 19–31.

(2006). Of pots and paradigms: interpreting the Intermediate Bronze Age in Israel/Palestine. In *Confronting the past: archaeological and historical essays on ancient Israel in honour of William G. Dever.* S. Gitin, J.E. Wright and J.P. Dessel, eds. 23–31. Winona Lake: Eisenbrauns.

Calcagnile L., Quarta G. and D'Elia M.(2013). Just at That Time: 14C Determinations and Analyses from EB IVA Layers. In: *Ebla and its landscape. Early state formation in the ancient Near East.* P. Matthiae and N. Marchetti eds. 415–424. Walnut Creek, CA: Left Coast Press.

Castel, C., Awad, N., Al-Kontar, R., Babour, T., Bano, M., Chiti, B., Cuny, A., Emery, A., Hammad, K., Munschy, M., Munos, S., Perello, B. and Wild, A. (2014). Rapport préliminaire sur les activités de la mission archéologique Franco-Syrienne d'Al-Rawda, travaux 2007–2010 (Part 1). *Akkadica* 135(1): 1–54.

Cohen, S.L. (2002). *Canaanites, chronologies, and connections: the relationship of Middle Bronze IIA Canaan to Middle Kingdom Egypt.* Studies in the Archaeology and History of the Levant 3, Winona Lake: Eisenbrauns.

(2012). Synchronisms and significance: re-evaluating interconnections between Middle Kingdom Egypt and the southern Levant. *Journal of Ancient Egyptian Interconnections* 4(3): 1–8.

(2017). Reevaluation of connections between Egypt and the southern Levant in the Middle Bronze Age in the light of the new higher chronology. *Journal of Ancient Egyptian Interconnections* 13: 34–42.

Cohen-Weinberger, A. (2016). A note on the provenance of Black Wheel-Made vessels from a burial cave west of Tel Hazor. *'Atiqot* 83: 21–23.

Cooper, L. (2006). The pottery from Tell 'Acharneh, part I: typological considerations and dating accordingly to excavated areas in the upper and lower towns, 1908–2002. In *Tell 'Acharneh 1998–2004: rapports préliminaires sur les campagnes de fouilles et season d'études.* M. Fortin, ed. 140–191. Subartu XVIII. Brussels: Brepols Publishers.

(2007). Exploring the heartland of the Early Bronze Age 'Caliciform' culture. *Bulletin of the Canadian Society for Mesopotamian Studies* 2: 43–50.

(2018). Half-empty or half-full? Past and present research on EB IV Caliciform goblets and their chronological and socio-economic implications. In *Ebla and beyond: ancient Near Eastern studies after fifty years of discoveries at Tell Mardikh. Proceedings of the international congress held in Rome, 15th–17th December 2014.* P. Matthiae, F. Pinnock and M. D'Andrea, eds. 181–208. Wiesbaden: Harrassowitz Verlag.

(2020). The Northern Levantine 'Caliciform' Tradition. In *New horizons in the study of the Early Bronze III and Early Bronze IV in the Levant.* S. Richard, ed. 111–118. University Park, PA: Eisenbrauns.

D'Andrea, M. (2012). The Early Bronze IV period in south-central Transjordan: reconsidering chronology through pottery technology. *Levant* 44(1): 17–50.

(2014a). La *Black Wheelmade Ware*: originalità e modelli stilistici, tipologici e tecnologici dalla Siria e dal Levante settentrionale in una peculiare produzione dipinta sud-levantina del tardo III millennio a.C. *Rendiconti Morali dell'Accademia Nazionale dei Lincei* s. IX, vol. 24 (2013): 181–220.

(2014b). *The southern Levant in Early Bronze IV: issues and perspectives in the pottery evidence.* Contributi e Materiali di Archeologia Orientale XVII. Roma: Sapienza Università di Roma.

(2015). Preliminary notes on some EB IVB Painted Simple Ware shards from Ebla. *Studia Eblaitica* 1: 205–209.

(2016). New data from old excavations: preliminary study of the EB IVB pottery from Area H at Tell Mardikh/Ebla, Syria. In *Proceedings of the 9th International Congress on the Archaeology of the Ancient Near East, 9–13 June 2014, University of Basel*. R.A. Stucky, O. Kaelin and H-P. Mathys, eds. 199–216. Wiesbaden: Harrassowitz Verlag.

(2017). Early Bronze IVB at Ebla: stratigraphy, chronology, and material culture of the late early Syrian town and their meaning in the regional context. *Annales Archéologiques Arabes Syriennes* LVII-LVIII: 131–164.

(2018a). The EB-MB transition in the southern Levant: contacts, connectivity and transformations. In *Proceedings of the 10th International Congress on the Archaeology of the Ancient Near East 25-29 April 2016, Vienna, Volume 1*. B. Horejs, C. Schwall, V. Müller, M. Luciani, M. Ritter, M. Guidetti, R.B. Salisbury, F. Höflmayer and T. Bürge, eds. 81–96. Wiesbaden: Harrasowitz Verlag

(2018b). The Early Bronze IVB pottery of Ebla: stratigraphy, chronology, typology, and style. Remarks from a work-in-progress. In *Ebla and beyond: ancient Near Eastern studies after fifty years of discoveries at Tell Mardikh*. P. Matthiae, F. Pinnock and M. D'Andrea, eds. 221–256. Wiesbaden: Harrassowitz Verlag.

(2019). Before the cultural *koinè*. Contextualising interculturality in the 'Greater Levant' during the Late Early Bronze Age and the Early Middle Bronze Age. In *The enigma of the Hyksos volume I. ASOR Conference Boston 2017 – ICAANE Conference Munich 2018 – Collected Papers*. M. Bietak and S. Prell eds. 13–46. Contributions to the archaeology of Egypt, Nubia and the Levant 9. Wiesbaden: Harrassowitz Verlag.

(2020a). Ebla and the south: re-considering inter-regional connections during Early Bronze IV. In *Broadening Horizons 5: civilizations in contact, Volume 1. From the prehistory of upper Mesopotamia to the Bronze Age societies of the Levant*. M. Iamoni, ed. 201–222. West & East, Monografie 2. Trieste: EUT.

(2020b). About stratigraphy, pottery and relative chronology: some considerations for a refinement of the archaeological periodization of the southern Levantine Early Bronze Age IV. In *New horizons in the study of the Early Bronze III and Early Bronze IV in the Levant*. S. Richard, ed. 395–416. Winona Lake: Eisenbrauns.

D'Andrea, M. and Vacca, A. (2015). The northern and southern Levant during the late Early Bronze Age: a reappraisal of the 'Syrian connection'. *Studia Eblaitica* 1: 43–74.

Dever, W.G. (1970). The 'Middle Bronze I' period in Syria-Palestine. In *Near Eastern archaeology in the twentieth century: essays in honor of Nelson Glueck*. J.A. Sanders, ed. 132–163. Garden City-New York: Doubleday.

(1971). The peoples of Palestine in the Middle Bronze I period. *Harvard Theological Review* 64: 197–226.

(1980). New vistas on the EB IV ('MBI') horizon in Syria-Palestine. *Bulletin of the American Schools of Oriental Research* 237: 35–64.

Dunand, M. (1954). *Les fouilles de Byblos II: 1933–1938*. Bibliothèque Archéologique et Historique 2. Paris: Librairie Orientaliste Paul Geuthner.

Échallier, J-C. and Braemer, F. (2004). Le matériel céramique. In *Khirbet al-'Umbashi: villages et campements de pasteurs dans le 'Désert Noir' (Syrie) à l'Âge du Bronze*. F. Braemer, J-C. Échallier and A. Taraqji, eds. 296–335. Bibliothéque Archéologique et Historique T.171. Beyrouth: Institut Français du Proche-Orient.

Eisenberg, E. (1985). A burial cave of the Early Bronze IV (MB I) near 'Enan. *'Atiqot* 17: 59–74. (English Series).

Epstein, C. (1985). Dolmen excavated in the Golan. *'Atiqot* 17: 20–58.

van Ess, M. (2008). First Results of the Archaeological Cleaning of the Deep Trench in the Great Courtyard of the Jupiter Sanctuary. In: *Baalbek/ Heliopolis. Results of Archaeological and Architectural Research 2002–2005: German-Lebanese colloquium, Berlin 2006*, M. van Ess, ed. 99–120. Bulletin d'Archéologie et d'Architecture Libanaises, Hors Série IV. Beirut: Ministère de la Culture, Direction Général des Antiquités.

Fugmann, E. (1958). *Hama: II.1. Fouilles et recherches de la Fondation Carlsberg 1931–1938: L'architecture des périodes pré-Hellénistiques*. Copenhagen: Nationalmuseet.

Garfinkel, Y. (1997). The Middle and Late Bronze Age phases in Area L. In *Hazor V: An Account of the Fifth Season of Excavation, 1968*. A. Ben-Tor and R. Bonfil, eds. 194–217. Jerusalem: Israel Exploration Society.

Genz, H. (2010). Reflections on the Early Bronze Age IV in Lebanon. In *Proceedings of the 6th International Congress on the Archaeology of the Ancient Near East May, 5th–10th 2008, 'Sapienza' – Università di Roma. Volume 2: excavations, surveys and restorations: reports on recent field archaeology in the Near East*. P. Matthiae, F. Pinnock, L. Nigro, N. Marchetti, with the collaboration of L. Romano, eds. 205–217. Wiesbaden: Harrassowitz Verlag.

(2014). Excavations at Tell Fadous-Kfarabida 2004–2011: an Early and Middle Bronze Age site on the Lebanese coast. In *Egypt and the southern Levant in the Early Bronze Age*. F. Höflmayer and R. Eichmann, eds. 69–87. Orient Archäologie, Band 31. Rahden: Verlag Marie Leidorf GmbH.

Genz, H., Badreshany, K. and Jean, M. (forthcoming). A view from the north: Black Wheel-made Ware in Lebanon. In *Transitions, urbanism, and collapse in the Early Bronze Age. Essays in honor of Suzanne Richard*. W.G. Dever and J.C. Long Jr, eds. Sheffield: Equinox

Genz, H., Daniel, R., Damick, A., Ahrens, A., el-Zaatari, S., Höflmayer, F., Kutschera, W. and Wild, E.M. (2010). Excavations at Tell Fadous-Kfarabida: preliminary report on the 2010 excavation season. *Bulletin d'Archéologie et d'Architecture Libanaises* 14: 241–274.

Getzov, N. (1995). Tombs of the Early and Intermediate Bronze Age in western Galilee. *'Atiqot* 27: 1*–18* (Hebrew Series), 211 (English Series).

Gitin, S. (1975). Middle Bronze I 'domestic pottery' at Jebel Qa'aqir: a ceramic inventory of cave G23. *Eretz Israel* 12: 46–62.

Greenberg, R. (2002). *Early urbanizations in the Levant: a regional narrative*. New approaches to anthropological archaeology. London: Leicester University Press.

(2017). No collapse: transmutations of Early Bronze Age urbanism in the southern Levant. In *The late third millennium in the ancient Near East: chronology, C14, and climate change*. Oriental Institute Seminars 11. F. Höflmayer, ed. 31–58. Chicago: The University of Chicago Press.

(2019). *The archaeology of the Bronze Age Levant. From urban origins to the demise of city-states, 3700–1000 BCE*. Cambridge: Cambridge University Press.

Greenberg, R., Horowitz, L.K., Lernau, O., Mienis, H.K., Khalaily, H. and Marder, O. (1998). A sounding at Tel Na'ama in the Hula valley. *'Atiqot* 35: 9–35.

Guy, P.L.O. (1938). *Megiddo tombs*. Oriental Institute Publications 33. Chicago: Oriental Institute of Chicago Press.

Helms, S. (1986). Excavations at Tell Umm Hammad, 1984. *Levant* 18: 25–49.

Höflmayer, F. (2014a). Dating catastrophes and collapses in the ancient Near East: the end of the first urbanization in the southern Levant and the 4.2 ka BP Event. In *Overcoming catastrophes: essays on disastrous agents characterization and resilience strategies in pre-classical southern Levant*. L. Nigro, ed. 117–140. Rome La Sapienza, Studies on the archaeology of Palestine and Transjordan 11. Rome: «La Sapienza» Expedition to Palestine and Transjordan.

(2014b). Egypt and the southern Levant in the late Early Bronze Age. In *Egypt and the southern Levant in the Early Bronze Age*. F. Höflmayer and R. Eichmann, eds. 135–141. Orient Archäologie, Band 31. Rahden: Verlag Marie Leidorf GmbH.

(2017). Introduction: the late third millennium BC in the ancient Near East and eastern Mediterranean. In *The late third millennium in the ancient Near East: chronology, C14, and climate change*. F. Höflmayer, ed. 1–29. Oriental Institute Seminars 11. Chicago: The University of Chicago Press.

Ingholt, H. (1934). *Rapport préliminaire sur sept campagnes de fouilles de Hama en Syrie (1932-1938)*. Archæologisk-kunsthistoriske Meddelelser I,3. København: Gyldendal.

Kaufman, B. (2013). Copper alloys from the 'Enot Shuni cemetery and the origins of bronze metallurgy in the EB IV-MB II Levant. *Archaeometry* 55(4): 663–690.

Kennedy, M.A. (2015). *The late third millennium BCE in the upper Orontes valley, Syria: ceramics, chronology and cultural connections*. ANES Supplementary Series 46. Leuven: Peeters.

(2016). The end of the 3rd millennium BC in the Levant: new perspectives and old ideas. *Levant* 48(1): 1–32.

(2019). A new EB IV cultural province in central and southern Syria: the view from Tell Nebi Mend. In *Pearls of the past. Studies on Near Eastern art and archaeology in honour of Frances Pinnock*. M. D'Andrea, M.G. Micale, D. Nadali, S. Pizzimenti and A. Vacca, eds. 429–448. Marru 8. Münster: Zaphon.

(2020). Horizons of cultural connectivity: north–south interactions and interconnections during the Early Bronze Age IV. In *New horizons in the study of the Early Bronze III and Early Bronze IV in the Levant*. S. Richard, ed. 327–346. University Park, PA: Eisenbrauns.

Kennedy, M.A., Badreshany, K. and Philip, G. (2018). Drinking on the periphery: the Tell Nebi Mend goblets in their regional and archaeometric context. *Levant*, doi: 10.1080/00758914.2018.

Kenyon, K.M. (1966). *Amorites and Canaanites*. The Schweich Lectures, 1963. London: Oxford University Press.

Köhler, E.C. and Thalmann, J-P. (2014). Synchronising early Egyptian chronologies and the northern Levant. In *Egypt and the southern Levant in the Early Bronze Age*. F. Höflmayer and R. Eichmann, eds. 181–206. Orient Archäologie Band 31. Rahden: Verlag Marie Leidorf GmbH.

Klengel, H. (1985). City and land of Damascus in the Cuneiform tradition. *Annales Archéologiques Arabes Syriennes* XXXV: 49–57.

Lazzarini, L. and Colombo, C. (1995). An archaeometric study of Bronze-Age pottery from Ebla-Syria. In *Estudios sobre ceràmica Antiga. Actes del simposi sobre ceràmica Antiga*. M. Vendrell-Saz, ed. 17–22. Barcelona: Barcelona Generalitat de Catalunya.

Maeir, A.M., with a contribution by Marcus, E. (2010). *'In the Midst of the Jordan.' The Jordan valley during the Middle Bronze Age (circa 2000–1500 BCE): archaeological and historical correlates*. Vienna: Österreichischen Akademie der Wissenschaften.

Mansfeld, G. (1970). Ein Bronzezeitliches steinkammergrab die Rafid im Wadi at-Taym. In *Bericht über die ergebnisse der ausgrabungen in Kamid el-Loz (Libanon) in den Jahren 1966 und 1967*. R. Hachmann, ed. 117–128. Bonn: Rudolf Habelt.

Marcus, E. (2003). Dating the early Middle Bronze Age in the southern Levant: a preliminary comparison of radiocarbon and archaeo-historical synchronizations. In *The synchronisation of civilisations in the eastern Mediterranean in the second millennium B.C. II. Proceedings of the SCIEM 2000-Euro conference Haindorf, 2nd–7th of May 2001*. M. Bietak, ed. 95–110. Contributions to the chronology of the eastern Mediterranean 4/Denkschriften der Gesamtakademie Band 19. Vienna: Österreichischen Akademie der Wissenschaften.

(2010). Appendix B: radiometric dates from the Middle Bronze Age Jordan valley. In *'In the Midst of the Jordan.' The Jordan valley during the Middle Bronze Age (circa 2000–1500 BCE): archaeological and historical correlates*, by A. Maeir. 243–252. Vienna: Österreichischen Akademie der Wissenschaften.

(2013). Correlating and combining Egyptian historical and southern Levantine radiocarbon chronologies at Middle Bronze Age IIa Tel Ifshar. In *Radiocarbon and the chronologies of Ancient Egypt*. A.J. Shortland and C. Bronk Ramsey, ed. 182–208. Oxford: Oxbow.

Marfoe, L. (1998). *Kamid el-Loz 14. The prehistoric and early historic context of the site: catalogue and commentary*. Saarbrücker Beiträge zur Altertumskunde. Band 41. Bonn: Dr. Rudolf Habelt GMBH.

Maritan, L., Mazzoli, C., Michielin, N., Morandi Bonacossi, D., Luciani, M. and Molin, G. (2005). The provenance and production technology of Bronze Age and Iron Age pottery from Tell Mishrifeh/Qatna, Syria. *Archaeometry* 47(4): 723–744.

Mathias, V.T. (2000). The Early Bronze Age pottery of Tell Nebi Mend in its regional setting. In *Ceramics and change in the Early Bronze Age of the southern Levant*. G. Philip and D. Baird, eds. 411–427. Sheffield: Sheffield Academic Press.

Mazzoni, S. (1982). La produzione ceramica del Palazzo G di Ebla e la sua posizione storica nell'orizzonte siro-mesopotamico del III millennio A.C. *Studi Eblaiti* V: 144–199.

(1985a). Elements of the ceramic culture of early Syrian Ebla in comparison with Syro-Palestinian EB IV. *Bulletin of the American Schools of Oriental Research* 257: 1–18.

(1985b). Frontières céramique et le haute Euphrate au Bronze Ancien IV. In *Mari: Annales de Recherches Interdisciplinaires 4. Actes du Colloque International du C.N.R.S. 620. À propos d'un cinquantenaire: Mari, Bilan et Perspectives*. 561–577. Paris: ERC.

(2002). The ancient Bronze Age pottery tradition in north-western central Syria. In *Céramique de l'Âge du Bronze en Syrie, I: La Syrie du sud et le vallée de l'Oronte*. M. Al-Maqdissi, V.

Matoïan and C. Nicolle, eds. 69–96. Bibliothéque Archéologique et Historique T.161. Beyrouth: Institut Français du Proche-Orient.

du Mesnil du Buisson, R. (1930). Compte rendu de la quatrième campagne de fouilles à Mishrifé-Qatna. *Syria* I: 146–163.

(1932). Une campagne de fouilles à Khan Sheikhoun. *Syria* XIII: 171–188, pl. LI.

(1935). Souran et Tell Masin. *Berytus* 2: 121–134.

Morandi Bonacossi, D. (2009). Tell Mishrifeh and its region during the EBA IV and the EBA-MBA transition. A first assessment. In *The Levant in transition. Proceedings of a conference held at the British Museum on 20–21 April 2004*. P.J. Parr, ed. 56–68. PEF Annuals IX. Leeds: Maney.

Morandi Bonacossi, D., Luciani, M., Barro, A., Canci, A., Cremaschi, M., Da Ros, M., Eidem, J., Finzi Contini, I., Iamoni, M., Intilia, A., Trombino, L., Sala, A. and Valsecchi, V. (2008). Tell Mishrifeh/Qatna 1999–2002: a preliminary report of the Italian component of the joint Syrian-Italian-German project. *Akkadica* 124: 97–118.

Mouamar, G. (2016). Tell Sha'īrat: une ville circulaire majeure du IIIe millénaire av. J-C. du territoire de la confédération des *Ib'al. Studia Eblaitica* 2: 71–101.

(2017a). De nouvelles données sur les gobelets de Hama: marqueurs de la chronologie et des échanges de Syrie centrale pendant la seconde moitié du 3e millénaire avant J-C. *Paléorient* 43(2): 69–89.

(2017b). Tell Ṣabḥ ah: a large circular city of the 3rd millennium BC in the Syrian steppe (Shamiya). *Studia Eblaitica* 3: 182–189.

(2018). The Early Bronze IVB Painted Simple Ware from Tell Sh'airāt: an integrated archaeometric approach. *Levant*, doi:10.1080/00758914.2018.1477295.

Nigro, L. (2003). Tell es-Sultan in the Early Bronze Age IV (2300–2000 BC). Settlement vs necropolis – a stratigraphic periodization. *Contributi e Materiali di Archeologia Orientale* IX: 121–158.

Palumbo, G. (1990). *The Early Bronze Age IV in the southern Levant. Settlement patterns, economy and material culture of a 'Dark Age'*. Contributi e Materiali di Archeologia Orientale III, Roma: Università di Roma 'La Sapienza'.

Philip, G. and Bradbury, J. (2010). Pre-Classical activity in the basalt landscape of the Homs region, Syria: implications for the development of 'sub-optimal' zones in the Levant during the Chalcolithic-Early Bronze Age. *Levant* 42(2): 136–169.

Pitard, W.T. (1987). *Ancient Damascus: a historical study of the Syrian city-state from the earliest time until its fall to the Assyrians in 732 B.C.E.* Winona Lake: Eisenbrauns.

Prag, K. (1974). The Intermediate Early Bronze-Middle Bronze Age: an interpretation of the evidence from Transjordan, Syria and Lebanon. *Levant* 6: 69–116.

(2009). The late third millennium in the Levant: a reappraisal of the north-south divide. In *The Levant in transition: Proceeding of a conference held at the British Museum on 20–21 April 2004*. P.J. Parr, ed. 80–89. PEF Annual IX. Leeds: Maney Publishing.

(2011). The domestic unit at Tall Iktanu: its derivations and functions. In *Daily life, materiality and complexity in early urban communities of the southern Levant: papers in honor of Walter E. Rast and R. Thomas Schaub*. M. Chesson, W. Aufrecht and I. Kuijt, eds. 55–76. Winona Lake: Eisenbrauns.

(2014). The southern Levant during the Intermediate Bronze Age. In *The Oxford handbook of the archaeology of the Levant*. M.L. Steiner and A.E. Killebrew, eds. 388–400. Oxford: Oxford University Press.

Regev, J., de Miroschedji, P., Greenberg, R., Braun, E., Greenhut, Z. and Boaretto, E. (2012). Chronology of the Early Bronze Age in the southern Levant: new analysis for a high chronology. *Radiocarbon* 54(3–4): 525–66.

Regev, J., Finkelstein, I., Adams, M.J. and Boaretto, E. (2014). Wiggle-matched 14C chronology of Early Bronze Megiddo and the synchronization of Egyptian and Levantine chronologies. *Ägypten und Levante/Egypt and the Levant* 24: 243–66.

Richard, S. (1980). Toward a consensus of opinion on the end of the Early Bronze Age in Palestine-Transjordan. *Bulletin of the American Schools of Oriental Research* 237: 5–34.

(1987). The Early Bronze Age in Palestine: the rise and collapse of urbanism. *Biblical Archaeologist* 50: 22–43.

(2010). Chapter 4: the Area C Early Bronze IV ceramic assemblage. In *Khirbet Iskander: final report on the Early Bronze Age C 'gateways' and cemeteries*. S. Richard, J.C. Long Jr, P.S. Holdorf and G. Peterman, eds. 69–111. American Schools of Oriental Research Archaeological Reports 14. Boston: American Schools of Oriental Research.

Richard, S. and D'Andrea, M. (2016). A Syrian goblet at Khirbat Iskandar, Jordan: a study of interconnectivity in the EB III/IV Period. *Studies on the history and archaeology of Jordan* XII: Transparent Borders. 561–586. Amman: Department of Antiquities Jordan.

Saghieh, M. (1983). *Byblos in the third millennium: a reconstruction of the stratigraphy and a study of the cultural connections*. Warminster: Aris & Phillips.

Schloen, D. (2017). In *The late third millennium in the ancient Near East: chronology, C14, and climate change*. Economic and political implications of raising the date for the disappearance of walled towns in the southern Levant. F. Höflmayer, ed. 59–71. Oriental Institute Seminars 11. Chicago: The University of Chicago.

Schwartz, G.M., Curvers, H.H., Dunham, S.S., Stuart, B. and Weber, J.A. (2006). A third-millennium B.C. elite mortuary complex at Umm El-Marra, Syria: 2002 and 2004 excavations. *American Journal of Archaeology* 110(4): 603–641.

Singer, I. and Dar, S. (1986). Middle Bronze I tombs at Hanita. In *The western Galilee antiquities*. M. Yedaya, ed. 49–65. Tel Aviv: Israel Antiquities Authority. (Hebrew).

Smithline, H. (2002). An Intermediate Bronze Age site at Horbat Qjshron. In *Eretz Zafon. studies in Galilean archaeology*. Z. Gal, ed. 21*–46*. Jerusalem: Israel Antiquities Authority.

Tadmor, M. (1978). A cult cave of the Middle Bronze Age I near Qedesh. *Israel Exploration Journal* 28: 1–30.

Tallon, M. (1964). Les monuments mégalithiques de Mengez. *Bulletin du Musée du Beyrouth* 13: 7–19.

Thalmann, J-P. (2006). *Tell Arqa - I: les niveaux de l'Âge du Bronze*. 3 vols. Bibliothéque Archéologique et Historique T.177. Beyrouth: Institut Français du Proche-Orient.

(2008). Tell Arqa et Byblos: essai de correlation. In *The Bronze Age in Lebanon: studies in the archaeology and chronology of Lebanon, Syria and Egypt*. M. Bietak and E. Czerny, eds. 61–78. Vienna: Österreichischen Akademie der Wissenschaften.

(2009). The Early Bronze Age: foreign relations in the light of recent excavations at Tell Arqa. In *Interconnections in the eastern Mediterranean: Lebanon in the Bronze and Iron Ages*.

Proceedings of the International Symposium Beirut 2008. C. Doumet-Serhal, ed. 15–28. Bulletin d'Archéologie et d'Histoire Libanaise Hors-Série VI. Beirut: Ministère de la Culture, Direction Général des Antiquités.

(2010). Tell Arqa: a prosperous city in the Bronze Age. *Near Eastern Archaeology* 73(2–3): 86–101.

Thalmann, J-P. and Roux, V. (2016). Évolution technologique et morpho-stylistique des assemblages céramiques de Tell Arqa (Liban, 3e millénaire av. J.-C.): stabilité sociologique et changements culturels. *Paléorient* 42(1): 95–121.

Vacca, A. (2014). Chronology and distribution of 3rd millennium BC flasks. In 'Šime ummiănka'. *Ascoltate l'ammaestramento. Scritti in onore del 75° compleanno di Paolo Matthiae da parte dei suoi allievi più giovani*. L. Romano and S. Pizzimenti, ed. 251–285. Contributi e Materiali di Archeologia Orientale XVI. Roma: Sapienza Università di Roma.

(2015). Before the Royal Palace G. The stratigraphic and pottery sequence of the west unit of the Central Complex: The Building G5. *Studia Eblaitica* 1: 1–32.

Vacca A., Mouamar, G., D'Andrea M. and Lumsden, S. (2018). A fresh look at Hama in an inter-regional context. New data from Phase J materials in the National Museum of Denmark. *Studia Eblaitica* 4: 17–58.

Vacca, A. and D'Andrea, M. (2020). The connections between the northern and southern Levant during EB III: re-evaluations and new vistas in the light of new data and higher chronologies. In *New horizons in the study of the Early Bronze III and Early Bronze IV in the Levant*. S. Richard, ed. 120–145. University Park, PA: Eisenbrauns.de.

de Vaux, R. (1946). Les Patriarches Hébreux et les découvertes modernes, I. *Revue Biblique* 53: 321–348.

Welton, L. and Cooper, L. (2014). Caliciform Ware. In *Associated regional chronologies for the ancient Near East and the eastern Mediterranean: interregional I. Ceramics*. M. Lebeau, ed. 325–354. Turnhout: Brepols.

Wilkinson, T.J., Philip, G., Bradbury, J., Dunford, R., Donoghue, D., Galiaststos, N., Lawrence, D., Ricci, A. and Smith, S.L. (2014). Contextualizing early urbanization: settlement cores, early states and agro-pastoral strategies in the Fertile Crescent during the fourth and third millennia BC. *Journal of World Prehistory* 27: 43–109.

Wright, G.E. (1938). The chronology of Palestinian pottery in Middle Bronze I. *Bulletin of the American Schools of Oriental Research* 71: 27–34.

Yadin, Y., Aharoni, A., Dunayevski, E., Dothan, T., Amiran, R. and Parrot, J. (1961). *Hazor III-IV: an account of the third and fourth season of excavation, 1957–1958*. Jerusalem: Israel Exploration Society.

5

Militarisation and the changing socio-political landscape of the northern Levant in the Early Bronze Age IVB

Melissa A. Kennedy
University of Western Australia

Scholars have argued that the overt beginnings of militarisation in the northern Levant can be traced back to the second millennium BC, specifically the early Middle Bronze Age.[1] This has variously been attributed to the development of complex, competing city-states, the rise of the so-called 'Amorite' kingdoms and a possible deterioration in the relationship between the 'desert' and the 'sown'.[2] However, analysis of the socio-economic and political landscape of the Orontes river valley and the surrounding regions during the final centuries of the third millennium BC (ca. 2300–2000 BC) suggests that this phenomenon can in fact be dated much earlier, to the EB IVB period, with the northern Levant distinguished by an increasingly militarised and fragmented political landscape.

At present, the Eblaite sequence, specifically Palace G and its associated cultural horizon, defines much of our archaeological and historical understanding of the EB

---

1   McLaren 2004; Burke 2008; Rey 2012.
2   Akkermans and Schwartz 2003, 297–306; Cooper 2006a, 35–36; Nichols and Webber 2006, 53–56.

IV period.³ This emphasis on the socio-political landscape of the early EB IV (EB IVA) has resulted in the EB IVB being largely ignored, a situation that is only now being addressed.⁴ Analysis of the extant evidence for western inland Syria suggests that not only were there significant changes in material culture throughout the EB IVB, but that the region's social and political landscape underwent significant transformation.⁵ This episode appears to have been marked by the apparent normalisation of militarisation: evidenced by the construction and/or enlargement of local settlement fortification systems. This phase of increased fortification activity may be associated with the destruction of Palace G, reflecting a sharp decline in Eblaite regional power and hegemony at the end of the third millennium BC.

The evidence for militarisation in the Early Bronze Age

Unfortunately, discussions of EB IV militarisation are complicated by several factors. Firstly, in contrast to the southern Levant, northern Levantine EBA defensive systems have rarely been explored either intensively or extensively.⁶ Secondly, when they have been identified they are frequently obscured or truncated by their later MBA counterparts.⁷ This phenomenon is observable throughout the Orontes river valley and in its hinterland, at sites such as Tell Tuqan,⁸ Ebla,⁹ Tell 'Acharneh¹⁰ and Qatna.¹¹

However, before EB IVB militarisation can be discussed, it is important to understand the earlier phases of urbanism and fortification activity in the region, as these developments are key to understanding this later phenomenon. It can also be argued that the initial appearance, decline, and subsequent re-emergence of fortification systems during the EBA mirrors the development of the Syrian Early Bronze Age urban experience.

Urbanism and fortification in the Syrian Early Bronze Age

Unfortunately, at present our understanding of the early EBA (EB I–III) in western inland Syria is limited, with archaeological evidence for these periods gleaned from a

---

3 Matthiae 1989; 2013, 49–50; Mazzoni 2002; 2013; Cooper 2006b, 63–66; 2010, 88; Matthiae and Marchetti (eds) 2013; Archi 2015; Biga 2015, 181–184.
4 Mazzoni 2013; Barge et al. 2014; Welton 2014; Kennedy 2015; 2016.
5 Cooper 2006b, 264–265; Matthiae 2009, 43–47; Peltenburg 2013, 250–251; Peyronel 2014, 123; Wilkinson et al. 2014; Kennedy 2016.
6 Matthiae 2001; Burke 2008; Rey 2012; Baffi 2013.
7 Burke 2008, 186–227; Cooper 2010, 90–91; Rey 2012, 90–95.
8 Baffi and Peyronel 2013, 198.
9 Matthiae 2000, 580–581.
10 Cooper 2006c, 150.
11 Morandi Bonacossi 2007, 72.

5 Militarisation and the changing socio-political landscape of the northern Levant in the Early Bronze Age IVB

few select sites, such as Tell Tayinat,[12] Ebla,[13] Tell Tuqan,[14] Hama[15] and Tell Nebi Mend.[16] This has complicated discussions of urban development in the region. However, on the basis of the extant evidence it would appear that the northern Levant was distinguished by a number of divergent trajectories or paths towards urban development. These trajectories or paths appear to have been influenced by a combination of both internal and external factors, such as geographic location, population density and trade.

Paolo Matthiae has divided western inland Syria's process of urbanisation into three stages.[17] The first stage equates to the local EB I–II and was distinguished by increases in settlement size and density.[18] The second stage equates to the EB III and the first major phase of urbanism.[19] Matthiae asserts that urbanism arose out the changing social and political realities of the region, with new mechanisms needed to regulate inter-site competition and the increased demand for raw materials.[20] Finally, stage three correlates with the EB IV and represents the mature phase of the urban process, with this period characterised by an exponential growth in settlement size and density, as well as an increase in hinterland site numbers.[21]

Stage 1 in the fortification process: the Late Chalcolithic to the EB II

The appearance of fortification systems in western inland Syria corresponds to Matthiae's description of this urban developmental trend. Like Matthiae's Stage 1,[22] the first phase of fortification activity can be dated within the Late Chalcolithic through to the EB II, and is aligned with the very beginnings of the urban phenomenon in the region. Fortifications dating to this phase (Late Chalcolithic/EB I/Phases 1 and 2/EME 2–3 on the Euphrates) have been identified mainly on the Euphrates and in the Jezireh,[23] as well as in isolated instances in the Orontes corridor and its hinterland (Figure 5.1). The best-preserved examples come from Tell Abou Danne on the Jabbul plain,[24] Habuba

---

12 Braidwood and Braidwood 1960.
13 Vacca 2015.
14 Vacca 2014.
15 Fugmann 1958; Thuesen 1988.
16 Kennedy 2015.
17 Matthiae 1993, 524–525.
18 Matthiae 1993, 524.
19 Matthiae 1993, 525.
20 Matthiae 1993, 526.
21 Matthiae 1993, 526; see Bartl and Al-Maqdissi 2014; Philip and Newson 2014.
22 Matthiae 1993, 528.
23 Novák 2015, 54–55.
24 Tefnin 1980, 184.

Kabira South,[25] Habuba Kabira North,[26] and Halawa on the Euphrates,[27] Tell Afis on the Jazr plain,[28] and potentially Tell Nebi Mend in the upper Orontes valley.

Tell Abou Danne is located approximately 25 km east of Aleppo on the Jabbul plain.[29] Excavated between 1975–83 by Roland Tefnin, the site has revealed an occupational sequence spanning the EB I–II, Middle Bronze Age, Late Bronze Age and Iron Age I–II as well as the Achaemenid, Hellenistic and Early Roman periods.[30] Niveaux VII (EB I–II) revealed the remains of a mudbrick wall, preserved in places to a height of 7.5 m. Associated with this horizon were ceramic types analogous to Hama K10–K5 and 'Amuq Phases F–G, with Chaff-Faced and Painted Wares predominating.[31] Further to the east, at Habuba Kabira South, a 10-ha walled settlement, dating to the Late Chalcolithic 5 (ca. 3400–3000 BC) has been identified.[32] At Habuba Kabira North on the west bank of the Euphrates, excavations of the earliest EBA horizons (Strata 2 and 3) on the south-eastern side of the settlement, fronting the Euphrates, have revealed a series of interconnected domestic complexes that utilised their exterior walls to form a larger perimeter wall.[33]

To the south, excavations at Halawa Tell B have revealed that the early EBA settlement (Level 1–2) was surrounded by a 2–3 m thick casemate wall.[34] This structure underwent numerous phases of strengthening and repair, including the addition of external buttresses.[35]

In western inland Syria, at present only two sites have revealed concrete evidence for fortification during this early phase, the best-known example of which is Tell Afis.[36] Located 15 km east of Ebla on the Jazr plain, excavations at the site have revealed an occupational sequence spanning from the Late Chalcolithic through to the Iron Age.[37] During the course of excavations in Area E, a large fortification wall (M.1155) dating to the Late Chalcolithic (Level 18) was identified.[38] This structure was excavated to a length of 9 m and was preserved to a height of 3 m. It was fashioned from large un-worked fieldstones and was lined with friable grey clay.[39] In section, at least two

---

25 Strommenger 1980.
26 Heusch 1980, 161.
27 Orthmann 1989, 85–86.
28 Giannessi 1998, 102.
29 Tefnin 1980, 184.
30 Tefnin 1980, 191–193.
31 Tefnin 1980, figs 22–23; Braidwood and Braidwood 1960, 232–241, 287; Thuesen 1988, 181–185.
32 Strommenger 1980.
33 Heusch 1980, 161.
34 Orthmann 1989, 87–88.
35 Orthmann 1989, 87–88.
36 Giannessi 199, 102.
37 Mazzoni 1998, 10–11.
38 Giannessi 1998, 102.
39 Giannessi 1998, 102.

5 Militarisation and the changing socio-political landscape of the northern Levant in the Early Bronze Age IVB

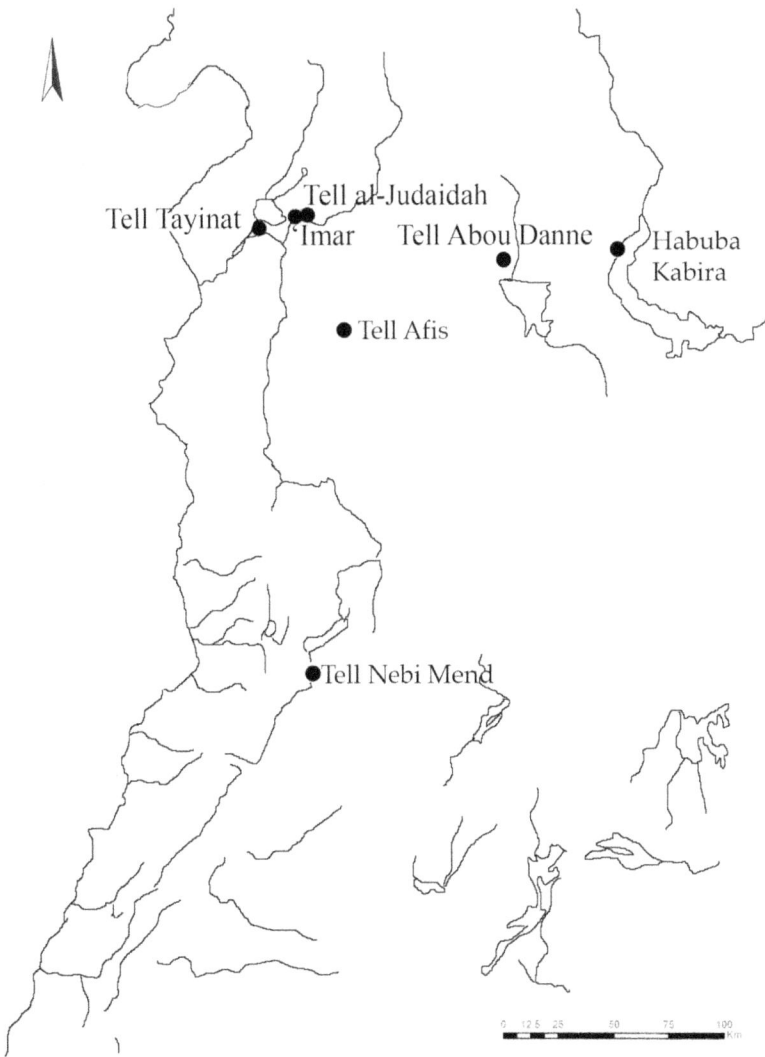

Figure 5.1: Early fortifications in the northern Levant and the Euphrates.

phases of construction are discernible.[40] Giannessi views the construction of this circuit wall as part of the wider Levantine phenomenon of monumentalising architecture and early urban development, with the best parallels for this structure found in the southern Levant, at the site of Jawa.[41]

Another possible fortification has been tentatively identified further south at the site of Tell Nebi Mend. Tell Nebi Mend is a 10 ha site located in the upper Orontes

---

40 Giannessi 1998, fig. 1.
41 Giannessi 1998, 105.

valley on the south-eastern end of the Homs-Tripoli Gap.[42] At present, early EBA (EB I–II) strata have only been identified in Trench VIII, which, due to its position on the north-eastern extremity of the site, suffered extensively from MBA pitting, erosion and deflation.[43] Despite these stratigraphic difficulties, a large north–south running feature or structure has been identified in what is currently known as the 'Yellow-Clay Phase' (Phase 13). This phase was marked by significant changes in settlement plan and orientation, and was distinguished by thick deposits of yellow clay (decayed mudbrick?) in places more than 1.00 m to 1.40 m thick. This deposit is reinforced by two parallels lines of fieldstone facing (Figure 5.2).[44] Although much uncertainty remains, this 'deposit' may in fact represent the eroded foundational materials of a large mudbrick circuit wall. This assertion is supported by the depositional make-up of this feature and the structural reinforcements of the fieldstone facing. On the basis of radiocarbon determinations, this horizon and structure dates to between 3200–3000 cal. BC.[45] If this feature were in fact a defensive structure it would make it one of the earliest extant fortification systems in the northern Levant, and contemporary with the first phase of fortification activity in the southern Levant, potentially suggesting a much earlier and wider urban phenomenon across the region.[46]

Excavations in the 'Amuq valley of the lower Orontes have also revealed evidence for early fortifications, potentially dating to Phases G and H of the 'Amuq sequence. Possible early fortifications have been identified at 'Imar, Chatal Höyuk, Tell Tayinat and Tell al-Judaidah.[47] However, the bulk of these constructions have not been explored in detail, with most identified during the course of rescue excavations associated with bulldozer cuts;[48] as such, the form and date of these structures cannot as yet be discussed in more detail.

It can be argued that the appearance of early fortification systems in both the Orontes corridor and its hinterland, as well as along the Euphrates, can be linked to nascent urbanism, which was characterised by increased settlement density and occupational intensification.[49] As settlements began to prosper and surpluses increased, new mechanisms of control were developed to stabilise and regularise the collective status quo.[50] This further entrenched the region's burgeoning social stratification and the socio-political domination of the region's major geo-political entities, such as Ebla and Mari.[51] A similar developmental trajectory has been recognised in the southern

---

42 Parr 1983, 101; Kennedy 2015, 38.
43 Kennedy 2015, 39–40.
44 Campbell 2012, 9.
45 Campbell 2012, 47.
46 Gibbins 2001; Bourke 2014, 5–6.
47 Yener et al. 1996, 67–68; Yener et al. 2000, 183–184.
48 Yener et al. 1996, 67; Yener et al. 2000, 192.
49 Esse 1989; Joffe 1993.
50 Matthiae 1993, 524; Cooper 2010, 90–91.
51 Akkermans and Schwartz 2003, 231; Cooper 2006b, 127; Lebeau 2011, 367–369; Rey 2012, 21–28; Peltenburg 2013, 243.

5 Militarisation and the changing socio-political landscape of the northern Levant in the Early Bronze Age IVB

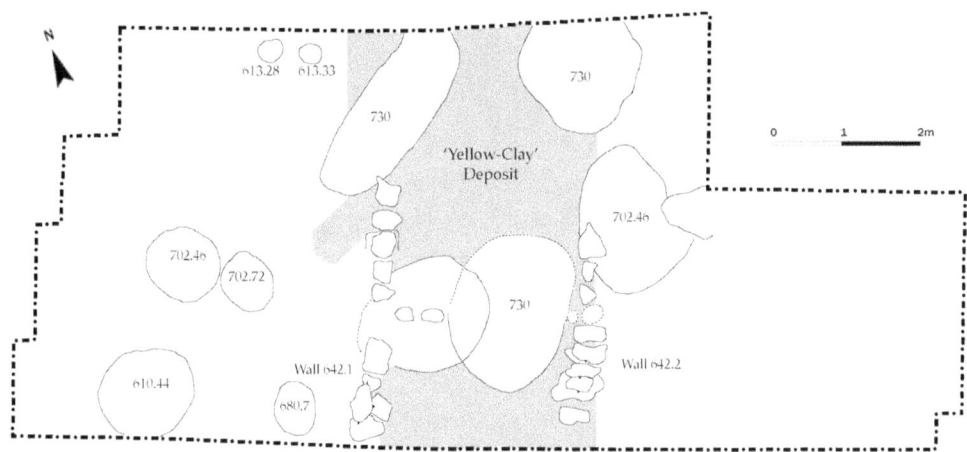

Figure 5.2: Possible early fortification from Tell Nebi Mend.

Levantine EB I–II, where the earliest fortifications dating to the EB IA–IB, such as those of Jawa,[52] Pella[53] and Beth Yerah,[54] have been cited as evidence for a developing urban landscape of increased centralisation and growing regional power.[55]

Stage 2 in the fortification process: the EB III–EB IVA

Stage 2 in this process of fortification and urbanisation correlates to the EB III and the early EB IV,[56] arguably the height of third millennium BC urbanism in western inland Syria, the Euphrates and the Jezireh (Figure 5.3).[57] This stage is characterised by a monumentalising tendency in civic architecture (secular, sacred and military), with several fortification systems, such as those of Habuba Kabira, significantly expanded during this period, with the circuit wall of the site almost doubling in size and width from 2.5 m to nearly 5 m.[58] This stage/period also witnessed for the first time the fortification of a number of key sites on the Lebanese coast,[59] the Jabbul plain,[60] and in

---

52 Helms 1991a, 12; Helms 1991b, 30–36.
53 Gibbins 2001, 90–93; Bourke 2014, 3–4.
54 Greenberg et al. 2012, 91, fig. 5.
55 Joffe 1993; Philip 2001, 163–168; Chesson and Philip 2003.
56 Early Northern Levant 3–5; Early Middle Euphrates 3–4; Early Jezireh 2–4.
57 Matthiae 1993, 524–525; Akkermans and Schwartz 2003, 235.
58 Heusch 1980, 166, 174.
59 Lauffray 2008, 289; fig. 154; Genz 2014, 70–71; Genz et al. 2016, 86–88; Genz et al. 2018, 55–59.
60 Schwartz et al. 2000, 426.

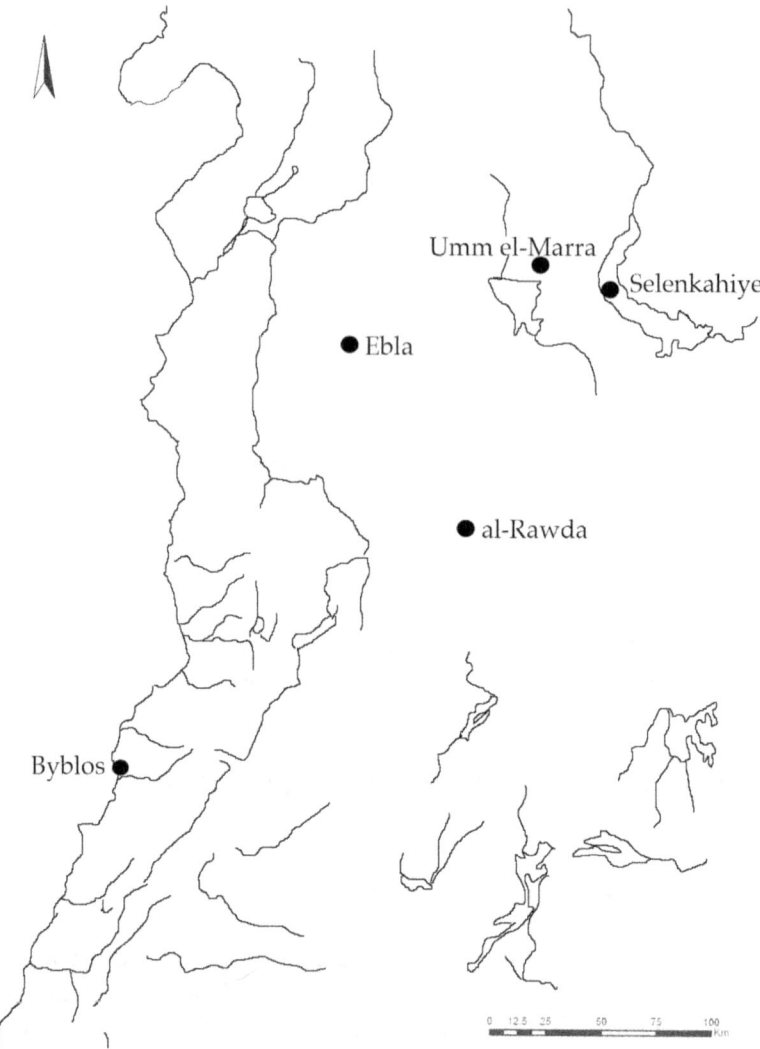

Figure 5.3: EB III-IVA fortifications in the northern Levant and Euphrates.

the Jezireh.⁶¹ Fortifications dating to this horizon have also been identified in 'Amuq valley/lower Orontes (Phase H).⁶²

In terms of architectural development, on the coast (Lebanon), this stage (EB III–IV) marks the first phase of monumental stone architecture.⁶³ Byblos is best illustrative of this phenomenon, with Dunand's excavations revealing a large stone fortification system, complete with square buttresses (3–4 m wide), a rampart and elaborate direct-axis

---

61   Pfälzner 2011, 138–145.
62   Yener et al. 1996, 67–68; Yener et al. 2000, 183–184.
63   Sagieh 1983, 130–131; Lauffray 2008, 289.

5 Militarisation and the changing socio-political landscape of the northern Levant in the Early Bronze Age IVB

gateways.[64] Excavations at Fadous-Kfarabida (Phases III–IV) also suggest that the site was fortified during this period. In Area I, a north-west to south-east fortification wall running parallel to the southern edge of the site was identified. This wall was associated with a large staircase which is believed to access one of the gateways of the fortification.[65] This structure has parallels with the *port nord-ouest* and the *porte nord-east* at Byblos.[66] Further evidence for this fortification system has also been identified in Area IV,[67] with the ceramic evidence potentially suggesting a somewhat earlier construction date, perhaps to the EB II–III (Phase II).[68]

To the east, mudbrick fortifications continued to dominate the military landscape of the Orontes,[69] Euphrates[70] and the Jezireh.[71] At Ebla beneath the later Middle Bronze Age fortifications in Area AA and Area V, the remains of a large mudbrick wall up to 6 m thick were identified.[72] Analysis of these bricks suggests they were identical in size and shape to those of Palace G, suggesting that these two structures were broadly contemporaneous.[73] Further to the east, excavations at Umm el-Marra on the Jabbul plain have revealed that during the EB IVA a large earthen rampart, as well as a glacis and a series of mudbrick revetments, surrounded the site.[74] Likewise, in the Jezireh, excavations at Tell Chuera have revealed that a large mudbrick fortification and a 15 m wide fosse encircled the site during this period.[75]

The EB IVA (Stage 2 in fortification development) is not only distinguished by an increase in the number and scale of defensive systems, but it also appears to have witnessed the birth of the symbolic frontier, *Très Long Mur* (TLM).[76] Located in the arid margins of the Syrian Shamiyeh, this structure may represent the first attempt to delineate an extended frontier or the boundary of a nascent regional polity or territory.[77] Surveys of this region have revealed that the wall measured approximately 220 km in length, running north–south in a roughly irregular arc from the Jabal 'Ubaysan in the north, past the Homs-Damascus Road in the south, and into the slopes of the Anti-Lebanon mountain range.[78] This dry stone-wall ranged in width from 0.90 to 1.1 m,

---

64 Saghieh 1983, 84; Lauffray 2008, 291–296, figs 155–158.
65 Genz 2014, 70.
66 Genz 2014, 71.
67 Genz et al. 2016, 86.
68 Genz et al. 2016, 88.
69 Matthiae 2000, 580–581.
70 Novák 2015, 55–61.
71 Pfälzner 2011, 143–144; Rey 2012, 21–29.
72 Matthiae 1998, 572–574; 2000, 580–581; 2009, 53; Pinnock 2009, 69.
73 Matthiae 2000, 580–581; Burke 2008.
74 Schwartz et al. 2000, 426.
75 Pfälzner 2011, 142–143.
76 Geyer 2002; Geyer et al. 2007; Geyer et al. 2010.
77 Geyer et al. 2007, 278–280.
78 Geyer et al. 2007, 278; Geyer et al. 2010, 62.

precluding its use as a defensive structure.[79] Instead, it has been interpreted as a symbolic frontier, marking the boundary between the 'desert' and the 'sown'.[80] However, the chronology and phasing of this imposing feature has been the subject of much debate, with Geyer et al. asserting that it can be dated to the very end of the third millennium BC, roughly contemporary with the Ur III Dynasty of southern Mesopotamia.[81] Barge et al. on the other hand have dated this structure earlier, to between ca. 2500–2200 BC, arguing for contemporaneity with the occupation of al-Rawda.[82] This assertion is based upon an unpublished Bayesian analysis from the site, which indicates that al-Rawda was abandoned during the early EB IVB, at ca. 2200 BC.[83] This coincides with the apparent collapse of the steppe settlement horizon, with most of the primary settlements associated with the al-Rawda system also abandoned at or around ca. 2200 BC.[84] This chronological horizon is also contemporary with the onset of the 4.2 kyr BP climatic event.[85] However, a number of settlements on the western edge of the steppe, such as Tell al-Ṣūr and Tell Munbatah, continued to be occupied and were significantly expanded throughout the last quarter of the third millennium BC.[86] Despite evidence for the continued occupation of some of the settlements located in the marginal zone, an earlier EB IV date for the TLM may be advocated, due to its purely symbolic nature and its position, located 10 km to the east of al-Rawda.[87]

Scholars have associated the construction of this feature with agricultural agistment for the production of wool, a commodity of increasing importance during the third millennium BC.[88] The EB IVA also corresponds to the height of Eblaite control and appears to have been a period of relative political stability, with perhaps the exception of conflict between Ebla and Mari for regional supremacy.[89] Conversely, the final centuries of the third millennium BC were marked by disruption.[90] During the MB I, the frontier of the central/eastern steppe became increasingly militarised, with numerous advance forts and relay towers identified to the east of the TLM, perhaps reflecting the

---

79 Geyer et al. 2010, 61.
80 Geyer et al. 2010, 67–69.
81 Geyer et al. 2010, 69. It should be noted that the dating of the TLM is somewhat contentious and tenuous as it has not been excavated and as such, any chronological designations are based purely on unstratified survey data. However, as no new evidence is likely forthcoming in the near future a later third millennium BC for this structure can be maintained.
82 Barge et al. 2014, 182.
83 Barge et al. 2014, 182.
84 Barge et al. 2014, 182.
85 Weiss et al. 1993; Fiorentino and Caracuta 2007; Riehl and Deckers 2012, 15–18; Weiss 2013.
86 Mouamar 2014, 97, 100; Peyronel 2014, 125.
87 Barge et al. 2014, 181.
88 Lafont 2010, 182; Barge et al. 2014, 182; Wilkinson et al. 2014, 57–59; Biga 2015, 182–183.
89 Archi and Biga 2003; Rey 2012, 129–130, 148; Biga 2013, 263–266; 2014, 204–205; 2015, 189–190; Bonechi 2016.
90 Kenyon 1966, 4–5; Schwartz 2007, 47–48; Kennedy 2016.

5 Militarisation and the changing socio-political landscape of the northern Levant in the Early Bronze Age IVB

increasingly fractious geo-political landscape of the region.[91] This scenario is reflected not only in the archives of the Ur III Dynasty,[92] but also in the later archives of Mari.[93]

One of the most interesting trends discernible during this stage of urban development and fortification activity is that as the key sites and 'central places' of the region, such as Ebla,[94] Tell Chuera,[95] al-Rawda[96] and Tell Leilan,[97] become more heavily fortified, there is a corresponding decline in the fortification of smaller sites in the Orontes corridor, such as those of Tell Nebi Mend and Tell Afis,[98] as well as the sites located in the Matkh Basin.[99] The apparent decline and abandonment of fortification systems in western inland Syria may be directly correlated with the strengthening centralisation of the mature EB III–EB IVA urban system. Indeed, with the rise of the 'central place' and/or larger regional polities, we appear to have an increasingly controlled and monitored landscape.[100] This feature is also reflected in the textual record of the late third millennium BC.[101] Moreover, as these mega-sites, especially Ebla, grew larger and larger, they controlled greater geographical areas, creating new territorial boundaries and spheres of cultural and economic influence and interaction. One possible way to ensure that control of these regions was maintained would be to regulate the creation and maintenance of local defensive systems, with only the larger regional centres of western inland Syria, such as Ebla, or implanted settlements or 'colonies' in territorial or geographic peripheries, such as the steppe, permitted to fortify during this horizon of urban florescence. Sites such as Tell al-Ṣūr and al-Rawda appear to have functioned as a 'central place' in the steppe settlement system.[102] Surveys in the immediate vicinity of al-Rawda have confirmed this in part, revealing that the site was surrounded by a series of towers, while the site itself was encircled by at least four defensive systems.[103] Al-Rawda seems to have functioned in a similar manner to that of the EB I–II site of Arad, in the eastern Negev of the southern Levant.[104] Arad operated as the central place in the Negev, connecting the desert trade networks of the Sinai with the northern cultivated zone.[105] Both Arad and al-Rawda appear to have acted as hubs of economic distribution, with Arad associated with the collection and distribution of copper and

---

91 Geyer et al. 2007, 279–280.
92 Sallaberger 2007, 433–435, 441–449; Sallaberger and Schrakamp 2015, 131.
93 Luke 1965; Matthews 1978.
94 Matthiae and Marchetti (eds) 2013; Archi 2015; Biga 2015.
95 Pfälzner 2011, 142–143.
96 Castel 2007, 285–286; Barge et al. 2014, 182–183.
97 Ristvet 2007, 193–195.
98 Giannessi 1998, 103–104; Mantellini et al. 2013, 250.
99 Baffi and Peyronel 2013, 194–200.
100 Biga 2013, 261; Cooper 2010, 89–90.
101 Archi and Biga 2003; Archi 2015; Biga 2015; Bonechi 2016.
102 Castel et al. 2004; 2005.
103 Castel et al. 2005, 57–58; Barge et al. 2014, 182–183.
104 Amiran et al. 1978; Amiran and Ilan 1996.
105 Joffe 1993, 80–82, 84.

al-Rawda with wool.[106] Moreover, both sites were positioned in environmental and geographic extremes, with Arad viewed as the embodiment of nomadic urbanisation.[107]

Control of the arid margins was potentially crucial to the overall prosperity and stability of the northern Levantine urban system, with the steppic margins possibly employed to pasture large flocks of sheep. Woollen textiles were essential to the strength and solidification of urban life-ways and the maintenance of the region's burgeoning elites.[108] Moreover, control of the east–west trade routes through the desert may well have been used as a means of regulating the Euphratean caravan route, funnelling trade away from possible rival principalities to the east, such as Mari, ensuring a ready supply of goods and exotic items to the 'kingdom(s)' of western inland Syria.[109]

Coinciding with this EB IVA increase in the scale of defensive architecture is an increase in militaristic iconography, particularly within the region's two major powers, Ebla and Mari. These take the form of ivory and shell inlays for mosaic panels, which depict soldiers, battle scenes and captives, as well as larger gypsum plaques that portray scenes of warfare.[110] These have been found primarily in elite and cultic contexts such as Palace G at Ebla,[111] and in the Temples of Ishtar, Nini-zaza and Ishtarat at Mari.[112] Although there is some debate as to whether these scenes were imported or locally produced, excavations in recent years at Mari have revealed evidence for workshops, suggesting a local hub of production.[113] This increasingly militaristic focus within the artistic landscape may echo the growing battle between Ebla and Mari for regional supremacy, a feature also reflected within the region's archives.[114] Moreover, the identification of these scenes in cultic contexts, particularly at Mari, may be indicative of a votive function, with these offered to the gods to ensure victory or in celebration of it. Analysis of the textual records has revealed that conflict between these two polities was considerable, with numerous wars between these two centres conducted over the course of the third millennium BC. Mari is now viewed as a contender for the destruction of Palace G at Ebla.[115]

Stage 3 in the fortification process: the EB IVB

Stage 3 in the fortification process correlates to the EB IVB and marks a distinct change in the fortification landscape of the northern Levant. This phase is characterised

---

106 Castel et al. 2004, 32–34; Barge et al. 2014, 182; Wilkinson et al. 2014.
107 Finklestein 1990.
108 Castel et al. 2004, 32–34; Wilkinson et al. 2014, 57–59; Kennedy 2016.
109 Kennedy 2016.
110 Margueron 2014, 144; Rey 2012, 142, fig. 83.
111 Matthiae 1980, 94; 2013a, pls 59–62.
112 Margueron 2014, 144–145.
113 Margueron 2014, 146.
114 Archi and Biga 2003; Archi 2015, 176–178; Biga 2015, 181–183; Bonechi 2016.
115 Archi and Biga 2003, 35; Lebeau 2012.

5 Militarisation and the changing socio-political landscape of the northern Levant in the Early Bronze Age IVB

by the destruction of Palace G and a decline in Eblaite hegemony.[116] During this phase a number of earlier defensive systems increased in size and scale, with major architectural modifications seen throughout the region, at sites such as Byblos (Figure 5.4).[117] Further to the east, on the Euphrates, the fortifications (buttresses) of Stratum 14 at Habuba Kabira were significantly reworked and extended during this period.[118] A similar scenario is also discernible at Selenkahiye. Selenkahiye was settled during the EB IVA, ca. 2400 BC, with the settlement surrounded by a simple defensive wall, which was severely damaged in a great conflagration, dated to ca. 2300/2200 BC. This destruction horizon has been attributed to the campaigns of the Akkadian kings.[119] The succeeding EB IVB phase, 'Late Selenkahiye', was marked by the construction of a much stronger fortification, with the defensive system/wall significantly expanded and in-filled during this period. This structure also included the construction of a number of large square bastions.[120] Further south at Mari, the fortifications of Ville III were renovated and expanded throughout this period. This included the addition of an earthen rampart, as well as a doubling in size of the inner and outer fortification lines.[121]

However, perhaps the most interesting feature of this stage is the renewed fortification of smaller, hinterland sites. The best examples of this phenomenon are found at Tell Kannâs,[122] Tell Munbatah,[123] Tell Sabkha,[124] and potentially Tell Tuqan,[125] and Tell Nebi Mend (Figure 5.4).[126] At Tell Kannâs on the Euphrates, fortifications were detected in the south-west and north-eastern sectors of the site. This system was distinguished by a large mudbrick wall on top of stone foundations, and was associated with a series of semi-circular towers and a glacis.[127] In the Ebla *chora*, surveys and investigations at Tell Munbatah (5.7 ha) and Tell Sabkha indicate that these sites were first fortified during the EB IVB, although earlier EB IVA occupation is discernible.[128] de Maigret has suggested that these sites functioned as control points, monitoring and regulating trade and exchange between the basalt plateau to the north and the steppe to the south, effectively functioning as gateway sites to the Jabbul plain and the Euphrates.[129] In regards to Tell Tuqan, as yet no clear evidence for fortification during the EB IVB can

---

116 Matthiae 2009, 55–59; Mantellini et al. 2013, 179; Mazzoni 2013, 50–51.
117 Lauffray 2008, 292–293.
118 Heusch 1980, 164–165; Cooper 2006a, 80–82; Novák 2015, 58.
119 Akkermans and Schwartz 2003, 278.
120 Meijer 2001, 3.86–3.89, 3.103–3.106.
121 Margueron 2014, 41–44.
122 Finet 1979, 83–86, figs 8–9.
123 de Maigret 1974, 249–250; Mantellini et al. 2013, 171.
124 Mantellini et al. 2013, 171.
125 Baffi and Peyronel 2013, 198–199; Peyronel 2014, 123–124, 126.
126 Kennedy 2015, 64.
127 Finet 1979, 83–86, figs 8–9.
128 de Maigret 1974, 264–266.
129 de Maigret 1974, 266; Mantellini et al. 2013, 171.

be discerned.[130] However, the site expanded rapidly throughout this period (25 ha); therefore, the existence of such a system cannot be ruled out, particularly in light of the aforementioned contemporary fortification of smaller sites.

At Tell Nebi Mend (Trench I), the transition from Phase N (EB IVA) to Phase M (EB IVB) witnessed the construction of a large structure. The shape and size (ca. 3.00 x 3.00 m) of this structure, as well as its site-peripheral position, running north–south, may suggest that this feature functioned as a tower or bastion, most probably associated with a larger (eroded) circuit-wall system (Figure 5.5).[131] Unfortunately, this structure was disturbed significantly by later intrusions such as refuse pits, Middle Bronze Age constructions as well as erosion. These factors have precluded the production of a coherent ground plan. However, this feature finds its best parallel in Bastion B at Selenkahiye, and is suggestive of defensive purpose.[132] A possible cut for a glacis or fosse has also been identified at the bottom of Trench III on the western side of the site.

Renewed fortification and the changing socio-political landscape of western inland Syria

This aforementioned evidence leads us to postulate the ebb and flow of fortification activity in western inland Syria and the ramifications of this for the urban phenomenon. On the basis of the extant evidence it would appear that the first phase of fortification, its decline and subsequent re-emergence during the EB IVB, can be correlated to the rise and decline of Ebla. In terms of the re-emergence of fortification activity, this may be traced back to a single event: the destruction of Palace G and a possible deterioration in Ebla's regional hegemony at ca. 2340/2280 BC or 2310–2300 BC.[133] Matthiae has previously suggested that this destruction event had little impact upon the region.[134] However, the evidence would suggest that the destruction of Palace G in fact had a profound effect, dramatically altering the region's urban experience and expression. It can be argued that prior to the destruction of Palace G, Ebla wielded significant regional power, controlling much of western inland Syria, the Orontes corridor and its desert margins to the east.[135] Its control of these strategic regions may have resulted in a regulation of inter-regional interaction, potentially stifling independent economic and cultural ventures between smaller 'peripheral' settlements. Evidence for this 'blocking' scenario can be seen within the ceramic horizon of Tell Nebi Mend during the EB IVA. Analysis of material related to this part of the sequence (Trench I) suggests that a strong degree of cultural insularity was present, with comparatively few external

---

130 Baffi and Peyronel 2013, 198–199.
131 Kennedy 2015, 64.
132 Meijer 2001, fig. 3.32.
133 Matthiae 2009, 54; Sallaberger 2007, 423, Table 1; Sallaberger and Schrakamp 2015a, Table 10.1.
134 Matthiae 2013a, 76.
135 Barge et al. 2014, 182; Biga 2014, 199–200; 2015, 181–184.

5 Militarisation and the changing socio-political landscape of the northern Levant in the Early Bronze Age IVB

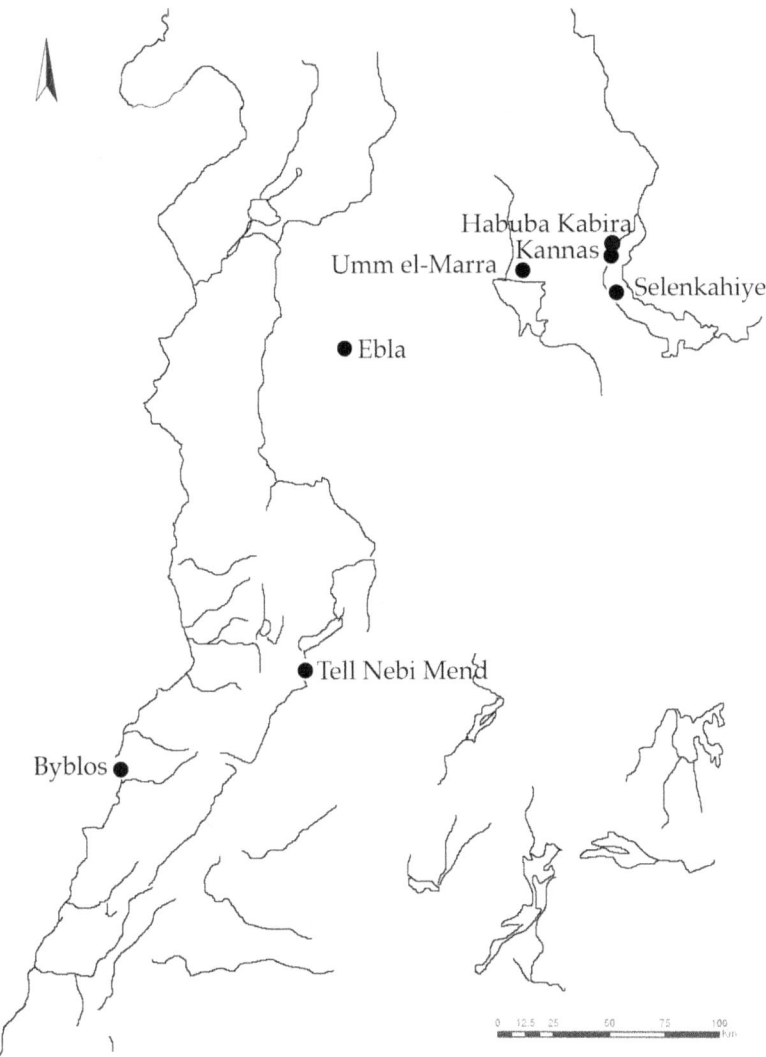

Figure 5.4: EB IVB fortifications in the northern Levant and the Euphrates.

ceramic links discernible within the sequence, particularly when compared to the subsequent EB IVB corpus.[136]

The removal of Ebla's ability to regulate and control western inland Syria in the post-Palace G landscape of the EB IVB may have resulted in a regional power vacuum, allowing settlements previously monitored and/or controlled by the Eblaite polity to expand both economically and culturally into regions previously prohibited.[137] Thus, the reappearance of fortifications during the EB IVB can be viewed as a manifestation of

---

136 Kennedy 2015, 261–266.
137 Kennedy 2015, 316; 2016.

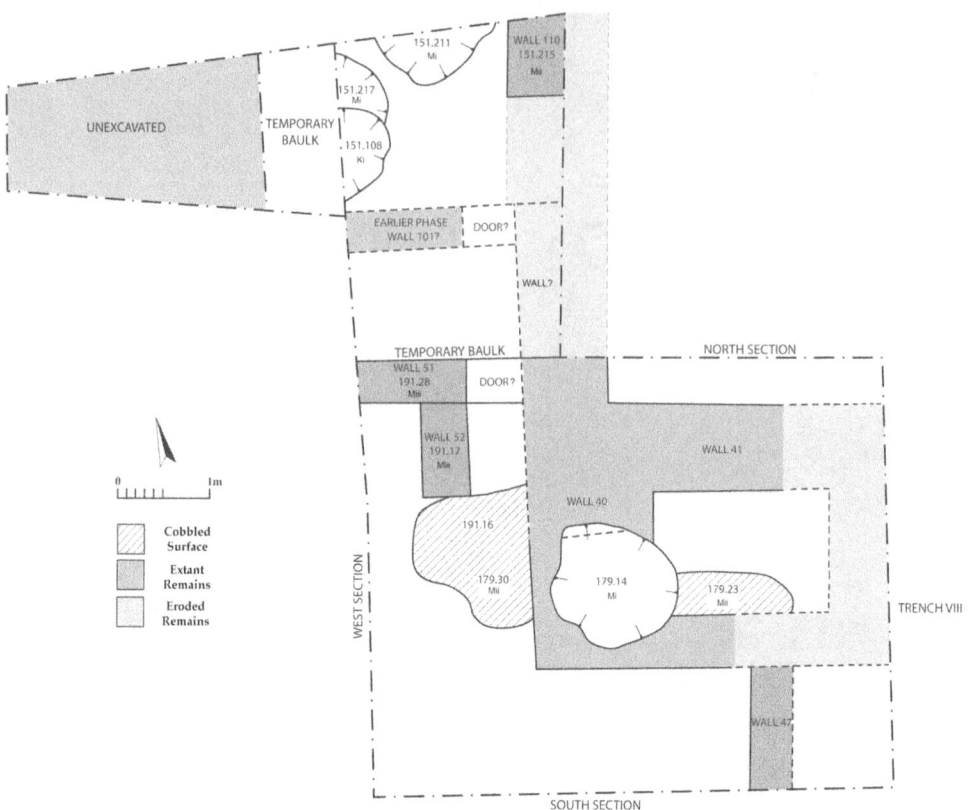

Figure 5.5: Potential EB IVB (Phase M) fortification at Tell Nebi Mend (Trench I).

this greater regional 'freedom'. Prior to the EB IVB, during the height of Ebla's regional hegemony, it can be speculated that Ebla maintained a large measure of control over its constituent parts, and by implication the region's economic interaction and cultural exchange. This 'imperial' regulation may account for the relative dearth of fortified EB IVA sites in the Orontes corridor, as centralised polities tend not to encourage the 'independence' that city walls epitomise.[138] On the basis of this assumption it may be that the absence of fortifications in the EB IVA may itself mark the footprint of the Eblaite state.

Contemporary evidence from the Euphrates would appear to support the supposition that increased regional hegemony came at the cost of localised fortification activity. Lisa Cooper posits that Ebla's control of the Euphrates was minimal and not readily visible within the cultural horizon of the region.[139] At present, no evidence for Eblaite military personnel or administrative faculty has been identified, with Cooper describing the relationship between Ebla and the Euphrates as 'hegemony without sovereignty'.[140] The

---

138 Ilan 1995, 316–317.
139 Cooper 2010, 89–90.
140 Cooper 2010, 92.

5 Militarisation and the changing socio-political landscape of the northern Levant in the Early Bronze Age IVB

semi-autonomous nature of the Euphratean settlements may account for the proliferation of fortification systems during the mid-third millennium BC.[141] As much of this region was allied to but not directly controlled by Ebla, settlements may have been free to fortify. Analysis of the Ebla archives indicates that the Eblaite elite fostered political alliances with independent centres, receiving tribute from these semi-autonomous polities, such as those located on the Euphrates. However, they appear to have maintained direct control over specific centres within their immediate regional territories, such as those located in the Orontes river valley, and its eastern and western peripheries.[142]

By contrast, in the Jezireh, Peter Pfälzner maintains that little evidence for fortification can be discerned during Periods EZJ 4 and EZJ 5.[143] Although the reuse of earlier EZJ 3 defensive systems could not be precluded,[144] the possibility remains, excluding the potential for population dispersal and climatic instability,[145] that the absence of fortification activity in this region may be indicative of Akkadian hegemony. The suppression of fortification systems may have been used as a means of maintaining control over this region, stifling potential insurrections. A similar scenario is attested to at Ebla itself, where there is evidence to suggest that at least part of the earlier EB IVA fortification system was dismantled after the destruction of Mardikh IIB1.[146] Throughout antiquity, victors have frequently dismantled the fortification systems of subjugated cities, as a symbolic act marking the end of their political independence.[147]

If the absence of regional fortification systems can be seen to mark the footprint of Eblaite control during the third millennium BC, we may reasonably ask how far did the reach of Ebla extend and how was control maintained? Textual sources indicate that during the early part of the EB IV, Ebla's territory extended from at least Carchemish in the north-east to as far south as Hama.[148] Archi contends that Ebla found extra-political ways to influence and maintain jurisdiction over its 'empire', through the control of key religious centres, such as that of Hadda of Halaba.[149] By controlling these centres of cultic significance, the rulers of Ebla were able to retain the loyalty of the believers. Naram-Sin enacted a similar policy in upper Mesopotamia, appointing his daughters to strategic high-priestess roles throughout greater Mesopotamia, at sites such as Tell Brak (Nagar) and Tell Mozan (Urkesh).[150]

The extent of Ebla's regional territory and strength during the EB IVB has not yet been ascertained, as fewer textual remains can be associated with this horizon. It is therefore possible that Ebla enjoyed a far less exalted position during the terminal

---

141 Meijer 2001, 103–106; Cooper 2006a, 79; Holland 2006, 28–31; Novák 2015, 55–57.
142 Archi and Biga 2003, 22; Cooper 2010, 90.
143 Pfälzner 2011, 144–145.
144 Pfälzner 2011, 145; Ristvet 2012, 242–244.
145 Peltenburg 2000; Weiss 2012, 4–5; 2013.
146 Matthiae 2013a, 67.
147 Postgate 1977, 124–127.
148 Archi 2010; Cooper 2010, 89–91.
149 Archi 2010.
150 Oates and Oates 2001, 383–386.

centuries of the third millennium BC. This is in part supported by evidence from the Matkh depression, which suggests that a number of settlements in the Ebla *chora*, such as Tell Tuqan, expanded both rapidly and significantly throughout the EB IVB period.[151] It would therefore appear that a number of larger regional entities, such as Tell Tuqan and potentially Hama, were now freed from more than titular interference.

The development and transition of the *Très Long Mur* between the EB IV and the MB I may reflect this changing socio-political landscape. However, key to this discussion is the date of this structure. At present, opinion is divided as to its chronological origin, with Barge et al. asserting that this was constructed sometime during the height of Ebla's regional hegemony,[152] while Geyer et al. have dated this structure to the terminal third millennium BC (Ur III Dynasty).[153] If the Geyer et al. chronology is correct, the potential remains for this symbolic frontier to be associated not with the 'kingdom' of Ebla and its eastern delineation, but with Hama. The assertion may be supported by the fact that Hama lies roughly at the geographic centre of this feature.[154] If this scenario is correct, what we may be seeing in the EB IVB period is the rise of the 'kingdom' of Hama. This new 'principality' may have taken advantage of the political vacuum left by the decline of Ebla, carving out its own economic and territorial niche. It may well be that the defining feature of the EB IVB period is the development of smaller regional entities or 'kingdoms' along the Orontes corridor, with these most probably focused around the major sites of the region, such as Hama, Qatna and Qadesh.

On the basis of this, it can be argued that the genesis of the Middle Bronze Age political landscape can be found within the EB IVB, rather than as a result of the destruction or decline of the Early Bronze Age settlement system. This is further reflected in the author's opinion by the fact that the EB IVB appears to be marked by an increasingly 'Balkanised' landscape, a feature which continued to be maintained during the MBA and is reflected within the later archives of Mari.[155] The potential for the later EBA origins of the MBA political system may also be evidenced in a number of architectural continuities, such as the Archaic Palace at Ebla, which has revealed both EB IVB and MB I horizons of occupation.[156] The continued use of this structure across the EB–MB chrono-cultural divide suggests a desire to maintain an ideological if not direct link between these two horizons. By reusing this important administrative structure, the Eblaite elite of the MB I may have sought to maintain a physical and ideological link with its 'imperial' past.[157] This link may have been utilised as a means of maintaining political legitimacy, although its reuse could also have been adopted as deliberate ploy by 'newcomers' to co-opt previous legitimacy. Either way, the continued

---

151 Baffi and Peyronel 2014, 12; Mantellini et al. 2013, 179–180.
152 Barge et al. 2014, 182.
153 Geyer et al. 2010, 69.
154 Geyer et al. 2007, fig. 7.
155 Matthews 1978; Sasson 2015.
156 Matthiae 2006, 87.
157 Matthiae 2006, 95; Kennedy 2015, 307–308.

5 Militarisation and the changing socio-political landscape of the northern Levant in the Early Bronze Age IVB

use of the Archaic Palace suggests an idealised identity of how the rulers of Ebla wished to be perceived; that is, within the context of past authority.

The post-Palace G horizon of the EB IVB was also concurrent with a dramatic upsurge in cultural interaction intensity. This is exemplified in the upper Orontes at Tell Nebi Mend. Throughout the EB IVB period (Phase M), the site demonstrates a much greater sense of economic and social mobility than during the preceding EB IVA period.[158] Analysis of the ceramic record revealed that Phase M was distinguished by a dramatic increase in inter-site parallels. However, this period of wider regional interaction was short-lived, at least at Tell Nebi Mend, with the transition from the EB IV (Phase M) to the MB I (Phase L) marked by sharply reduced assemblage variability and an accompanying decline in inter-site interaction, with parallel-counts in most instances almost halved.[159] This decline is suggestive of economic contraction and a growing horizon of cultural insularity, which was possibly curtailed by the emergence of a newly reconfigured landscape and the rise of old and new geo-political entities; specifically the re-emergence of Ebla and the beginning of the Middle Bronze Age world. However, this was a very different world from the more cohesive earlier EBA; Hama remained strong, Qadesh rose in ascendency, Tell Atchana was founded in the 'Amuq,[160] and a number of smaller sites continued upon their own, distinct developmental trajectory, with the northern Levant and upper Mesopotamia marked by a developing horizon of north-south and east-west cultural and political fragmentation.

Conclusion

On the basis of the extant evidence from western inland Syria it would appear that the development and utilisation of fortification systems in the Early Bronze Age can be divided into three distinct stages, which loosely correspond to the various phases of urban development in the region. As the urban phenomenon strengthened, the creation of territorial kingdoms resulted in a decline in settlement independence, one possible manifestation of which is the absence of fortification systems. This state of affairs continued until the destruction of Palace G, which was accompanied by a significant weakening of Ebla's regional control. A direct consequence of this decline would appear to be the re-emergence of 'hinterland' settlement independence, at sites such as Tell Tuqan, Tell Munbatah and Tell Nebi Mend. A corollary of this growing regional independence and political fragmentation is the apparent refortification of previously monitored and controlled settlements, as well as a rise in multi-polar, inter-regional interaction. This horizon of developing political fragmentation laid the foundations for the Middle Bronze Age geo-political landscape, with a number of the region's major powers of the second millennium BC, such as Hama, Qadesh

---

158 Kennedy 2015, 304.
159 Kennedy 2015, 304–305.
160 Yener 2005, 100–103.

and Qatna, increasing in size and complexity throughout this episode. New territorial boundaries were drawn, setting the stage for their greatest expression, the urban zenith of the second millennium BC.

References

Akkermans, P.M.M.G. and Schwartz, G.M. (2003). *The archaeology of Syria: from complex hunter-gathers to early urban societies (ca. 16,000-300 BC)*. Cambridge: Cambridge University Press.

Amiran, R. and Ilan, O. (1996). *Early Arad II: the Chalcolithic and Early Bronze Age city I. Sixth to eighteenth seasons of excavations, 1971-1978, 1980-1984*. Jerusalem: Israel Exploration Journal.

Amiran, R., Paran, U., Shiloh, Y., Brown, R., Tsafrir, Y. and Ben-Tor, A. (1978). *Early Arad: the Chalcolithic settlement and Early Bronze city*. Jerusalem: The Israel Exploration Society

Archi, A. (2010). Hadda of Halab and his temple in the Ebla period. *Iraq* LXXXII: 3-17.

(2015). The chronology of Ebla and synchronisms with Abarsal, Tuttul, Nagar and Nabada, Mari, Kish. In *Associated regional chronologies for the Ancient Near East and the eastern Mediterranean: history and philology*. Vol. III. W. Sallaberger and I. Schrakamp, eds. 163-180. Turnhout: Brepols.

Archi, A. and Biga, M.G. (2003). A victory over Mari and the fall of Ebla. *Journal of Cuneiform Studies* 55: 1-44.

Baffi, F., Fiorentino, R. and Peyronel, L. eds. (2014). *Tell Tuqan excavations and regional perspectives: cultural developments in inner Syria from the Early Bronze Age to the Persian/Hellenistic period. Proceedings of the international conference, May 15th-17th 2013, Lecce*. Lecce: Congedo Editore.

Baffi, F. and Peyronel, L. (2013). Trends in village life: the Early Bronze Age phases at Tell Tuqan. In *Ebla and its landscape: early state formation in the ancient Near East*. P. Matthiae and N. Marchetti, eds. 195-214. Walnut Creek: Left Coast Press.

Baffi, F. and Peyronel, L. (2014). Tell Tuqan and the Matkh basin in a regional perspective: thoughts and questions raised by the international conference. In *Tell Tuqan excavations and regional perspectives: cultural developments in inner Syria from the Early Bronze Age to the Persian/Hellenistic period. Proceedings of the international conference, May 15th-17th 2013, Lecce*. F. Baffi, R. Fiorentino and L. Peyronel, eds. 9-34. Lecce: Congedo Editore.

Barge, O., Castel, C. and Élie Brochier, J. (2014). Human impact on the landscape around al-Rawda during the Early Bronze IV. In *Settlement dynamics and human-landscape interaction in the dry steppes of Syria*. D. Morandi Bonacossi, ed. 173-185. Studia Chaburensia Vol. 4. Wiesbaden: Harrassowitz Verlag.

Bartl, K. and Al-Maqdissi, M. (2014). Archaeological prospecting on the middle Orontes river survey work between ar-Rastan and Qal'at Šhayzar. In *New prospecting in the Orontes region: first results of archaeological field work*. K. Bartl and M. Al-Maqdissi, eds. 61-78. Orient-Archäologie Band 30. Rahden: Verlag Marie Leidorf GmbH.

Biga, M.G. (2013). Defining the *chora* of Ebla: a textual perspective. In *Ebla and its landscape: early state formation in the ancient Near East*. P. Matthiae and N. Marchetti, eds. 259-267. Walnut Creek: Left Coast Press.

5 Militarisation and the changing socio-political landscape of the northern Levant in the Early Bronze Age IVB

(2014). The Syrian steppes and the Kingdom of Ibal in the third millennium B.C.: new data from the Ebla texts. In *Settlement dynamics and human-landscape interaction in the dry steppes of Syria*. D. Morandi Bonacossi, ed. 199–208. Studia Chaburensia Vol. 4. Wiesbaden: Harrassowitz Verlag.

(2015). The geographical scope of Ebla: commerce and wares. Some remarks. *Associated regional chronologies for the ancient Near East and the eastern Mediterranean: history and philology.* Vol. III. W. Sallaberger and I. Schrakamp, eds. 181–190. Turnhout: Brepols.

Bonechi, M. (2016). Strife in Early Bronze Syria: lexical, prosopographical, and historical notes on the Ebla texts. *Revue Internationale d'Histoire Militaire Ancienne* 3: 17–54.

Bourke, S.J. (2014). Urban origins in the Early Bronze Age Jordan valley: recent discoveries from Pella in Jordan. In *Egypt and the southern Levant in the Early Bronze Age*. F. Höflmayer and R. Eichmann, eds. 3–18. Orient-Archäologie 31. Rahden: Verlag Marie Leidorf GmbH.

Braidwood, R.J. and Braidwood, L.S. (1960). *Excavations in the plain of Antioch I: the early assemblages Phases A–J*. The University of Chicago Oriental Institute Publications No. LXI. Chicago: University of Chicago Press.

Burke, A. (2008). *'Walled up to heaven': the evolution of Middle Bronze Age fortification strategies in the Levant*. Studies in the archaeology and history of the Levant 4. Winona Lake, Indiana: Eisenbrauns.

Campbell, M. (2012). *Tell Nebi Mend: Trench VIII*. Masters thesis, Durham University, Durham, United Kingdom.

Castel, C. (2007). Stratégies de subsistence et modes d'occupation de l'espace dans la micro-région d'al-Rawda au Bronze Ancien final (Shamiyeh). In *Urban and natural landscapes of an ancient Syrian capital: settlement and environment at Tell Mishrifeh/Qatna and in central-western Syria*. D. Morandi-Bonacossi, ed. 283–294. Studi Archeologici su Qatna 01. Udine: Forum.

Castel, C., Al-Awad, N., Barge, O., Boudier, T., Cuny, A., Delattre, I., Joannès, F., Moulin, B. and Sanz, S. (2004). Rapport préliminiaire sur les activités de la première mission archéologique Franco-Syrienne dans la micro-région d'al-Rawda (Syrie interieure): la campagnes de 2002. *Akkadica* 125(1): 27–77.

Castel, C., Archambault, D., Barge, O., Boudier, P., Courbon, A., Cuny, A., Gondet, S., Herveux, L., Isnard, F., Martin, I., Monchambert, J-Y., Moulin, B. and Sanz, S. (2005). Rapport préliminaire sur les activités de la mission archéologique Franco-Syrienne dans la micro-région d'al-Rawda (Shamiyeh): deuxième et troisième campagnes (2003 et 2004). *Akkadica* 126(1): 51–96.

Chesson, M.S. and Philip, G. (2003). Tales of the city? 'Urbanism' in the Early Bronze Age Levant from Mediterranean and Levantine perspectives. *Journal of Mediterranean Archaeology* 16(1): 3–16.

Cooper, L. (2006a). *Early urbanism on the Syrian Euphrates*. London: Routledge.

(2006b). The pottery from Tell 'Acharneh, part I: typological considerations and dating accordingly to excavated areas in the upper and lower towns, 1998–2002. In *Tell 'Acharneh 1998–2004: rapports préliminaires sur les campagnes de fouilles et season d'études*. M. Fortin, ed. 140–191. Brussels: Brepols.

(2006c). The demise and regeneration of Bronze Age urban centres in the Euphrates valley of Syria. In *After collapse: the regeneration of complex societies*. G.M. Schwartz and J.J. Nichols, eds. 18–37. Tucson: University of Arizona Press.

(2010). States of hegemony: early forms of political control in Syria during the 3rd millennium BC. In *The development of pre-state communities in the ancient Near East: studies in honour of Edgar Peltenburg*. D. Bolger and L.C. Maguire, eds. 87–96. Oxford: Oxbow.

Esse, D.L. (1989). Secondary state formation and collapse in Early Bronze Age Palestine. In *L'urbanisation de la Palestine à l'âge du Bronze Ancien*. P. de Miroschedji, ed. 81–96. British Archaeological Reports, International Series 527. Oxford: British Archaeological Reports.

Finet, A. (1979). Bilan provisoire des fouilles Belges du Tell Kannâs. In *Archaeological projects from the Tabqa dam project – Euphrates valley Syria*. D.N. Freedman, ed. 79–96. Annual of the American Schools of Oriental Research 44. Cambridge, MA: American Schools of Oriental Research.

Finkelstein, I. (1990). Early Arad: urbanisation of the nomads. *Zeitschrift des Deutschen Palästina-Vereins* 106: 34–50.

Fiorentino, G. and Caracuta, V. (2007). Palaeoclimatic signals inferred from carbon stable isotope analysis of Qatna/Tell Mishrifeh archaeological plant remains. In *Urban and natural landscapes of an ancient Syrian capital: settlement and environment at Tell Mishrifeh/Qatna and in central-western Syria*. D. Morandi-Bonacossi, ed. 153–160. Studi Archeologici su Qatna 01. Udine: Forum.

Fugmann, E. (1958). *Hama: II.1. Fouilles et recherches de la Fondation Carlsberg 1931–1938: L'architecture des périodes pré-Hellénistiques*. Copenhagen: Nationalmuseet.

Genz, H. (2014). Excavations at Tell Fadous-Kfarabida 2004–2011: an Early and Middle Bronze Age site on the Lebanese coast. In *Egypt and the southern Levant in the Early Bronze Age*. F. Höflmayer and R. Eichmann, eds. 69–91. Orient-Archäologie 31. Rahden: Verlag Marie Leidorf GmbH.

Genz, H., Riehl, S., Çakırlar, C., Slim, F. and Damick, A. (2016). Economic and political organization of Early Bronze Age coastal communities: Tell Fadous-Kfarabida as a case study. *Berytus* 55: 79–119.

Genz, H., Damick, A., Berquist, S., Makinson, M., Wygnanska, Z., Mardini, M., Peršin, M., Raad, N., Alameh, J., Ahrens, A., El-Dana, N., Edwards, J. and El-Zaatari, S. (2018). Excavations at Tell Fadous-Kfarabida: preliminary report on the 2014 and 2015 seasons of excavations. *Bulletin d'Archéologie et d'Architecture Libanaises* 18: 37–78.

Geyer, B. (2002). Expansion and decline of Syria's arid margin. *The Arab world geographer* 5(2): 73–84.

Geyer, B., Awad, N., al-Dbiyat, M., Calvet, Y. and Rousset, M-O. (2010). Un 'Très Long Mur' dans la steppe Syrienne. *Paléorient* 36(2): 57–72.

Geyer, B., al-Dbiyat, M., Awad, N., Barge, O., Besançon, J., Calvet, Y. and Jaubert, R. (2007). The arid margins of northern Syria: occupation of the land and modes of exploitation in the Bronze Age. In *Urban and natural landscapes of an ancient Syrian capital: settlement and environment at Tell Mishrifeh/Qatna and in central-western Syria*. D. Morandi-Bonacossi, ed. 269–281. Studi Archeologici su Qatna 01. Udine: Forum.

5 Militarisation and the changing socio-political landscape of the northern Levant in the Early Bronze Age IVB

Giannessi, D. (1998). Area E – Late Chalcolithic, Early, Middle and Late Bronze I Ages: architecture and stratigraphy. In *Tell Afis (Siria): the 1988–1992 excavations on the acropolis.* S.M. Cecchini and S. Mazzoni, eds. 101–122. Pisa: Edizioni Ets.

Gibbins, S. (2001). Early Bronze Age fortifications on Tell Husn (Pella). In *Australians uncovering ancient Jordan: fifty years of Middle Eastern archaeology.* A. Walmsley, ed. 89–94. Sydney: University of Sydney Press.

Greenberg, R., Paz, S., Wengrow, D. and Iserlis, M. (2012). Tel Bet Yerah: hub of the Early Bronze Age Levant. *Near Eastern Archaeology* 75: 88–107.

Helms, S.W. (1991a). Introduction. In *Excavations at Jawa 1972–1986: excavations and explorations in the Hashemite Kingdom of Jordan.* A.V.G. Betts, ed. 6–18. Edinburgh: Edinburgh University Press.

(1991b). Stratigraphy. In *Excavations at Jawa 1972–1986: excavations and explorations in the Hashemite Kingdom of Jordan.* A.V.G. Betts, ed. 19–54. Edinburgh: Edinburgh University Press.

Heusch, J-C. (1980). Tall Habuba Kabira im 3. und 2. jahrtausend: die entwiclung der Baustruktur. In *Le Moyen Euphrates: Zone de Contacts et d'Échanges.* J-C. Margueron, ed. 159–178. Strasbourg: Travaux du Centre de Rescherches sur le Proche-Orient et la Grèce Antiques 5.

Holland, T.A. (2006). *Excavations at Tell es-Sweyhat, Syria: archaeology of the Bronze Age, Hellenistic, and Roman remains at an ancient town on the Euphrates river.* Oriental Institute Publications No. CXXV. Chicago: University of Chicago Press.

Ilan, D. (1995). The dawn of internationalism: the Middle Bronze Age. In *The archaeology of society in the Holy Land.* T.E. Levy, ed. 297–319. London: Leicester University.

Joffe, A.H. (1993). *Settlement and society in the Early Bronze I and II southern Levant: complementarity and contradiction in a small-scale complex society.* Monographs in Mediterranean Archaeology 4. Sheffield: Sheffield Academic Press.

Kennedy, M.A. (2015). *The late third millennium BCE in the upper Orontes valley, Syria: ceramics, chronology and cultural connections.* Ancient Near Eastern Studies Supplement 46. Peeters: Leuven.

(2016). The end of the third millennium BC in the Levant: new perspective and old ideas. *Levant* 48(1): 1–32.

Kenyon, K.M. (1966). *Amorites and Canaanites.* London: Oxford University Press.

Lafont, B. (2010). Contribution de la documentation Cunéiforme à la connaissance du 'Très Long Mur' de la steppe Syrienne. *Paléorient* 49: 73–89.

Lauffray, J. (2008). *Fouilles de Byblos: l'urbanisme et l'architecture.* Tome VI. Bibliothéque Archéologique et Historique T.182. Beyrouth: Institut Français du Proche-Orient.

Lebeau, M. ed. (2011). *Associated regional chronologies for the Ancient Near East and the Eastern Mediterranean: the Jezirah.* Vol. I. Turnhout: Brepols.

Lebeau, M. (2012). Dating the destructions of Ebla, Mari and Nagar from radiocarbon with reference to Egypt, combined with stratigraphy and historical data. In *Stories from long ago Festschrift für Michael D. Roaf.* H. Baker, K. Kaniuth and A. Otto, eds. 301–321. AOAT 397. Münster: Ugarit-Verlag.

Luke, J.T. (1965). *Pastoralism and politics in the Mari period: a re-examination of the character and political significance of the major west Semitic tribal groups on the middle Euphrates, ca. 1828–1758 B.C.* Michigan: University Microfilms, Inc. (1975).

de Maigret, A. (1974). Tell Munbatah, un novo sit della cultura 'Caliciform' nella Siria del nord. *Oriens Antiquus* 13: 249–297.

Mantellini, S., Micale, M.G. and Peyronel, L. (2013). Exploring diversity: the archaeological landscape of the Eblaite chora. In *Ebla and its landscape: early state formation in the ancient Near East*. P. Matthiae and N. Marchetti, eds. 163–194. Walnut Creek: Left Coast Press.

Margueron, J-C. (2014). *Mari: capital of northern Mesopotamia in the third millennium: the archaeology of Tell Hariri on the Euphrates*. Oxford: Oxbow Books.

Matthews, V.H. (1978). *Pastoral nomadism in the Mari kingdom (ca. 1850–1760 BC)*. Cambridge: Cambridge University Press.

Matthiae, P. (1980). *Ebla: an empire rediscovered*. C. Holme, trans. London: Hodder & Stoughton.

(1989). The destruction of the Ebla royal palace: interconnections between Syria, Mesopotamia and Egypt in the late EB IVA. In *High, middle or low? Acts of an international colloquium on absolute chronology held at the University of Gothenburg, 20th–22nd August 1987*. P. Åström, ed. 163–169. Gothenburg: Åströms.

(1993). On this side of the Euphrates: a note on the urban origins of inner Syria. In *Between the rivers and over the mountains: archaeologica Anatolica et Mesopotamica Alba Palmieri Dedicata*. M. Frangipane, H. Hauptmann, M. Liverani, P. Matthiae and M. Mellink, eds. 523–530. Rome: University of La Sapienzia Press.

(1998). Les fortification d'Ébla paléo-Syrienne fouilles à Tell Mardikh (1995–1997). *Comptes-rendus de l'academie des inscriptions et Belles-Lettres* 1998: 557–588.

(2000). Nouvelles fouilles à Ebla (1998–1999): forts et palais de l'enclinte urbaine. *Comptes-rendus de l'académie des inscriptions et Belles-Lettres* 2000: 567–610.

(2001). A preliminary note on the MB I-II fortifications system at Ebla. *Damaszener Mitteilungen* 13: 29–51.

(2006). The Archaic Palace at Ebla: a royal building between Early Bronze Age IVB and Middle Bronze Age I. In *Confronting the past: archaeological and historical essays on ancient Israel in honour of William G. Dever*. S.J. Gitin, E. Wright and J.P. Dessel, eds. 85–103. Winona Lake: Eisenbrauns.

(2009). Crisis and collapse of Ebla from EB IVA and EB IVB. *Scienze dell'Antichità* 15: 43–83.

(2013a). Crisis and collapse of Ebla from EB IVA and EB IVB. In *Studies on the archaeology of Ebla 1980–2010*. F. Pinnock, ed. 57–94. Weisbaden: Harrassowitz Verlag.

(2013b) The IIIrd millennium in north-western Syria: stratigraphy and architecture. In *Archéologie et histoire de la Syrie I: la Syrie de l'époque Néolithique à l'Âge du Fer*. W. Orthmann, P. Matthiae and M. Al-Maqdissi, eds. 181–198. Weisbaden: Harrassowitz Verlag.

Mazzoni, S. (1998). Materials and chronology. In *Tell Afis (Siria): The 1988–1992 excavations on the acropolis*. S.M. Cecchini and S. Mazzoni, eds. 101–122. Pisa: Edizioni Ets.

(2002). The ancient Bronze Age pottery tradition in north-western central Syria. In *Céramique de l'Âge du Bronze en Syrie, I: la Syrie du sud et le vallée de l'Oronte*. M. Al-Maqdissi, V. Matoïan and C. Nicolle, eds. 69–96. Bibliothéque Archéologique et Historique T.161. Beyrouth: Institut Français du Proche-Orient.

(2013). Tell Afis and the Early-Middle Bronze Age transition. In *Syrian archaeology in perspective celebrating 20 years of excavations at Tell Afis: proceedings of the international meeting percorsi di archeologia Siriana Pisa, 27-28 November 2006*. S. Mazzoni and S. Soldi, eds. 31–80. Pisa: Edizioni ETS.

5 Militarisation and the changing socio-political landscape of the northern Levant in the Early Bronze Age IVB

McLaren, P.B. (2004). *The military architecture of Jordan during the Middle Bronze Age: new evidence from Pella and Rukeis*. British Archaeological Reports British Series 1202. Oxford: British Archaeological Reports.

Meijer, D.J.W. (2001). Architecture and stratigraphy. In *Selenkahiye: final report on the University of Chicago and University of Amsterdam excavations in the Tabqa reservoir, northern Syria, 1967–1975*. M. van Loon, ed. 3.35–3.126. Leiden/Istanbul: Nederlands Historisch-Archaeologisch Institut.

Morandi-Bonacossi, D. (2007). Qatna and its hinterland during the Bronze and Iron Ages: a preliminary reconstruction of urbanism and settlement in the Mishrifeh region. In *Urban and natural landscapes of an ancient Syrian capital: settlement and environment at Tell Mishrifeh/Qatna and in central-western Syria*. D. Morandi-Bonacossi, ed. 65–90. Studi Archeologici su Qatna 01. Udine: Forum.

Mouamar, G. (2014). Tell al-Şūr/al-Sankarī: une nouvelle agglomeration circulaire du Bronze Ancien IV à la lisière de la steppe Syrienne. In *Tell Tuqan excavations and regional perspectives: cultural developments in inner Syria from the Early Bronze Age to the Persian/Hellenistic period. Proceedings of the international conference, May 15th–17th 2013, Lecce*. F. Baffi, R. Fiorentino and L. Peyronel, eds. 95–114. Lecce: Congedo Editore.

Nichols, J.J. and Weber, J.A. (2006). Amorites, onagers, and social reorganization in Middle Bronze Age Syria. In *After collapse: the regeneration of complex societies*. G.M. Schwartz and J.J. Nichols, eds. Tucson: University of Arizona Press.

Novák, M. (2015). Urbanism and architecture. In *Associated Regional Chronologies for the Ancient Near East and the Eastern Mediterranean: Middle Euphrates*. Vol. IV. U. Finkbeiner, M. Novák, F. Sakal and P. Sconzo, eds. 41–84. Turnhout: Brepols.

Oates, D. and Oates, J. (2001). Archaeological reconstructions and historical commentary. In *Excavations at Tell Brak. Nagar in the third millennium B.C.* Vol. 2. D. Oates, J. Oates and H. McDonald, eds. 379–394. Cambridge: McDonald Institute of Archaeological Research.

Orthmann, W. (1989). *Halawa 1980–1986*. Bonn: Rudolf Habelt Verlag.

Parr, P.J. (1983). The Tell Nebi Mend project. *Annales Archeologiques Arabes Syriennes* 33(2): 18–45.

Pfälzner, P. (2011). Architecture. In *Associated Regional Chronologies for the Ancient Near East and the Eastern Mediterranean: the Jezirah*. Vol. I. M. Lebeau, ed. 137–200. Turnhout: Brepols.

Peltenburg, E. (2000). From nucleation to dispersal: late third millennium BC settlement pattern transformations in the Near East and Aegean. In *La Djéziré et L'Euphrate Syriens de la protohistoire à la fin du IIe millénaire Av. J-C. Tendances dans l'Interprétation historique des données Nouvelles*. O. Rouault and M. Wäfler, eds. 183–206. Subartu VII. Brussels: Brepols.

(2013). Conflict and exclusivity in Early Bronze Age societies of the middle Euphrates valley. *Journal of Near Eastern Studies* 72(2): 233–252.

Peyronel, L. (2014). Living near the lake: the Matkh region (Syria) during the Early and Middle Bronze Ages. In *Tell Tuqan excavations and regional perspectives: cultural developments in inner Syria from the Early Bronze Age to the Persian/Hellenistic Period. Proceedings of the international conference, May 15th–17th 2013, Lecce*. F. Baffi, R. Fiorentino and L. Peyronel, eds. 115–162. Lecce: Congedo Editore.

Philip, G. (2001). The Early Bronze I–III Ages. In *The archaeology of Jordan*. B. Macdonald, R. Adams and P. Bienkowski, eds. 163–232. Sheffield: Sheffield Academic Press.

Philip, G. and Newson, P. (2014). Settlement in the upper Orontes valley: a preliminary statement. In *New prospecting in the Orontes region: first results of archaeological field work*. K. Bartl and M. Al-Maqdissi, eds. 33–40. Orient-Archäologie Band 30. Rahden: Verlag Marie Leidorf GmbH.

Pinnock, F. (2009). EB IVB-MB I in northern Syria: crisis and change of a mature urban civilization. In *The Levant in transition: proceeding of a conference held at the British Museum on 20–21 April 2004*. P.J. Parr, ed. 69–79. PEF Annual IX. Leeds: Maney Publishing.

Postgate, N. (1977). *The first empires*. Oxford: Phaidon.

Rey, S. (2012). *Poliorcétique au Proche-Orient à l'Âge du Bronze: fortifications urbaines, procédés de siège et systèmes défensifs*. Bibliothéque Archéologique et Historique T.197. Beyrouth: Institut Français du Proche-Orient.

Riehl, S. and Deckers, K. (2012). Environmental and agricultural dynamics in northern Mesopotamia during the Early and Middle Bronze Age. In *Looking north: the socioeconomic dynamics of the northern Mesopotamian and Anatolian regions during the late third and early second millennium BC*. N. Laneri, P. Pfälzner and S. Valentini, eds. 11–24. Studien zur Urbanisierung Nordmesopotamiens, Serie D, Band 1. Wiesbaden: Harrassowitz Verlag.

Ristvet, L. (2007). The third millennium city wall at Tell Leilan, Syria: identity, authority and urbanism. In *Power and architecture: monumental public architecture in the Bronze Age Near East and Aegean*. J. Bretschneider, J. Driessen and K. Van Lerberghe, eds. 183–211. Leuven: Peeters.

(2012). Resettling Apum: tribalism and tribal states in the Tell Leilan region, Syria. In *Looking north: the socioeconomic dynamics of the northern Mesopotamian and Anatolian regions during the late third and early second millennium BC*. N. Laneri, P. Pfälzner and S. Valentini, eds. 37–50. Studien zur Urbanisierung Nordmesopotamiens, Serie D, Band 1. Wiesbaden: Harrassowitz Verlag.

Saghieh, M. (1983). *Byblos in the third millennium: a reconstruction of the stratigraphy and a study of the cultural connections*. Warminster: Aris & Phillips.

Sallaberger, W. (2007). From urban culture to nomadism: a history of upper Mesopotamia in the late third millennium. In *Sociétés humaines et changement climatique à la fin du trosième millénaire: une crise a-t-elle eu lieu en Haute Mésopotamie? Actes du colloque de Lyon 5–8 Décembre 2005*. C. Kuzucuoğlu and C. Marro, eds. 417–456. Varia Anatolica 19. Paris/Istanbul: Institut Français d'Études Anatoliennes-Georges Dumézil.

Sallaberger, W. and Schrakamp, I. (2015). The Third Dynasty of Ur and other late 3rd millennium dynasties. In *Associated regional chronologies for the Ancient Near East and the eastern Mediterranean: history and philology*. Vol. III. W. Sallaberger and I. Schrakamp, eds. 131–134. Turnhout: Brepols.

Schwartz, G.M. (2007). The Early-Middle Bronze transition: evidence from Umm el-Marra and western Syria. In *From relative chronology to absolute chronology: the second millennium BC in Syria-Palestine, proceedings of the international colloquium, Rome, 29th November – 1st December 2001*. P. Matthiae, F. Pinnock, L. Nigro and L. Peyronel, eds. 511–530. Contributi del Centro Linceo Interdisciplinare 'Beniamino Segre'. No. 117. Rome: Bardi Editore, Editore Commerciale.

5 Militarisation and the changing socio-political landscape of the northern Levant in the Early Bronze Age IVB

Schwartz, G.M., Curvers, H., Gerritsen, F., MacCormack, J., Miller, N. and Webber, J. (2000). Excavations and survey on the Jabbul plain, western Syria: the Umm el-Marra Project 1996–1997. *American Journal of Archaeology* 104: 419–462.

Strommenger, E. (1980). *Habuba Kabira, eine stadt vor Jahren*. Mainz: Philipp von Zabern.

Tefnin, R. (1980). Deux campagnes des fouilles au Tell Abou Danné (1975–1976). In *Le moyen Euphrates: zone de contacts et d'échanges*. J-C. Margueron, ed. 179–200. Strasbourg: Travaux du Centre de Rescherches sur le Proche-Orient et la Grèce Antiques 5.

Thuesen, I. (1988). *Hama: the pre- and proto-historic periods: fouilles et recherches de la foundation Carlsberg, 1931–1938*. Copenhagen: Nationalmuseet.

Vacca, A. (2014). The Tuqan IC pottery sequence from Area P south. In *Tell Tuqan excavations and regional perspectives: cultural developments in inner Syria from the Early Bronze Age to the Persian/Hellenistic period. Proceedings of the international conference, May 15th–17th 2013, Lecce*. F. Baffi, R. Fiorentino and L. Peyronel, eds. 45–84. Lecce: Congedo Editore.

(2015). Before the Royal Palace G. The stratigraphic and pottery sequence of the west unit of the central complex: the Building G5. *Studia Eblaitica* 1: 1–32.

Wilkinson, T.J., Philip, G., Bradbury, J., Dunford, R., Donoghue, D., Galiaststos, N., Lawrence, D., Ricci, A. and Smith, S.L. (2014). Contextualizing early urbanization: settlement cores, early states and agro-pastoral strategies in the Fertile Crescent during the fourth and third millennia BC. *Journal of World Prehistory* 27(1): 43–109.

Weiss, H. (2012). Quantifying collapse: the late third millennium Khabur Plains. In *Seven generations since the fall of Akkad*. H. Weiss, ed. 1–24. Studia Chaburensia Vol. 3. Wiesbaden: Harrassowitz Verlag.

(2013). The northern Levant during the Intermediate Bronze Age: altered trajectories 2200–1900 BCE. In *The Oxford handbook of the archaeology of the Levant: c. 8000–332 BCE*. M. L. Steiner and A.E. Killebrew, eds. 367–387. Oxford: Oxford University Press.

Weiss, H., Courty, M-A., Witterstrom, W., Guichard, F., Senior, L., Meadow, R. and Curnow, A. (1993). The genesis and collapse of third millennium north Mesopotamian civilisation. *Science* 261: 995–1004.

Welton, L. (2014). Revisiting the 'Amuq sequence: a preliminary investigation of the EB IVB ceramic assemblage from Tell Tayinat. *Levant* 46(3): 339–370.

Yener, K.A. (2005). Alalakh Spatial Organisation. In *The 'Amuq Valley Regional Projects, volume 1: surveys in the plain of Antioch and Orontes delta, Turkey, 1995–2002*. K.A. Yener, ed. 99–144. Oriental Institute Publications No. CXXXI. Chicago: University of Chicago Press.

Yener, K.A., Wilkinson, T.J., Branting, S., Friedman, E.S., Lyon, J.D. and Reichel, C.D. (1996). The Oriental Institute 'Amuq Valley Projects, 1995. *Anatolica* XXII: 49–84.

Yener, K.A., Edens, C., Harrison, T.P., Verstraete, J. and Wilkinson, T.J. (2000). The 'Amuq Valley Regional Projects, 1995–1998. *American Journal of Archaeology* 104(2): 163–220.

6

Evolutions of pottery production over a millennium

Petrographic analysis of the EB ceramic assemblage from Tell Arqa

Mathilde Jean
Université Paris 1, Panthéon-Sorbonne

Although understanding craft production and its evolution through time allows the documentation of socio-economic organisation in past societies, it requires using detailed data to reach the most plausible interpretation. It also means studying assemblages from uninterrupted stratigraphic sequences, covering long periods of time and multiple aspects of the assemblage, such as: selection of raw materials and their provenance, manufacturing processes, morpho-functional typology and decoration style. The Early Bronze Age pottery assemblage from Tell Arqa fits these criteria and is, therefore, an excellent candidate to undertake this kind of comprehensive analysis. In order to do so, a multidisciplinary program was initiated in 2010 on the Tell Arqa materials to document technological issues and reconstruct craft productions and the socio-economic development of the site. The petrographic study presented hereafter is part of the program and enables us to reconstruct the first step of pottery production: the selection of raw materials.

Tell Arqa is located at the opening of the Homs Gap, in the southern part of the Akkar plain (northern Lebanon), 6 km from the Mediterranean coast and 12 km south of the Nahr el-Kebir (Figure 6.1). The top of the tell is about 140 m above sea

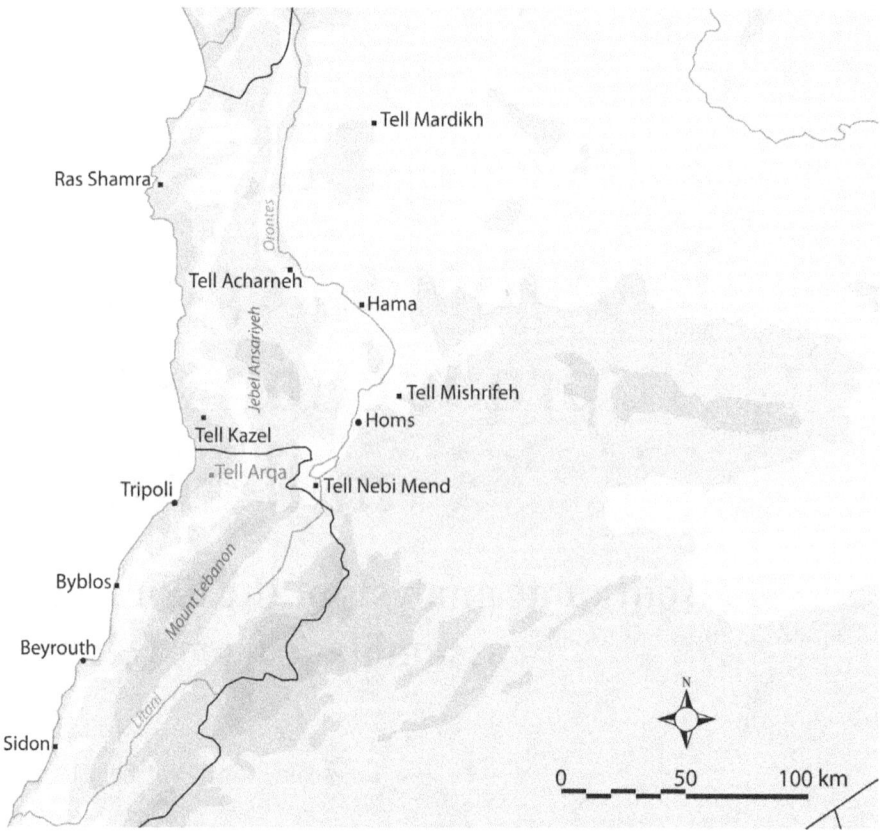

Figure 6.1: Geographic location of Tell Arqa in the Akkar plain, northern Lebanon (background map: M. Sauvage).

level and covers 4.5 ha.[1] Along with Tell Kazel and Tell Jamous, Tell Arqa is one of the three main sites of the Akkar plain during the Bronze Age.[2]

The first remains were dug up by E. Will from 1972 to 1974,[3] and the medieval fortress was unearthed by P. Leriche in 1975.[4] Since 1978, J.-P. Thalmann has headed excavations, with these focusing on the Bronze Age sequence. Until 2012, he documented occupation from the beginning of the third millennium BC to the Mameluk period, uncovering a rich and uninterrupted Early Bronze Age sequence,[5] which corresponds to Early Central Levant in ARCANE chronology.[6] The aim of the project was to establish a chronological reference for the Bronze Age Central Levant. The ceramic study was

---

1. Thalmann 2006a, 7.
2. Thalmann 2006a, 211; 2007.
3. Will et al. 1973; Thalmann 1978.
4. Leriche 1983.
5. Thalmann 2006a; 2010; 2016.
6. The full ARCANE chronological table can be found on the website of ARCANE project (http://www.arcane.uni-tuebingen.de/).

6 Evolutions of pottery production over a millennium

Phase	Stratum	Date	ARCANE Chronology	Conventional Chronology
T	20	3100 BC — 2900 calBC	ECL 2	EB II
T	19			
S	18	2800 BC — 2700/2650 calBC	ECL 3	EB II/III
R	17	2450 ± 50 calBC	ECL 4	EB III
P	16	2250 ± 50 calBC	ECL 5	EB IV A
P	15	2000 ± 50 calBC	ECL 6	EB IV B

Table 6.1: Early Bronze Age sequence of Tell Arqa and correspondence with the ARCANE and conventional chronologies. (The 'BC' dates are estimates while the 'cal. BC' are 14C dates. Thalmann 2006, 230–231; Cichocki 2007; Thalmann 2016, fig. 34).

one of the foremost goals of the mission, including typo-chronology, technology and petrography to reach a complete overview of the ceramic assemblage and to give the most convincing vision of pottery production during the third millennium BC. Petrography is a way to understand the processes of selection and treatment of raw materials, and thus to reconstruct the boundaries of the territory exploited by the potters around the production site. It can therefore be used as a good indication of the socio-economic characteristics of pottery production. The first outcomes of the petrographic study are presented hereafter.[7]

General framework: archaeological sequence

The Bronze Age excavation was focused on the western edge of the tell. In this location, the Bronze Age strata represent the most important part of the stratigraphic sequence, which is 16 m high for the third millennium BC. The strata (Strata 20–15) represent

---

7   The issues related to provenance will not be addressed in this chapter.

four chronological phases (Phase T to Phase P) from ca. 3100 BC (beginning of EB II/ECL 2) to 2000 BC (end of EB IVB/ECL 6; see Figure 6.2).[8]

The excavation revealed houses along the edge of the tell, bordering a small street. The EB pottery thus comes from domestic contexts only. The typical architectural style of the EB northern Lebanese coast consists of mudbrick walls on stone foundations, supported by wooden posts on stone bases positioned against the walls. This architectural form appears at Tell Arqa at the beginning of Phase S (EB II–III/ECL 3, ca. 2800 BC) and is observed until the end of Phase P (EB IVB/ECL 6, ca. 2000 cal. BC).[9] Moreover, the stratigraphic sequence is marked by two instances of destruction by fire. The first defines the end of Phase S (Stratum 18A; 2700/2650 cal. BC), while the second occurs during Phase P (Strata 16A and 16B, 2250 ± 50 cal. BC).[10] The exceptional preservation of the burnt strata provides a unique snapshot of life at the site, with *in situ* assemblages offering a *longue durée* perspective of ceramic change and a unique insight into material culture.

Ceramic assemblage: typo-chronology

Typo-chronological and technological investigations have been conducted on the ceramic materials by J-P. Thalmann[11] and V. Roux.[12]

The typological study evidenced two main features: local characteristics,[13] and a general trend towards progressive diversification of the ceramic repertoire.[14] During Phase T, pottery shapes are almost limited to carinated platters, storage jars and cooking pots, with jugs and hemispherical bowls also represented (Figure 6.2).

From Phase S onwards, open forms become rare, most probably due to a significant change in consumption habits. Although carinated platters were present at the very beginning of Phase S, once they disappear, they are not replaced by any other open shape. The ceramic assemblage from Phase S consists of hemispherical bowls (of which two-thirds at least served as lamps, as indicated by burning on the rims),[15] handled pots, globular pots without handles, jugs (globular or elongated, with large flat to very narrow bases and large to narrow necks), small jars, large storage jars and globular cooking pots. Scarcer shapes, including basins, are also occasionally encountered (Figure 6.3).

During Phase R, the repertoire of pottery shapes evolves and includes the new four-spouted lamps, handled cups, jugs (with flat base and flaring neck, or narrow

---

8   Thalmann 2010, fig. 4; 2016.
9   Thalmann 2006b.
10 Thalmann 2006a, 19–28; 2010, 88–90.
11 Thalmann 2006a; 2010; 2016.
12 Roux 2013; Roux and Thalmann 2016.
13 Limited typological parallels can be drawn from the Tell Arqa ceramic assemblage. See the detailed analysis in Thalmann 2006a; 2016.
14 All details about ceramic typo-chronology can be found in Thalmann 2006a; 2010; 2016.
15 Thalmann 2012, 177.

6 Evolutions of pottery production over a millennium

base and narrow neck), globular pots, storage jars and cooking pots (Figure 6.4). The handled cups then become a diagnostic feature of the assemblage until the end of the third millennium BC, revealing a change towards drinking culture: it seems to be the local expression of the goblet tradition evidenced throughout the Levant during this period.[16]

Finally, the ceramic repertoire from Phase P is the most diversified. Among small vases, handled cups are the most common, although bowls and goblets of different types are also attested. Four-spouted lamps, jugs with large to narrow necks and trefoil rims, globular pots, small jars, large storage jars and cooking pots complete the assemblage. Rarer types also occur: miniature vases, stands, storage jars with rich decoration (R3 jars), medium jugs and jars with painted decoration and baking trays (Figure 6.5).

Surface treatments evolve according to the chronological phases and are especially useful for dating the Arqa pottery.[17] During Phase T, all vessels are vertically burnished. Then, surface treatments differ on large vessels and medium to small ones. Phase S small and medium shapes are pattern-burnished, while larger vessels are pattern-combed. Pattern-combing continues during Phase R on large vases, along with horizontal combing, while small and medium vessels are vertically burnished. Finally, horizontal combing and vertical burnishing continue during Phase P, the former on large vessels and the latter on small and medium ones. Medium to large storage vases may display impressed decoration at the base of the neck. Slipping is almost never observed, and painting occurs rarely, on very specific productions, mostly from Phase P (cf. jars and jugs with white painted horizontal and wavy bands).[18]

To sum up, one major change occurs in pottery typology between Phase T and Phase S. The carinated platters from Phase T disappear without being replaced by any other open shape, while handled drinking vessels appear by the beginning of Phase S. This shift in the repertoire reveals a significant break in consumption habits at that time, from sharing food to drinking in individual cups.[19] Then, during Phase S onwards, the pottery shapes evolve in a more continuous way, and although the repertoire becomes more diversified, no sharp change is observed within the general morphology of the vessels. The handled pots from Phase S become smaller, transforming into the handled cups of Phases R and P. Likewise, the narrow-base jugs from Phase S evolve into the jugs with narrower bases from Phase R. Cooking pots are globular and only exhibit rim variations over time. Thus, by the end of Phase T (EB II/ECL2), the pottery assemblage demonstrates significant evolution with a progressive diversification of the repertoire.

---

16 Bunimovitz and Greenberg 2004.
17 Roux and Thalmann 2016, Table 2.
18 Thalmann 2006a, pls 60, 1–2; 64–65.
19 Bunimovitz and Greenberg 2004.

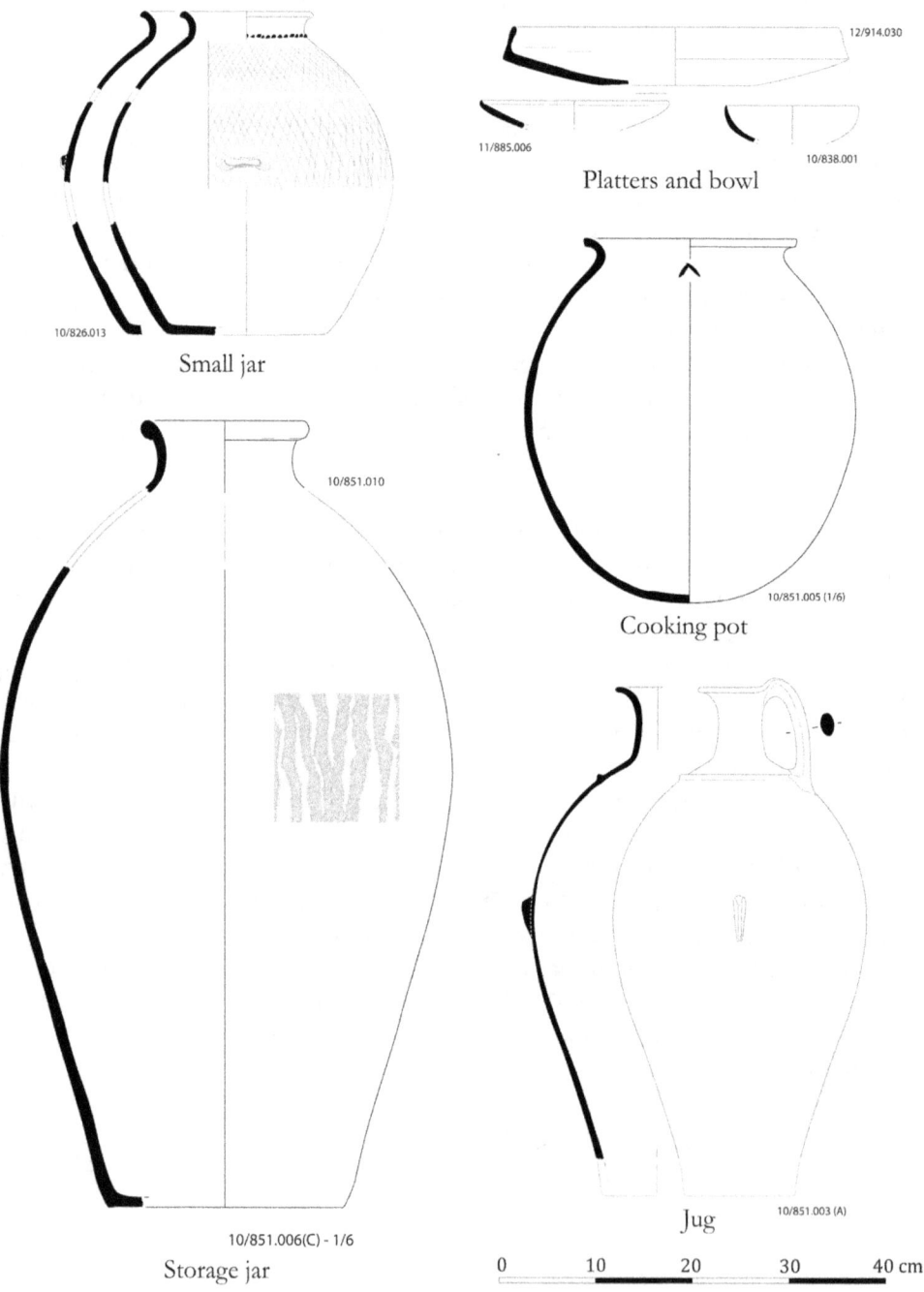

Figure 6.2: Ceramic types from Phase T (after Thalmann 2016, pl. 1–7).

6 Evolutions of pottery production over a millennium

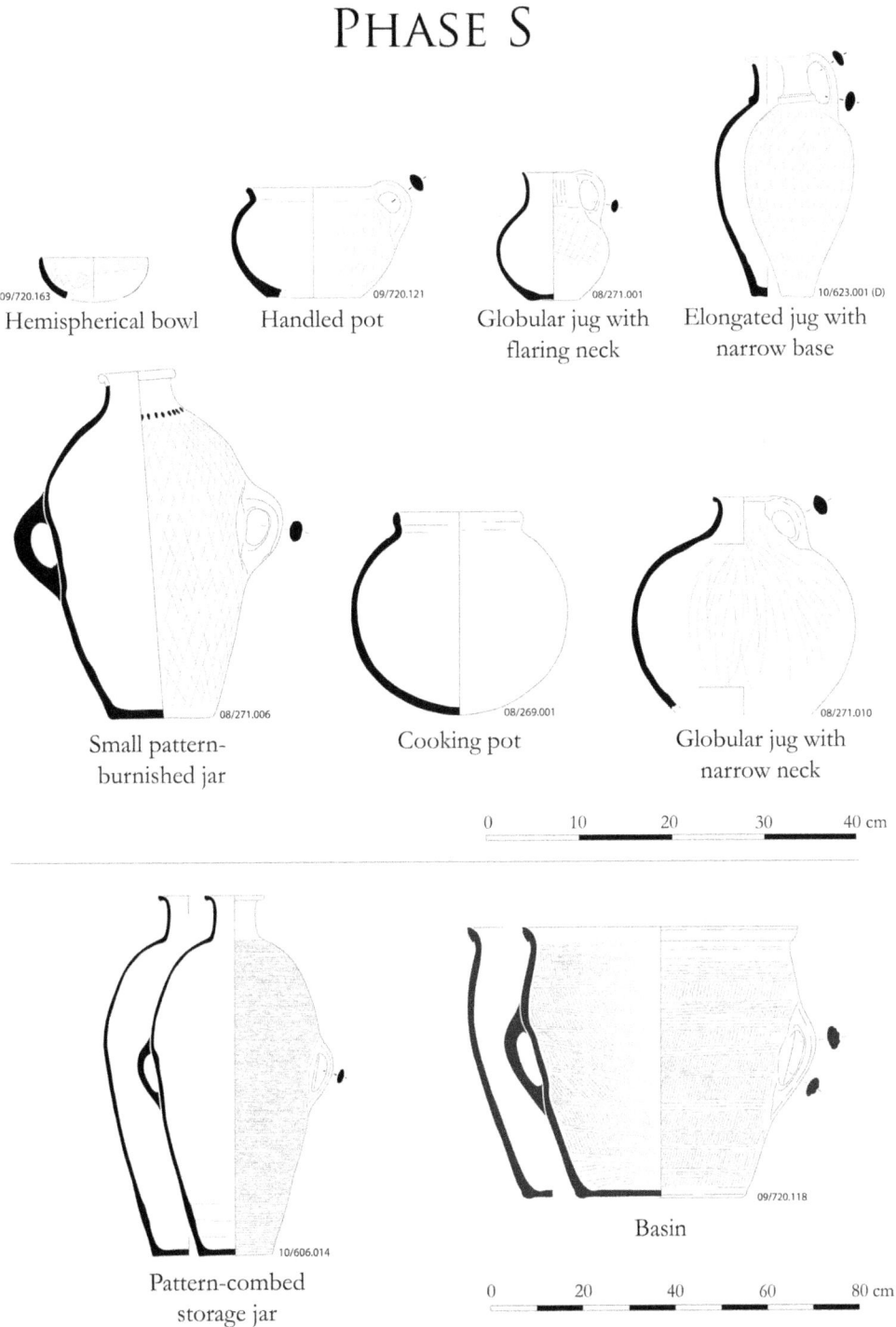

Figure 6.3: Ceramic types from Phase S (after Thalmann 2009, pl. 1-2; 2016, pl. 8-22).

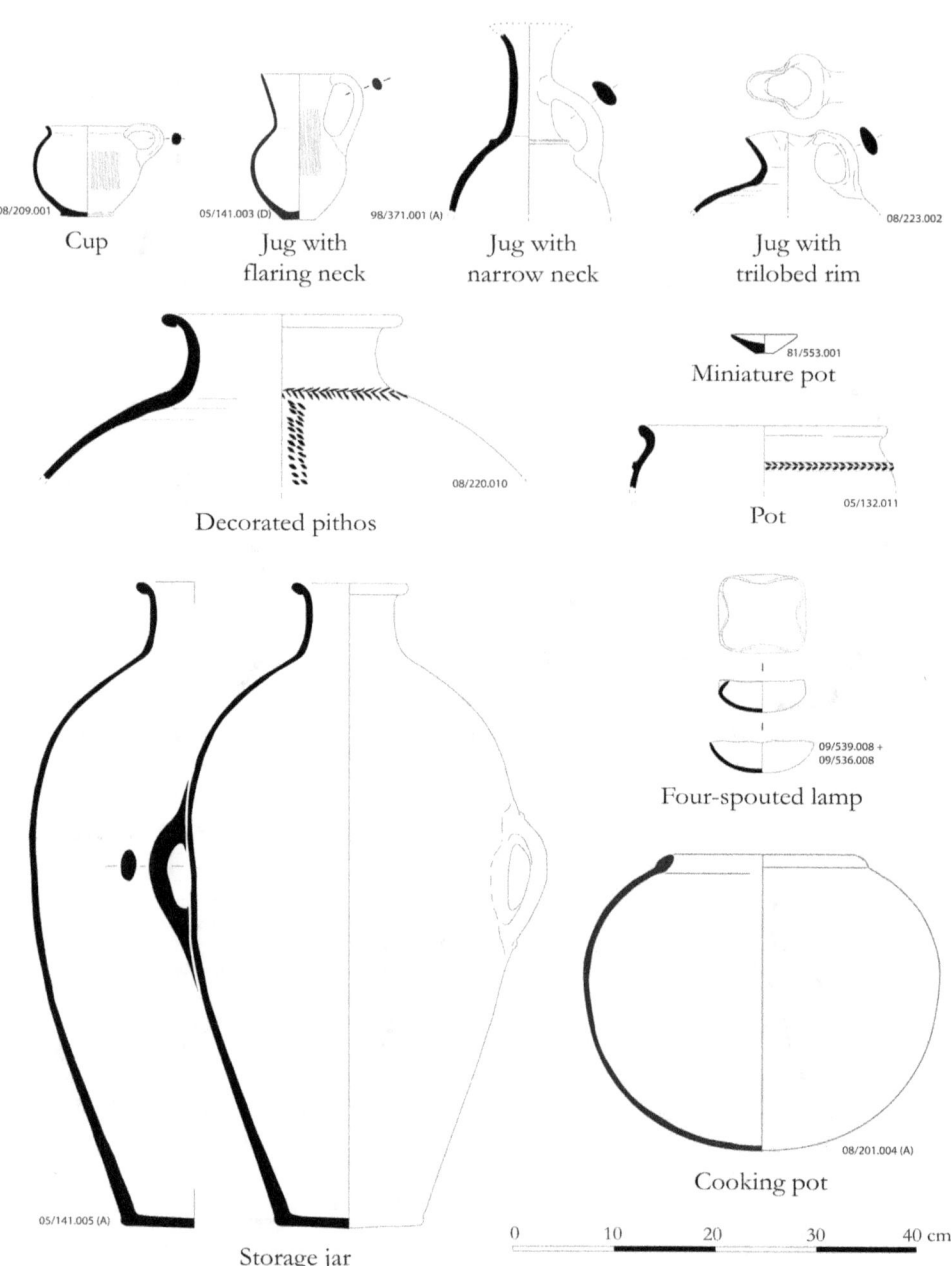

Figure 6.4: Ceramic types from Phase R (after Thalmann 2006, pl. 46–55; 2016, pl. 23–28).

Manufacturing processes

The technological investigation evidenced continuity in the manufacturing processes. One main *chaîne opératoire* is identified: on a basalt fly-wheel stone, the flat bases are made of a spiral coil, and a peripheral coil is added before building the wall with pinched coils.[20] Fast rotation (Rotary Kinetic Energy/RKE, as defined by Roux)[21] was used for fashioning vessels from Phase T onwards, at first in a limited way, before becoming common during the third millennium BC. During Phase P, RKE is used in the making of almost all vessels. The determining factor in the diffusion of the use of fast rotation is the substitution of basalt fly-wheel stone for the more efficient Palestinian *tournette* during Phase P, which is eventually replaced by the *tenon tournette* at the very end of the third millennium BC. This manufacturing process is evidenced in the making of all ceramic shapes, from goblets to storage jars, with the exception of cooking pots.[22] However, different surface treatments are used within this *chaîne opératoire*, depending on the chronological phases: vertical or pattern burnishing, horizontal or pattern combing are the most common. Internal combing is only observed during Phase S on the internal surface of storage jars. Since it is not visible from the outside, this surface treatment cannot be considered as decoration but is more probably a technical feature to join the coils of the jar body together.[23]

A second *chaîne opératoire* has been evidenced in the making of cooking pots. The base and walls are built with pinched coils. Then the body is shaped using slow rotation. This method differs from the first one because of the rounded bases, possibly made by scraping the base when leather-hard, and a self-slip is obtained by smoothing the surface with a wet hand.[24]

Finally, the technological study highlighted a strong continuity throughout the third millennium BC. Only one main *chaîne opératoire* is used to make the entire assemblage (except cooking pots) and the use of RKE continues throughout the millennium. The Palestinian *tournette* is introduced during Phase P without any social or technical rupture. In fact, only surface treatments evolve according to chronological progression. As stated by Roux,[25] this implies a strong social homogeneity and stability among the potters, and suggests the specialisation of potters from Phase T onwards.

Petrographic study: aims of the study

The selection of raw materials is the basis of pottery production, as it determines the aspect and qualities of the products. Therefore, the petrographic study may highlight

---

20 Roux and Thalmann 2016.
21 Courty and Roux 1995.
22 Roux 2013, 321.
23 Thalmann 2016.
24 Roux and Thalmann 2016.
25 Roux 2013, 323.

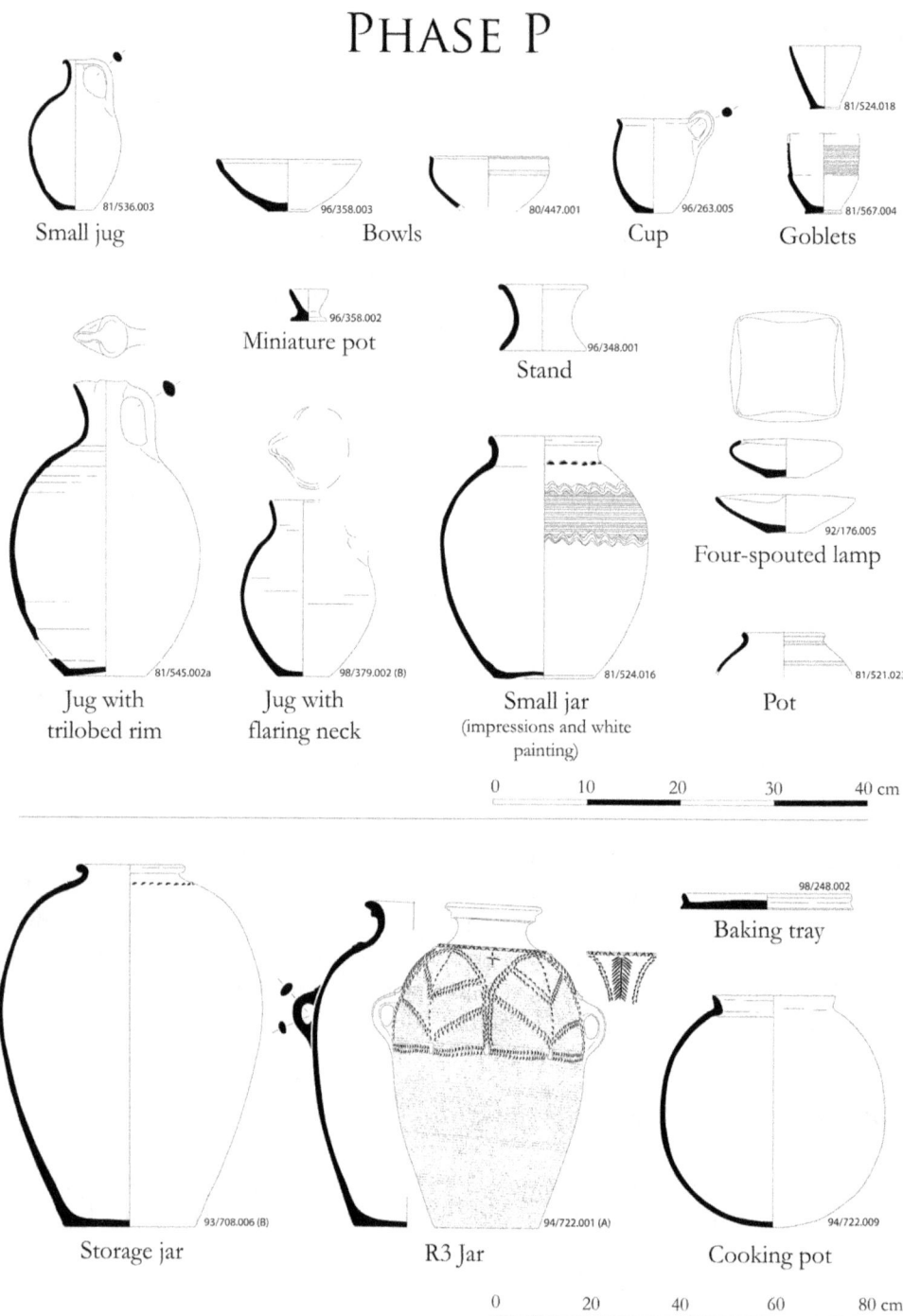

Figure 6.5: Ceramic types from Phase P (after Thalmann 2006, pl. 54–79).

important characteristics of the organisation of the production. The first step in this work was to distinguish and characterise different fabrics. The results were then correlated to the archaeological, chronological, typological and technological data. The study aimed to examine the correlations between the selection of raw materials and the typological and technological features of the ceramic assemblage, in order to offer new interpretations on the organisation of pottery production and its socio-economic implications. It would also enable an assessment of the degree of craft specialisation present at Tell Arqa during the third millennium BC.

Methodology and sampling

The petrographic study was conducted on two scales of analysis. Macroscopic observations were carried out by naked eye and stereomicroscope, while microscopic data was collected by observing thin sections under a polarising microscope. Thorough macroscopic registration includes description of the matrix colours (surfaces and core), and frequency, colours, size and shape of the non-plastic inclusions. Microscopic analysis gives further description of the matrix (colours in PPL and XPL, optical activity), identification of the mineralogy of the inclusions and description of their frequency, size and shape.

During the macroscopic study, a set of 1359 diagnostic sherds from identified shapes and securely stratified contexts were considered. The samples were distributed among the chronological phases of the third millennium BC and the morpho-functional classes (Figure 6.6). The results led to the development of macroscopic groups.

In order to avoid eventual quantitative bias in this first sampling – limited to diagnostic sherds – a complementary approach was implemented. Closed and well-documented archaeological contexts were chosen and a second corpus of potsherds from these contexts was analysed regardless of any typological consideration. This second dataset of 2447 sherds from Phases T (n = 502), S (n = 528) and P (n = 1417) was distributed among the macroscopic groups.[26] This methodology enables us to consider the actual proportions of each fabric within the assemblage. Residual materials from other chronological phases, representing 1% to 6% of the sampling, were excluded. As Phase R did not provide a closed archaeological context suitable for this type of analysis – the proportion of residual sherds is too high – Phase R data was thus limited to the first set of macroscopic observations on diagnostic sherds.

Among the diagnostic sherds from the macroscopic study, 74 samples were selected for thin section analysis.[27] They represent the chronological phases and the typological diversity of the assemblage. The microscopic analysis gave a further documentation of the samples and led to the definition of microscopic groups that have been correlated to the macroscopic ones. In this way, macroscopy enables us to consider very large samplings – thousands of samples – while microscopy gives thorough data on fabrics. Both methods are thus complementary and need to be conducted together.

---

26 Roux and Thalmann 2016.
27 This number of samples is likely to increase in the future.

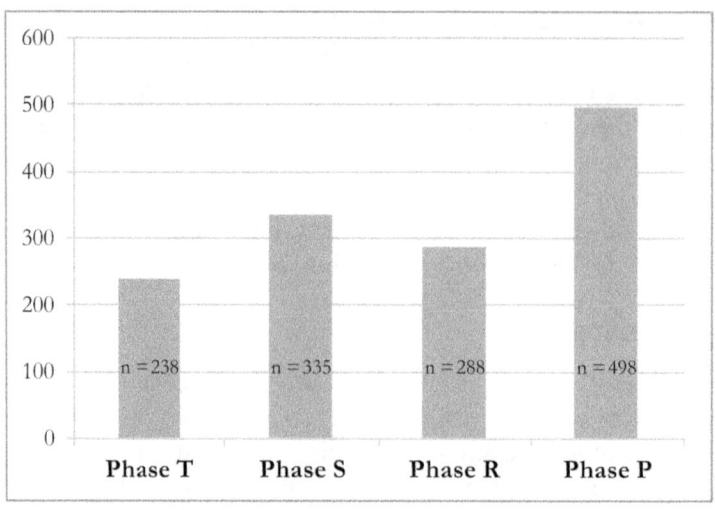

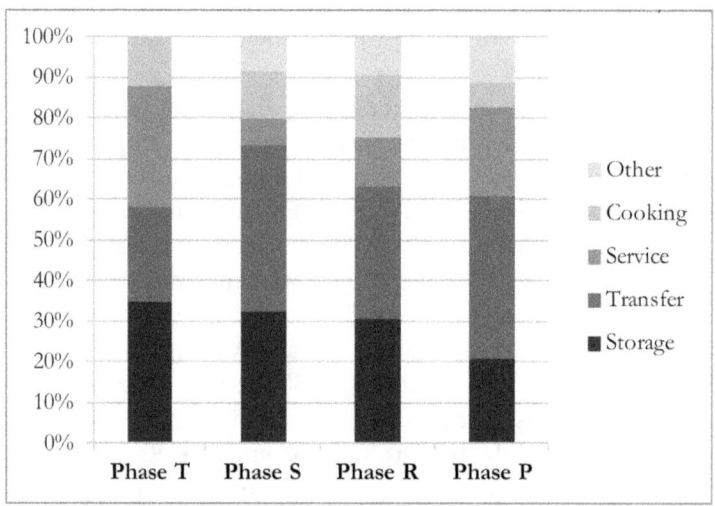

	Phase T	Phase S	Phase R	Phase P
Storage	34.45 %	32.24 %	30.56 %	20.68 %
Transfer	22.69 %	40.90 %	32.64 %	39.96 %
Service	29.41 %	6.57 %	11.81 %	22.09 %
Cooking	12.19 %	11.64 %	15.62 %	5.82 %
Other	1.26 %	8.65 %	9.37 %	11.45 %

Figure 6.6: Repartition of diagnostic samples from the first dataset selected for the macroscopic analysis. Top: number of studied diagnostic samples per chronological phase. Middle and bottom: repartition of the studied diagnostic samples per chronological phase and morpho-functional class. 'Storage' corresponds to storage jars; 'Transfer' to medium vases (jugs, small jars, pots); 'Service' to platters, cups and goblets; and 'Cooking' to cooking pots and baking trays.

6 Evolutions of pottery production over a millennium

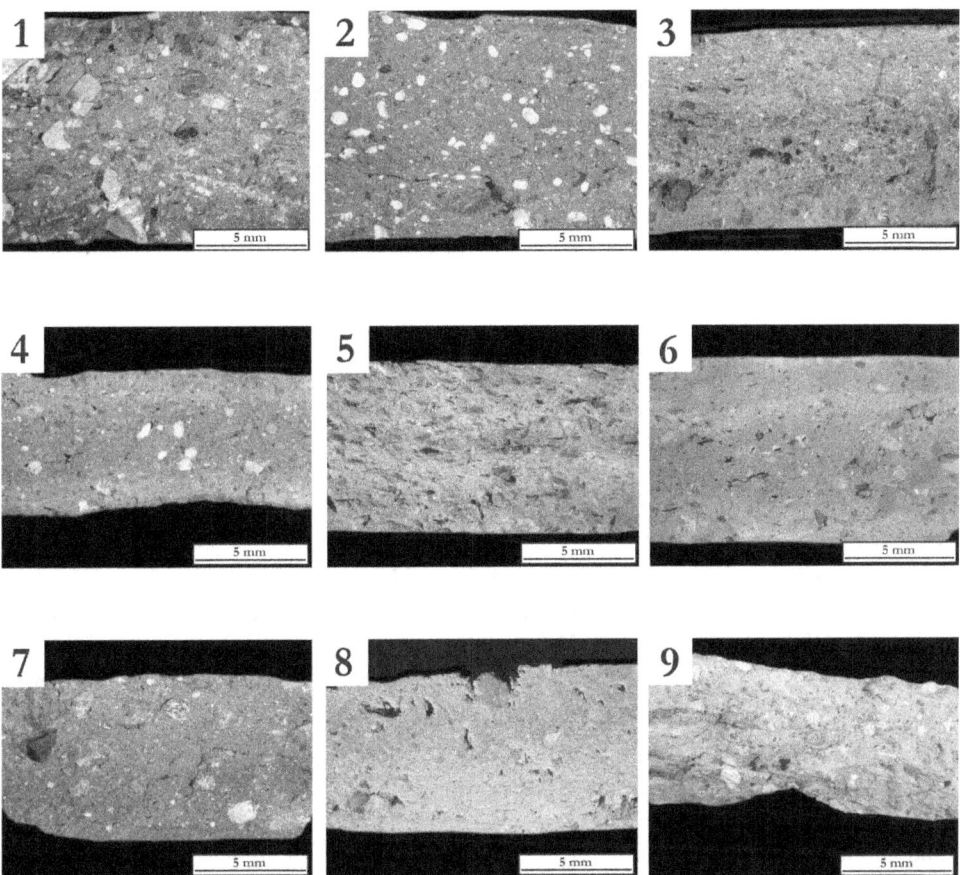

Figure 6.7: Illustrations of the nine petrographic groups (macrophotographs under stereomicroscope).

Results: nine petrographic groups

The petrographic analysis revealed a good correspondence between the macro and microscopic groups. Nine petrographic groups have been defined – regarding primarily the nature and characteristics of the non-plastic inclusions. The macroscopic features of the nine groups are presented below (Figure 6.8).[28]

Group 1: Samples from group 1 contain a high percentage of coarse non-plastic inclusions (25–30%, up to very coarse sand or granules),[29] characterised by rhombohedral calcite inclusions. The matrix is usually red-brown to black in colour. Other non-plastic inclusions are limestone, quartz grains, iron-rich argillaceous clasts and foraminifera. The samples may also contain some vegetal inclusions. Group 1

---

28 The results of microscopic observations, a further petrographic description and microphotographs of the groups are given in Jean 2018.
29 According to the Wentworth grain size classification.

demonstrates a higher variability than the other groups, regarding the matrix colour and the relative proportions of inclusions.

Group 2: Samples from group 2 usually contain around 20–25% non-plastic inclusions. The matrix ranges from red-brown to dark grey in colour. The non-plastic inclusions are mainly rounded limestone and rounded quartz grains, in all grain size classes but mostly coarse to very coarse sands. Other non-plastics are red to black angular iron-rich argillaceous clasts, and foraminifera.

Group 3: Samples from group 3 contain approximately 20% non-plastic inclusions, including rounded limestone, foraminifera, iron-rich argillaceous clasts and angular quartz grains. The matrix is red-brown to grey in colour.

Group 4: Samples from group 4 contain 20–30% non-plastic inclusions. The matrix is usually light brown to red-brown. Rounded quartz grains are predominant; some limestone inclusions and foraminifera are also present. Iron-rich argillaceous clasts are less common.

Group 5: Samples from group 5 contain 20–25% non-plastic inclusions. The matrix is usually orange to grey or red. The non-plastic inclusions include mainly Argillaceous Rock Fragments (ARFs),[30] of rounded shape and low sphericity, with a preferential fracture plane in the direction of elongation of the grains. The ARFs' colours vary as the surrounding matrix does and the ARFs are enclosed by a void, demonstrating their argillaceous composition with a high shrinkage rate. They are mostly oriented alongside the surfaces and give a very specific aspect to the fabric. Other inclusions consist of a few limestone and quartz grains.

Group 6: Samples from group 6 contain around 25% non-plastic inclusions. The matrix is light orange to grey in colour. The sand-sized inclusions are limestone and quartz grains, ARFs and iron-rich argillaceous clasts. Voids of organic origin may be observed in some samples.

Group 7: Samples from group 7 contain 25–30% non-plastic inclusions. The matrix is usually brown to dark grey-black in colour. The presence of rounded basalt to basalt-dolerite grains is specific to this group, along with limestone, iron-rich argillaceous clasts and some quartz grains.

Group 8: Samples from group 8 contain 15–20% non-plastic inclusions. The matrix is much lighter in colours, ranging from beige to pink and greenish-grey shades. The inclusions are grey chert, quartz grains, limestone and a few iron-rich argillaceous clasts. The overall proportion of siliceous material is higher than in the other groups and the samples do not contain foraminifera.

Group 9: Samples from group 9 contain about 20% non-plastic inclusions. The matrix is grey to red-brown in colour. The non-plastic inclusions are mostly rounded limestone with some quartz grains, iron-rich argillaceous clasts and foraminifera.

In some groups, several variants may have been distinguished – but all samples share the main characteristics of the group. The non-plastic inclusions, whose mineralogy has been confirmed in thin sections, are consistent with the local geological environment

---

30 As defined by I.K. Whitbread (1986).

6 Evolutions of pottery production over a millennium

surrounding Tell Arqa and its wider region.[31] This corroborates the idea previously drawn from the typological examination that pottery production is predominantly of local origin and local shapes.

Petrography and chronology

The principal outcome of the petrographic analysis is a demonstrated and strong link between fabrics and chronology. The results are detailed hereafter in the light of the chronological, typological and technological data.

Description of the results

The petrographic data demonstrates an evolution in the selection of raw materials throughout the third millennium BC. As mentioned previously, two datasets were analysed. The first one is constituted of diagnostic samples (Figure 6.9). To carry out a more accurate quantitative analysis, a second dataset from well-documented and secure archaeological contexts was considered, regardless of any typological selection (Figure 6.10).

Repartition of diagnostic samples from the first dataset observed in macroscopy among the petrographic groups and chronological phases.

Repartition of the samples from the second dataset (no typological consideration) observed in macroscopy among the petrographic groups and chronological phases.[32]

The chronological division of the petrographic groups provides important results, highlighting the fabric changes over time (Figures 6.8–6.9). During Phase T, groups 5 and 6 are the most common: group 5 represents the bulk of the assemblage. Subsequently it is only observed in very low proportions during Phase S, before disappearing during Phase R. Group 6 also disappears during Phase S. Group 2 is present from the beginning of the EBA in small proportions, becoming more common during Phase S and disappearing before Phase P. Group 4 is only identifiable during Phases S and R, while groups 7 and 9 are typical of Phase P. Group 8 is represented in low proportions during Phases R and P. The percentage progression of group 3 is one of the most interesting results: this fabric, which appears during Phase T (Stratum 19), progressively increases until it reaches a very high percentage of production during Phase P. During Phase P, this group accounts for a significant proportion of the assemblage, up to 85%. In contrast, group 1 is present in relatively stable proportions (about 10–15%) throughout the third millennium BC.

Here, the comparison between the two datasets is useful. In the first dataset (that of the diagnostic sherds; Figure 6.8), the proportions of rarer groups are higher than in the entire assemblage (second dataset, no typological selection; Figure 6.9). Conversely, the proportions of the most common groups are lower in the first sampling. It clearly

---

31 The microscopic data are further developed in Jean 2018.
32 As mentioned, archaeological contexts from Phase R were not reliable enough to carry out this analysis without using typo-chronological data: the groups proportions are here reconstructed from Phase S and Phase P.

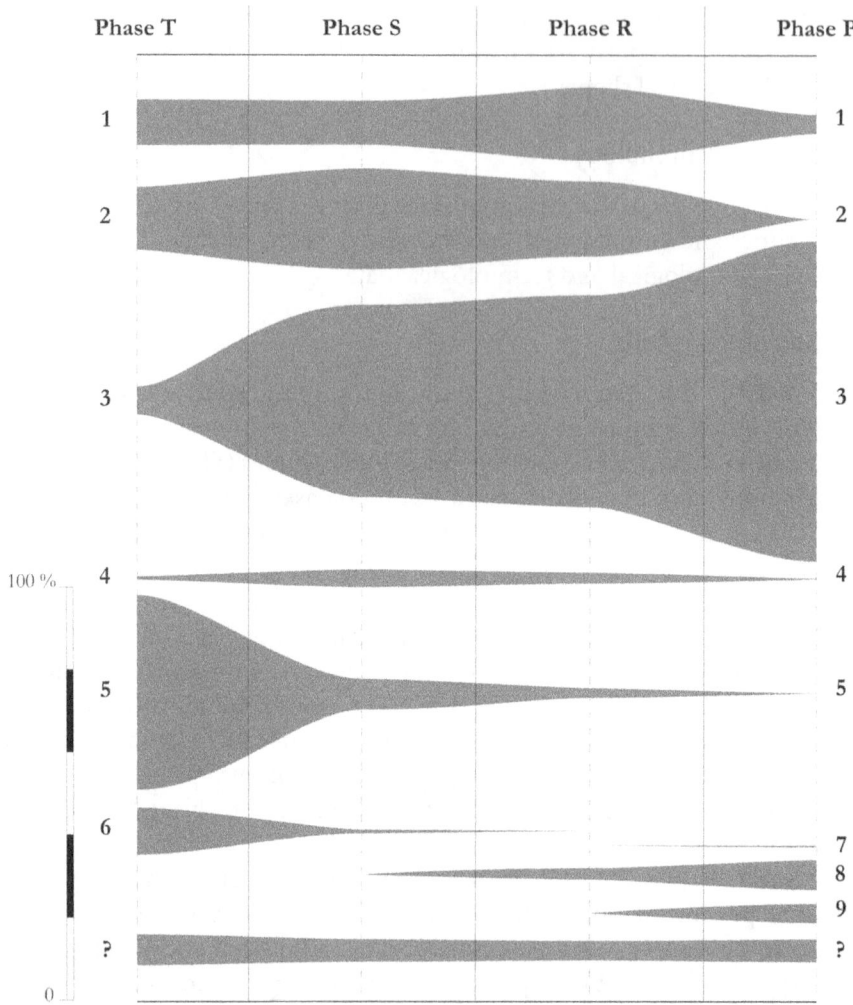

	Phase T	Phase S	Phase R	Phase P
1	10.92 %	10.45 %	17.71 %	4.62 %
2	15.13 %	24.48 %	18.40 %	0.00 %
3	6.72 %	46.57 %	51.04 %	77.31 %
4	0.84 %	4.48 %	2.78 %	0.20 %
5	47.06 %	7.45 %	2.43 %	0.00 %
6	11.34 %	0.90 %	0.00 %	0.00 %
7	0.00 %	0.00 %	0.00 %	0.40 %
8	0.00 %	0.00 %	2.78 %	7.23 %
9	0.00 %	0.00 %	0.00 %	4.62 %
?	7.99 %	5.67 %	4.86 %	5.62 %

Figure 6.8: Repartition of diagnostic samples from the first dataset observed in macroscopy among the different petrographic groups.

6 Evolutions of pottery production over a millennium

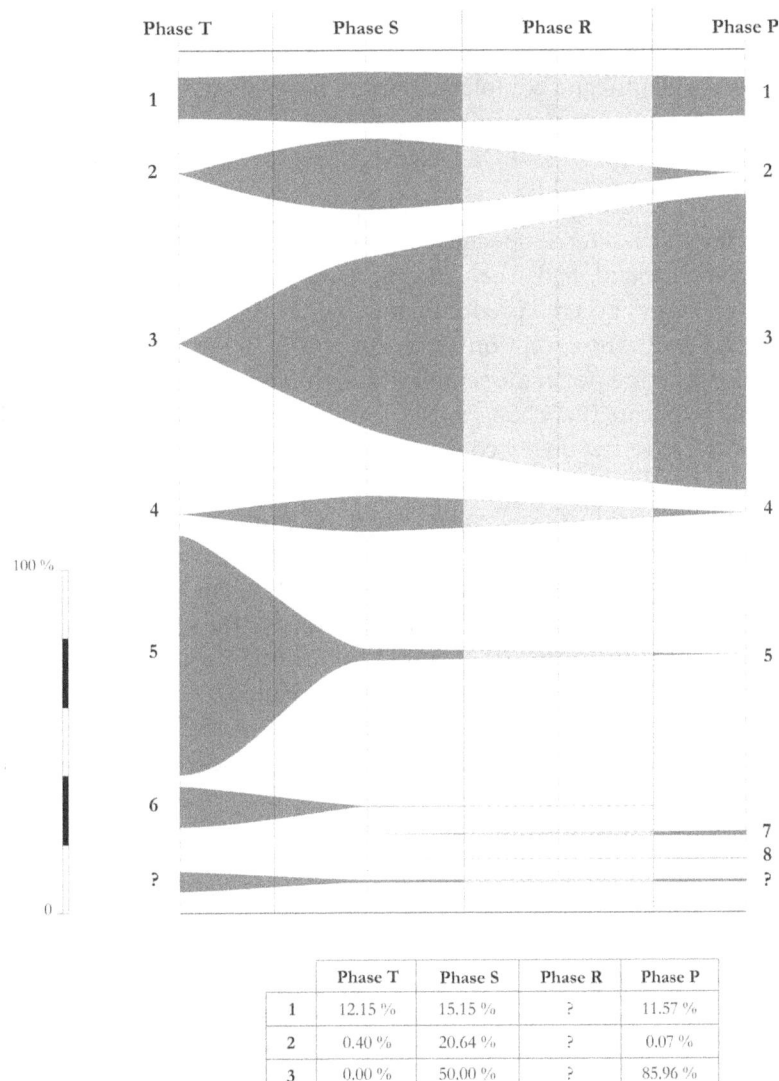

	Phase T	Phase S	Phase R	Phase P
1	12.15 %	15.15 %	?	11.57 %
2	0.40 %	20.64 %	?	0.07 %
3	0.00 %	50.00 %	?	85.96 %
4	0.00 %	9.85 %	?	0.00 %
5	69.72 %	3.41 %	?	0.00 %
6	11.75 %	0.19 %	?	0.00 %
7	0.00 %	0.00 %	?	0.40 %
8	0.00 %	0.00 %	?	1.34 %
9	0.00 %	0.00 %	?	0.00 %
?	5.98 %	0.76 %	?	0.92 %

Figure 6.9: Repartition of the samples from the second dataset (non diagnostic and diagnostic sherds) observed in macroscopy among the different petrographic groups. The samples from documented archaeological contexts were analysed without any selection or typological consideration. As Phase R strata did not provide a closed archaeological context suitable for this work, no quantitative analysis could be lead on the assemblage from Phase R without considering the typo-chronological data. The proportions of the petrographic groups for Phase R are reconstructed here from the proportions obtained for Phase S and Phase P.

indicates that the typological selection of pottery during the excavation implies an over-representation of peculiar types, and then of unusual fabrics. The use of a non-sorted dataset is helpful and complementary to balance out the bias.

Interpretation

The results indicate that the selection of raw materials varied through time. Some of the fabric groups characterise specific periods: groups 5 and 6 were preferred during Phase T and then abandoned. Then groups 2 and 3 are used during Phases S and R; while during Phase P, group 3 predominates, with this fabric group used to make all kinds of vessels (with the exception of cooking pots). Groups 4, 6, 7 and 8 constitute a low percentage of the pottery assemblage (Figures 6.9–6.10).

It therefore appears that changes do affect the pottery production processes, but they seem progressive and do not constitute a sudden break. For instance, the presence of group 3 since the end of Phase T and its gradual development until Phase P reveals a likely continuous production. Second, the stable proportion of group 1 among the assemblage across the millennium is a marker of consistency. The only change we could really highlight occurs by the end of Phase T, when the main fabrics of that period (groups 5 and 6) disappear to be replaced during the subsequent phase by very different fabrics (groups 2 and 3). This shift is correlated with the change of pottery shapes already underlined: disappearance of open platters and emergence of drinking vessels. To sum up, the petrographic results show a progressive evolution of the pottery production processes, as the typological and technological studies suggested, with the exception of the transition between Phases T and S, which could correspond to a deeper cultural change at the site.

Chronological value of petrographic observations

The results also indicate that petrographic observations may be used as a chronological indicator. As some fabrics characterise chronological phases, the identification of the fabric provides a significant element for dating. In that manner, a potsherd identified as group 5 is likely to belong to Phase T. The evolution of fabrics, correlated with the archaeological phases, may therefore offer important chronological insight into the Tell Arqa pottery sequence, even at a macroscopic scale. This should however be combined with archaeological, typological and technological observations to reach an accurate dating.

Organisation of pottery production

Conversely, the evolution of the selection of raw materials reflects changes in the organisation of pottery production. The abandonment of a raw material in favour of another may be related to several possibilities: inaccessibility of a supply source; changes in the manufacturing processes; surface treatments or firing modes that necessitate the adaptation of the fabrics; functional choices depending on the appreciation of the raw materials' qualities by the potter; or even preference for some specific colours or aspects of fabric. At this point of the petrographic analysis, it is not possible to determine which of these factors (maybe several of them) led to these observable changes.

However, we are able to propose some interpretations. Group 1, because of its stability over time, is an exception. The presence of calcite, probably crushed and added to the natural clay, is probably related to the function of the vessels, all made for cooking. Tempering the clay with calcite is thus probably a functional choice to enhance the resistance of the fabric.[33]

Apart from group 1, the potters always preferred one or two fabrics during each chronological phase: group 5 during Phase T, groups 2 and 3 during Phases S and R, and group 3 during Phase P. The synchronous variability of fabrics is thus restricted, which may suggest a limited number of production places or workshops. The other groups are related to marginal productions that may be local, or from a smaller independent workshop; or perhaps they may be exogenous.[34]

In addition, group 3 represents a very high proportion of the EB IV assemblage. It reveals a trend towards standardisation of the fabrics until Phase P, correlated with the standardisation of manufacturing processes and the diffusion of wheel-coiling.[35] According to Roux's hypothesis, the continuity of the manufacturing processes reveals a homogeneous social group of potters. It is thus possible that both the standardisation of fabrics and the introduction of wheel-coiling occur within the context of homogeneous pottery production, and do not necessarily reveal a change in organisation. However, it may also reflect the growth of a pre-existing workshop delivering its production to the whole site. In terms of craft specialisation, the continuity in pottery production and the related homogeneity of the social group may suggest the specialisation of the potters from Phase T onwards. The relatively small number of groups of ceramic raw materials for a period of a thousand years moves in this direction, suggesting that the pottery production had been in the hands of a restricted group of specialised craftsmen since the beginning of the EBA.

Conclusion

The petrographic analysis of the EBA ceramics from Tell Arqa offers new data to interpret pottery production. First, the chronological value of the petrographic observations is now attested in a comprehensive approach, which means that typological and technological features also need to be considered. The petrographic analysis corroborates the main trends evidenced by the typological and technological studies, demonstrating the existence of progressive changes in the selection of raw materials. It also confirms the evolution of manufacturing processes, within a general continuity throughout

---

33 Shoval et al. 1993.
34 The issue of identification of exogenous ceramics in the Tell Arqa assemblage is not discussed here.
35 Roux 2013, 321.

the third millennium BC. The trend towards standardisation in the selection of raw materials and manufacturing processes is associated with a gradual diversification of the repertoire of pottery shapes. These conclusions support the hypothesis about the early specialisation of the Arqa potters, from Phase T onwards.

The petrographic study also highlights new features in the evolution of pottery production. It especially evidenced marginal productions, identified in low proportions across the entire assemblage. However, these need to be further analysed to determine their provenance and production framework. These uncommon potteries may have been produced by small local workshops; or were possibly exogenous. In this perspective, their study can contribute to the reconstitution of the trade networks in the EBA northern Levant. Moreover, a further analysis of the petrographic results along with archaeological and other pottery data will improve our knowledge of craft production during the third millennium BC.

Acknowledgements

This chapter is based on a 2016 state of research of my PhD, which I defended in 2019; the samplings and results could vary as the work is progressing, but we may consider the general framework reliable. I am very grateful to Dr Jean-Paul Thalmann, who gave me the opportunity to study the Tell Arqa ceramics and guided me in this work. I am also indebted to Pr Pascal Butterlin and Dr Sophie Méry, who supervised my PhD research and read the drafts of this chapter. Many thanks to J.-M. Pannecoucke for revising the English of this chapter. Finally, I would like to thank Dr Melissa Kennedy for inviting me to contribute to this book.

References

Bunimovitz, S. and Greenberg, R. (2004). Revealed in their cups: Syrian drinking practices in Intermediate Bronze Age Canaan. *Bulletin of the American School of Oriental Research* 334: 19–31.
Cichocki, O. (2007). Analysis of charcoal samples from Early Bronze Age strata at Tell Arqa. *Archaeology and History in Lebanon* 26–27: 99–109.
Courty, M-A. and Roux, V. (1995). Identification of wheel throwing on the basis of ceramic surface features and microfabrics. *Journal of Archaeological Science* 22: 17–50.
Jean, M. (2018). Pottery production at Tell Arqa (Lebanon) during the 3rd millennium BC: preliminary results of petrographic analysis. *Levant*, doi.org/10.1080/00758914.2018.1454239.
Leriche, P. (1983). Les défenses orientales de Tell Arqa au Moyen Age. *Syria* LX(1–2): 111–132.
Maritan, L., Mazzoli, C., Michielin, V., Morandi-Bonacossi, D., Luciani, M. and Molin, G. (2005). The provenance and production technology of Bronze Age and Iron Age pottery from Tell Mishrifeh/Qatna (Syria). *Archaeometry* 47(4): 723–744.

Roux, V. (2013). Spreading of innovative technical traits and cumulative technical evolution: continuity or discontinuity? *Journal of Archaeological Method and Theory* 20(2): 312–330.

Roux, V. and Thalmann, J-P. (2016). Évolution technologique et morpho-stylistique des assemblages céramiques de Tell Arqa (Liban, 3e millénaire av. J-C.): stabilité sociologique et changements culturels. *Paléorient* 42(1): 101–127.

Shoval, S., Gaft, M., Beck, P. and Kirsh, Y. (1993). Thermal behaviour of limestone and monocrystalline calcite tempers during firing and their use in ancient vessels. *Journal of Thermal Analysis* 40: 263–273.

Thalmann, J-P. (1978). Tell Arqa (Liban nord), campagnes I-III (1972–1974), chantier and rapport préliminaire. *Syria* LV(1–2): 1–151.

(2006). *Tell Arqa I. Les niveaux de l'âge du Bronze.* Bibliothèque Archéologique and Historique T.177. Beyrouth: Institut Français du Proche-Orient.

(2006b). Nouvelles données sur l'architecture domestique du Bronze Ancien IV à Tell Arqa (Liban). *Comptes-rendus des séances de l'Académie des Inscriptions et Belles-Lettres* 150: 841–873.

(2007). Settlement patterns and agriculture in the Akkar plain during the late Early and early Middle Bronze Ages. In *Urban and natural landscapes of an ancient Syrian capital: settlement and environment at Tell Mishrifeh/Qatna and in central-western Syria: proceedings of the international conference held in Udine, 9–11 December 2004.* D. Morandi-Bonacossi, ed. 219–232. Studi archeologici su Qatna 1. Udine: Forum.

(2010). Tell Arqa: a prosperous city during the Bronze Age. *Near Eastern Archaeology* 73(2–3): 86–101.

(2012). *Ex Oriente Lux*: l'invention de la lampe au Proche-Orient. In *Aux marges de l'archéologie: hommage à Serge Cleuziou.* J. Giraud and G. Gernez, eds. 175–185. Paris: De Boccard.

(2016). Rapport préliminaire sur les campagnes de 2008 à 2012 à Tell Arqa. *Bulletin d'Archéologie et d'Architecture Libanaises* 16: 15–78.

Welton, L. (2014). Revisiting the 'Amuq sequence: a preliminary investigation of the EB IVB ceramic assemblage from Tell Tayinat. *Levant* 46(3): 339–370.

Whitbread, I.K. (1986). The characterisation of argillaceous inclusions in ceramic thin section. *Archaeometry* 28(1): 79–88.

Will, E., Dentzer, J-M. and Thalmann, J-P. (1973). La première campagne de fouilles à Tell 'Arqa (Liban nord). *Bulletin du Musée de Beyrouth* 36: 61–79.

7

The 1968 survey in the Beqa' of Lebanon and its relevance to the archaeology of the central Levant ca. 2500–2000/1900 BC

Kay Prag
Manchester Museum

In 1968 I made a brief survey in the Beqa' of Lebanon to explore three principal questions: to investigate the relevance of the Beqa' as a land route between the north and south Levant to our understanding of the cultural changes appearing during the Intermediate Bronze Age (IBA) in the south; to look at the nature of the 'borders' between the regional, less urban archaeology of the south and the then hardly known urban Early Bronze IV (EB IV) archaeology of Syria; and what connections, if any, could be observed between the differing archaeologies of the north and south. In this chapter, the term IBA will be used to describe the archaeological assemblages of the second half of the third millennium in the south Levant, and EB IV will be applied to a similar chronological period in the north Levant.

The report on the survey made to the Department of Antiquities of the Lebanon dated 18 September 1968 began as follows.

> Between August 9th and 20th [1968] I visited and sherded sites in the Biqa'a valley to look at the type of occupation in this area from the mid-third to the mid-second

millennium BC. In this time twenty-four sites were visited, mostly those listed in Copeland and Wescombe's "Inventory of Stone Age Sites in Lebanon. Part II" as having Early Bronze or Middle Bronze occupation. Approximately twenty-nine bags of pottery were collected, the material consisting in the main of Early Bronze and Middle Bronze sherds. Sherds of earlier periods were also kept and a note made of later occupation, with usually a representative type fragment included in the collection eg. a glazed or imported sherd. The purpose of the survey was to establish whether or not pottery typical of the Intermediate Early Bronze-Middle Bronze Age period in Palestine and Transjordan occurred in the Biqa'a, and if so, to what extent. After visiting these sites, and recovering a uniform sample in nearly all cases, it seems fairly certain, without excavation, that it does not – at least north of the Litani Gorge area. In general, the Early Bronze Age sherds related only in part to Hama J, and more nearly to Byblos, coastal Syria and Palestine. The Middle Bronze Age sherds had close connections in particular with Hama H, but also with Palestine – this after preliminary examination only. The homogeneity of the sherd types suggested that it would be pointless to look further at this stage.

I should acknowledge my indebtedness and gratitude to the institutions and people who were so helpful with the project. Firstly to the Department of Antiquities in Lebanon for the permission to undertake the survey, and then to the French Institute in Beirut in the person of the then Director, Dr Daniel Schlumberger, both for the kind hospitality extended, for access to the library and for facilitating in every way my work in Lebanon and during a subsequent visit to Syria. Without this support the project would hardly have been possible. The late Gerald Lankester Harding and the late Mrs L. Copeland are gratefully remembered both for their encouragement and for giving me much time and assistance. The Department of Antiquities of Syria most kindly facilitated a brief visit to Syria in every way possible at the time, including access to the museums in Damascus and Aleppo. The project was funded by the G.A. Wainwright Near Eastern Archaeological Fund from the University of Oxford, and as Senior Scholar (1967–68) of the British School of Archaeology in Jerusalem.

Byblos

The conclusions drawn from the survey were summarised in a doctoral thesis,[1] and further summarised in the subsequent summary publication.[2] At that time it was appropriate to open a discussion of the later third millennium pottery of the Lebanon with what was then almost the only published material of that date from the country, from the coastal site of Byblos, despite the stratigraphic problems involved with the excavation of that site. Since then Saghieh has contributed much to the resolution of the Byblos stratigraphy, not least in attempting to relate the architecture to the associated

---

1 Prag 1971, 206–217.
2 Prag 1974, 69–116, especially 87.

7 The 1968 survey in the Beqa' of Lebanon and its relevance to the archaeology of the central Levant ca. 2500–2000/1900 BC

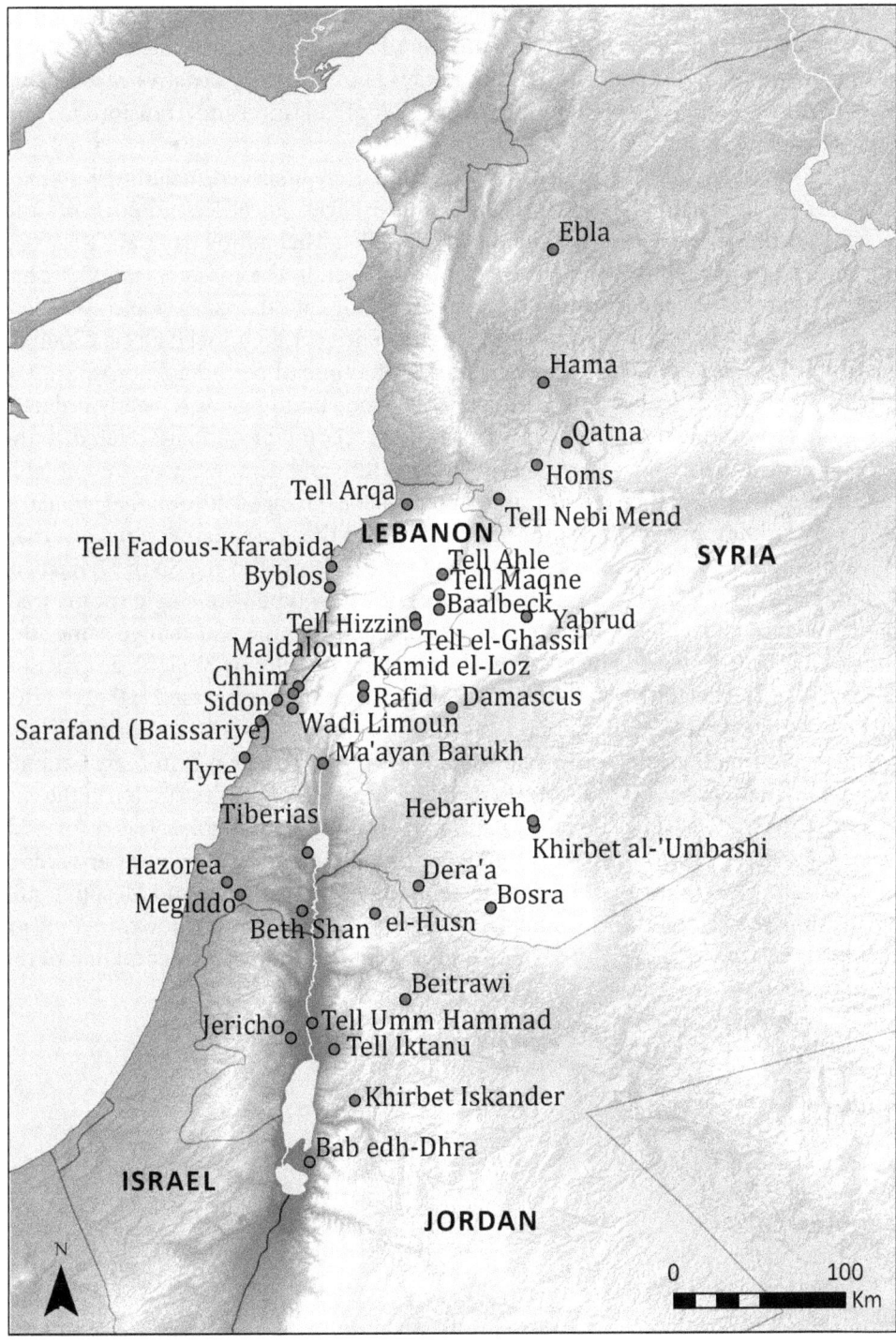

Figure 7.1: Map of main sites cited in the text (map by N. Khalaf).

finds;³ and more recently there is Lauffray's monumental publication of the architecture.⁴ Despite the many new insights to be considered below, the actual objects excavated at Byblos still offer relevant information because of the largely negative relationship of Byblos in the late third millennium to the IBA of Palestine and Transjordan. This was, in itself, illuminating.⁵

Since the work on Byblos, much more work has been published, including Kuschke's 1972 survey in the northern Beqa',⁶ the major excavations at Kamid ed-Loz,⁷ and Marfoe's detailed descriptions of the Beqa',⁸ as well as Thalmann's work at Tell Arqa,⁹ but there has still been relatively little excavation, even in the coastal areas. Genz has summarised the evidence for the more recent findings at other sites (Figure 7.1).¹⁰

Dunand's Installation VI at Byblos,¹¹ to which he gave an initial date ca. 2700 BC, was published as a well-planned town existing at a time of remarkable prosperity in Egypt, which was reflected at Byblos itself. The stone buildings were neatly ordered. The pottery typology derived from that of the preceding period and related to the general EBA horizon of the Levant. The architecture and ceramics were remarkably homogeneous for the whole period, and pottery shapes changed little on that evidence. What evolution there was, was internal.¹² This, and the close connections of urban Byblos with Egypt continued right up to the time of Pepi II in the Sixth Dynasty of Egypt.¹³ During this long period some houses of a new type with single rooms were built at Byblos and some new pottery types appeared. But the real change came after the total destruction of the Installation VI town and temples by fire (the destruction at the end of Saghieh's EBA Period KIV). Dunand dated this event ca. 2150–2125 BC. The following period (Saghieh's JI/II) was much more fully described by Saghieh, and correlated chronologically to the late Akkadian and Ur III periods in Mesopotamia (Period JI/JII, perhaps ca. 2200–2000 BC) and in the debris of the destruction at the end of Period JI/II an Ur III period tablet naming Ib-Dadi, 'ensi' of Byblos, was recovered. The two noteworthy points of this find were that the name of the governor/ruler is linguistically West Semitic, and that other contacts between Byblos and Mesopotamia at this time reinforced the view that there were influences and/or newcomers from the north-east arriving at Byblos over a considerable period in the second half of the third millennium BC.

---

3   Saghieh 1983.
4   Lauffray 2008.
5   Also noted by Saghieh 1983, 107.
6   Kuschke 1976.
7   Hienz 2010.
8   Marfoe 1995; 1998.
9   Thalmann 2006; 2012.
10 Genz 2010.
11 Dunand 1937; 1950; 1952; 1954; see also Lauffray 2008.
12 Dunand 1952, 84.
13 See Lauffray 2008, 286.

7 The 1968 survey in the Beqaʻ of Lebanon and its relevance to the archaeology of the central Levant ca. 2500–2000/1900 BC

The fall of Byblos Period KIV appears to have been later than events brought about by the end of the Early Dynastic III period in Mesopotamia ca. 2370 BC, and the collapse of urban civilisation in Palestine ca. 2500 BC (this last date is based on the revised chronology following the reassessment of 14C dates).[14] This chronology suggests a longer-lasting and more stable EBA period for the country within the hegemony of Byblos; and even if outside influences were appearing at Byblos before the end of the period, as the excavator contended and is clear, it suggests that though the destruction of Installation VI proposed by Dunand may bear some relationship to the new influences in Palestine, in both time and geographical distance, they need not necessarily be identical.[15] The pottery typology in general shows that they are not; the goblets and the cups by which both areas are characterised show that even though a common origin is likely, they have been subject to disparate influences and developments. The finds at Byblos have a considerable amount in common with the much more recent excavations at Tell Arqa, ca. 60 km north-east of Byblos,[16] where however a major destruction was dated earlier, to ca. 2400 BC, and thereafter there was an internal continuity to ca. 2000 BC despite another destruction ca. 2200 BC.

The innovating features at Byblos which can be associated with those in Transjordan and Palestine were quite difficult to extract, given the form of Dunand's publication, but Saghieh's work on collecting and organising the relevant assemblages is helpful. There are finds at Byblos which reflect the elements of a common third millennium diffusion throughout the Levant, and there is pottery clearly reflective of Syrian material in her Periods JI/JII.[17] Some elements of the assemblages are discussed briefly here.

Four-spouted lamps

Dunand illustrated some 10 four-spouted lamps from Byblos; at least three examples were illustrated in his Volume I, two of which have a flat base while that of the third from a late level, has a round base and is burnished; seven flat-based examples were illustrated in his Volume II (see Table 7.1). Their attribution ranged from Levels IV to XXXIII, but were concentrated in Levels XX to XXIV (cotes 24.20–23.20), which in the arbitrary stratigraphy of Byblos was mainly in the later part of Installation VI and its destruction period. This suggests the flat-based, four-spouted lamps were reasonably common in both Periods K and J, and it may be chance that the only round-based lamp illustrated is from a late/disturbed context. A round-based four-spouted lamp without registration number was however attributed by Dunand to the EB II period.[18] Saghieh refers to six

---

14 See Regev et al. 2012.
15 Although there are as yet no published radiocarbon dates from Byblos, it should be noted that recent radiocarbon determinations from Fadous-Kfarabida have dated the EB III–IV transition to ca. 2500 cal. BC – see Höflmayer et al. 2014.
16 Thalmann 2006.
17 Saghieh 1983, 23.
18 Dunand 1952, pl. IV.

Table 7.1: Four-spouted lamps published by Dunand (1937–1958) and Saghieh (1983).

Lamp base	Reg. no.	Page ref.	Fig.	Plate	Level
Round + burnish	1777	I. 119	-	CXLIX	IV
Flat	5304	I.358	281	-	XXX
Flat	5411	I.370 Saghieh 52	288 14	CLII	XXXIII KIII
Flat	10562	II.375 Saghieh	- 5	CCVIII	VIII Late context
Flat	11684	II.468	503	-	VI-X
Flat (EB II)	16773	II.862	969	-	XX
Flat + hollow tube through centre	16798	II.864	1008	CCVIII	XX
Flat	18293	II.1000	1138	-	XXIII
Flat	18388	II.1006 Saghieh 18	1126 7d	-	XXIII JI/JII
Flat	18756	II.1028 Saghieh 18	1182 7d	-	XXIV JI/JII
Disk	7624	Saghieh 73	21	-	JI/JII
Flat	13474	Saghieh 12	-	-	KIV

lamps in her re-analysis, two from Periods KIII–IV, three from JI/JII, and one from a late context. It seems that the majority of early lamps from Byblos were flat-based.[19]

This distribution also indicates that their appearance at Byblos before Period JI/JII is clear, and parallels the presence of a flat-based, four-spouted, stone lamp at Tell Mardikh before the destruction of that site, which occurred in the earlier Akkad period (cat. No. 41 from Royal Palace G).[20] The four-spouted lamp is found in Hama Levels J8–4, usually with a low disc or flattish base.[21] These occurrences also indicate that these lamps appear considerably earlier than the Installation VI/Period KIV destruction at Byblos, but precise dating is impossible on present data. At Arqa, these lamps are common in the EB IV period (ca. 2400–2000 BC), with this type first appearing during the EB III;[22] all those illustrated have flat bases, but the bases are smaller than is common in the southern Levant in the IBA (as also at Hama), and the fabric is darker, one being dark grey, the rest shades of dark brown to reddish in colour. A four-spouted lamp with

---

19 Saghieh 1983.
20 Matthiae et al. 1995, 282.
21 Fugmann 1958, fig. 58: 3H372.
22 See Thalmann 2006, pl. 79: 1–8; 2012, 177–180, fig. 6.

7 The 1968 survey in the Beqaʻ of Lebanon and its relevance to the archaeology of the central Levant ca. 2500–2000/1900 BC

flat base was found at Tell Fadous-Kfarabida,[23] and inland from Byblos; many others almost all with flat or flattish bases have been found in a cave in the Qadesha valley.[24]

In the south, in the IBA tombs at Jericho, four-spouted lamps are common, but there seems to be no particular distinction in the use of flat, disk and round-based lamps, though more round-based lamps were found.[25] From the tell at Jericho, only two four-spouted lamps with bases were illustrated, and they had flat bases.[26] A similar pattern is visible at Tell Umm Hammad slightly further north in the Jordan valley where they are rare in the settlement but common in its cemetery at Tiwal esh-Sharqi.[27]

The appearance of the single-spouted lamp in late IBA contexts in the south (e.g. at Beitrawi, with rounded base) may be contemporary with the introduction of this type of lamp in the north at the beginning of the MBA.[28] In southern MB II tombs where single-spouted lamps are characteristic, they all have the smaller flat/disc and round bases that are in use throughout the period. One would assume that the broad flat base of the IBA would be safer for an oil-filled lamp, so why the small flat and round bases became the norm by the MBA seems slightly odd, but perhaps to do with a change to fully wheel-made manufacturing techniques. Earlier, perhaps the flat-based lamps were in domestic use, and round-based lamps more common in funerary use.

Cups

Cups in burnished fabric, of a type vaguely comparable to cups in Phase 1 at Iktanu,[29] at Byblos range between Dunand's Levels XIX and XXVI, but the best parallels occur in Level XXII[30] and Level XXVI,[31] a considerable number of which arbitrary levels pre-date the arbitrary level of the Period KIV destruction. A large range of miniature votive cups in this shape are also attributed to Period JI/JII by Saghieh.[32] At Arqa, cups with similar bases appear already in the late EB III and continue in use in EB IV.[33]

---

23 Genz 2009, pl. 2: 3.
24 Beayno et al. 2002, fig. 5; pls 1: 10–11; 3: 12–13; 5: 6–8.
25 Kenyon 1960; 1965, 47.
26 Kenyon and Holland 1983, fig. 19: 20; fig. 20: 14.
27 Tubb 1990, 94; Kennedy 2015a, 15–16.
28 Prag 1995, fig. 3: 3.
29 Prag 1971, fig. 16.7; 2011, fig. 9, top left.
30 Dunand 1937, 321; fig. 257: 4404.
31 Dunand 1937, 345; fig. 275: 5149; pl. CLXVII.
32 Saghieh 1983, pl. XLVI.
33 Thalmann 2006, pl. 47: 1, 31–32.

Teapots

Much more directly linked to the southern assemblages, however, is a 'teapot' noted by Saghieh.[34] The 'teapot' has a globular body, flat base and a cylindrical spout on the shoulder, a blackish fabric with white horizontal painted lines on the shoulder and below the rim. It is the only one of its kind at Byblos and so is probably an import to Byblos,[35] most likely from the hill country to the south-east (see below), and belongs in the group of white-painted grey wares common in the Megiddo region.[36] At Megiddo, round-based, single-spouted lamps occur with white-painted grey 'teapots' in Tombs 217B and 877C2, which may suggest that in this area the flat-based four-spouted lamp gave way first to a round-based then to the single-spouted lamp under the influence of the early MBA characteristic single-spout lamp.

The Byblos teapot occurs within an assemblage of pottery much of which is typical of Hama J and regions to the north and east of Byblos in the EB IV period,[37] but the assemblage includes some pottery of the MBA, and it is uncertain whether this reflects a very late date in Period JI/JII, continued use of the structure from EB IV into the MBA or is due to stratigraphic contamination. It is notable, however, that it is in this assemblage that the four-spouted lamp with small disk base noted above occurs (see Table 7.1).[38]

Trefoil-mouth jugs

One of the 'truly diagnostic' new vessels fairly common in the JI/JII assemblage at Byblos is the trefoil-mouth jug with horizontal/spiral bands of cream paint.[39] This jug shape, and the white painted decoration, is also very common at Arqa in the EB IV.[40] It is also found in Building P4 associated with Royal Palace G at Mardikh.[41]

Beyond Byblos

These assemblages in coastal Lebanon and Syria can briefly be compared with the evidence from the rest of Lebanon, where relatively few sites of the third millennium BC have been excavated since the 1960s.

---

34 Reg. no. 7585, see Area VI, from the Temple Tower; Saghieh 1983, fig. 21 and pl. XLII, pottery of Periods JI/JII; for another discussion of this structure; Lauffray 2008, 414–415.
35 Saghieh 1983, 93.
36 For more detail regarding this tradition in the southern Levant, see Bechar 2015.
37 See Dunand 1950; 1954, 115–123; Saghieh 1983, 95–98; Moumar 2017; 2018; Kennedy et al. 2018.
38 Reg. no. 7624.
39 For example, reg. no. 7590; Saghieh 1983, 96; fig. 21; pl. XLII.
40 Thalmann 2006, pl. 58.
41 Marchetti and Nigro 1995–1996, 9–36.

7 The 1968 survey in the Beqa' of Lebanon and its relevance to the archaeology of the central Levant ca. 2500–2000/1900 BC

Cemeteries of IBA Palestinian type were discovered in the 1950s and 1960s in the foothills south of Beirut, mainly in the Sidon hinterland. I am grateful to the various excavators and owners for allowing me to see the pottery in 1968, especially to the late Roger Saidah for the Sidon region cemeteries,[42] and to Madame N. Alameddine for a visit to Khallet el-Khazen. The range of ceramics from these sites is fairly extensive but the final assessment will have to await publication of this material, which is still in the National Museum in Beirut (my thanks for this recent information to Mrs A.M. Afeiche).

A cemetery at Wadi Limoun,[43] excavated by G. Simson in 1958 and later by R. Saidah,[44] contained much pottery of Palestinian IBA type, which except for the grey ware teapot noted above, is entirely without parallel at Byblos. Pottery from Wadi Limoun (Graves 7 and 8) included cups, goblets and white-painted grey teapots, and a jar with drooping lugs at the rim which directly parallels a jar from Ma'ayan Barukh (from Wadi Limoun Grave 7, no. 2; cf. photo 87 from Ma'ayan Barukh).[45] A grave at Majdalouna contained cups, jars with envelope ledge handles, and jars decorated with band-combing and incised lines in IBA style. Similar comments apply to the material from Chhim and a tomb at Sarafand (Baissariye), the latter with about 38 pots, one of which had a vestigial ledge handle. The late IBA connections between north Palestine and these grave groups are clear.

G.E. Wright listed his preferences for the order of dating of the Megiddo IBA tombs,[46] and many vessels from these Lebanese assemblages fall within his latest group. There are particularly close links between the Lebanese cemetery groups and Tombs 877A2 and 4l at Megiddo. This dating would fit the view that the Lebanese foothill cemeteries represent a relatively late and secondary move northwards from Palestine: that they are an offshoot of an established group of IBA people in the Beth Shan–Megiddo–Hazorea area. Some of the Lebanese cemeteries may be earlier, but, given the almost complete lack of evidence for this material from Byblos, it seems likely that they will also prove to be derived immediately from north Palestine, or belong in the development of a distinct regional group. Apart from the possibility of a link with the north coast and a metal trade, these groups show no direct north Levantine influences. The evidence would suggest that until ca. 2200 BC, Byblos exercised a reasonable control over the coastal routes and the adjacent Lebanese foothills and that the 'Palestinian' groups did not move northwards until at about this time the power and prosperity of Byblos were interrupted, and her attention was afterwards taken up with northern and north-eastern contacts. Thus the southern groups, appearing at a late stage of the Palestinian IBA period, remained established in a poor way, perhaps leading a semi-nomadic existence in the wooded foothills during the redevelopment of Byblos in Periods JI/JII and only disappeared during the renewed prosperity in the Middle Bronze Age.

---

42 Saidah 1967, 171.
43 Copeland and Wescombe 1966, 161.
44 Saidah 1967, 171.
45 See Amiran 1969.
46 Wright 1961, 87; chart 4.

To what extent these groups moved into the coastal area is not clear; just one vessel at Byblos and some pottery at Tyre (Levels XX and XIX) marks their presence,[47] and these may be imports from groups in the foothills, perhaps associated with exchanges of animal products with urban communities. On the extreme western edge of the site of Tyre no associated architecture of this period has yet been excavated, just sherds associated with reddish earth and sea pebbles in Stratum XX, and black earth and larger stones in Stratum XIX. Some of the pottery from both these strata is EB II/III in date, but in Stratum XIX there are two envelope ledge handles, and two dark grey teapots and one jug, two of which have white painted decoration and which compare very closely with the material from Majdalouna noted above. There is also a tiny carnelian disk bead, which is not uncommon in the south Levant at this period; and notably an Egyptian quartz cylinder seal which Ward dated to the Old Kingdom,[48] and although he preferred an early date, perhaps Dynasties 3 and 4, and a later importation to Tyre, noted that the type was most common from Dynasty 5 onwards and could have found its way to Tyre 'at any time during the Old Kingdom'; so may well be an import contemporary with other finds of the Egyptian Dynasties 5 and 6 at Byblos. There is thus more evidence at Tyre for the presence of the southern groups, but mixed with a potential urban presence as at Byblos. These deposits in St. XX and XIX at Tyre were followed by heavy accumulations of sand on the site.

In the south Levant, IBA occupation on the coast remains very rare.[49]

The 1968 Beqa' survey

It is concluded that a reflection of this evidence is visible in the Beqa' of Lebanon. During the survey in the summer of 1968, about 30 sites were visited throughout the whole length of the Beqa' and part of the Wadi et-Teim (see Figure 7.2 and Table 7.2).[50] As noted above, the major purpose of this survey was to assess whether pottery comparable to the southern IBA pottery existed in the Beqa', and attention was mainly focused on revisiting the EBA and MBA sites listed by Copeland and Wescombe with this in mind, though a few new sites were discovered.[51] The evidence obtained during this work was the same for the whole area, apart from the grave at Rafid (the pottery from the cist grave at Rafid was seen courtesy of Professor Hachmann at Kamid el-Loz).

---

47 Bikai 1978, 6; pls LIV–LVI.
48 Ward in Bikai 1978, 83–87.
49 Prag 1974, 70; 2014: 389; cf. Genz 2010, 207.
50 Saidah 1969, 141–142; Marfoe 1995, 94; n. 112; 1998, 179.
51 Copeland and Wescombe 1965; 1966.

7 The 1968 survey in the Beqaʻ of Lebanon and its relevance to the archaeology of the central Levant ca. 2500–2000/1900 BC

The Early Bronze Age II–III

The pottery recovered during this survey in the Beqaʻ indicates a development separate to some extent from that of Syria, coastal Lebanon and Palestine. Hand-made pottery of a type comparable particularly to that of Hama K (i.e. pre-2400 BC on the excavators' dates) and to that of the Levantine EBA generally is readily discernible throughout the Beqaʻ, and with some reference to Hama J. A representative collection of the material is illustrated in Figure 7.3 and Figure 7.4.

The ledge handle is a type fossil of the EBA and IBA throughout the third millennium BC in the south and, as noted above, is found at Majdalouna and Tyre in coastal Lebanon. It is not present at Byblos. Mrs Copeland and Miss Tufnell found just a single ledge handle of Palestinian type at Tell Ahle in the Beqaʻ, of 'plain rounded form but the widest part is slightly turned up and pressed in', and we found another at Tell Ahle, a flat plain ledge.[52] Both these may belong to the early Arab period when the site was also occupied. Another ledge handle, straight ended, rather than sloping, was found at Tell Maqne and attributed by us to a similar late date. But these three examples, regardless of their probable late date, are rare examples of ledge handles from the Beqaʻ, and the Palestinian ledge handle is certainly not a typical form there, reinforcing a 'northern' pattern in the EBA in the Beqaʻ.

The Early Bronze IV

The best parallels for pottery from the Beqaʻ with that of the IBA are given in Figure 7.3: 10–19. They are generally not close. Figure 7.3: 10 may be a four-spouted lamp fragment, but there is hardly enough to be certain. It appears to have a flat base. This piece and another body fragment from Tell Serhan (Figure 7.4: 37) are made of a dark grey-black ware, with lighter tinges of brown to red. They are hand-made, and almost metallic. The nearest parallel for the fabric is with the Megiddo painted teapots, but they are much closer to the grey/red/brown fabrics at Arqa, where the vessels were wheel-made. It seems likely, however, that Figure 7.4: 37 may be a fragment of Base Ring Ware. Figure 7.3: 11 was included in this group, but it is a very simple form.

Body-combing in this chapter refers to vertical, oblique or pattern-combing covering most of the body of the vessel, as opposed to band-combing, which is restricted to groups of horizontal straight and/or wavy bands of lines usually confined to the shoulders of jars. Sherds with body-combing were common, and those illustrated (Figure 7.3: 7–9) are all of rough pattern-combing or diagonal combing; pattern-combing was well entrenched in the Beqaʻ in the EBA as at Byblos, and it is difficult to say whether these vessels were still being mass produced during EB IV, although pattern-combed vessels have been identified in smaller quantities in the EB IV deposits of Tell Arqa and Tell Fadous-Kfarabida.[53] As the north Palestine–south Lebanon IBA pottery does not

---

52   Copeland and Wescombe 1966, 54.
53   Thalmann and Sowada 2014, 358.

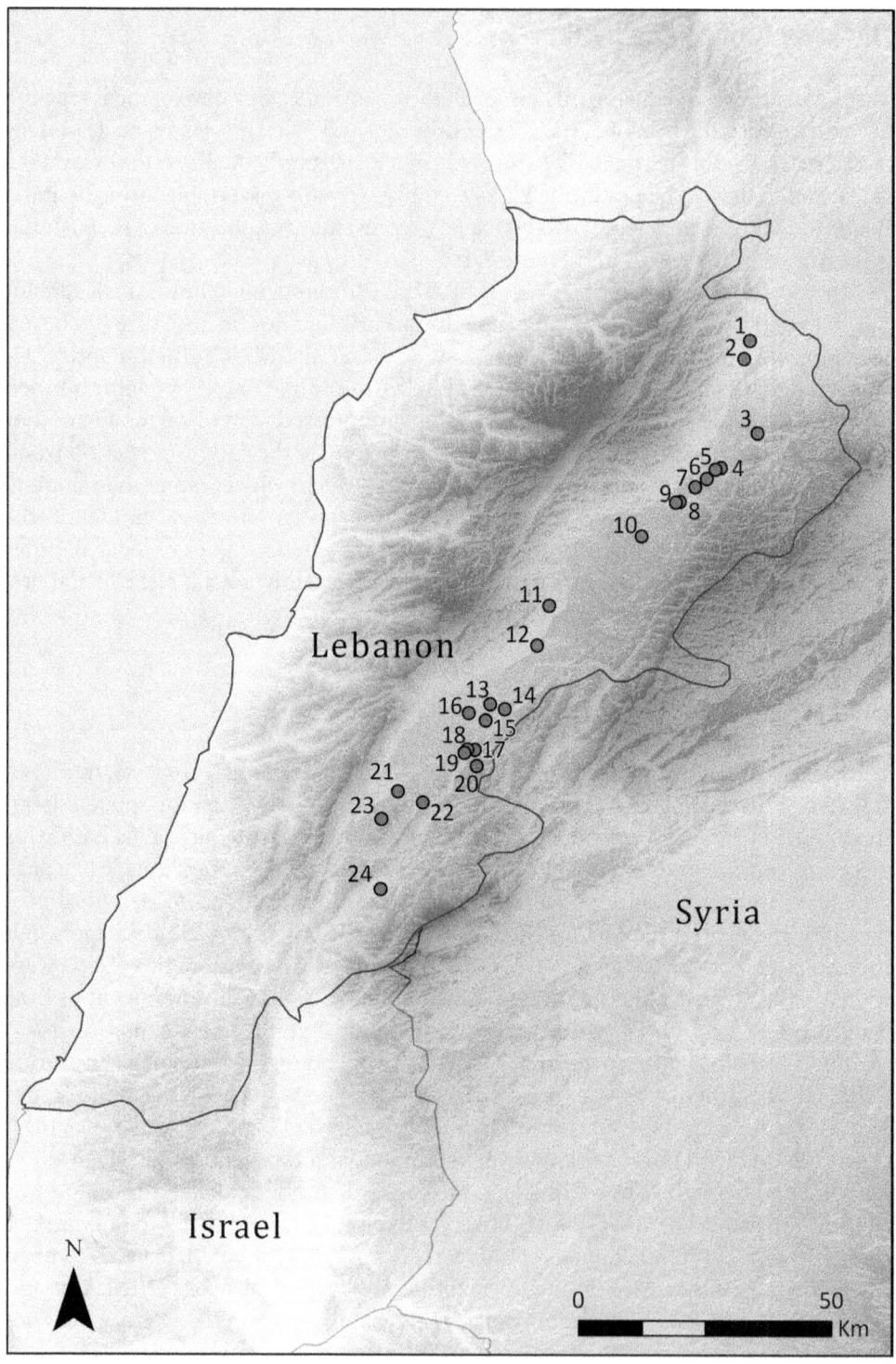

Figure 7.2: Map of sites survyed during the 1968 survey of the Beqa' (map by N. Khalaf).

7 The 1968 survey in the Beqa' of Lebanon and its relevance to the archaeology of the central Levant ca. 2500–2000/1900 BC

Table 7.2: Sites surveyed and sherded during the 1968 survey of the Beqa'.

No.	Site	No.	Site
1.	Hermel I	13.	Tell Serhan
2.	Hermel IV	14.	Tell Neba'a Faour I
3.	Ras Baalbek Railway Station	15.	Tell Derzenoun
4.	Tell Labwe North	16.	Tell Bar Elias
5.	Tell Qasr Labwe	17.	Mejdel Anjar II
6.	Tell es-Hassan	18.	Tell Saatiye North
7.	Wadi Bourra	19.	Tell Saatiye South
8.	Tell Rasm el-Hadeth	20	Tell Ain el-Meten
9.	Tell Neba'a Chatt	21.	Tell ej-Jisr
10.	Tell Maakne	22.	Kamed el-Loz
11.	Ain Hachbai	23.	Baaloul
12.	Tell Ain Cherif	24.	Tell ez-Zeitoun

appear to have body-combing, it rather supports the view that all the Beqa' fragments are in the EBA II/III tradition, though the plain diagonal combing such as Figure 7.3: 7 was not uncommon, and on this fragment is allied to a strap handle, a form especially typical of the IBA. The typical IBA body-combing in the south is normally done more lightly, with long oblique strokes on much thinner fabrics (see, for example, Figure 7.5: 2). Figure 7.3: 16 is not quite of Transjordan IBA form; Figure 7.3: 17 is wheel-made; Figure 7.3: 18 is quite similar to hand-made IBA moulded bands; Figure 7.3: 19 displays a painting technique similar to that of 'trickle-painted' IBA vessels from the Megiddo and el-Husn region in the south, but being wheel-made should perhaps be attributed to the MBA, particularly as the decoration is bichrome in dull red and black paint, whereas all the IBA examples have monochrome red-painted decoration. However, the painted decoration fits the style of the IBA material, rather than the MBA jugs where the trickle-painted vertical lines are suspended from a band above, but do not reach the lower painted band as on the IBA examples.[54] For a summary of pottery of this period in the Beqa', see Marfoe 1998, section 4.4.3.[55]

Genz refers to an EB IV teapot spout from Baalbek but this hand-made spouted teapot,[56] with light reddish to pink fabric, dark red painted decoration and crooked spout seems more likely to be EBA than IBA, or at best the EBA tradition influenced by the IBA. The small body sherd with straight and wavy band-combing and poor

---

54 For MBA juglets, see Amiran 1969, pl. 24: 17, 19 from Megiddo, Catanzariti 2010–2011, figs 1 and 2 from Kamid el-Loz; Genz and Sader 2010–2011, fig. 5: 3–4 from Tell Hizzin; Saidah 1993–4, 137–210 from Beirut.
55 Marfoe 1998.
56 Genz 2010, 208; Van Ess 2008, 110–111; pl. 2: 9.

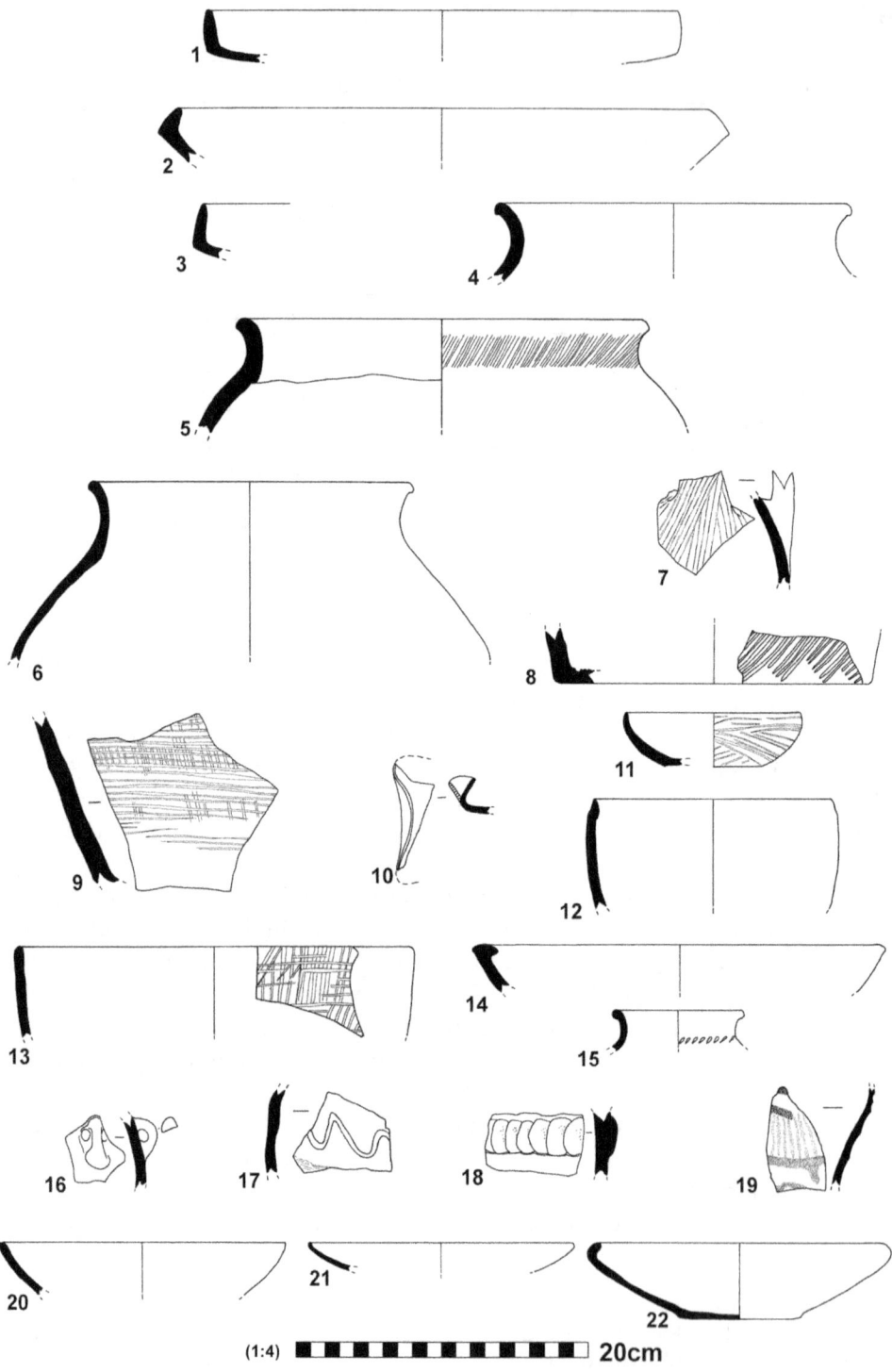

Figure 7.3: Beqa' survey 1968: 1-9: Early Bronze Age; 10-19: later third millennium BC; 20-22: Middle Bronze Age.

7 The 1968 survey in the Beqa' of Lebanon and its relevance to the archaeology of the central Levant ca. 2500–2000/1900 BC

No.	Site	Description	Parallels
1.	Ain Hachbai	Bowl, carinated, fabric: pink-buff, hardish fired, smooth burnish, light red slip inside; temper fine to small grey, red and white. Very worn outside.	Hama K6–5, K3 and J7
2.	Ain Hachbai	Bowl, carinated, fabric: hard grey; temper: fine to medium grey and white.	Hama J8
3.	Zeitoun	Bowl, carinated, fabric: pink-red, possible traces of red slip outside, fairly worn; temper: fine to medium grey and red.	Hama K6 and J8
4.	Ain Hachbai	Jar, everted rim, fabric: red-buff, grey core; temper: a lot of small to medium grey and white.	Hama K10, K2 and J8
5.	Tell Maqne	Jar, everted rim, fabric: fine cooking pot ware, brown to pink; temper: small to medium grey and white. Hand-made with horizontally smoothed rim, junction of neck and shoulder marked; faint oblique combing on neck.	Hama J7 and J4
6.	Der Zenoun	Jar, everted rim, fabric: fine red-brown-black mottled cooking pot ware(?); temper: small to medium grey and white grits, rim horizontally smoothed, slight junction on interior between neck and shoulder; fire blackened.	Hama K7, J8. For further material of similar type see Copeland and Wescombe; and summary in Marfoe. It appears to relate more closely to the Syrian ceramic assemblage than to that of Palestine, but the bowls are also typical of the southern Levant in a tradition going back to EB I.
7.	Rasm el-Hadeth	Strap handle, fabric: hard grey, buff slip, body-combed; temper: small to medium grey and white.	Paralleled at Tell Maqne where it is dated to EB II/III, which is probably correct. Flat-based storage jars with patterned body-combing.

No.	Site	Description	Parallels
8.	Ain Hachbai	Jar base, fabric: heavy grey with red-grey surface, medium-hard fired; broad bands of diagonal combing; temper: medium.	Classic form in EB III in the south
9.	Der Zenoun	Jar body sherd, fabric: grey hard fired, red at surface, pattern-combed; temper: small to large grey and white.	Classic form in EB III in the south
10.	Tell Serhan	Four-spouted lamp(?), fabric: thin, hard, wheel-made, almost metallic-fired dark grey, self slip; temper: fine to small grey and white.	N/A
11.	Der Zenoun	Small bowl, plain upright rim, flat base, fabric: hard fired, pink-buff ware, light grey core, surface wiped or irregularly combed, base rough, interior uneven; temper: fine to large grey and white.	N/A
12.	Tell Hassan	Small bowl, slightly inset rim, fabric: dull buff ware, poorly wheel-made, well fired; temper: some straw, fine grey and white, with occasional large white.	N/A
13.	Der Zenoun	Medium bowl, plain upright rim, fabric: dark red-buff gritty ware, exterior pattern-combed; temper: small to medium grey and white.	N/A
14.	Der Zenoun	Medium bowl, inverted rim, fabric: dark pink-drab ware, self slip mottled pink to black; burnished inside and out, wheel-made(?); temper: small grey and white.	N/A
15.	Der Zenoun	Jar, everted rim, fabric: red to grey ware, red slip, hard fired, stabbed row at base of neck; temper: grey and white.	N/A
16.	Ain Hachbai	Lug handle, fabric: grey-drab, rather worn red slip outside; temper: fine to medium grey and white.	N/A

7 The 1968 survey in the Beqa' of Lebanon and its relevance to the archaeology of the central Levant ca. 2500-2000/1900 BC

No.	Site	Description	Parallels
17.	Tell Hassan	Body sherd with incised wavy line, fabric: pink, roughly wheel-made; temper: small to large grey.	N/A
18.	Ain Hachbai	Body sherd with impressed applied band, fabric: gritty with thick dark grey core, fired red-buff at surface, dark red slip outside; temper: fine to medium.	N/A
19.	Zeitoun	Jar shoulder, fabric: cream, self-slip with black (horizontal) and light-red (vertical, trickle) painted decoration, wheel-made; temper: small to medium grey, red and white.	N/A
20.	Der Zenoun	Medium bowl, fabric: hard cream, cream slip with vertical burnish inside and possibly outside, wheel-made; temper: small grey and white grits.	Qatna – Iamoni and Morandi Bonacossi 2010–2011, fig.12: 8.
21.	Ain el-Meten	Medium bowl with up-curved rim, fabric: fine, thin hard cream ware, honey-cream slip, finely hand burnished, radial inside, radial and horizontal outside, wheel-made; temper: very fine white.	Hama H5
22.	Tell Serhan	Medium bowl, incurved rim, small flat base, fabric: hard fired, roughly wheel-made, drab buff, pink surface or slip; temper: fine to medium grey and white.	Bowl with incurved rim and a low disk base is unlike pottery from Tell Nebi Mend (pers. comm. M. Kennedy), but there are similar bowls from MBA Arqa (Thalmann 2006, pl. 80: 10; Level 14c; and cf. Du Mesnil du Buisson 1948, pl. LXXIX: Z141; Baghouz)

context may equally date to the MBA as the IBA.[57] Marfoe refers to an unstratified EB IV/MB I painted teapot from Tell Ghassil. Otherwise the evidence for IBA/Grey Ware pottery currently seems largely restricted to burials in the Beqaʻ.[58]

We found no painted fragments of the Hama J wares, nor of the IBA Megiddo cream-painted grey wares in 1968. This may have been due to chance in survey work, but was striking. It may also be due to the fact that we were looking at settlement sites, and these appear to be sparse in the later third millennium BC. Marfoe recorded 79 EB II/III sites in the Beqaʻ, and 72 of the MBA, but just 16 possible sites for EB IV.[59] The Kuschke Survey in the northern Beqaʻ did not discriminate EB IV from EB and MBA sites, registering 10 EBA and 14 MBA sites.[60] Painted goblet fragments of Hama J type were found readily at Qatiné on the Lake of Homs,[61] just north of the arid zone and the drop in the course of the Orontes which form the modern Syrian border at the northern end of the Beqaʻ.[62] The pottery from Qatiné is very close to that of Tell Nebi Mend while that from the Beqaʻ 1968 survey is less close and has a more southern look.[63] These statements simply strengthen Marfoe's conclusion that 'the present evidence would suggest that although the Beqaʻ possesses affinities with other regions, it cannot claim membership in either the Syrian or Palestinian patterns'.[64] His conclusion was strengthened by the absence of Rafid-type Grey Ware material at Kamid el-Loz.

The presence of IBA grey wares in the Beqaʻ is linked thus far to tombs in the Beqaʻ, at Tell Hizzin (location and type of tomb unknown),[65] and at Rafid in the Wadi et-Teim (large stone-built tomb).[66] The Wadi et-Teim, not the Litani valley, is the main route through from the Beqaʻ to the south.[67]

The case for an IBA influence/presence/occupation in the Beqaʻ is not very strong but a mere influence would emerge much more clearly in excavation than surface survey. There are elements of the Beqaʻ assemblage that can be paralleled in Hama J, and which suggest that there is no break in the occupation of the Beqaʻ during the EB IV/IBA. However, it seems that the tombs at Rafid and Hizzin are the only clear evidence of the presence of IBA assemblages so far, and though it may be chance that Rafid is on the direct route from Palestine, it may rather suggest that the Beqaʻ was not deserted but perhaps more sparsely populated during EB IV, and these probably nomadic groups

---

57   Van Ess 2008, pl. 3: 3.
58   Marfoe 1998, 164.
59   Marfoe 1995.
60   Kuschke et al. 1976, 151.
61   Personal observation.
62   Marfoe 1998, 23.
63   Pers. comm. M. Kennedy.
64   Marfoe 1995, 98.
65   Genz and Sader 2008; Genz 2010–2011, 209–210, figs 2–5.
66   Mansfeld 1970.
67   For its environment and modern patterns of transhumance and refuge, see Marfoe 1998, 166.

7   The 1968 survey in the Beqa' of Lebanon and its relevance to the archaeology of the central Levant ca. 2500–2000/1900 BC

were restricted to the fringes of the fertile agricultural central Beqa' and to the foothills south of Sidon. The cist graves at Yabrud may also point to this conclusion: see below.

The Middle Bronze Age

Excavations at Kamid el-Loz and other recent excavations have revealed widespread occupation and prosperity in the MBA in Lebanon. In the Beqa', many wheel-made types of pottery paralleling those of Hama H (excavators' dates post-1900 BC) were found in the 1968 survey.

In the north Beqa', in the vicinity of Hermel,[68] and in the plain of Akkar, some work has been done on a variety of dolmens, tumuli and other megalithic remains.[69] The finds from the Hermel region, as so often for remains of this nature, have had dates attributed ranging through Arab, Byzantine, Roman, Iron Age, Middle Bronze Age and the Neolithic periods. At the Mengez sites in the plain of Akkar, where nearly 50 tombs or monuments were looked at, all of them previously looted, a considerable number of finds were made, including a Canaanean flint (from MSE 2). From the total 30 kg of sherds recovered from all the tombs, several main periods of Bronze Age occupation or use were deduced,[70] one of which the excavator attributed to the MBA, and one vessel in particular (a cup from QM 1) he compared to an IBA type; but with its bands of blue paint below the rim, it would seem to belong to a date at least approaching the MBA. Some of this pottery can be vaguely fitted to a late stage of the period with which we are concerned, but it has no direct parallels as yet. Data on the wares is also lacking in the publication. The graves were mainly of a large cist type, a tradition with very early origins which continued into the Middle Bronze Age (e.g. Sidon, Tell Hizzin, Baghouz).

From the central Beqa' comes further evidence of possible nomadic traces at the site of Tell el-Ghassil approximately 18 km south of Baalbeck.[71] At the base of a deep trench there were Chalcolithic sherds and above them evidence of buildings dating to the EBA. This was followed by a period without any architecture, but with a number of crude stone fireplaces. The pottery associated with these includes jars with band-combing, and seems to parallel that of Hama H, being in all cases wheel-made. Professor Baramki most kindly gave me access to his collections in the Museum of the American University in Beirut. In the photograph of the jars from this level, the pottery seemed very similar to that of Palestine; but all the pieces seen in the Museum were of the Hama H type. Other MBA evidence from the central Beqa', which links cist burials with the MBA, came from the brief excavations at Tell Hizzin. The graves contained pottery comparable to that of the MBA pottery from Kafr Djarra on the coast, and the site produced a statue fragment inscribed with the name of Sebekh-hotep IV

---

68   Tallon 1958; 1959.
69   Tallon 1964; Steimer-Herbet 2000.
70   Steimer-Herbet 2000, 16–17.
71   Baramki 1961.

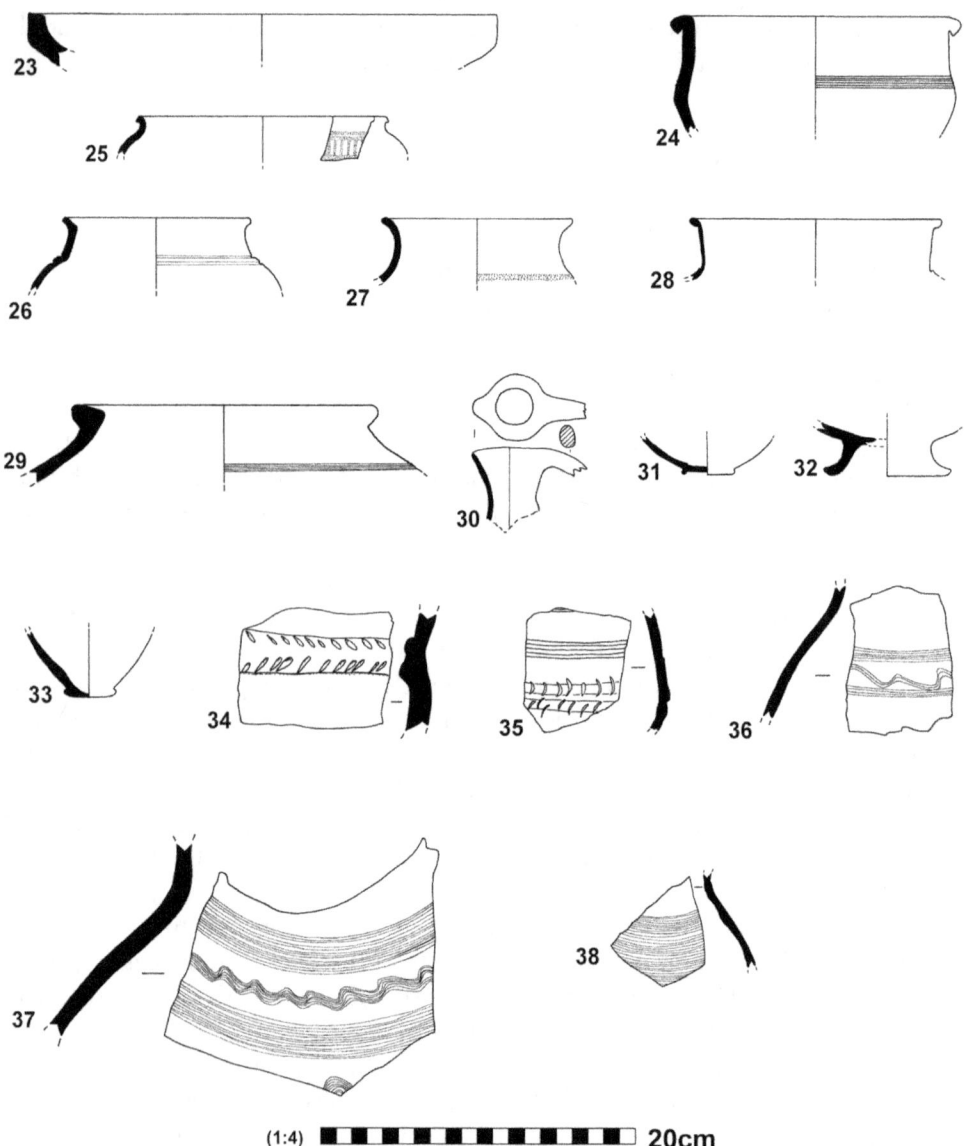

Figure 7.4: Beqa' survey 1968: pottery of the Middle Bronze Age.

No.	Site	Description	Parallels
23.	Der Zenoun	Medium bowl, carinated, fabric: red, grey core, red well-burnished slip inside and out, but very worn outside; temper: small grey and white.	Qatna – Iamoni and Morandi Bonacossi 2010–2011, fig. 6: 4

7 The 1968 survey in the Beqaʻ of Lebanon and its relevance to the archaeology of the central Levant ca. 2500–2000/1900 BC

No.	Site	Description	Parallels
24.	Ain el-Meten.	Deep bowl, out-turned rim, fabric: pink ware, well fired, wheel-made, horizontal band-combing above slight carination; temper: fine to small grey and white grits.	Qatna – Da Ros and Iamoni 2010–2011 fig. 6: 13; Iamoni and Morandi Bonacossi, 2010–2011, fig. 11: 1, 3
25.	Der Zenoun	Jar, short everted rim, fabric: well-fired buff, pink-buff slip, matt red painted decoration, wheel-made; temper: fine.	N/A
26.	Tell Hassan	Jar, slightly in-turned neck, everted gutter rim, incised lines on shoulder, fabric: wheel-made, hard fired, pink, buff slip; temper: small to medium grey and white, traces of straw.	N/A
27.	Rasm el-Hadeth	Jar, everted rim, fabric: soft greenish-buff, traces of matt black paint; hand-made(?); temper: small to medium grey and white.	N/A
28.	Der Zenoun	Jar, upright neck, everted rim, slight grooving on neck, fabric: thin, hard, wheel-made, cream; temper: fine.	Hama H; Tell Burak – Badreshany and Kamlah 2010–2011, fig. 13: 1
29.	Tell Hassan	Jar, short everted rim, fabric: hard, rather heavy grey-buff, buff slip, horizontal band-combing on shoulder, wheel-made; temper: medium grey.	Kamid el-Loz – Catanzariti 2010–2011, fig. 11: 4; MBA tomb at Amman in Harding 1953, fig. 8.75
30.	Zeitoun	Trefoil-mouth juglet, loop handle from rim, fabric: pink-buff, handle has grey core; temper: fine to medium grey, red and white, possibly grog.	Hama H
31.	Ain el-Meten	Ring base, closed vessel, fabric: fine metallic grey, fired buff-drab at surface, smooth vertical burnish on outer surface, wheel-made; temper: very fine.	Hama H5
32.	Der Zenoun	Pedestal base, fabric: gritty grey-cream, cream slip, wheel-made; temper: fine to medium grey and white.	Tell el-Burak – Badreshany and Kamlah 2010–2011, fig. 24: 5–8

No.	Site	Description	Parallels
33.	Tell Hassan	Disk base, closed vessel, fabric: gritty pink-buff gritty, hardish fired, outside pink-buff with traces of vertical burnish, inside grey, wheel-made; temper: fine to small grey and white.	Hama H; Tell Burak – Badreshany and Kamlah 2010–2011, fig. 29; Qatna – Iamoni and Morandi Bonacossi 2010–2011, fig. 13; 52
34.	Zeitoun	Body sherd from a large vessel, applied band with herring-bone incisions, fabric: deep-pink; crudely wheel-made; temper: small to large grey, red and white, with traces of straw.	Hama H; Tell Burak – Badreshany and Kamlah 2010–2011, fig. 29; Qatna – Iamoni and Morandi Bonacossi 2010–2011, fig. 13; 52
35.	Ain el-Meten	Body sherd with horizontal band-combing and two applied bands with stabbing, fabric: hard fired grey, drab at surface; temper: small to medium grey and white.	Hama H; Kamid el-Loz – Catanzariti 2010–2011, fig. 12: 13; Fadous-Kfarabida – Genz 2010–2011, fig. 13; MBA tomb at Amman, Harding 1953, fig. 9: 100
36.	Tell Hassan	Body sherd with straight and wavy band-combing, fabric: roughly wheel-made, buff; temper: small to large grey.	Hama H; Kamid el-Loz – Catanzariti 2010–2011, fig. 12: 13; Fadous-Kfarabida – Genz 2010–2011, fig. 13; MBA tomb at Amman, Harding 1953, fig. 9: 100
37.	Zeitoun	Body sherd with straight and wavy band-combing, fabric: heavy wheel-made, hard, red to grey drab; temper: numerous small to medium grey and white.	N/A
38.	Der Zenoun	Body sherd, fabric: grey-black ware with tinges of brown, hand-made, shallow combing or wiping, metallic; temper: fine. Base Ring Ware(?)	N/A

7 The 1968 survey in the Beqa' of Lebanon and its relevance to the archaeology of the central Levant ca. 2500–2000/1900 BC

(ca. 1700 BC), although these statues do not appear to be contemporary with their archaeological context.[72]

This further indication that in Syria and Lebanon band-combing is associated with the wheel-made pottery of the MBA gives cause for thought about the relative chronologies of Syria and Palestine in the IBA and MBA. There is no clear evidence to show which area has priority, but band-combing is a decorative motif ideally produced on wheel-made pottery. The present gap in the distribution of band-combing between the south Palestine-Transjordan sites and the North Syrian coastal sites, the Beqa' and at Hama perhaps infers an independent creation in each area, though it seems a little unlikely.

Into Syria

It was not a good time in 1968 to explore sites in south Syria, an area of considerable relevance in a search for answers to the same questions addressed in Lebanon, but the courtesy and help of the Department of Antiquities in Syria is gratefully acknowledged. It had been hoped to visit the only excavated site of the period, at Khirbet al-Umbashi (and possibly Hebariyeh), a site well to the north-east of any other known occurrence of IBA pottery, and only 90 km from Damascus, but at the time the whole south of the country was under military control. As all pottery from the excavations in 1933 appeared to be lost,[73] the only evidence at the time for the ceramics from Umbashi was a few published photographs of poor quality.[74] The possible IBA pottery included four fragments of finger-moulded bands, one sherd with raised bands with incision (MBA?), two sherds with rows of oblique parallel incisions, five body-combed sherds (one EBA pattern-combed?) and three fragments of envelope ledge handles of well-developed and over-lapping types, the latter clearly deriving from the IBA of the south Levant. More recently a substantial project at the site has confirmed the presence of a major pastoral economy with stone-built structures including tombs in this very marginal area, which extended over much of the third and second millennia with again a few sherds associated with the remains to show contact with the IBA of the south.[75]

In the more fertile regions, at Bosra, excavation has revealed EB II/III pottery, and a few fragments of EB IV Syrian pottery found in later contexts.[76]

At Dera'a, a series of cists, tumuli and various megalithic remains with mixed contents have been excavated, but only the major finds were published.[77] These appear to belong principally to the Middle and Late Bronze Ages. These megalithic remains lie in an area west of Dera'a station. Albright visited the splendid tell at Dera'a, where he claims to have found remains of all ages from the EBA to the present; but as his visit

---

72 Chéhab 1949–1950, 109; Genz and Sader 2010–2011; Aherns 2015.
73 Pers. comm. M. Dunand.
74 Dubertret and Dunand 1954–1955, 59–76; pl. VII, 1–2.
75 Braemer et al. 2004, 37; Prag forthcoming.
76 Seeden 1986, 23; pl. 18: 150–151.
77 Nasrallah 1950.

took place many years ago, this general statement will not include a clear recognition of IBA type pottery.[78]

The Dera'a region was the probable source of two un-provenanced vessels in the Damascus Museum (permission to study and draw them in 1968 courtesy of the Department of Antiquities of Syria). One jar (Figure 7.5: 1) is a completely typical IBA hand-made jar, flat-based and fat, with large envelope ledge handles, and a row of stabbing at the base of the neck; it is not of a very late IBA type, and it extends the Syrian distribution of hand-made wares. The second jar (Figure 7.5: 2), said to be from the same area, has some different features. It shows many of the normal traits of IBA jars in Transjordan – a flared neck, globular body and flat base; it has completely typical oblique body-combing.[79] The painting is closely paralleled at el-Husn.[80] The slight ridge rather than an applied and impressed band at the base of the neck on the outer wall is a slight oddity, as are loop handles on the body (though the strap section is very typical of IBA in the south); of particular interest is that it is coil-built, the traces showing clearly in the walls. This technique of manufacture is typical of the IBA at sites such as Iktanu. The direct parallel for this jar is that from Tiberias, which repeats every feature (including the coil building) except for the ridge on the neck.[81]

Further north, and filling a nicely intermediate position between Hama and the IBA of the south, are two un-provenanced jugs, both acquired from a dealer in the region of Homs and being registered together, presumably deriving from the same source (Figure 7.5: 3–4). They make an interesting pair, both with trefoil mouth, very much in the pattern of the trefoil-mouth jugs which were such a diagnostic vessel in Byblos Period JI/JII but lacking the cream paint (see above); unpainted jugs with trefoil mouths appear in the latest IBA strata at Iskander and Bab edh-Dhra in the far south. Both the jugs from 'the Homs region' have similar stabbed 'potter's marks' at the base of the handle, short stabbed rows which are familiar in central Transjordan and the Jordan valley, particularly on jug handles. One vessel is fatter, probably coil-built pottery, over-fired to a greenish-grey colour, with greenish black paint and slightly warped, familiar in over-fired vessels from poorly controlled kilns at Tell Iktanu in the south. The handle is missing, but on the more technologically advanced Homs vessel (Figure 7.5: 4) the strap handle is familiar in the south, but the vessel is slimmer, wheel-made and the red-painted decoration on the body is familiar from the Megiddo region. Although in so many ways a pair, these jugs nonetheless show marked transitional features.

Finally there is Yabrud, located on the eastern side of the Anti-Lebanon Range, north-east of Damascus, just east of the northern Beqa', where in 1964–65 excavations uncovered a settlement with silos and pottery of Hama J type, dated not just by painted goblets etc. to the EB IV, but by an Egyptian blue faience scarab and a Byblos-style male bronze figurine.[82] Adjacent to the EB IV settlement were nine cist graves which

---

78 Albright 1925, 16.
79 cf. Beitrawi, Prag 1995, fig. 3: 1.
80 Harding 1953, fig. 1: 8.
81 Tzaferis 1968, fig. 5: 11.
82 Abou Assaf 1967, Taf. VI.

7 The 1968 survey in the Beqa' of Lebanon and its relevance to the archaeology of the central Levant ca. 2500–2000/1900 BC

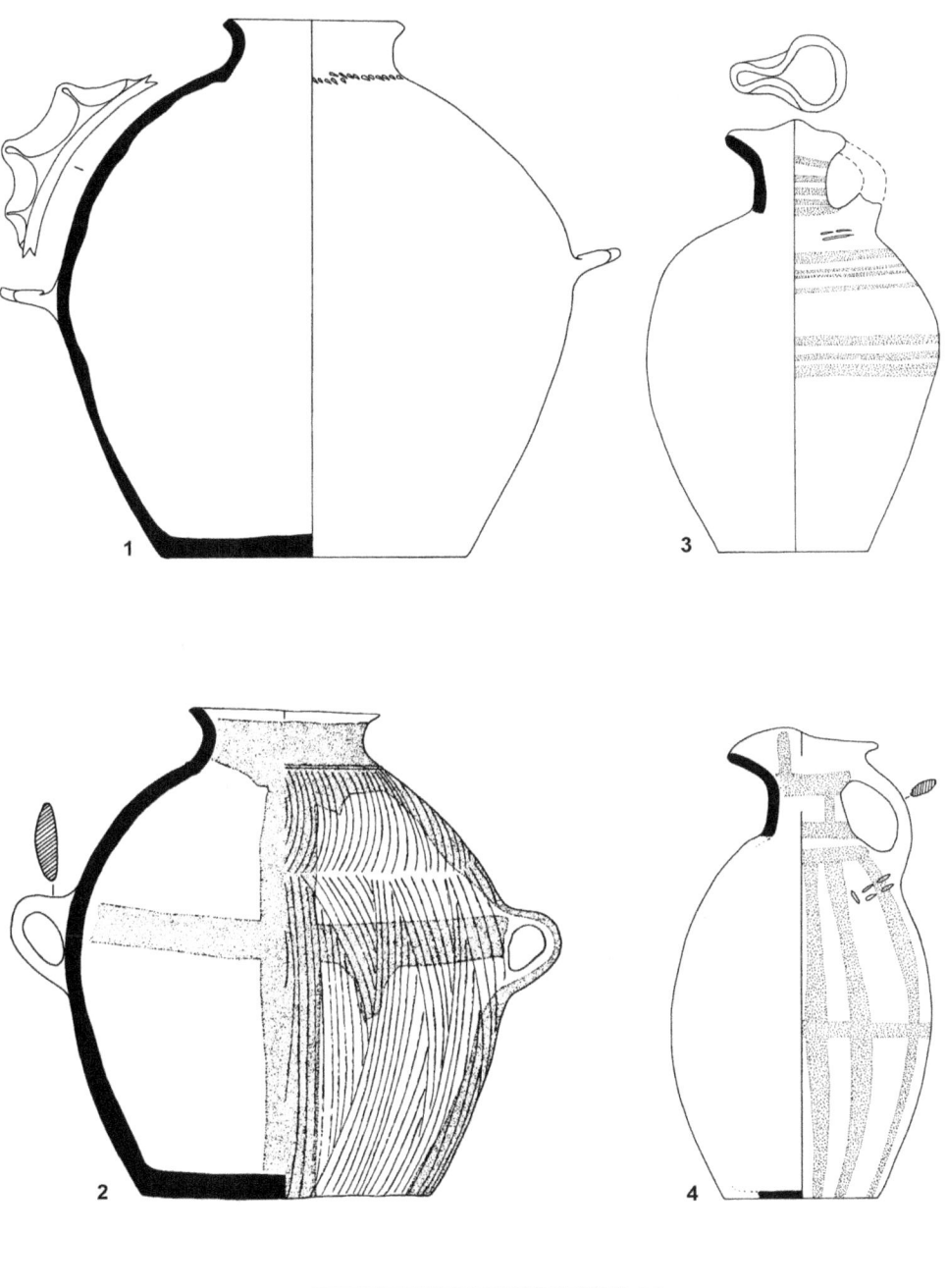

Figure 7.5: Late third millennium BC pottery in the National Museum, Damascus.

appear to have been originally used in the IBA (Grey Ware teapots). The cist graves themselves were oriented north/south in three rows, a pattern similar to that of the IBA cist graves at Tell el-'Ajjul,[83] also in the cemeteries of small cist graves south of Iktanu,[84] and to some extent also in the west cemetery at 'Umbashi.[85] Abou Assaf dated the cist graves later than the adjacent settlement, to continuous MBA use ca. 2100–1500 BC. In their earliest 'teapot' phase the earliest date may well be correct. He interpreted the EB IV occupation of the adjacent settlement with its silos as that of semi-nomads, a description which may also apply to the first IBA users of the cist graves. He concluded that the users (but perhaps just the MBA re-users) of the cist graves were the sedentary occupants of the tell in the modern settlement of Yabrud itself. He noted that the stratigraphy was unclear, and the presence of a MB I cooking pot in his fourth millennium BC occupation confirms this.[86] Yabrud, in the foothills of the Anti-Lebanon, seems to represent a genuine 'border' zone, between the urban north on the cusp of the Hama J to H transition and the intrusion northwards of the late IBA 'grey ware' cultural group. To the east, the agricultural area of south Syria appears to be another very intermediate regional zone, which more clearly reflects the combined influences of both the north and the south, but where the northern more urban influences were stronger. This, and the marginal areas further east, was an area which was very open geographically to ancient and modern routes of migration from the Euphrates, as well as to the urban fashions and technologies of the north.

Without further excavation in the inland regions of the central Levant, such hypotheses are based on too little solid evidence. What we have to date appears to imply the development of a fragile, shifting late IBA regionalism in parts of the central Levant towards the end of the third millennium BC, often based in marginal zones and wooded foothills, with slight extensions into the coastal areas. To what extent there is a chronological overlap between such groups and between different regions will be dependent on radiometric dating. Too much is still dependent on burial evidence. Perhaps, as in the south, the settlement evidence will be slower to emerge and provide evidence for more complex societies, and enlarge our interpretations.

This chapter was completed in February 2016 and I am very grateful to the anonymous referees and especially to Dr Kennedy for updating a number of references and providing the maps.

---

83 Petrie 1932: pl. LI; Kennedy 2015b; Prag forthcoming.
84 Prag 1990, fig. 7.
85 Braemer et al. 2004, fig. 401.
86 Abou Assaf 1967, Trench I, Layer 1; taf. VI: 31.

7 The 1968 survey in the Beqa' of Lebanon and its relevance to the archaeology of the central Levant ca. 2500-2000/1900 BC

References

Abou Assaf, A. (1967). Der friedhof von Yabrud. *Annales Archéologiques Arabes Syriennes* 17: 55–68; abb 1–21; taf. I–VI.

Ahrens, A. (2015). The Egyptian objects from Tell Hizzin in the Beqa'a valley (Lebanon): an archaeological and historical reassessment. *Ägypten und Levante* 25: 201–222.

Albright, W.F. (1925). Bronze Age mounds of northern Palestine and the Hauran: the spring trip of the School in Jerusalem. *Bulletin of the American Schools of Oriental Research* 19: 5–19.

Amiran, R. (1969). *Ancient Pottery of the Holy Land.* Jerusalem: Masada Press.

Badreshany, K. and Kamlah, J. (2010–2011). Middle Bronze Age pottery from Tell el-Burak, Lebanon. *Berytus* 53–54: 81–113.

Baramki, D. (1961). Preliminary report on the excavations at Tell el-Ghassil. *Bulletin du Musée de Beyrouth* XVI: 87–102.

Beayno, F., Mattar, C. and Abdul-Nour, H. (2002) Mgharet al-Hourriyé (Karm Saddé, Caza de Zgharta): rapport préliminaire de la fouille de 2001. *Bulletin d'Archéologie et de l'Architecture Libanaises* 6: 135–178.

Bechar, S. (2015). A reanalysis of the Black Wheel-Made Ware of the Intermediate Bronze Age. *Tel Aviv* 42(1): 27–58.

Bikai, P.M. (1978). *The pottery of Tyre.* Warminster: Aris & Phillips.

Braemer, F., Échallier, J-C. and Taraqji, A. (2004). *Khirbet al Umbashi: villages et campements de pasteurs dans le 'désert noir' (Syrie) à l'âge du Bronze.* Bibliothèque Archéologique et Historique T.171. Institut français du Proche Orient: Beirut.

Catanzariti, A. (2010–2011). Middle Bronze Age ceramic vessels from Kamid el-Loz. *Berytus* 53–54: 47–80.

Chéhab, M. (1949–1950). Chronique. *Bulletin du Musée de Beyrouth* IX: 107–117.

Copeland, L. and Wescombe, P.J. (1965). Inventory of Stone Age sites in Lebanon. Part I. *Mélanges de l'Université Saint-Joseph de Beyrouth* 41: 29–176.

(1966). Inventory of Stone Age sites in Lebanon. Part II. *Mélanges de l'Université Saint-Joseph de Beyrouth* 42: 1–174.

Da Ros, M. and Iamoni, M. (2003). The Bronze and Iron Age pottery: a preliminary account. *Akkadica* 124: 177–196.

Dubertret, L. and Dunand, M. (1954–1955). Les gisements ossifères de Khribet el Umbachi et de Hebariyeh (Safa) et les installations correspondantes: note préliminaire. *Annales archéologiques Arabes Syriennes* 4–5: 59–76.

Dunand, M. (1937). *Fouilles de Byblos* I: *1926–1932.* Geuthner: Paris.

(1950–1954). *Fouilles de Byblos* II: *1933–1938.* Atlas (1950) Text (1954). Librairie d'Amérique et d'Orient Adrien Maisonneuve: Paris.

(1952). Byblos au temps du Bronze Ancien et de la conquête Amorite. *Revue Biblique* 59: 82–90.

van Ess, M. (2008). First results of archaeological cleaning of the deep trench in the Great Courtyard of the Jupiter sanctuary. In *Baalbeck/Heliopolis: results of archaeological and architectural research 2002–2005.* M. van Ess, ed. 99–120. *Bulletin d'Archéologie et de l'Architecture Libanaises.* Hors-Série IV.

Fugmann, E. (1958). *Hama: II.1. Fouilles et recherches de la Fondation Carlsberg 1931–1938: L'architecture des périodes pré-Hellénistiques.* Copenhagen: Nationalmuseet.

Genz, H. (2009). Tell Fadous-Kfarabida: regional connections in the Early Bronze Age. *BAAL Hors-Série* VI: 107–116.

(2010). Reflections on the Early Bronze Age IV in Lebanon. In *Proceedings of the 6th International Congress of the Archaeology of the Ancient Near East 5–10 May 2009*, Sapienza – Università di Roma. Vol. 2. P. Matthiae, F. Pinnock, L. Nigro and N. Marchetti, eds. 205–217. Wiesbaden: Harrassowitz.

Genz, H. and Sader, H. (2008). Tell Hizzin: digging up new material from an old eExcavation. *Bulletin d'Archéologie et d'Architecture Libanaises* 12: 183–201.

(2010–2011). Middle Bronze Age pottery from Tell Hizzin, Lebanon. *Berytus* 53–54: 133–146.

Harding, G.L. (1953). A Middle Bronze Age tomb at Amman. *Palestine Exploration Fund Annual* VI: 14–26.

Heinz, M. (2010). Kamid el-Loz: intermediary between cultures: more than 10 years of archaeological research in Kamid el-Loz (1997–2007). *Bulletin d'Archéologie et de l'Architecture Libanaises Hors-Série* VII. Ministère de la Culture. Direction Général des Antiquitiés.

Höflmayer, F., Dee, M., Genz, H. and Riehl, S. (2014). Radiocarbon evidence for the Early Bronze Age Levant: the site of Tell Fadous-Kfarabida (Lebanon) and the end of the Early Bronze III period. *Radiocarbon* 56(2): 529–542.

Iamoni, M. and Morandi Bonacossi, D. (2010–2011). The Middle Bronze Age I – III pottery sequence from the Italian excavations at Mishrifeh/Qatna, Syria: archaeological contexts and ceramic evidence. *Berytus* 53–54: 181–212.

Kennedy, M.A. (2015a). Life and death at Tell Umm Hammad: a village landscape of the southern Levantine EB IV. *Zeitschrift des Deutschen Palästina-Vereins* 131: 1–28.

(2015b). EB IV stone-built cist-graves from Sir Flinders Petrie's excavations at Tell el-'Ajjul. *Palestine Exploration Quarterly* 147(2): 104–129.

Kennedy, M.A., Badreshany, K. and Philip, G. (2018). Drinking on the periphery: the Tell Nebi Mend goblets in their regional and archaeometric context. *Levant*, doi.org/10.1080/00758914.2018.1442076.

Kenyon, K.M. (1960). *Excavations at Jericho I: the tombs excavated in 1952–1954*. London: British School of Archaeology in Jerusalem.

(1965). *Excavations at Jericho II: the tombs excavated in 1952–1958*. London: British School of Archaeology in Jerusalem.

Kenyon, K.M. and Holland, T.A. (1983). *Excavations at Jericho V: the pottery phases of the tell and other finds.* London: British School of Archaeology in Jerusalem.

Kuschke, A., Mittmann, S. and Müller, U. (1976). *Archäologischer survey in der nördlichen Biqa', Herbst 1972.* Beihefte zum Tübinger Atlas des Vorderen Orients 11. Wiesbaden: Reichert Verlag.

Lauffray, J. (2008). *Fouilles de Byblos VI: l'urbanisme et l'architecture.* Bibliothéque Archéologique et Historique T.182. Beyrouth: Institut Français du Proche-Orient.

Mansfeld, G. (1970). Ein bronzezeitliches steinkammergrab bei Rafid im Wadi at-Taym. In *Bericht über d. ergebnisse d. ausgrabung in Kamid el-Loz (Libanon) in den jahren 1966 und 1967.* R. Hachmann, ed. 117–128 and Tfl. 38–39. Saarbrücker Beiträge zur Altertumskunde 7. Bonn: Rudolf Habelt Verlag.

7 The 1968 survey in the Beqa' of Lebanon and its relevance to the archaeology of the central Levant ca. 2500-2000/1900 BC

Marchetti, N. and Nigro, L. (1995-1996). Handicraft production, secondary food transformation and storage in the public building P4 at EB IVA Ebla. *Berytus* 42: 9-36.

Marfoe, L. (1995). *Kāmid el-Lōz. 13: the prehistoric and early historic context of the site*. Revised, enlarged and prepared for publication by R. Hachmann and C. Misamer. Saarbrücker Beiträge zur Altertumskunde, Bd. 41. Bonn: Dr. Rudolf Habelt GMBH.

(1998). *Kamid el-Lōz 14: settlement history of the Biqa' up to the Iron Age*. Revised by R. Hachmann and prepared for publication by C. Misamer and M. Froese. Saarbrücker Beiträge zur Altertumskunde, Bd. 53. Bonn: Dr. Rudolf Habelt GMBH.

Matthiae, P., Pinnock, F. and Scandone Matthiae, G. eds. (1995). *Ebla: alle origini della civiltà urbana: trent'anni di scavi in Siria dell'Università di Roma "La Sapienza"*. Milan: Electa.

du Mesnil du Buisson, Le Comte (1948). *Baghouz: L'Ancienne Corsôte*. Leiden: Brill.

Mouamar, G. (2017). De nouvelles données sur les gobelets de Hama : marqueurs de la chronologie et des échanges de Syrie centrale pendant la deuxième moitié du IIIe millénaire av. J-C. *Paléorient* 43(2): 69-89.

(2018). The Early Bronze IVB Painted Simple Ware from Tell Sh'aïrat: an intergrated archaeometric approach. *Levant*, doi.org/10.1080/00758914.2018.1477295.

Nasrallah, J. (1950). Tumulus de l'Âge du Bronze dans le Hauran. *Syria* XXVII: 314-331.

Petrie, W.M.F. (1932). *Ancient Gaza II*. British School of Archaeology in Egypt: London

Prag, K. (1971). *A study of the Intermediate Early Bronze-Middle Bronze Age in Transjordan, Syria and Lebanon*. D.Phil thesis, University of Oxford. Oxford: United Kingdom.

(1974). The Intermediate Early Bronze-Middle Bronze Age: an interpretation of the evidence from Transjordan, Syria and Lebanon. *Levant* 6: 69-116.

(1990). Preliminary report on the excavations at Tell Iktanu, Jordan, 1989. *Annual of the Department of Antiquities of Jordan* 34: 119-128.

(1995). The 'built tomb' of the Intermediate Early Bronze-Middle Bronze Age at Beitrawi, Jordan. In *Trade, contact and the movement of peoples in the Eastern Mediterranean: studies in honour of J. Basil Hennessy*. S.J. Bourke and J-P. Descœudres, eds. 103-113. Mediterranean Archaeology Supplement 3. Sydney: Meditarch.

(2011). The domestic unit at Tall Iktanu, its derivations and functions. In *Daily life, materiality, and complexity in early urban communities of the southern Levant: papers in honor of Walter E. Rast and R. Thomas Schaub*. M. Chesson, W. Aufrecht and I. Kuijt, eds. 55-76. Winona Lake: Eisenbrauns.

(2014). The southern Levant during the Intermediate Bronze Age. In *The Oxford Handbook of the Archaeology of the Levant c. 8000 - 332 BC*. M. Steiner and A. Killebrew, eds. 388-400. Oxford: Oxford University Press.

Forthcoming. Kenyon, Jericho and the Amorites. In *Digging up Jericho past, present and future*. B. Finlayson, R. Sparks and B. Wagemakers, eds. Oxford: Archaeopress.

Regev, J., Miroschedji, P. de, Greenberg, R., Braun, E., Greenhut, Z. and Boaretto, E. (2012). Chronology of the Early Bronze Age in the southern Levant: new analysis for a High Chronology. *Radiocarbon* 54(3-4): 525-566.

Saghieh, M. (1983). *Byblos in the third millennium B.C: a reconstruction of the stratigraphy and a study of the cultural connections*. Warminster: Aris & Phillips.

Saidah, R. (1967). Chronique. J. Fouilles varies. *Bulletin du Musée de Beyrouth* 20: 171.

(1969). Archaeology in the Lebanon, 1968-1969. *Berytus* 18: 119-175.

(1993–1994). Beirut in the Bronze Age: the Kharji tombs. *Berytus* 41: 137–210.

Seeden, H. (1986). Bronze Age village occupation at Busra: AUB excavations on the northwest tell 1983–1984. *Berytus* 34: 11–81.

Steimer-Herbet, T. (2000). Étude des monuments mégalithiques de Mengez (Liban) d'après les carnets de fouilles du R. P. M. Tallon (1959–1969). *Syria* 77: 11–21.

Tallon, M. (1958). Monuments mégalithiques de Syrie et du Liban. *Melanges de l'Université de Saint-Joseph* XXXV: 213–234.

(1959). Tumulus et mégalithes du Hermel et de la Beqaʻ nord. *Melanges de l'Université de Saint-Joseph* XXXVI: 89–111.

(1964). Les monuments mégalithiques de Mengez. *Bulletin du Musée de Beyrouth* XVII: 7–19, pls. I–VII.

Thalmann, J-P. (2006). *Tell Arqa: Les niveaux de l'Âge du Bronze*. Bibliothèque Archéologique et Historique T.177. Beirut: Institut Français du Proche Orient.

(2008). Tell Arqa et Byblos: essai de correlation. In *The Bronze Age in Lebanon: studies in the archaeology and chronology of Lebanon, Syria and Egypt*. M. Bietak and E. Czerny, eds. 61–78. Vienna: Österreichischen Akademie der Wissenschaften.

(2012). Ex Oriente lux, l'invention de la lampe au Proche-Orient. In *Aux marges de l'archéologie. Hommage à Serge Cleuziou*. J. Giraud and G. Gernez, eds. 175–185. Travaux de la Maison René-Ginouvès 16. Paris: De Boccard.

Tubb, J.N. (1990). *Excavations at the Early Bronze Age cemetery of Tiwal esh-Sharqi*. British Museum Press: London.

Tzaferis, V. (1968). A Middle Bronze I cemetery in Tiberias. *Israel Exploration Journal* 18: 15–19.

Ward, W.A. (1978). Appendix B: The Egyptian Objects. In *The Pottery of Tyre*. P. Bikai, ed. 83–87. Warminster: Aris & Phillips.

Wright, G.E. (1961). The archaeology of Palestine. In *The Bible and the ancient Near East: essays in honor of William Foxwell Albright*. G.E. Wright, ed. 73–112. New York: Routledge & Kegan Paul.

8

Sequence, chronology and culture at Tell Nebi Mend in the Middle and Late Bronze Ages

Stephen J. Bourke
University of Sydney

Introduction

This chapter is offered in part to address the question of 'second millennium BC developments', following on from the age of first cities in the Early Bronze Age of the Orontes corridor. In many of the chief sites considered in these proceedings (Tell Afis, Ebla, Hama, Qatna), substantial Early Bronze Age strata (fourth-third millennia BC) are followed by extensive Middle Bronze Age horizons, facilitating comparative analysis seeking to tease out the differences between the two urban horizons. At Tell Nebi Mend, the nature and physical extent of EBA occupation (if not its duration) remains obscure, with relatively small areas of fourth-third millennia BC date exposed.[1] It is therefore difficult to contextualise the second millennium BC occupation at Nebi Mend in the light of preceding history. At other sites, the restoration/restructuring of major fortification traces, the rebuilding/remodelling of citadels, and the intensification of lower town occupation, are all features of the changing urban landscape across the two urban ages.

At Tell Nebi Mend, EBA occupation is apparently restricted to the upper tell, with only very small areas of the later EBA horizons excavated.[2] It was felt useful to summarise the main features of the Middle and Late Bronze Age strata at Tell Nebi

---

1   Kennedy 2015; this book.
2   Kennedy 2015; this book.

Figure 8.1: Map of sites mentioned in text.

Mend, first because such has yet to be placed in the public domain, and second because it will facilitate region-wide comparative analyses between EBA and MB–LB urban development and settlement landscape studies. As well, providing comparative datasets may be considered especially timely, as recent big-data syntheses are moving to consider regional and inter-regional changes to urban design and hinterland exploitation across traditional timelines,[3] foregrounding generic concerns with climate, landform and population, while de-emphasising the particular and historical agencies traditionally held to dominate such analyses.

This short summary of the second millennium BC sequence at Tell Nebi Mend is mindful of the larger trends in Syro-Mesopotamian urban and landscape studies, but seeks to highlight the significance of the particular circumstances at work in shaping

---

3   Wilkinson et al. 2014.

8 Sequence, chronology and culture at Tell Nebi Mend in the Middle and Late Bronze Ages

the history of occupation at Nebi Mend and in its hinterland through the ages. It is suggested herein that such particular circumstances (changing modes of imperial warfare for one) may well be of significance in understanding the settlement history of other major centres of the Orontes catchment, in danger of being 'evened-out' of the picture in the unfolding era of big-data.

Tell Nebi Mend: site description and excavation history

The site of Tell Nebi Mend is located in the upper Beqa' valley, at the confluence of the Orontes river (Nahr al-Asi) and one of its main tributaries, the Mukadiyah (Ain et Tannur; Figure 8.1). The site is situated at the point where the east-west Homs/Tripoli road meets the inland north-south highway running along the upper Orontes valley and on into the northern Beqa'. Protected on two sides by water, Nebi Mend combines the advantages of a rich agricultural plain with an easily defensible site, dominating important trade routes that run nearby.[4]

The settlement consists of a double-mounded upper and lower tell, together approximately 10 ha in size, rising some 30 m above the surrounding flat plain (Figure 8.2). A walled enclosure of probable MBA date runs east/west along the south side of the lower mound, linking the Orontes and Mukadiyah. This enclosure wall continues west of the latter river before turning north some 400 m beyond the western river's modern course.[5] An approximately 40 ha area was contained within this ramparted enclosure, and potentially more if the enclosure walls continued north and east to join the Orontes immediately north of the mounded tell, as seems likely.[6]

French Excavations (1921-22)

The first exploration of Tell Nebi Mend began with the pioneering two-season (1921–22) French Mission under Maurice Pézard.[7] Investigations concentrated on the north-east quadrant of the upper tell, in two contiguous irregular exposures, Tranches A and B. Tranche A was an approximately 70 x 14 m rectangular cut through the body of the mound, sampling Byzantine through Middle Bronze Age horizons (Figure 8.3).[8] Tranche B abutted the north-eastern edge of Tranche A, and sampled Byzantine through Late Bronze Age strata across a three-step terraced area roughly 70 x 30 m in extent (Figure 8.3).[9] Pézard divided the strata uncovered into four main architectural horizons, corresponding broadly to Middle Bronze II ('Amorite'), Late Bronze II ('Syro-Hittite'), Iron Age II ('Syro-Phenicien'), and Late Hellenistic ('Seleucides').[10]

---

4   Parr 1983, 100–103; Parr (ed.) 2015, 2–10.
5   Parr (ed.) 2015, 346–347, fig. 9.1.
6   Parr (ed.) 2015, 356–358.
7   Pézard 1931.
8   Pézard 1931, 3–11.
9   Pézard 1931, 11–12.
10 Pézard 1931, 3–75.

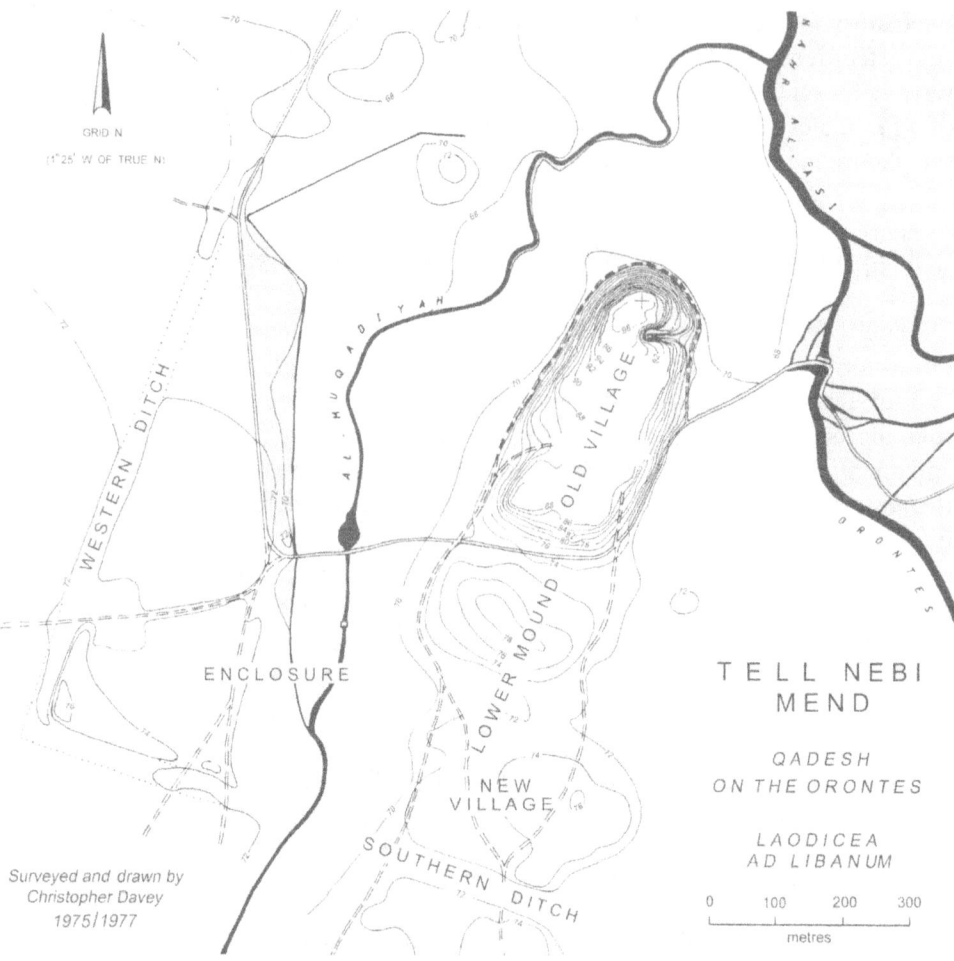

Figure 8.2: Overall contour plan of Tell Nebi Mend (after Parr ed. 2015).

In the early 1920s, the whole of the Orontes valley was terra incognita, and Pézard's excavations among the very first to plumb second millennium BC deposits. His technique, while very loose seen against present practice, compares well with du Mesnil du Buisson's work at Qatna,[11] and is not so very inferior to that of Braidwood at Judaidah,[12] and Ingolt at Hama.[13] Given the soundness of the majority of what were (of necessity, given his death in 1923) only preliminary observations, Pézard's achievements were considerable, and should be acknowledged as an important foundation on which later French, American and Danish archaeologists built.[14]

---

11 du Mesnil du Buisson 1935.
12 Braidwood and Braidwood 1960, 1–11.
13 Ingolt 1940.
14 Parr (ed.) 2015, 14–20.

8 Sequence, chronology and culture at Tell Nebi Mend in the Middle and Late Bronze Ages

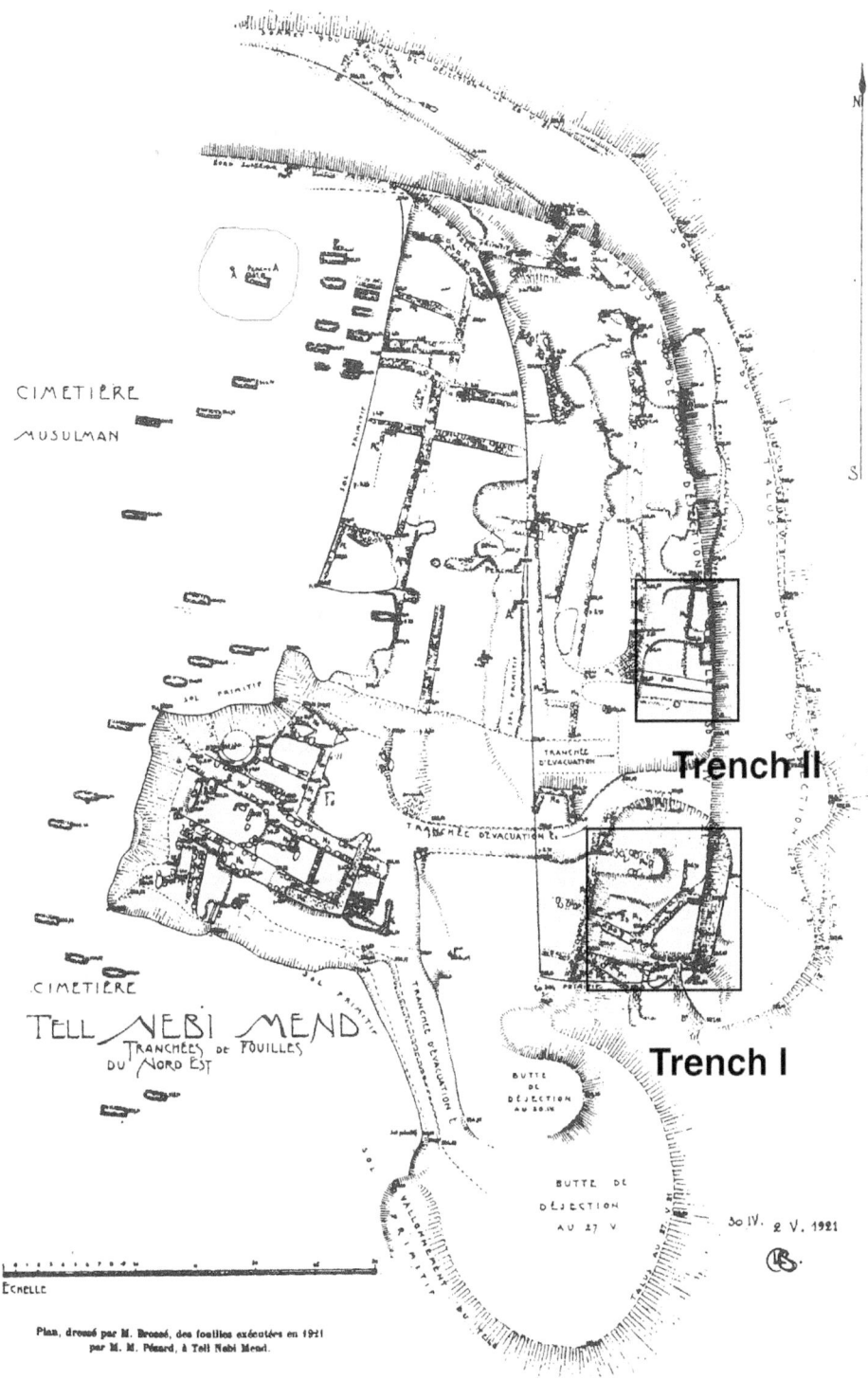

Figure 8.3: Upper tell overview of Tell Nebi Mend, Pézard and UCL London Exposures.

Table 8.1: Excavated areas at Tell Nebi Mend.

Excavated Area	MB I	MB II	MB III	LB I	LB II
Trench I	5 x 10m	15 x 25m	25 x 25m	5 x 15m	5 x 15m
Trench II	n/a	n/a	n/a	5 x 5m	25 x 25m
Trench III	3 x 11m	15 x 25m	25 x 25m	15 x 25m	10 x 15m
Trench VII	3 x 11m	3 x 11m	n/a	n/a	n/a
Trench VIII	3 x 15m	3 x 15m	5 x 15m	n/a	n/a
Trench VI/IX	2 x 65m	n/a	n/a	n/a	n/a

British Excavations (1975-95)

The second mission to the site, from the Institute of Archaeology, University College London, under the direction of Peter Parr, worked for 12 field seasons over the 20-year life of the project.[15]

Excavations on the central mound were concentrated on two major exposures (see Table 8.1). The first of four trenches (I, II, V and VIII) was located on the north-eastern slopes of the upper mound, within (Trench I) and to the east (Trench VIII) of Pézard's Tranche A, and within the southern margins (Trench II) and slightly upslope to the west (Trench V) of the more irregular Tranche B. The second main focus of excavation on the upper mound (Trench III) was located on the untouched western side of the upper tell, positioned slightly to the south of Pézard's Tranche A, itself located on the eastern slopes.

Two isolated trenches on the south side of the upper mound were laid across distinct contour intervals around the middle (Trench IV & Trench VII) reaches of the high tell, to investigate the placement and dating of possible gate and fortification lines.[16] Finally, two long thin trenches (Trenches VI and IX) were laid out across the main structural features of the lower embankment wall,[17] to determine its date and sequence of construction.

Essentially complete second millennium BC stratigraphic sequences were recovered from Trench I (east upper tell) and Trench III (west upper tell), supplemented by important (but less comprehensive) sequences of MBA (Trenches VI-IX) and LBA (Trench II) strata recovered from elsewhere across the ruin field (Table 8.1).

Broadly speaking, the more complete later Middle through earlier Late Bronze Age sequences covered around 1250 m² of excavated area, which were supplemented by less complete earlier MBA (200 m²) and later LBA (625 m²) excavated areas.

---

15 Parr (ed.) 2015, 22–27.
16 Parr (ed.) 2015, fig. 1.18.
17 Parr (ed.) 2015, fig. 9.1.

8 Sequence, chronology and culture at Tell Nebi Mend in the Middle and Late Bronze Ages

Absolute chronology and radiometric dating

The Trench I second millennium BC sequence consists of 10 main strata (Phases A–M), defined by architecture and associated sequential deposits, with Phase A the latest (LB II) and Phase M the earliest (MB I). Most chronological data derive from comparative ceramic analysis sourced to this Trench I master sequence. This is derived from a form-based typology of more than 900 elements, with individual phased assemblages tied to major architectural horizons, each defined by varying frequencies of individual forms over time.[18]

Radiometric data

There are a number of radiometric dates from second millennium BC strata at Tell Nebi Mend, derived from sorted charcoal samples, and processed at British Museum laboratories (see Figure 8.4; Table 8.2).[19] Unfortunately, there were technical problems with analytic procedures in the mid-1980s, and although 'generic corrections' were later applied once the errors were assessed,[20] the results remain problematic. They are presented here with all caveats in place.

Commentary

The ceramic-derived relative chronology for the second millennium BC strata in Trenches I and III (supplemented by MBA from VII and LBA from II) posited a relatively uninterrupted sequence of occupation across the entire millennium. Taken very broadly, this is confirmed by the 14C data. In Trench I Area 171, the earliest MBA strata began with layer I 171.24. Contexts immediately below this (I 171.25–30) in Area 171 were all very probably EB IV period in date, so an EB IV reading for sample I 171.28 seems quite reasonable, although the heavily pitted stratigraphy in this area makes definitive statements hazardous.

The firmly third millennium BC date (I 151.33) seems far too early for its secure later MBA context,[21] with this later MBA attribution supported by upwards of two metres of earlier MBA occupation below 151.33. It should therefore probably be seen as residual. The early MBA date derived from what seems to be a Late Bronze Age I (ca. fifteenth century BC) burnt floor layer (I 200.85), associated with flimsy architecture,[22] also seems residual, perhaps deriving from structural timbers associated with the monumental MB II Phase G architectural complex.

---

18 Bourke 1993, 167–168.
19 Burleigh et al. 1984, 72.
20 Bowman 1990, 59–62, 77.
21 Bourke 1993, 162–163.
22 Bourke 1993, 161.

Table 8.2. Tell Nebi Mend radiometric dates (MB-LB).

Sample ID	Context	Material	Expected Date	^{14}C Age $\pm 1\sigma$	Calibrated Age Range (BC)		Assessment
					1σ (68.2%)	2σ (95.4%)	
BM2946	I 171.28	Wood charcoal	EB IV	3780±60	2298–2056	2456–2032	EB IV
BM2947	I 151.33	Wood charcoal	MB/LB	3730±50	2201–2039	2289–1979	EB IV
BM2933	I 200.85	Wood charcoal	LB I	3580±110	2122–1768	2275–1641	MB I-II
BM2029R	VII 100.16	Wood charcoal	MB I	3540±110	2026–1701	2198–1616	MB I-II
BM2040R	III 204.17	Charcoal	LB II	3370±120	1870–1510	1974–1414	MB I-LB I
BM2035R	III 206.15	Wood charcoal	LB II	3230±110	1657–1396	1768–1225	LB I-II
BM2032R	III 206.24	Wood charcoal	LB II	3160±70	1507–1307	1611–1263	LB I-II
BM2037R	III 206.35	Charcoal	LB II	2940±250	1431–845	1771–518	LB I-IA II
BM2033R	III 203.63	Wood charcoal	LB II-IA I	2430±110	750–405	806–234	IA II-Hell

The southern tell stratigraphy recorded in the narrow exposure of Trench VII first noted a series of thin wash/debris layers (VII 100.17–19), containing predominantly EB IV ceramic material, laid over sterile deposits. These EB IV deposits were cut through by a massive east-west running mudbrick wall, probably defensive in nature. An early MBA date for this wall is not unreasonable, given the scant deposits of earlier materials below, and the (apparently early) MBA ceramics associated with the wall (VII 100.13–16). Of course, the large standard deviation for this assay is not helpful, and allows for a date spanning much of the MBA.

The sequence of five assays from Trench III were selected to 'bracket' the use-life of the last phase of what ceramics suggested to be an LB II architectural complex, the rooms and courtyards of which represented the bulk of the exposed horizons in Trench III. The depositionally earliest samples (III 204.17 and III 206.35) were associated with the last constructional phase before the final destruction horizon. Sample III 204.17 was drawn from pit fill, with the pit in question cut from a floor associated with the penultimate phase before the fiery destruction. As several earlier structural phases containing Cypriot and Mycenaean pottery underlay this horizon, the Late Bronze Age IIB attribution seems reasonably secure. However, the 14C reading, falling considerably earlier (within the MB/LB date range), should probably be seen as residual, although the large standard deviation is again unhelpful.

The second assay (III 206.35) derives from one of the most intriguing deposits excavated on the site. It is drawn from material within a pit, cut from floor levels associated with the penultimate architectural phase before the fiery destruction horizon. Complicating interpretation is the fact that the pit penetrated into foundation deposits associated with wall construction belonging to the earlier phase, potentially combining pit fill from one occupational sub-phase with constructional debris associated with an earlier sub-phase. This is especially unfortunate when we consider the contents.

8 Sequence, chronology and culture at Tell Nebi Mend in the Middle and Late Bronze Ages

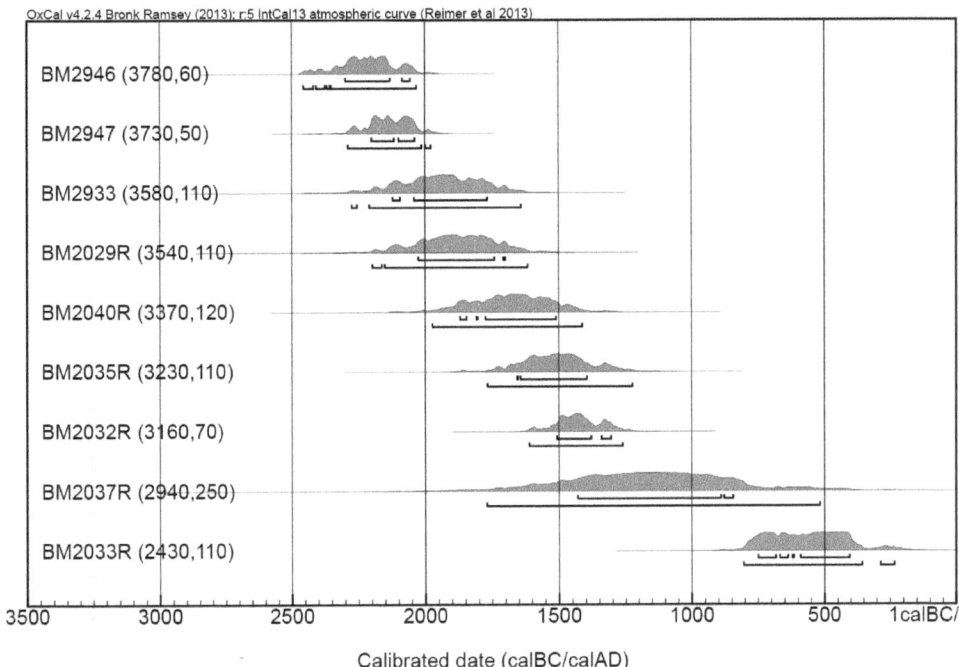

Figure 8.4: Tell Nebi Mend radiometric dates (MB-LB).

Along with imported Cypriot White Slip II and Base Ring II pottery, a Mycenaean IIIA2 chalice/goblet, and a Mycenaean IIIB stirrup jar, there were several near complete platter-bowls, shallow bowls and jars. As well, there were a number of miniature platter-bowls, upright shallow bowls and several trefoil-lipped juglets, these last consistent with foundation-deposit offerings. The potential combination of a cultic offering deposit and wall foundational materials is especially regrettable, as the deposit also contained fragments of several ring kernoi, and a unique ceramic incised 'sandal', perhaps better described as a 'foot-shaped' dedicatory plaque. The deposit of complete, semi-complete, miniature and full-size locally made ceramics, along with foreign imports and cultic paraphernalia, is unique at Nebi Mend. A radiometric date for this extraordinary find would have been welcomed. However, the assay from III 206.35 has a huge standard deviation, making any hope of an exact placement illusory, as potential dates range from the Late Bronze Age I through to the later Iron Age II, while foreign imported pottery would suggest an LB IIA depositional date.

Two samples (III 206.15 and III 206.24) were drawn from the fiery destruction horizon of the building complex. Both derive from the same deposit, dug in two sequences. The expected date for the destruction fell somewhere within the LB II period, perhaps towards the end of the thirteenth century BC. Taken together the assays might allow for a date within the LB II period, but not particularly late in that period. However, again, as the solid charcoal samples could well derive from constructional timbers associated with the last-phase rebuilding of the complex, a date within the fourteenth century BC for this refurbishing event would not be unreasonable.

The final sample (III 203.63) derived from a large dump deposit that overlay and sealed the civic complex of the final Bronze Age phase. Excavators felt the combination of rubbish (bone, ash and ceramics) and the direction of the tip lines suggested walls were still standing to a reasonable height when the in-filling operations began. However, the date (which falls unhelpfully within the Hallstatt Plateau) countenances an Iron Age IIB–C through early Classical date for the deposit, which seems unlikely, as this 'dump' horizon was sealed by several substantial phases of Iron I–II architecture, one associated with a coherent assemblage of diagnostic later Iron II ceramics. Therefore, it may be that the sample derives from intrusive material. Classical and Late Antique period pits, along with occasional modern owl nests, were encountered across the upper reaches of Trench III, so this occurrence is not entirely unexpected.

Summary

Although the radiometric dataset is both inadequate in size and problematic in both composition and processing procedure, a sequence spanning the entire second millennium BC is broadly indicated by the radiometric assays. Additional short-life radiometric samples are currently being processed, and should lead to a far better definition of the sequential phasing within this second millennium BC horizon. However, until the new datasets are processed and analysed, ceramic-derived assemblage groups and their associated architecture still provide the best guide to settlement intensity across the millennium of occupation under discussion.

Settlement history

Stratigraphically, the later Middle Bronze Age and most Late Bronze Age horizons are adequately sampled, but earlier Middle Bronze Age horizons are only known from relatively small soundings on the upper mound.[23] These were supplemented by long thin entrenchments across huge earthen embankments in the lower town, which often could not sample occupational strata associated with the earthworks, as these lay below the modern water table.[24]

The MB I period (ca. 2000–1800 BC)

The Trench I stratigraphic sequence encountered two phases of MB I period architecture (Trench I Phases K and L) in the north sounding, and one (Phase K) in the south sounding, sealed below three phases of ever more substantial MB II period architecture (Trench I Phases G, H and J). Both soundings below the MB II horizons were of limited extent (4 x 6 m and 3 x 4 m respectively), and preserved only short fragments of mudbrick walling, alongside plaster floors, numerous pits, several plaster-sealed

---

23　Parr (ed.) 2015, 23; Kennedy 2015, 40–41.
24　Parr (ed.) 2015, 353–359.

8 Sequence, chronology and culture at Tell Nebi Mend in the Middle and Late Bronze Ages

benches, and in one case an intra-mural burial below a floor. The impression is of a sequence of well-founded but modest architectural phases, with no indication of any function beyond the purely domestic.

The MB I ceramic assemblage from Trench I is relatively small (approximately 50 unique forms in an assemblage of around 2500 sherds), and not particularly diagnostic for sorting out individual sub-periods within the MB I. The predominant cooking pot forms are the flat-based wide-mouthed upright piecrust-flanged examples, common to all Orontes valley sites in the earlier MBA. Tall narrow-necked and short-necked jar forms, and platter, shallow and carinated bowl forms are all long-lived. Indeed, the use-life of most of the Trench I MB I forms extends well into the MB II period, which might imply that the earliest phases of the MBA were not sampled in the Trench I soundings. However, there is a considerable frequency of EB IV forms (fine bowls in particular) in the earliest MBA assemblages from Trench I, which may imply a relatively early start date for the Trench I MB I horizons. This suggested early start date is given some limited support by the radiocarbon dates, however problematic. So, while it remains unclear precisely when within the MB I period occupation begins, once commenced, occupation was apparently uninterrupted through six successive MBA building phases.

The Trench III exposure on the western side of the upper mound has a reasonably extensive later MBA through LBA sequence. However, the earlier horizons of the MBA were sounded via a long thin (3 x 11 m) trench across the upper fortification lines, predominantly sampling the western (outer) side of the earthen embankment, as well as a 3 x 5 m long slot-trench across the dry fosse excavated into the underlying bedrock, which lay immediately west of the embankment. The presence of any external wall lines west of this 4 m wide fosse could not be determined, as the modern water table intervened at the Late Roman period horizons.

Besides the embankment and the fosse (Trench III Phase J), other MB I period constructions detected in the slot-trench were modest, consisting largely of bedrock cuts and levelling fills east and upslope of the fosse, which should probably be considered as sub-phases within the main Phase J embankment constructional horizon. The Trench III MB I ceramic assemblage was equally restricted, with upwards of 40% by number being (apparently) EB IV residual material, even though no dedicated EB IV horizon underlay basal MB I deposits at the foot of the slope, although such deposits may have existed upslope to the east of the rampart. This stratigraphic procession (MBA strata directly on bedrock), and the high frequency of EB IV materials among the earliest MB I assemblage, might imply an early date within the MB I period for the construction of the upper tell embankment, although there is (as yet) no radiometric data to support such an assertion.

On the southern slopes of the upper tell, the Trench VII exposure sought to explore an additional stretch of what was assumed to be the same embankment/wall construction, again through a narrow (3 x 11 m) trench laid across a marked contour 'step' that seemed to indicate a major underlying irregularity. Both the earthen embankment and remains of a topping mudbrick wall (approximately 1.5 m thick) were duly detected running east–west across the middle reaches of the trench. Only thin deposits of wash/fill layers containing EB IV sherds overlay bedrock in this area, which were in turn overlaid by embankment fills. Associated occupational strata were detected against the inner face of the mudbrick wall, with ceramics typologically MB I in date. A single 14C date (VII 100.16) was not inconsistent with dating derived from the ceramic assemblage, although the large standard deviation frustrated any surety in the matter.

In the lower town, Trench VI (1 x 65 m long) and Trench IX (2 x 35 m long) were positioned to sample the upper metre of embankment fills that flanked the deep ditch, although the base of the deep ditch could not be fully excavated, as the modern water table intervened once again.[25] There was no trace of wall lines on top of the embankment in either trench exposure, although a significant remodelling of the embankment surface in Trench IX by Late Roman period burials suggested that post-Bronze Age activity in the area may have removed any Bronze Age structures that once existed on top of the rampart.

Bronze Age ceramic materials deriving from the two long strip-trenches were sparse, with less than a hundred Bronze Age sherds recovered from all excavation units. The majority (85%) dated to the later EBA period(s), with around 15% by number of MBA date. The high percentage of EBA sherds in the rampart fills may hint at some form of lower town settlement in the later third millennium BC, but as putative pre-Roman occupation in the embankment area must lie well below the current water table, any such remain hypothetical. Of the MBA sherds, none was clearly diagnostic of any particular phase within the MBA. That said, several of the fabric/form combinations occurred early within the MBA sequence, although these do have a reasonably long use-life across MB I–II horizons. While it seems likely that the lower town embankment was constructed at some stage (perhaps early) within the MBA, the slight evidence to hand offers no confidence in a more precise dating.

The MB II period (ca. 1800–1600 BC)

The MB II horizons in Trench I were considerably more substantial architecturally than MB I predecessors, featuring at least two phases (Phases H and G) of increasingly monumental mudbrick architecture, with a less grand earliest MB II phase (Phase J) exposed only in small soundings (4 x 6 m and 3 x 4 m), previously mentioned (see Figure 8.5). Trench I Phase G architecture was by far the most monumental complex of brick rooms encountered across the site in UCL excavations. The exterior east wall (Trench I Wall 1) of the associated complex was first detected in Pézard's excavations (his 'Mur X'), where Mur X was suggested to be a fortification wall.[26] While the 3.5 m thick Wall 1 may well have served this purpose, the carefully designed series of associated small square rooms (many plaster-lined and several sporting plastered benches) uncovered by British excavators in the 1980s suggests that something more than a simple trace-wall existed in this place (see Figure 8.5).[27]

---

25 Parr (ed.) 2015, 346–353.
26 Pézard 1931, 3–7.
27 Parr 1983, 106.

8 Sequence, chronology and culture at Tell Nebi Mend in the Middle and Late Bronze Ages

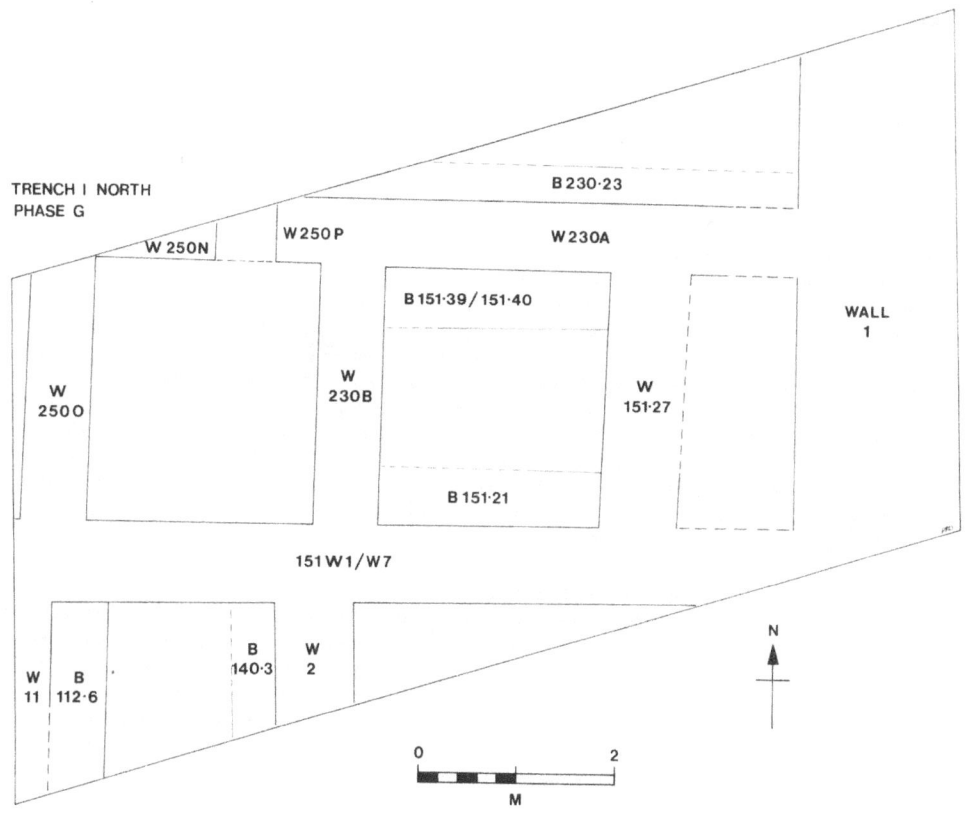

Figure 8.5: Trench I, plan of Phase G, Wall I and 'stronghold' complex.

The complex of small rooms[28] closely resembles the 'fortress/stronghold' structures encountered in several places along the Ebla embankment.[29] While it is generally felt the Ebla embankment dates to the MB I period,[30] the strongholds are less securely dated, as they are better known for their destruction assemblages than for constructional data.[31] While the excavators imply that the strongholds and the rampart were constructed over a short period of time in the MB I,[32] it seems more likely that these strongholds were constructed in the MB II to reinforce lengthy embankment lines at their relatively weak central regions,[33] perhaps responding to mass-assault tactics, compound-bows and siege towers employed by the considerably larger armies of the later MBA.[34]

---

28   Parr 1983, 106, fig. 3; Bourke 1993, 162–163, fig. 8.
29   Burke 2008, 200–204, figs 39–41.
30   Pinnock 2001, 25–29, figs 11–13.
31   Peyronel 2007.
32   Pinnock 2001, 22, fn.12.
33   Burke 2008, 49.
34   Burke 2008, 27–29, 33–36.

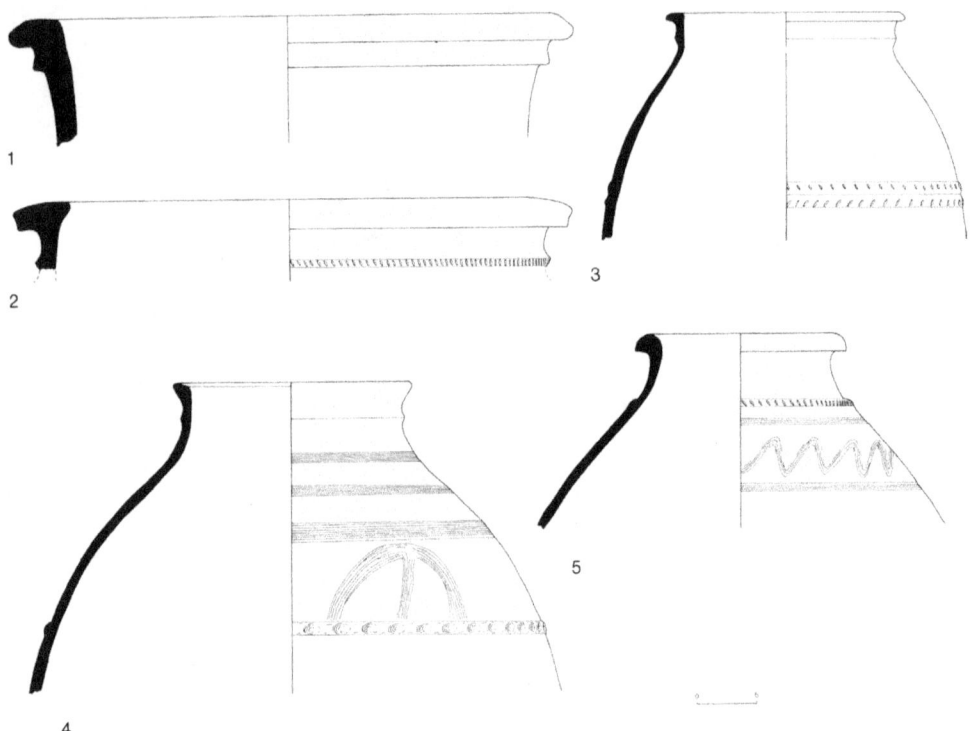

Figure 8.6: Tell Nebi Mend, Trench I, MBA ceramics (storage jars).

Ceramic evidence suggests the Trench I Phase G complex was constructed around 1650 BC, although the single relevant radiometric date (I 151.33) is considerably earlier and is probably residual (see Figures 8.6–8.8). A sherd from a Cypriot WP IV Pendent-Line Style jug was recovered from deposit I 151.33.[35] Pendent-Line Style jugs have a date range between 1750–1650 BC, suggesting that if the sherd was a contemporary deposit at TNM, then a seventeenth century BC date range for Phase G occupation is not unreasonable.

Earlier MB II Phase H architecture (directly below Phase G) can be viewed as a less monumental precursor to the succeeding phase,[36] although overall structural plans remain rather sketchy. At least one major n/s wall (Wall 33) was around 2 m thick, and ran directly below Phase G Wall I/Mur X. The orientation of associated (but smaller) plaster-lined walls and plastered benches seems to echo the later Phase G constructions. Ceramic assemblages suggest an MB II construction date around 1750 BC, with thin layers of burnt black destruction marking the end of the horizon across the trench, perhaps a century later.

---

35 Eriksson et al. 2000, 205–208.
36 Bourke 1993, 163–164, fig. 9.

8 Sequence, chronology and culture at Tell Nebi Mend in the Middle and Late Bronze Ages

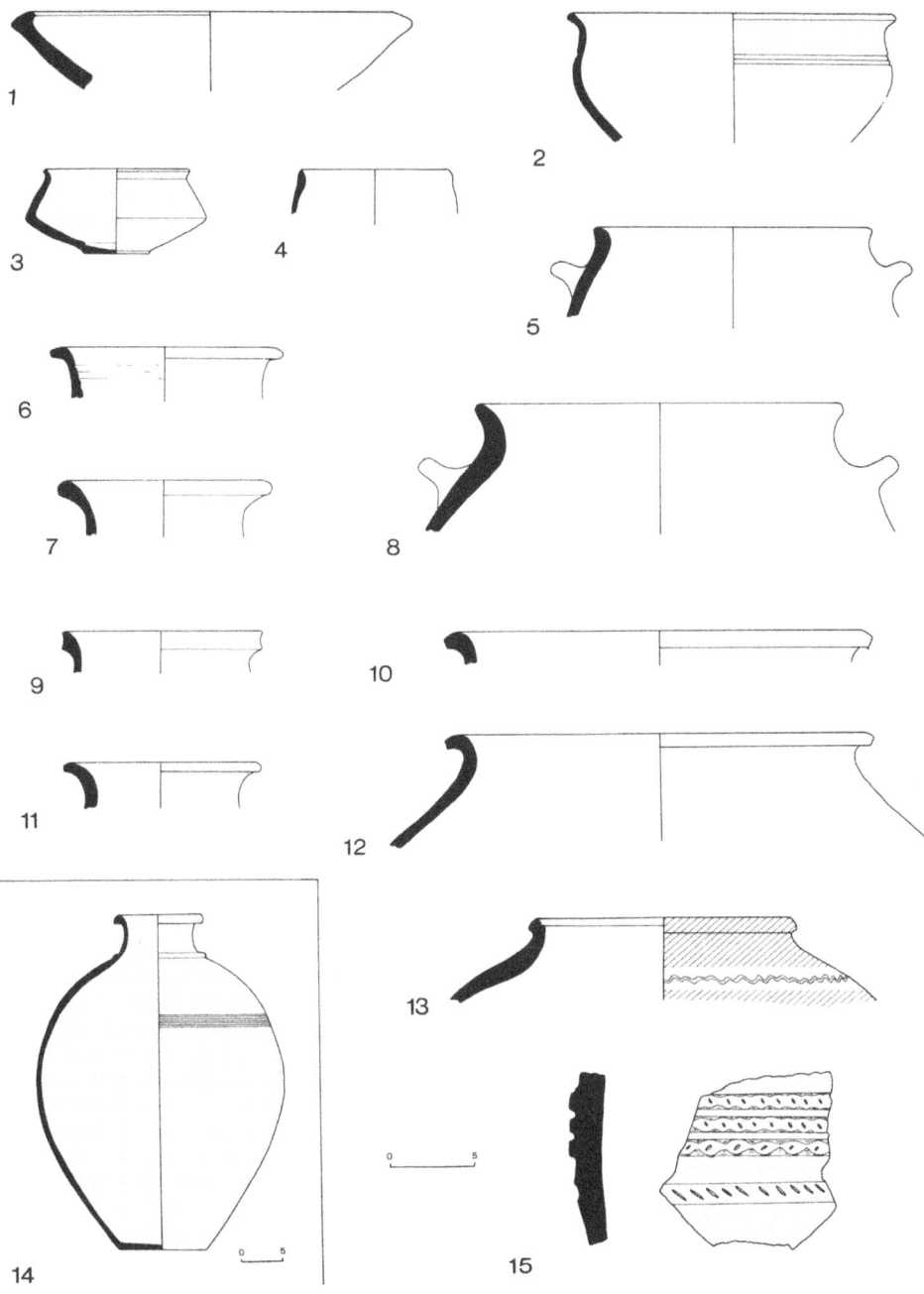

Figure 8.7: Tell Nebi Mend, Trench I, MBA ceramics (bowls/cooking pots/jars).

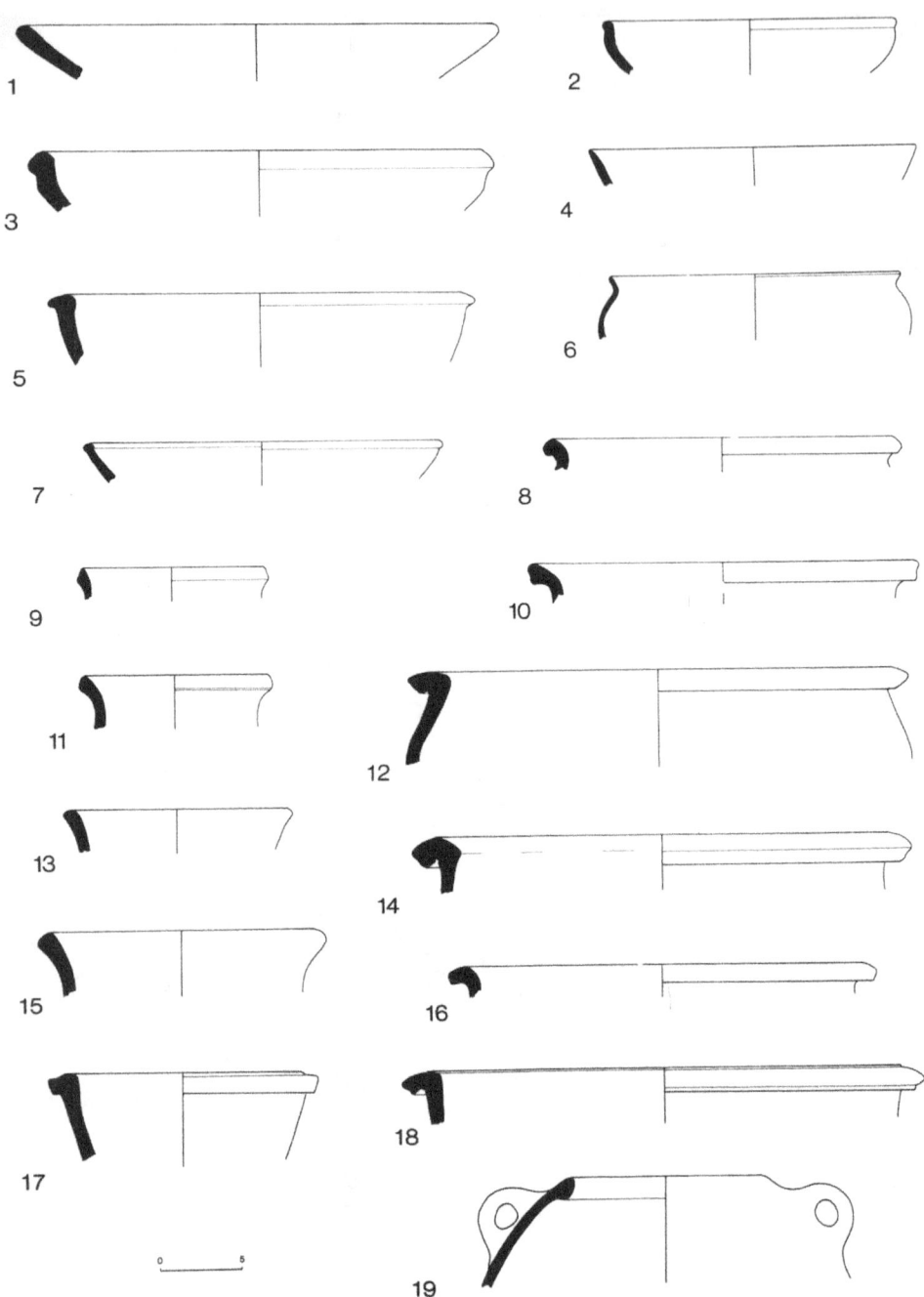

Figure 8.8: Tell Nebi Mend, Trench I, MBA ceramics (bowls/jars).

8 Sequence, chronology and culture at Tell Nebi Mend in the Middle and Late Bronze Ages

The earliest of the MB II phases, Trench I Phase J, is only known from the two small soundings previously mentioned. These soundings (especially the 4 x 6 m South Sounding) nonetheless recorded fragments of neatly built walls, thick white plaster floors, plaster-lined pits and at least one sub-floor burial. This phase included several similarly executed rebuilds, featuring 'stiffening' walls built hard against previous plastered wall faces, suggesting a reasonably lengthy period of occupation. Although the small areas excavated made it hard to characterise the constructions functionally, there was nothing in architectural form or built features that mandated anything other than prosperous domestic structures. The restricted ceramic assemblages from the soundings indicated an early MB II date for the horizon, predominantly within the nineteenth century BC. There was no suggestion of destruction or disruption at the end of Phase J.

MB II horizons in western Trench III seem to have been reasonably extensive, although investigations were confined to several disconnected soundings within a strip never more than 10 m wide or 25 m long, running along the western edge of the exposure. One major phase of architecture (Trench III Phase G), rebuilt several times, dominated the horizon. Constructions were set against (and eventually laid over) the inner face of the upper tell embankment. Walls were substantial (up to a metre thick), and normally built on massive stone footings. Several rooms featured plastered benches and well-laid white plaster floors.

It was difficult to gain a reliable impression as to the function of the structure or structures running along the western edge of the tell, as only the outer western limits were sampled, but the presence of what appear to be long corridor rooms with benches, abutting open square rooms with plastered floors, is not inconsistent with known civic/administrative structures elsewhere.[37] There was minimal evidence for storage of staples, pit installations, food preparation facilities, or domestic cooking/serving ceramics.

Ceramics from the putative civic/administrative complex suggested occupation across the MB II period, with construction in the late eighteenth/early seventeenth centuries BC, and occupation extending down into the early sixteenth century BC. There is some evidence for localised disruption in some rooms at the end of the occupational span, but it is not possible to determine if the entire west tell suffered a similar destruction/abandonment event to that documented in Trench I, as the testimony from disconnected soundings remains equivocal.

One earlier phase (Trench III Phase H) of MB II architecture was detected in a small (approximately 4 x 5 m) probe against the inner slope of the embankment, below the earliest Phase G plaster floors. Short lengths of relatively substantial stone wall-footings were detected in the probe, but it was not possible to determine anything further concerning the nature or function of the constructions. A very restricted ceramic assemblage suggested (tentatively) a date within the eighteenth century BC for the horizon.

---

37 Pinnock 2001, 13, figs 5–8.

Thin MB II period deposits were present in the Trench VII exposure, overlying the more substantial MB I horizons, and abutting the inner face of what is taken to be the upper tell fortification wall. These ephemeral MB II deposits were sealed by Hellenistic period wash levels. There was no evidence for disruption or destruction at the end of the MBA sequence, with thick Classical period wash/erosion lines overlying the fortification complex. The depth of the erosion lines suggests significant post-Bronze Age erosion has taken place in this southern region of the upper tell, removing any evidence for later MBA occupation in Trench VII.

As previously mentioned, a small number of the MBA sherds recovered from the upper deposits of the embankment trenches (Trenches VI and IX) were likely to be MB II in date. However, they were, for the most part, recovered from contexts that had been disturbed by Late Roman period activities, and therefore cannot serve to clarify the date for the construction of the embankment, or the length of MBA occupation associated with it, beyond the bare observation of their presence, which implies continued occupation within the embankment beyond the MB I period.

The LB I period (ca. 1600–1400 BC)

Pézard's deep cut through the upper tell stratigraphy (Tranche A) removed all LBA strata before halting at some stage in the later MBA.[38] The UCL Trench I excavations commenced approximately at the level of Pézard's stopping point. While the primary aim of Trench I fieldwork was to explore MBA and earlier strata below Pézard's 'stop line', soon after excavation began, it became apparent that some idea of the subsequent history of occupation was needed to more fully understand the use-life of Pézard's 'Mur X' (UCL Trench I Wall I) and the complex of rooms with which it was associated. With this realisation in mind, a 15 x 4 m expansion (Trench I Area 200) was opened into the north face of Pézard's Tranche A.[39] Although only relatively small areas of LBA occupational horizons were sampled, the carefully excavated Trench I Area 200 sequence provided a full record of LBA occupation in the north-eastern corner of the upper tell (see Figure 8.9).[40]

Two phases of LB I period occupation (Trench I Phases E and F) were encountered in the Area 200 excavations, set above and in places cut into the levelled-off destruction/abandonment horizons that sealed all MBA occupation in the area. Both phases of LB I architecture were characterised by flimsy thin-walled domestic structures with beaten earth floors and outdoor cooking facilities. Both phases were set back considerably to the west of Wall I/Mur X, implying some recession of settlement area in the early phases of the LB I.

As well, three simple pit burials were encountered in the peripheries of the Trench I excavation area (164.5, 200.6 and 603.4). All were found dug into destruction debris, and each was positioned in wall corners of the defunct Phase G complex, suggesting these

---

38 Pézard 1931, 4; Parr 1983, 106.
39 Bourke 1993, 158–164.
40 Bourke 1993, 189–190.

8 Sequence, chronology and culture at Tell Nebi Mend in the Middle and Late Bronze Ages

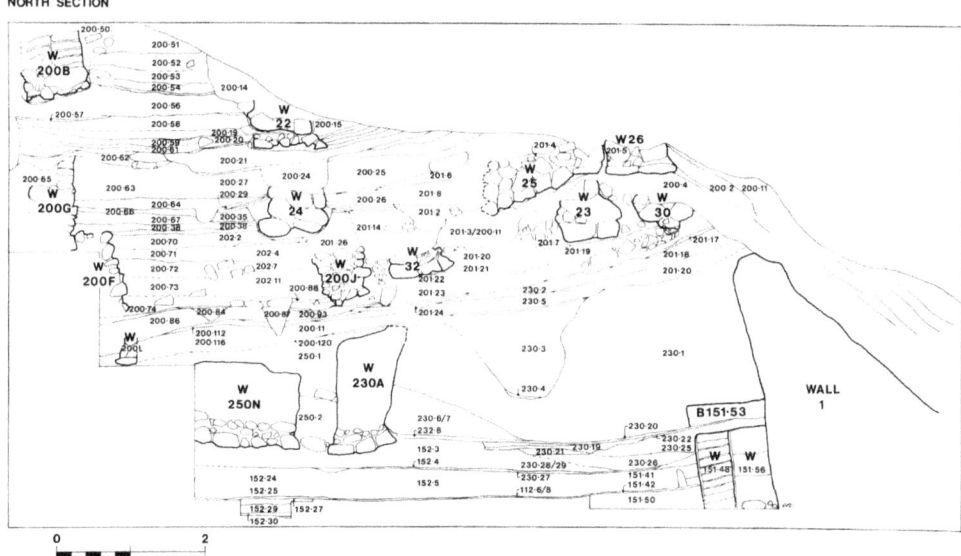

Figure 8.9: Trench I, north section, Area 200. MB-LB Phases A-G.

walls may well have been at least partly visible at the time of interment. Pézard's compilers listed four pit burials,[41] which Pézard took to be LB I in date.[42] Some uncertainty surrounds the exact stratigraphic positioning of all burials (both Pézard and UCL), as the horizons from which they were cut were removed without comment during the course of Pézard's work, although position and orientation makes it probable that at least two of Pézard's burials were cut into the thick debris layers which sealed UCL Phase G architecture, in the southern reaches of what became UCL Trench I.[43]

UCL Jar Burial 603.4 contained a carinated bowl, along with a faience scarab, a faience pendant and a number of stone beads. The other jar burials (200.6 and 164.5) were much less complete, although large pieces of storage jars were recovered from all three. The scarab from 603.4, although difficult to date, fits broadly within an early New Kingdom horizon, consistent with its assumed stratigraphic position.

If there was a short interruption to settlement in the area of Trench I after the Phase G complex fell out of use, and substantial erosional lines sealing the complex supports this scenario, then it may be that the area was used as a burial field during this short break in occupation. This 'break' in settlement, for perhaps 50 years across the MB/LB period, was followed by the two phases (Trench I Phases E and F) of fitful LB I occupation, which are best placed within the fifteenth century BC.

---

41 Pézard 1931, 72–74.
42 Pézard 1931, 64.
43 Pézard 1931, Pl. B, bottom right.

Figure 8.10: Trench III, schematic plan of multi-phase (MB-LB) architecture, Phases A-G.

In western Trench III, an area approximately 10 x 5 m in extent was exposed below the more substantial LB II period civic structures that covered much of the excavated area (Figure 8.10). This revealed parts of at least two phases (Trench III Phases E and F) of relatively well-built stone wall-footings, and at least three sub-phases of associated white plaster floors. Although the wall-footings and floors were reasonably substantial, it seemed probable that they had been set back somewhat from the western edge of the LB I period tell, the surface of which sloped inwards at this point.

While this suggestion of settlement recession might imply relatively reduced circumstances during the LB I, the region of the LB I sounding in the western tell seems to have suffered heavily from erosion in the MB/LB period, complicating interpretation. There was minimal overlap with the preceding quite substantial MB II period structures, which aligned more certainly with the edge of the tell. Although the LB I horizons were exposed over a relatively limited area, the broad similarity of

8 Sequence, chronology and culture at Tell Nebi Mend in the Middle and Late Bronze Ages

wall alignments and constructional details may imply continuity of function across the MB–LB transition.

There was no trace of LBA period ceramics among the assemblages drawn from the southern trench on the upper tell (Trench VII), nor from either of the strip-trenches (Trenches VI and IX) in the embankment area. Post MBA-period erosion had been very heavy across the southern reaches of the site, removing any Late Bronze and Iron Age occupational traces that may once have existed. Given the evidence from the Egyptian Qadesh battle reliefs,[44] it seems probable that extensive LBA horizons (at least) should have existed in the southern upper tell, perhaps in association with lower fortified zones, but they are no longer in evidence.

The LB II period (ca. 1400–1200 BC)

In many ways, the Late Bronze Age II period is the best documented across the upper tell of Nebi Mend. Although there is little lateral coverage of LB II horizons in the UCL Trench I excavations, there is nonetheless a four-phase (Trench I Phases A–D) occupational sequence recorded in the Area 200 exposure, cut into the north face of Pézard's Tranche A.[45] This sequence is duplicated in the minor baulk-straightening exercise positioned along the southern edge of UCL Trench I (Area 500), which cut less deeply into the south face of Pézard's Tranche A (see Figure 8.11).[46]

The earliest LB II period Phase D materials consist of the Pézard-truncated and much disturbed traces of two north–south wall lines forming part of one structure.[47] Only with the succeeding Phase C materials does some coherence come into the record. Although sharply truncated by Pézard's cut, Phase C preserves fragments of four walls, built of neat red and yellow brick laid upon quite substantial basalt stone foundations.[48] It seems very likely that these wall lines preserve parts of three small rooms, either pebble-paved or with thick rammed mud floors. A plastered pit installation and a small hearth were positioned in two room corners. The Phase C materials seem best placed within the fourteenth century BC, with this horizon ending in a fiery destruction (see Figure 8.11).

The traces of the latest LB II Phase A and B horizons in Trench I did not project far into the Area 200 excavation area,[49] but enough was visible to demonstrate that they were nonetheless architectural phases of some sophistication, featuring 90 cm thick walls, plastered benches and well-laid plaster floors. Phase B contained a piece of a Mycenaean IIIB1 stirrup jar, which would support the general thirteenth century BC date proposed for these two architectural phases.

---

44   Parr (ed.) 2015, 360.
45   Bourke 1993, 158–160.
46   Bourke 1991, 21, fn.13, fig. 6.
47   Bourke 1993, 158, fig. 5.
48   Bourke 1993, 158, fig. 4.
49   Bourke 1993, 158.

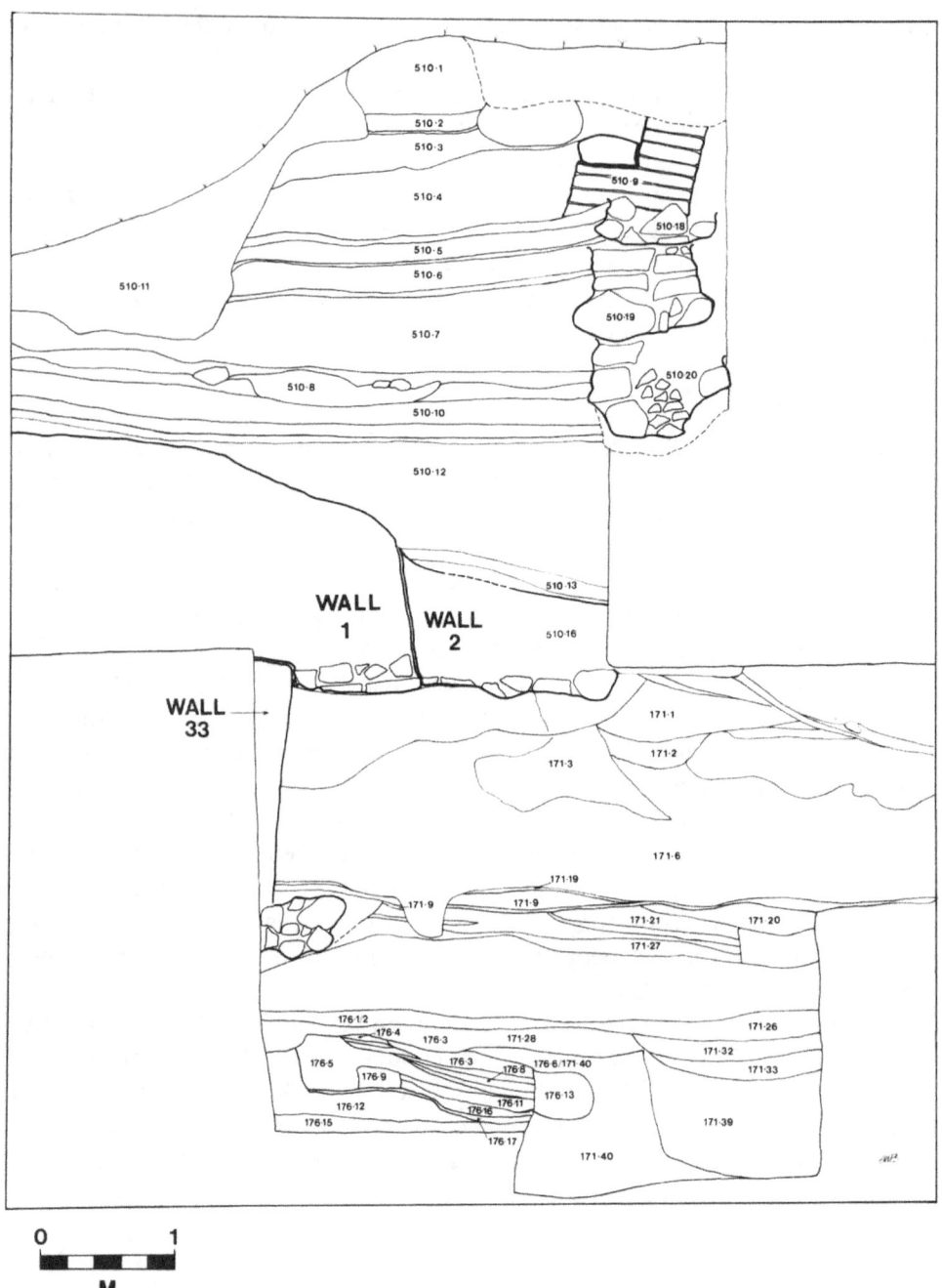

Figure 8.11: Trench I, south section, Area 500. MB-LB Phases A-J.

8 Sequence, chronology and culture at Tell Nebi Mend in the Middle and Late Bronze Ages

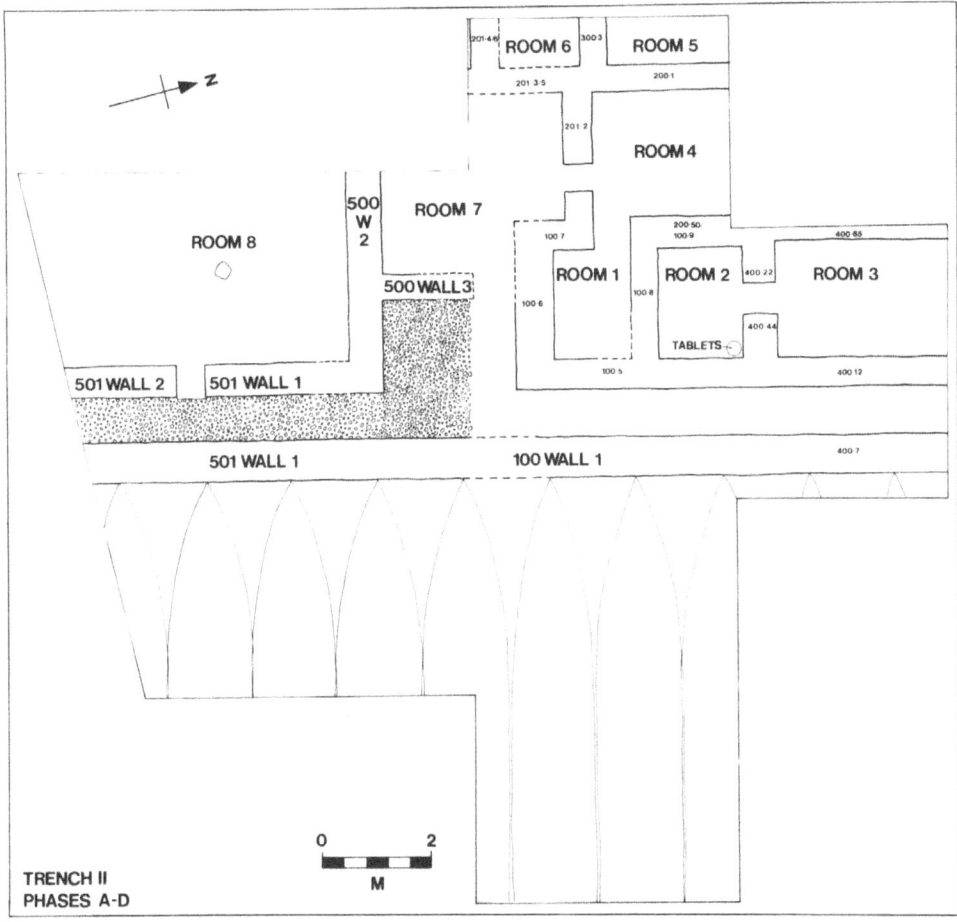

Figure 8.12: Trench II, schematic plan of civic complex building, Phases C-D.

UCL Trench II[50] was placed over the central/southern area of Pézard's Tranche B exposure.[51] At its maximal extent, Trench II excavations achieved an approximately 25 x 25 m exposure of LB II horizons, below Pézard's somewhat irregular terraced 'stop line' in Tranche B. UCL excavators uncovered one major horizon of architecture (Trench II Phases C–D) across the entire area. Small probes (Areas 800 and 1000) beneath floor levels of the main horizon sampled one phase of earlier architecture (Trench II Phase E), while scraps only of two later phases (Trench II Phases A and B), preserved in the far western reaches of the Trench II exposure, survived Pézard's clearance across the Tranche B excavation area.

Highlights of UCL Trench II excavations include the famous 'Tablet House' discoveries of 1975, which produced the five clay tablets that finally secured the identity

---

50   Parr 1983, 107; Bourke 1991, 31–37, fig. 13.
51   Pézard 1931, Pl. A, upper right; Bourke 1991, fig. 3.

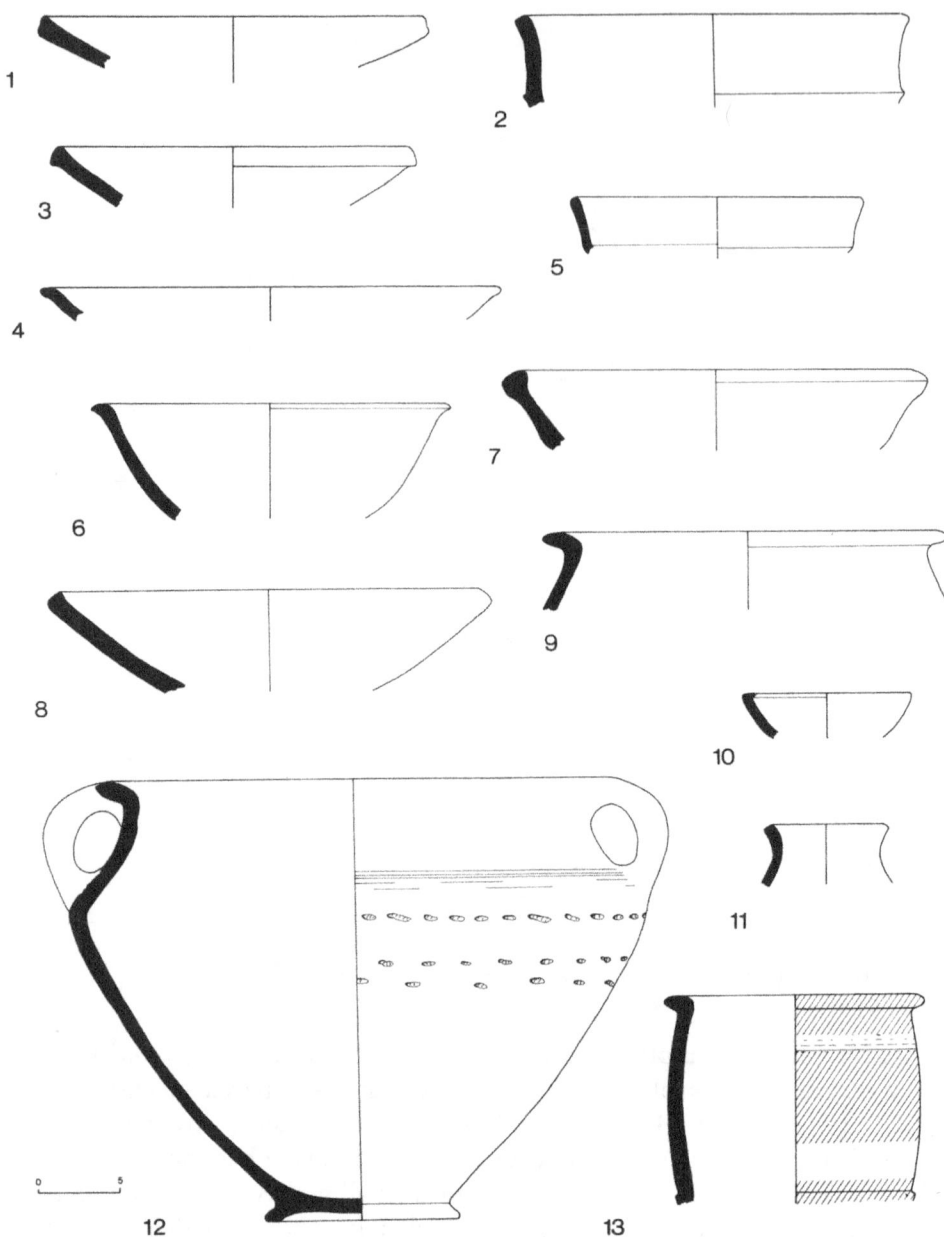

Figure 8.13: Tell Nebi Mend, Trench II, LBA ceramics (bowls/jars).

of the site (see Figure 8.12).⁵² Further excavations in Trench II in the 1980s and 1990s more fully exposed two sub-phases of a neatly constructed administrative complex, built against the eastern slope of the upper tell, in all probability associated with Pézard's Walls U and Z.⁵³ The tablets were associated with the destruction debris of the later (Phase C) sub-phase of this complex.

This mudbrick and stone complex featured well-built mud-plaster lined, brick-walled rooms, all featuring thick yellow plaster floors. Access to each was gained through long flanking corridors, which ran around the north and eastern sides of a large pebble-paved courtyard, located south of the northern complex of brick rooms, from which the tablets derived. It seems probable that a matching complex of small rooms existed to the south of the courtyard, but most traces of these had been lost to post-Pézard erosion. This erosion was considerable in the region of the northern edge of Pézard's deeper Tranche A explorations, which unluckily coincided with the area of construction flanking the south side of the pebble-paved courtyard (see Figure 8.12).

Traces of the southern room system and abutting pebbled courtyard floors were recorded in the Trench I Area 200 Phase C horizons.⁵⁴ It has been suggested previously that this horizon might be related broadly to Pézard's 'Niveau 4' or Syro-Hittite phase, and dated within the fourteenth century BC. Associated Egyptian Blue Painted pottery and a number of diagnostic Mycenaean IIIA2 and Cypriot LC IIA sherds typical of the 'Amarna' horizon (see Figure 8.13) lends credence to this scenario, as does Millard's analysis of the clay tablets, which he dated broadly to the period 1320–1295 BC.⁵⁵ The administrative complex was destroyed in a fiery conflagration, which reduced the surrounds to vitrified rubble.

On the western side of the upper mound, UCL Trench III excavations uncovered a well-preserved building complex, exposed across the entire excavated area.⁵⁶ It featured neat red and yellow mudbrick superstructures laid over massive basalt stone footings. Walls were often around a metre thick, and in places preserved to a height of more than two metres. The complex as exposed consisted of parts of seven rooms, six relatively small and arranged around a larger central hall. This complex was rebuilt several times over what was probably more than a century of continued occupation, and four distinct phases of use (Trench III Phases A–D) are currently allocated to this complex, although further subdivision may be required as the final occupation phases, recorded in increasingly small areas of excavation upslope to the east, are yet to be fully integrated into the master stratigraphy of the trench.

The complex was probably constructed early in the fourteenth century BC, with its various sub-phases of use stretching across the fourteenth and thirteenth centuries BC. Significant amounts of Late Cypriot II Base Ring and White Slip wares, Mycenaean IIIA

---

52 Millard 2010, 227.
53 Pézard 1931, pl. B, central east.
54 Bourke 1993, 158, fig. 4.
55 Millard 2010, 234.
56 Parr 1983, 107, fig. 4, pl. IV.

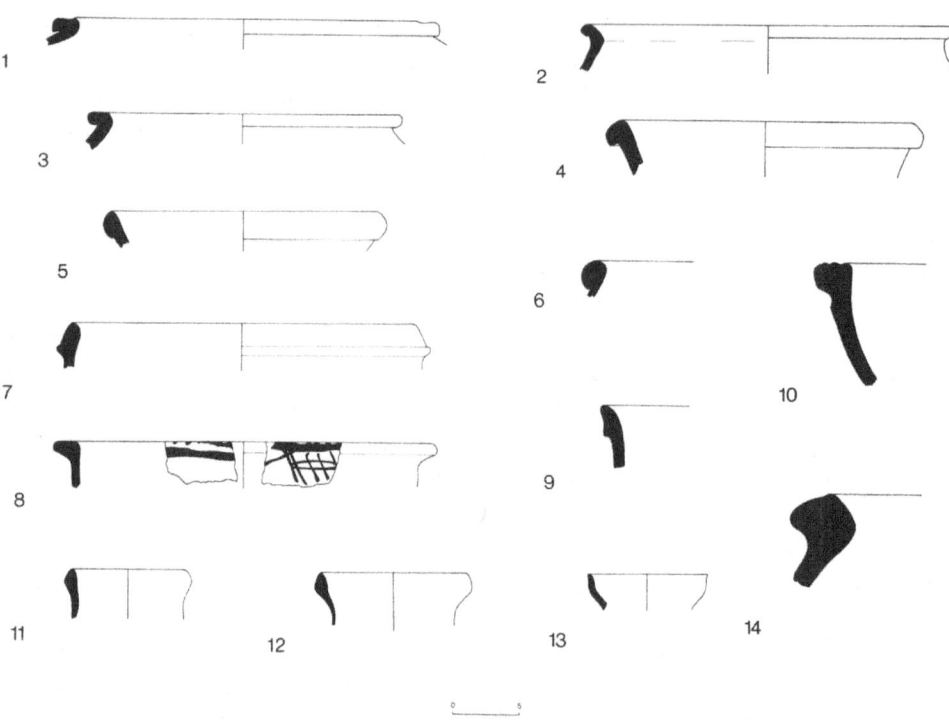

Figure 8.14: Tell Nebi Mend, Trench II, LBA ceramics (jars).

materials, and smaller amounts of Egyptian and Egyptianising ceramics, were recovered from the various horizons associated with the structure, adding some support to the chronology of use largely derived from local forms (see Figures 8.14–8.15). Precisely what function this complex served remains unclear. Parr originally suggested a civic function,[57] but was non-committal as to whether this was administrative or military.

In addition, further analysis of the fourteenth century BC horizons has identified elaborate cult/ritual deposits as well, suggesting that the complex may well have served a number of different functions, although certainly of a major civic form. The complex suffered one major destruction, towards the end of the fourteenth century BC (at the end of Phase C). It may be that the final Bronze Age horizon (Phase A) also suffered disruption at some stage within the twelfth century BC, although the circumstances surrounding the end of occupation in this complex remains unclear. A simple abandonment of an increasingly poorly maintained structure may well be a better reading of the problematic final horizons, than seeking to identify a particular moment of final disruption.

As mentioned earlier, there are few traces of LB I–II occupation in the southern upper tell (Trench VII) or embankment (Trenches VI and IX) deposits, and these are restricted to a few problematic body-sherd readings. The extensive erosional activity

---

57 Parr 1983, 107.

8 Sequence, chronology and culture at Tell Nebi Mend in the Middle and Late Bronze Ages

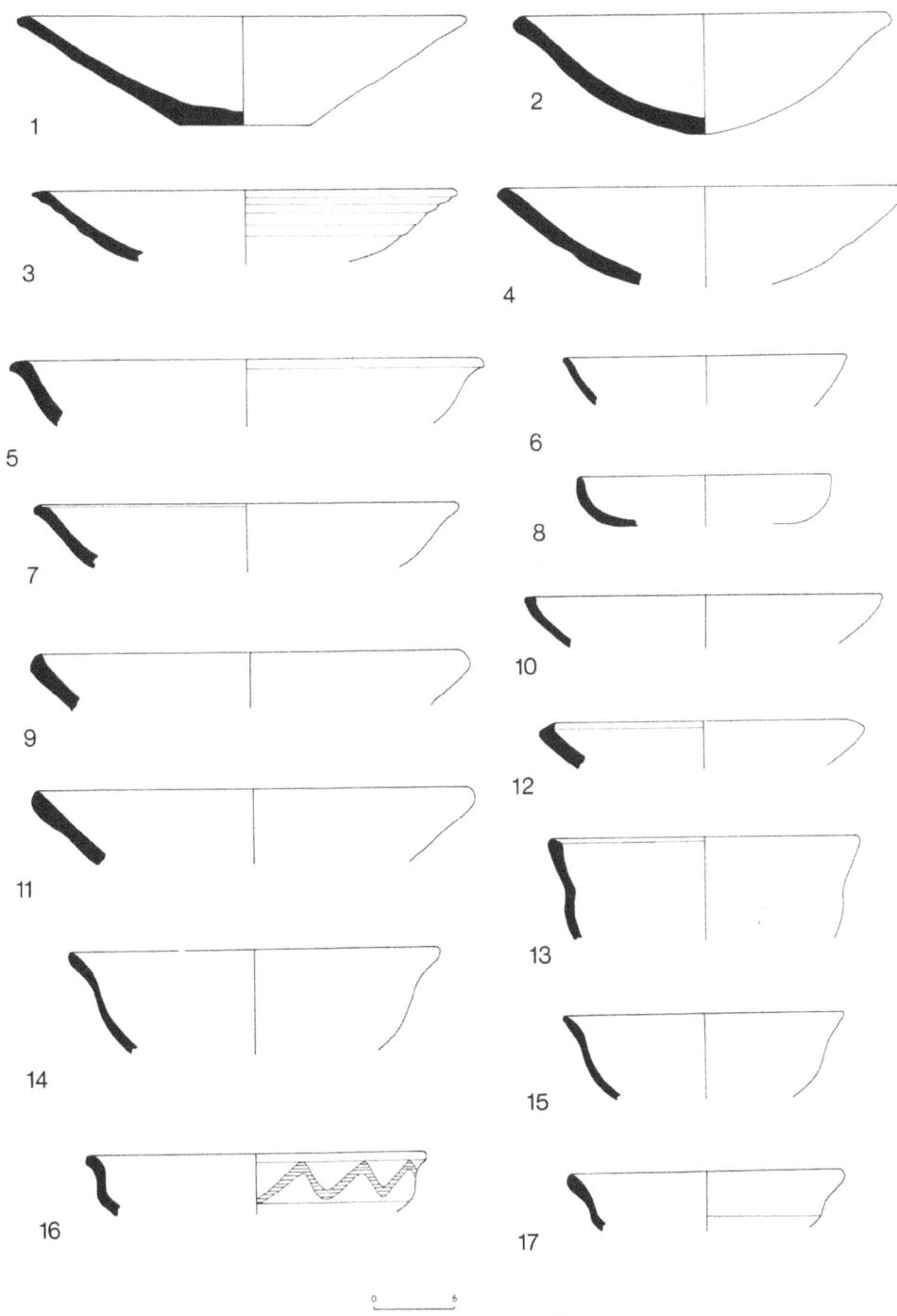

Figure 8.15: Tell Nebi Mend, Trench II, LBA ceramics (bowls).

on the southern upper tell, and Classical period remodelling of the lower regions, would seem to have removed all trace of the LB II horizons in these areas, although Egyptian inscriptional evidence implied that it did once exist.

Summary of settlement history

While MB I period occupation at Tell Nebi Mend is evidenced across both the upper tell and lower embankment areas, only in the Trench I exposure on the north-east corner of the upper tell has a long sequence of occupation been exposed.[58] The BM radiocarbon datasets provide limited support for occupation from an early period within the MB I.[59] The large rampart fortifications are difficult to date, as most associated occupational strata remain deeply buried (Trench III), or are now below the water table (Trenches VI and IX). Nonetheless, comparable fortifications at Qatna and Ebla would seem to have been constructed at some stage within the MB I period,[60] although a more precise determination within that period cannot yet be assayed. The few traces of MB I period structures uncovered in Trench I are consistent with prosperous domestic occupation.

MB II period occupation is found in abundance across all areas of the site. Massively built multi-room structures occupy much of the excavated area of Trench I. In Trench III, traces of similarly monumental structures were detected along the western escarpment, while thick occupation layers were associated with the MB I circuit wall in the southern reaches of the upper tell (Trench VII). Although much disturbed by later activity, lower tell MB II occupation is indicated by a consistent presence within the sherd assemblages of Trenches VI and IX. All in all, the consistent density of MB II period sherdage across all areas explored (even those where MB II strata were not reached) indicates the MB II was a period of dense occupation across the ruin-field, perhaps the most extensive in the pre-Classical history of the site.

Late Bronze Age strata are closely documented (if little exposed) within the Trench I margins, but were extensive across both Trenches II and III, indicating significant continuity of occupation from the MBA. There is some evidence for a temporary interruption to occupation in the early LB I period, but thereafter occupation soon returns to a level of sophistication rarely matched in pre-Classical horizons. There is clear evidence for a major disruption towards the end of the fourteenth century BC, and if the textual evidence can be trusted, this is not related to the Hittite conquest, but more likely in reaction to it.

Nonetheless, recovery from this site-wide late fourteenth century BC destruction event was rapid, with little indication of reduced circumstances in its wake. A consistent presence of Cypriot and Mycenaean imports both before and after the destruction horizon is characteristic, although there are rather less of both as the LB II unfolds. In the later LB II horizons new elements within the assemblage may be characterised

---

58　Bourke 1991; Kennedy 2015.
59　Bowman et al. 1990.
60　Burke 2008, 48–50.

as strongly Egyptianising, if not actually Egyptian imports. Charting the final years of LBA occupation is made problematic by the increasingly small excavation areas available for review. This said, there is no clear indication of a major terminal Bronze Age destruction horizon at Tell Nebi Mend, merely evidence for decay and ultimate abandonment of poorly maintained but once impressive structures. However, these final Bronze Age horizons include rare sherds of 'local' LH IIIC pottery and a number of clay spool weights, suggesting the presence of new elements within the assemblage, appearing at some stage within the twelfth century BC.

Discussion

The early years of the Middle Bronze Age seem to witness a sharp militarisation of the Orontes settlement landscape, with major rampart fortifications a feature of most regional centres on or adjacent to the Orontes watershed. Massive rectilinear ramparts are constructed early in the MB I at Qatna[61] and Ebla,[62] and very probably in strategic settlements such as Tell es-Sur,[63] Tell Nebi Nour,[64] Tell Afis[65] and Tell Tuqan,[66] in the border zones of both these regional hubs. Although difficult to date precisely, it seems probable that the lower town ramparts at Tell Nebi Mend date to the MB I, probably responding to the same insecurities and rivalries that prompted similar fortification in nearby major settlements such as Hama,[67] 'Acharneh,[68] and very probably other significant sites such as Qarqur and Atchana along the Orontes watershed.[69]

While a first 'wave of fortification' in the EB IV period indicates that militarised landscapes were nothing new,[70] the massive scale of the MBA ramparts and their employment in large and small centres alike, suggests that some significant change in strategic priorities[71] and/or military tactics may have occurred early in the MBA.[72] As well, recent observations on urban layout would suggest that many of the MB I earthen ramparts encompassed substantial empty spaces,[73] underlining the fact that most lower town ramparts were not 'settlement-girdles' designed to stiffen and expand

---

61 Al-Maqdissi 2013; Morandi-Bonacossi 2014.
62 Pinnock 2001.
63 Mouamar 2014.
64 Moussli 1989–90.
65 Mazzoni 2013; Baffi and Peyronel 2014.
66 Baffi 2014.
67 Thuesen 2000; Thuesen and Ribbe 2000.
68 Fortin et al. 2014.
69 Woolley 1995; Casana 2009; Yener 2010; 2015.
70 Kennedy, this book.
71 Baffi and Peyronel 2014, 15–16.
72 Burke 2008, 29–36, fig. 3.
73 Morandi-Bonacossi 2014, 282–283; Rey 2014, 102–104.

high mounded occupation areas,[74] although many upper tell/citadel fortification walls may well have served the multiple purposes of defence/isolation, mound stabilisation and the expansion of elevated areas available for monumental construction. It would seem that the Tell Nebi Mend upper tell was likewise ringed by such a fortification/stabilisation wall, considering the evidence from the Trench I, III and VII excavations, while the lower town was equipped with extensive ramparts, going on the evidence garnered from the Area VI and IX strip trenches.

Whatever the purpose of the massive ramparts of the MB I, the onset of the MB II period ushered in further change. While a general increase in within-settlement density, with an accompanying elaboration of civic/religious architecture is everywhere apparent,[75] changes to military architecture are also evident. In the hinterland of Tell Nebi Mend, even very small tell settlements of under two hectares almost without exception now sport massive brick fortification walls,[76] and the main centres construct massive multi-storey brick fortress complexes on top of their ramparts,[77] while gateways become heavily fortified strongpoints in their own right.

It may be that another change in strategic circumstance prompted this change in fortification stance, towards encastled rampart lines, and hinterland defence in depth.[78] Early MBA military operations tended towards siege activity perhaps undertaken by relatively small household military forces.[79] In the MB II period, the move towards large infantry forces seems to have accelerated,[80] with the clash of regional field armies not uncommon, especially once the Hittite Old Kingdom began to feature more heavily in north Syrian affairs.[81] It seems probable that the Trench I Phase G multi-roomed brick-walled complex on the north-eastern rim of Tell Nebi Mend[82] should be viewed in the same light as the Ebla 'fortress castles' documented in recent work,[83] representing one element in an overall strengthening of the regional fortification systems.

At Tell Nebi Mend, the Late Bronze I period remains enigmatic. Archaeologically, the period is one of recession, if not outright abandonment, if the Trench I sequence may be generalised to the rest of the site, which the less clear-cut evidence from Trench III would favour. The Trench I Phase E–F horizons are characterised by thin-walled flimsy domestic structures. These followed a period of probable abandonment characterised by deep erosion layers and occasional burials placed within abandoned structures. And yet, this period of abandonment and impoverished first reoccupation would seem to stand chronologically immediately before the zenith of Qadesh's albeit

---

74 *Contra* Parr 1968, 44.
75 Morandi-Bonacossi 2014, 275–279; Pinnock 2001, 17–22; Baffi and Peyronel 2014, 17–19.
76 Philip and Bradbury 2016, 386–387.
77 Pinnock 2001; Peyronel 2007.
78 Baffi and Peyronel 2014, 17.
79 Burke 2008, 27–41.
80 Van de Mieroop 2004, 99–108.
81 Van de Mieroop 2004, 112–115.
82 Bourke 1993, 162–163, fig. 8.
83 Pinnock 2001, 21, figs 13–15; Peyronel 2007.

8 Sequence, chronology and culture at Tell Nebi Mend in the Middle and Late Bronze Ages

short-lived moment of regional prominence, as coalition war-leader of an alliance that shook political structures from the Taurus to the Sinai.[84]

The archaeological evidence would seem to be sharply 'out of step' with what we assume to be the political clout of what should be a newly eminent LB I period kingdom. It may be that the archaeological horizons sampled in UCL excavations are not representative of the wealth and power of the day, although LB I strata are thin and patchy whenever encountered on the upper tell and absent completely from the lower settlement, so the evidence (or its lack) from Trench I is consistent with that from all other excavated areas. Of course, these archaeological circumstances may simply reflect the fact that political and economic power need not go hand in hand. After all, short-term political movements of great force (think the Mahdists in Sudan in the later nineteenth century AD) can flash and recede without leaving much trace upon the built landscape. Even so, the Egyptian view of the world implies in Qadesh a polity of some power and influence, and such is nowhere evident in the archaeology of the LB I period city, nor indeed in associated hinterland sites, which are bare of all but trace presences during this period.

The impoverished LB I archaeological horizon at Tell Nebi Mend finds a strong echo in the record at Qatna, where a short-term disruption to central administration, featuring reuse of previously civic areas as burial grounds is documented.[85] Further north, it might be argued that LB I period horizons are poorly in evidence at Atchana,[86] Ebla[87] and Hama,[88] suggesting that the LB I period was one of deep recession across the entire Orontes watershed.

All this being said, we still face the quandary of explaining the sudden rise of an apparently Hurrian-led north/central Levantine coalition of kings able to project power (and compel alliances) deep into the southern Levant,[89] notionally at a time when the archaeological evidence would suggest a period of recession and decay in precisely the assumed heartland of the entity.[90] While we can ignore the problem by stating that archaeological and historical scenarios need not be in harmony,[91] such dismissals do not advance debate. A more productive line of inquiry may suggest that the traditional historical associations of LB I archaeological assemblages needs reassessing. One way of harmonising historical and archaeological datasets might be to reposition the historical activities of the Thutmosid warrior pharaohs of the late Sixteenth and early Fifteenth centuries BC (falling within the LB IA period as currently formulated) into the later phases of the Middle Bronze Age,[92] lowering the date for the

---

84 Redford 1992, 155–160; 2003.
85 Morandi-Bonocossi 2014, 280.
86 Fink 2010.
87 Colantoni 2014.
88 Thuesen and Ribbe 2000; Nigro 2002.
89 Na'aman 1994.
90 Gonen 1984.
91 Dever 1998.
92 Dever 1987.

end of the MBA well into the fifteenth century BC, and thus reducing the time span of LB I assemblages to little more than 50 years (ca. 1450–1400 BC).

This would begin to account for the thin horizons of occupation currently attributed to the LB I period at Tell Nebi Mend, and more generally across the Orontes watershed.[93] Of course, it may well be that the Egyptian view of the world was deeply coloured by the need to create a casus belli for aggressive moves into the central Levant,[94] as larger events in the northern Levant, specifically Mitannian expansion west of the Euphrates,[95] threatened to remake the political map in a way decidedly unfavourable to Egyptian interests.[96] The justification for vigorous Egyptian intervention in a region racked by poverty and recession (LB IA) makes little sense militarily, but is perhaps more understandable if one suggested that it took place in response to a perceived growing threat (late MBA).[97]

Whatever the circumstances of the LB I period, whether a short-impoverished postscript to a more prosperous MBA, or the product of destructive adventurism by Egyptian and Mitannian imperial armies, economic and political stability returned to the region with the Egyptian-Mitannian détente of the late fifteenth century BC. Archaeological circumstances record renewed prosperity across the Orontes watershed early in the LB IIA period. At Tell Nebi Mend, elaborate courtyarded administrative complexes were constructed on the north-east summit (Trench II Phases C–D) and on the central western periphery (Trench III Phases A–D). It may be that Pézard's monumental 'Syro-Hittite' complex,[98] located on the upper north-east slope, also dates from this period. Many of the hinterland settlements show signs of renewed occupation in the early LB II, with the presence of fine-ware imports spread across a number of often quite small sites, indicating the return of a modest prosperity to the hinterland.[99] The tablets associated with the Trench II Phase D–C administrative complex document widespread contacts across northern Syria,[100] and exotic animals and elite hunting practices,[101] along with the import of Cypriot, Mitannian and Mycenaean fine-ware ceramics, all indicate revived economic fortunes.

At some stage around the late fourteenth or early thirteenth centuries BC, Tell Nebi Mend suffers what on current indications (deep destruction debris layers in Trenches I, II and III) is suggested to be a site-wide destruction. Both major civic/administrative complexes bear the marks of a severe destruction, which the tablet evidence would imply happening towards the end of the fourteenth century BC at the earliest,[102] well

---

93 Fink 2010, 143; Morandi-Bonacossi 2014, 280.
94 Redford 2003.
95 Wilhelm 1996, 17–19; Burney 1997, 185–188; Kuhne 1999, 207–218.
96 Klengel 1992; Van de Mieroop 2004.
97 Bourke 1991, 294–297.
98 Pézard 1931, 11–12, Pl. B; Bourke 1993, 158.
99 Philip and Bradbury 2016, 387.
100 Millard 2010, 232–235.
101 Grigson 2015, 167–168, 180.
102 Millard 2010, 234–235.

after the Hittite takeover in central Syria. Similarly, extensive destructions at Atchana,[103] 'Acharneh,[104] and most especially at Qatna,[105] are more generally associated with the Hittite conquest under Suppiluliuma. Archaeological evidence alone is unlikely to be able to differentiate between a destruction at ca. 1335 BC and one occurring at ca. 1300 BC, so it is perhaps important to recognise that any apparent 'horizon of destruction' across the Orontes watershed may represent at least two quite separate events, although they are very likely to be linked geopolitically.

The Orontes valley undergoes many trials in the hundred years between 1350–1250 BC, with multiple potential destructive agents on offer, from Hittite conquerors to Egyptian revanchists, and no doubt opportunistic internecine raiding when situations permitted. It would be a mistake to 'join the dots' and suggest that all destructions were the work of a northern conqueror, or a southern revanchist. Whatever the specifics of individual destruction events, it is clear that many prominent sites in the Orontes valley were destroyed in this period.

The conditions of life in the subsequent LB IIB period (most of the thirteenth century BC) are difficult to assess. Coastal centres such as Ugarit seem to have maintained a modest prosperity throughout the LB II,[106] while thirteenth century BC occupation at nearby centres, such as Atchana[107] and Qatna,[108] seems sharply reduced. At Tell Nebi Mend, occupation resumed soon after the LB IIA destruction, with some evidence (especially in Trench III) for the rebuilding of administrative complexes essentially on previous lines, suggesting high culture and civic/administrative functions recovered rapidly. When considering the faunal remains from the rebuilt Trench III complex, there is evidence for luxury novelties, arguably Egyptian-influenced, with the presence of Nile perch and Egyptian geese noteworthy.[109]

That said, there are indications of settlement decline in the Nebi Mend hinterland, as many of the small sites show little or no evidence for occupation in the thirteenth century BC,[110] with a telling absence of fine-ware imports on sites at any distance from the Orontes river. It may be that the constant military activity in the region in the first half of the thirteenth century BC proved particularly hard on the agricultural underpinnings of the smaller sites,[111] far away from the better defended river-lands. Evidence tends to suggest that the hinterland region was significantly depopulated over the course of the thirteenth century BC and only thinly settled by period's end.

The fate of Nebi Mend at the end of the Bronze Age remains unclear. The main exposures in Trenches I and II record very little evidence datable to the LB IIB, but then

---

103 Fink 2010.
104 Fortin et al. 2014.
105 Luciani 2008; Iamoni 2014; Dopper 2017.
106 Yon 2006; McGeough 2007.
107 Fink 2010, 142–143.
108 Luciani 2014; Dopper 2017.
109 Grigson 2015, 177–180.
110 Philip and Bradbury 2016, 384–385.
111 Murnane 1985.

much of the relevant strata had been removed in Pézard's earlier excavations. In Trench III there is some evidence bearing on this period, but it is neither extensive nor easy to interpret. The final occupational horizons in the area of the main administrative complex continue into the twelfth century BC without apparent break or sign of destruction. There is some evidence for the slow decay of the previously substantial architectural complex, with flimsy structures, fragmented occupation deposits and much evidence of pitting within what had become by the end of the period a largely ruined building. The later twelfth century BC occupation may be described as ephemeral, located within largely abandoned structures, amidst actual ruins.

It is during this still-obscure twelfth century BC occupational horizon that intriguing new elements appear within the ceramic repertoire, echoing similar ceramic and non-ceramic materials found at Tell Tayinat[112] and various coastal sites during this period.[113] Such elements include basket-handled jars and pyxides, apparently locally produced Mycenaean IIIC-inspired painted wares, and unfired spool-shaped clay loom weights. While caution is necessary when interpreting what is still a small assemblage, it may be argued that the appearance of these new features hints at changing cultural associations at Tell Nebi Mend in particular, and the Orontes corridor more generally. This may mark the beginning of the slow recession of inland west Syrian cultural traditions, which for more than a millennium had looked to Mesopotamia for innovation, and the rise of Mediterranean littoral influences (both Phoenician and Cypro-Greek). These growing Mediterranean influences usher in a new age of post-imperial sub-regional statelets, which develop a more maritime-mercantile outlook, and come to characterise the unfolding age of Iron.

References

Al-Maqdissi, M. (2013). From Tell Sianu to Qatna: some common features of inland Syrian and Levantine cities in the second millennium B.C. In *Cultures in contact: from Mesopotamia to the Mediterranean in the second millennium BC*. J. Aruz, S. Graff and Y. Rakic, eds. 74–83. New Haven: Yale University Press.

Baffi, F. (2014). The defences at Tell Tuqan in the 2nd millennium B.C. In *Tell Tuqan excavations and regional perspectives: cultural developments in inner Syria from the Early Bronze Age to the Persian/Hellenistic period. Proceedings of the international conference, May 15th–17th 2013, Lecce*. F. Baffi, R. Fiorentino and L. Peyronel, eds. 163–188. Lecce: Congedo Editore.

Baffi, F. and Peyronel, L. (2014). Tell Tuqan and the Matikh basin in a regional perspective: thoughts and questions raised by the international congress. In *Tell Tuqan excavations and regional perspectives: cultural developments in inner Syria from the Early Bronze Age to the Persian/Hellenistic period. Proceedings of the international conference, May 15th–17th 2013, Lecce*. F. Baffi, R. Fiorentino and L. Peyronel, eds. 9–34. Lecce: Congedo Editore.

---

112 Janeway 2006–2007.
113 du Pied 2006–2007.

8 Sequence, chronology and culture at Tell Nebi Mend in the Middle and Late Bronze Ages

Bourke, S. (1991). *The transition from the Middle to the Late Bronze Age in the northern Levant: the evidence from Tell Nebi Mend, Syria.* Ph.D thesis, Institute of Archaeology, UCL, London, United Kingdom.

(1993). The transition from the Middle to the Late Bronze Age in Syria: the evidence from Tell Nebi Mend. *Levant* 25: 155–195.

Bowman, J., Ambers, J. and Leese, M. (1990). Re-evaluation of British Museum radiocarbon dates issued between 1980 and 1984. *Radiocarbon* 32(1): 59–79.

Braidwood, R.J. and Braidwood, L.S. (1960). *Excavations in the plain of Antioch I: the early assemblages Phases A-J.* The University of Chicago Oriental Institute Publications No. LXI. Chicago: University of Chicago Press.

Burke, A. (2008). *"Walled up to heaven": the evolution of Middle Bronze Age fortification strategies in the Levant.* Studies in the Archaeology and History of the Levant 4. Winona Lake, Indiana: Eisenbrauns.

Burleigh, R., Ambers, J. and Matthews, K. (1984). British Museum radiocarbon measurements XVII. *Radiocarbon* 26(1): 59–74.

Burney, C. (1997). Hurrians and Indo-Europeans in their historical and archaeological context. *al-Rafidan* 17: 175–193.

Casana, J. (2009). Alalakh and the archaeological landscape of Mukish: the political geography and population of a Late Bronze Age kingdom. *Bulletin of the American Schools of Oriental Research* 353: 7–37.

Colantoni, A. (2014). The Late Bronze I pottery at Tell Mardikh/Ebla and its relations with the Middle Bronze II tradition. In *Recent trends in the study of Late Bronze Age ceramics in Syro-Mesopotamia and neighbouring regions.* M. Luciani and A. Hausleiter, eds. 103–114. Orient-Archäologie 32. Rahden: Verlag Marie Leidorf GmbH.

Dever, W. (1987). The Middle Bronze Age: the zenith of the urban Canaanite era. *Biblical Archaeologist* 50: 148–177.

Dever, W. (1998). Hurrian incursions and the end of the Middle Bronze Age in Syria-Palestine: a rejoinder to Nadav Na'aman. In *Ancient Egyptian and Mediterranean studies in memory of William A. Ward.* L. Lesko, ed. 91–110. Providence: Brown University.

Dopper, S. (2017). *Ein form typenkatalog der spätbronzezeitlichen keramik Westsyriens und der Levante.* Qatna Studien 7. Wiesbaden: Harrassowitz Verlag.

Dornemann, R. (2003). Seven seasons of ASOR excavations at Tell Qarqur, Syria 1993–1999. In *Preliminary excavation reports and other archaeological investigations: Tell Qarqur and Iron I sites in the north-central highlands of Palestine.* N. Lapp, ed. 1–141. Boston: American Schools of Oriental Research.

Eriksson, K., Hennessy, B. and Bourke, S. (2000). A Middle Cypriot WP IV sherd from Tell Nebi Mend, Syria. *Aegyptum und Levante* 10: 205–210.

Fink, A. (2010). *Late Bronze Age Tell Atchana (Alalakh): stratigraphy, chronology, history.* BAR International Reports 2021. Oxford: Archaeopress.

Fortin, M., Cooper, L. and Boileau, M-C. (2014). Rapport préliminaire et études céramologiques sur les campagnes de fouilles 2009 et 2010 à Tell 'Acharneh, vallée du Ghab, Syrie. *Syria* 91: 173–220.

Fugmann, E. (1958). *Hama: II.1. Fouilles et recherches de la Fondation Carlsberg 1931–1938: L'architecture des périodes pré-Hellénistiques.* Copenhagen: Nationalmuseet.

Gonen, R. (1984). Urban Canaan in the Late Bronze period. *Bulletin of the American Schools of Oriental Research* 253: 61–73.

Grigson, C. (2015). The fauna of Tell Nebi Mend (Syria) in the Bronze and Iron Age – a diachronic overview. Part 2: Hunting, Fowling and Fishing. *Levant* 47(2): 164–185.

Iamoni, M. (2014). Transitions in ceramics, a critical account and suggested approach: case-study through comparison of the EBA-MBA and MBA-LBA horizons at Qatna. *Levant* 46(1): 4–26.

Ingolt, H. (1940). *Rapport preliminaire sur sept Campagnes de fouilles a Hama en Syrie (1932–1938)*. Copenhagen: Nationalmuseet.

Janeway, B. (2006–2007). The nature and extent of Aegean contact at Tell Ta'yinat and the vicinity in the early Iron Age: evidence of the Sea Peoples? *Scripta Mediterranea* 27–28: 123–146.

Kennedy, M.A. (2015). *The late third millennium BCE in the upper Orontes valley, Syria: ceramics, chronology and cultural connections*. Ancient Near Eastern Studies Supplement 46. Peeters: Leuven.

Klengel, H. (1992). *Syria 3000 to 300 B.C.* Berlin: Akademie.

Kuhne, C. (1999). Imperial Mitanni: an attempt at historical reconstruction. In *Studies in the civilization of Nuzi and the Hurrians 10: Nuzi at Seventy-five*. D. Owen and G. Wilhem, eds. 203–221. Winona Lake, Indiana: Eisenbrauns.

Luciani, M. (2008). The Late MB to early LBA in Qatna with special emphasis on decorated and imported pottery. *The Bronze Age in the Lebanon*. M. Bietak and E. Czerny, eds. 115–126. Vienna: ÖAW.

(2014). The northern Levant (Syria) during the Late Bronze Age: small kingdoms between supra-regional empires of the international age. In *The Oxford handbook of the archaeology of the Levant, c. 8000–332 BCE*. M. Steiner and A. Killebrew, eds. 509–523. Oxford: Oxford University Press.

Matthias, V. and Parr, P. (1989). The early phases at Tell Nebi Mend: a preliminary account. *Levant* 21: 13–32.

Mazzoni, S. (2013). Tell Afis and the Early-Middle Bronze Age transition. In *Syrian archaeology in perspective celebrating 20 Years of excavations at Tell Afis: proceedings of the international meeting percorsi di archeologia Siriana Pisa, 27–28 November 2006*. S. Mazzoni and S. Soldi, eds. 31–80. Pisa: Edizioni ETS.

McGeough, K. (2007). *Exchange relationships at Ugarit*. Leuven: Peeters. Ancient Near Eastern Studies Supplement 26. Peeters: Leuven.

du Mesnil du Buisson, R. (1935). *Le site archeologique de Mishrife-Qatna*. Paris: Paul Geuthner.

Millard, A. (2010). The Cuneiform tablets from Tell Nebi Mend. *Levant* 42: 226–236.

Morandi Bonacossi, D. (2007). Qatna and its hinterland during the Bronze and Iron Ages: a preliminary reconstruction of urbanism and settlement in the Mishrifeh region. In *Urban and natural landscapes of an ancient Syrian capital: settlement and environment at Tell Mishrifeh/Qatna and in central-western Syria*. D. Morandi Bonacossi, ed. 65–90. Studi Archeologici su Qatna 01. Udine: Forum.

(2014). Some considerations on the urban layout of second millennium BC Qatna. In *Tell Tuqan excavations and regional perspectives: cultural developments in inner Syria from the Early Bronze Age to the Persian/Hellenistic period. Proceedings of the international conference,*

May 15th-17th 2013, Lecce. F. Baffi, R. Fiorentino and L. Peyronel, eds. 275–296. Lecce: Congedo Editore.

Moussli, M. (1984). Tell Homs (Qal'at Homs). *Zeitschrift des Deutschen Palastina-Vereins* 100.1: 9–11.

(1989–90). Tell Safinat-Nouh. *Archiv fur Orientforschungen* 37: 300–308.

Murnane, W. (1985). *The road to Kadesh: a historical interpretation of the battle reliefs of King Sety I at Karnak*. Studies in Ancient Oriental Civilisation No. 42. The Oriental Institute of the University of Chicago: Chicago.

Na'aman, N. (1994). The Hurrians and the end of the Middle Bronze Age in Palestine. *Levant* 26: 175–187.

Nigro, L. (2002). The Middle Bronze Age pottery horizon of northern inner Syria on the basis of stratified assemblages of Tell Mardikh and Hama. *Céramique de l'âge du Bronze en Syrie I: la Syrie de sud et la vallée de l'Oronte*. M. Maqdissi, V. Matoian and C. Nicolle, eds. 97–128. Bibliothèque Archéologique et Historique T.161. Beirut: Institute Francois du Proche Orient.

Parr, P. (1968). The origin of the rampart fortifications of Middle Bronze Age Palestine and Syria. *Zeitschrift dea Deutschen Palastina-Vereins* 84(1):18–45.

(1983). The Tell Nebi Mend Project. *Annales Archéologique Arabes Syriennes* 31: 99–117.

Parr, P. ed. (2015). *Excavations at Tell Nebi Mend, Syria. Volume 1*. Levant Supplementary Series 16. Oxford: Oxbow Books.

Peyronel, L. (2007). Late Old Syrian fortifications and Middle Syrian re-occupation on the western rampart at Tell Mardikh-Ebla. *The synchronisation of civilisations in the eastern Mediterranean in the second millennium B.C. III*. M. Bietak and E. Czerny, eds. 61–139. Vienna: SCIEM 2000.

Pézard, M. (1931). *Qadesh: Mission Archeologique à Tell Nebi Mend 1921-1922*. Paris: Paul Geuthner.

Philip, G. and Bradbury, J. (2016). Settlement in the upper Orontes valley from the Neolithic to the Islamic period: an instance of punctuated equilibrium. In *La Geographie Historique de l'Oronte. De l'Epoque d'Ebla a l'Epoque Medieval*. D. Paravre, ed. 375–399. Syria Supplement IV. Beirut: Institute Francois du Proche Orient.

du Pied, L. (2006–2007). The early Iron Age in the northern Levant: continuity and change in the pottery assemblages from Ras el Bassit and Ras ibn Hani. *Scripta Mediterranea* 27–28: 161–185.

Pinnock, F. (2001). The urban landscape of Old Syrian Ebla. *Journal of Cuneiform Studies* 53:13–33.

Redford, D. (1992). *Egypt, Canaan and Israel in ancient times*. Princeton: Princeton University Press.

(2003). *The wars in Syria and Palestine of Thutmose III*. Leiden: Brill.

Rey, S. (2014). The fortifications of Mari: preliminary results of the 2006–2010 excavations in the east city. In *Proceedings of the 8th International Congress on the Archaeology of the Ancient Near East. Volume 2*. P. Bielinski, M. Gawlikowski, R. Kolinski, D. Lawecka, A. Soltysiak and Z. Wygnanska, eds. 101–116. Wiesbaden: Harrassowitz Verlag.

Schwartz, G. (2018). The value of the vestigial: from Middle to Late Bronze in Ebla and western Syria. In *Ebla and beyond: ancient Near Eastern studies after fifty years of discoveries at Tell Mardikh*. P. Matthiae, F. Pinnock and M. D'Andrea, eds. 439–474. Wiesbaden: Harrassowitz Verlag.

Sievertsen, U. (2014). Late Bronze Age pottery from the middle Orontes survey: a preliminary overview. In *Recent trends in the study of Late Bronze Age ceramics in Syro-Mesopotamia and neighbouring regions*. M. Luciani and A. Hausleiter, eds. 159–176. Orient-Archäologie 32. Rahden: Verlag Marie Leidorf GmbH.

Singer, I. (2011). The historical context of two Tell Nebi Mend/Qadeš letters. *Kaskal: rivista di storia, ambiente e culture del vinino oriente antico* 8: 161–175.

Thuesen, I. (2000). Hama in the Middle Bronze Age: a new interpretation. In *Between Orient and Occident: Studies in Honour of P.J. Riis*, J. Lund and P. Pentz, eds. 11–21. Copenhagen: Nationalmuseet.

Thuesen, I. and Ribbe, W. (2000). Hama, the Middle Bronze Age reconsidered – a ceramic typology of periods, J, H and G. In *Proceedings of the 1st International Congress on the Archaeology of the Ancient Near East*. P. Matthiae, F. Pinnock, L. Nigro and N. Marchetti, eds. 1637–1664. Rome: La Sapienza.

Van der Mieroop, M. (2004). *A history of the ancient Near East ca. 3000–323 BC*. Oxford: Blackwell Publishing.

Venturi, F. (2014). The Late Bronze Age sequence at Tell Afis. In *Tell Tuqan excavations and regional perspectives: cultural developments in inner Syria from the Early Bronze Age to the Persian/Hellenistic period. Proceedings of the international conference, May 15th-17th 2013, Lecce*. F. Baffi, R. Fiorentino and L. Peyronel, eds. 297–324. Lecce: Congedo Editore.

Wilhelm, G. (1996). The Hurrians in the western parts of the ancient Near East. *Michmanin* 9: 17–30.

Wilkinson, T., Philip, G., Bradbury, J., Dunford, R., Donoghue, D., Galiatsatos, N., Lawrence, D., Ricci, A. and Smith, S. (2014). Contextualizing early urbanisation: settlement cores, early states and agro-pastoral strategies in the Fertile Crescent during the fourth and third millennia BC. *Journal of World Prehistory* 27(1): 43–109.

Woolley, C. (1955). *Alalakh. An account of the excavations at Tell Atchana in the Hatay 1937–1949*. Oxford: Oxford University Press.

Yener, A. (2010). *Tell Atchana: ancient Alalakh. Vol. 1. The 2003–2004 Excavation Seasons*. Istanbul: KUP.

(2015). A monumental Middle Bronze Age apsidal building at Alalakh. In *Nostoi: indigenous culture, migration and integration in the Aegean islands and western Anatolia in the Late Bronze and early Iron Ages*. N. Stampolidis, C. Maner and K. Kopanias, eds. 485–498. Istanbul: Koç University Press.

Yon, M. (2006). *The city of Ugarit at Tell Ras Shamra*. Winona Lake, Indiana: Eisenbrauns.

Index

9th International Congress on the Archaeology of the Ancient Near East 1
'Adabal 98
Afeiche, A. M 207
Akkadian 2, 161, 165, 202
Akkar plain 3, 5, 114, 117, 121, 177
Alalahu. *See Tell Tayinat*
Alalakh. *See Tell Atchana*
Alameddine, N. 207
alcohol 6. *See also beer, wine*
Algaze, G. 21
alluviation 20
al-Maqdissi, M. 11, 57
al-Rawda 48, 57, 114, 158–159
Amorites 149, 231
'Amuq sequence 3, 17, 21–22, 27, 56, 154
'Amuq valley 3, 156–157
'Amuq Valley Regional Project (AVRP) survey 18
Anatolia 21, 31, 61, 74
Arad 159
ARCANE Project 3, 18, 75
Archaic Palace 34, 95–96, 166
Archi, A. 38, 165
Argillaceous Rock Fragments (ARFs) 190
Arslantepe 21, 23
Assaf, A. 224
Associated Regional Chronologies for the Ancient Near East and the Eastern Mediterranean. *See ARCANE Project*

Badreshany, K. 106, 219–220
Baffi, F. 55
Bartl, K. 11
Bayesian analysis 10, 158

beer 74–76. *See also alcohol*
Beqa' valley 3, 5, 9, 231
Beth Shan 207
Beth Yerah 6, 155
Biga, M. G. 38
Bosra 221
bottles 109, 114, 117–118, 125
bowls 5, 8, 21, 23, 36–37, 61–74, 76, 88–89, 94, 114, 121, 180–182, 213–215, 218, 237, 239
    carinated 67
    Coba 21
    shallow 21, 61, 62, 237
    vertical 36, 215
Bronze Age
    Early 2–3, 6, 8–9, 17, 27, 31, 54, 56, 91, 150, 166–167, 177–179, 200, 209, 229
    Late 10–11, 57, 152, 221, 229–238, 249, 256
    Middle 10, 137, 149, 152, 157, 162, 166–167, 200, 207, 217, 229–231, 238, 257–259
Bunimovitz, S. 106, 131
Byblos 127, 156–157, 161, 200–209, 222

Carlsberg Expedition to Phoenicia 56
Çatal Höyük 35
Cecchini, S. M. 55
cemeteries 205, 207–208, 224
Centre for Dating and Diagnostics of the University of Salento (CEDAD) 58
ceramics
    Black Wheel-made Ware (BWW) 7–9, 104–112, 124–137
    Brittle Orange Ware (BOW) 27, 30–31, 36, 40, 52

Caliciform Ware 5, 47–59, 63, 69–75
chronology of 129, 254
Cooking Ware (CW) 52, 61, 63, 63–66, 76, 136
divergence of 3
Grey Ware 7–9, 72–73, 106–108, 117, 121–126, 133–139, 206–207, 216, 224–225
homogenisation of 47, 63
Multi-Brush Painted Ware 25, 61
Painted Simple Ware (PSW) 123–128, 131–133, 138
Plain Simple Ware (PLSW) 25, 30
province 7, 52, 137
Red-Black Burnished Ware (RBBW) 27, 30, 39–40, 52, 73
Reserved Slip Ware (RSW) 25, 30, 39, 40, 89
Simple Ware (SW) 52–53, 61, 62, 63, 72, 76–77
Smeared Wash Ware (SWW) 34, 36–37, 39
Trickle-Painted Ware (TPW) 9
wheel made 205, 209, 217–218, 221–222
chaîne opératoire 185–186
Chalcolithic period 3, 20–25, 40, 55, 87, 151–152, 217
Circles Building 6
Cooper, L. 51, 73, 133, 134–135, 164
Copeland, L. 200, 208–209
cultural connection 4, 8
cuneiform 50, 76
cups 5, 25, 35, 39, 51, 61, 67–73, 180, 203–207
Cyma Recta 89

Damascene 129, 135, 138–139
Damascus
  Museum 9
Damascus Museum 9, 222
D'Andrea, M. 6–8, 125
de Maigret, A. 161
Denmark, National Museum of 51, 72
Dera'a region 9, 222
Dever, W. G. 103
Dornemann, R. H. 58
Dunand, M. 202–205

Early Dynastic 2, 203
Early Transcaucasian Culture (ETC) 31, 37
Ebla *chora* 4–5, 8, 161, 166
  Acropolis of 93
  hegemony 8, 38, 150, 161–167
  political control 39
  Red Temple 92–93
economic interaction 1, 164
Egypt 202
Euphrates river 121
Euphrates valley 1, 75

fortifications 151–152, 154–157, 161–165, 256–257
French Institute in Beirut 200
Fugmann, E. 73

Galilee 113
Geyer, B. 158, 166
Ghab basin 48, 121
Giannessi, D. 153
goblets 4–7, 31–36, 39, 51–61, 63–77, 90, 106–109, 113–133, 181, 185, 203, 207, 216, 222, 237
  communal drinking 5
  corrugated 5, 34–35, 61, 69, 73, 77, 114–117
  'Grey Ware' 7, 121, 125
  miniature/votive 6, 90, 205
  painted 5, 39, 51, 216, 222
Greenberg, R. 106, 131

Habuba Kabira 151–155, 161
Hachmann, R. 208
Hadda of Halaba 165
Halawa 152
Hama 5, 17, 20–23, 25, 30, 50–58, 62–63, 72–74, 77, 111–112, 114–117, 121–122, 124–125, 127, 131, 135–136, 151–152, 165–167, 200, 204–224, 229, 232, 257–259
Hatay region 17
Hauran 4, 7–10
Hazor. *See Tell Waqqas*
Homs, Lake of 216
Homs-Tripoli gap 39
Homs-Tripoli Gap 9, 154
Hulah valley 7–9

Index

Ibal tribal confederation 137
Ibbi-Zikir 38
Idlib. *See Tell Matsuma*
Ingholt, H. 56, 72, 114
invasionists 103
Irkab-Damu 38
Iron Age 11, 58–60, 90, 152, 217, 231, 237–238, 249
Išar-Damu 38
Islahiye 31, 40
Italian Archaeological Expedition to Syria (MAIS) 54

Jabbul lake 98
Jabbul Plain 121, 151–157, 161
Japanese archaeological expedition of the Ancient Orient Museum 55
Jawlan 127, 136
Jebel Arbayin 88
Jemdet Nasr period 88
Jericho 205
Jezireh 2, 155–157, 165
Jordan 205, 222
jugs 180–181, 206, 207, 208, 211, 237, 242

Kamid el-Loz 216–217
Karkemish 98
Kennedy, M. 117, 123, 224
Khirbat an-Na'ima 106
Khirbet al-'Umbashi 4, 133, 138
Khirbet ed-Dabab 4
Khirbet Kerak Ware 90
Khirbet Kishron 113
Khirbet Qadish 113
kilns 222
Kurban Höyük 75
Kuschke 202, 216

lamps 180, 203–209
Lancaster Harding, G. 200
Lebanon 3, 8–9, 48, 62, 105–106, 127–129, 135, 156–157, 177, 199–200, 206–209, 209, 217–224
  Baalbeck 217
  Beirut 200, 207, 217
  Department of Antiquities of the 199
  Majdalouna 207–209

Tyre 9, 208–209
Leriche, P. 178
Levant
  Central 3, 6–9, 178, 224, 259–260
  Northern 1–11, 17–18, 31–34, 36, 38, 48, 50–55, 62–63, 73–77, 103, 114, 131, 135, 149–151, 154, 160, 167, 196, 260
  Southern 2–10, 63, 103–106, 111, 117–121, 125–139, 150, 153–154, 159, 204, 259
limestone 87–88, 90, 189–190

Ma'ayan Barukh 207
Mahdists 10, 259
Mameluk period 178
Mardikh 50, 58, 88–91, 95–96, 165, 206
Marfoe, L. 9, 202, 211, 216
Mari 98, 154, 158–161, 166
Matkh region 88, 98
Matthiae, P. 54, 151, 162
Mazzoni, S. 55, 72, 88, 103, 106, 114, 125
Mediterranean 2–3, 11, 88, 177, 262
Megiddo. *See Tell Mutesellim*
Mesopotamia 2, 8, 11, 74, 87, 158, 165–167, 202–203, 230, 262
migrationists 103
militarisation 8, 149–150, 257
monumentalism 90, 153, 155
Mouamar, G. 57, 114, 123
Moumassakhin 124, 133, 138
Mount Hermon 106
mudbrick 57, 93–96, 152–157, 161, 180, 236, 238–240, 253
Museum
  Damascus Museum 9, 221, 222
  National Museum in Beirut 207
  National Museum of Denmark 51, 72

Nahr el-Kebir 177
Nahr el-Quweiq river 55
Naram-Sin 165

Orontean region 20, 25, 31
Orontes 1–11, 18–25, 31, 35, 38–40, 48–51, 54, 58, 61–63, 63, 71–74, 77, 88, 98, 105–106, 114–139, 149–157, 162–167, 216, 229–232, 239, 257–262

Palestine 105–109, 200–203, 207–209, 209, 216–221
Palestinian *tournette* 185
Palumbo, G. 103
Pella 155
Pepi II 202
petrography 8, 124, 179
Petrography 191
Pfälzner, P. 165
Philistines 11
Phoenicians 11
pilgrimage 98
population 3, 20, 27–30, 34, 50, 56, 98, 151, 165, 230
pottery. *See Calciform Ware, ceramics*
Prag, K. 9, 103, 199

Qadesh 10, 166–168, 249, 258
Qal'at er-Rus 23, 38
Qatiné 216
Qatna. *See Tell Mishrifeh*
Qoueiq 31

radiocarbon dating 11, 51, 54–61, 69–72, 75–77, 239
Ras Shamra 20–23, 36–38, 62
Roux, V. 180, 185
Ruj basin 48

Saghieh, M. 200–206
Saidah, R. 207
Schlumberger, D. 200
Schwartz, G. 56
Sebekh-hotep IV 217
Selenkahiye 161–162
Settlement Landscape of the Orontes valley from the Fourth through to the Second Millennia BC, The 1
silos 56–58, 90, 222. *See also storage areas*
cereal storage 6, 50
Simson, G. 207
socio-political centralisation 3
storage areas. *See silos*
storage jars 7, 76, 180–181, 185, 247
Sudan 10, 259
Syria
    Aleppo 152, 200
Damascus 9, 124, 138, 200, 221–222
Simiriyan 121

Tabqa Dam 61
tartaric acid 75
teapots 51, 61, 109–111, 113, 125, 206–211, 224
Tefnin, R. 152
Tell Abu Mreir 55, 61
Tell 'Acharneh 121
Tell Afis 20–23, 25, 55, 61, 69, 87, 152, 159, 229
Tell Ahmar/Til Barsip 76
Tell Al-Ṣūr 48, 57, 61, 71, 158–159
Tell Arqa 8–9, 38–39, 62, 114, 121, 126, 177–180, 187, 191, 194, 202–203, 209
Tell Atchana 37, 55, 61, 167
Tell Beydar 76
Tell Chuera 157–159
Tell el-'Ajjul 224
Tell el-'Ashari 133
Tell el-Ghassil 217
Tell el-Waqqas 106, 125, 129, 134, 137
Tell Hizzin 216–217
Tell Judaidah 20, 25, 34
Tell Kannâs 161
tell Mardikh 47
Tell Mardikh 5, 17, 25, 50, 54, 58–61, 67, 73–74, 96, 204. *See also Ebla chora*
    Palace G 5–6, 31–34, 37–39, 50, 54, 54–55, 58, 69–67, 75–77, 89–97, 135, 149–150, 157, 160–167, 204–206
Tell Mastuma 49, 55, 61, 62
Tell Mishrifeh 50, 57, 61–63, 71, 121–124, 137–138
    Royal Palace 57
Tell Munbatah 158–161, 167
Tell Mutesellim 109
Tell Nebi Mend 1, 4, 8–11, 20–21, 39, 74, 111, 117, 121–124, 127–131, 137–138, 151–153, 159–163, 167, 216, 229–261
Tell Qarqur 48, 58, 69
Tell Sabkha 161
Tell Sh'aīrat 48, 57, 121–131, 137–138
Tell Suffane 55, 61, 69
Tell Sukas 38, 62
Tell Tayinat 3, 18, 30, 34, 35–37, 151, 154

Index

Tell Tuqan 25, 31, 36, 50, 55, 58–62, 87, 150–151, 161, 166–167, 257
Tell Umm el-Marra 114
Tell Waqqas 109, 135
Tel Na'ama 106, 129
Temple of the Rock 6, 34, 88, 93–96
textiles 75, 160
Thuesen, I. 56
Tilbeshar Höyük 74
Titriş Höyük 75
tombs 9, 50, 57, 109, 113, 125, 129, 129–133, 205–207, 216–217, 221
Transjordan 7, 129, 134, 200–203, 211, 221–222
Très Long Mur (TLM) 157–159, 166
Tufnell, O. 209
Turkey 17, 20
Turri, L. 11

'Ubaid ceramics 20, 23
ugula 38
Umm el-Marra 114, 157
urbanisation 4, 31, 34, 50, 74–77, 87, 97, 138, 151, 155, 160
Ur III 2, 96, 158–159, 166, 202
Uruk period 97
    influence 21

Vacca, A. 5, 8, 47, 125

Wadi et-Teim 208, 216
Welton, L. 3–4, 17, 51
Wescombe, D. 200, 208
Will, E. 178
wine 74–76. *See also alcohol*
wool 158–160. *See also textiles*

Yabroud 133, 138

www.ingramcontent.com/pod-product-compliance
Lightning Source LLC
Chambersburg PA
CBHW060303010526
44108CB00042B/2641